Library of
Davidson College

ATLANTIC STUDIES ON SOCIETY IN CHANGE
NO. 46

Editor-in-Chief Béla K. Király

Associate Editor Peter Pastor

Assistant Editor Albert A. Nofi

War and Society in East Central Europe
Vol. XXVII

THE PRESS DURING THE
HUNGARIAN REVOLUTION OF
1848-1849

DOMOKOS G. KOSÁRY

Social Science Monographs, Boulder, CO
Atlantic Research & Publications, Inc., Highland Lakes, NJ
Distributed by Columbia University Press

1986

Copyright © 1986 by Domokos G. Kosáry
Library of Congress Card Catalog Number 85-61725
ISBN 0-88033-091-0
Printed in the United States of America

TABLE OF CONTENTS

Preface to the Series   vii
Acknowledgments   ix
Map   x
CHAPTER ONE 1
   Antecedents: The Press Before 1848
CHAPTER TWO 10
   Hungary and the European Revolutions
CHAPTER THREE 12
   The Last Feudal Diet and the Press
CHAPTER FOUR 25
   The March Revolution in Pest and the Freedom
     of the Press
CHAPTER FIVE 32
   The Press Laws of 1848
CHAPTER SIX..................................... 43
   The Press and the Political Spectrum
CHAPTER SEVEN 57
   Conservative Papers in a Period of Change
CHAPTER EIGHT................................. 67
   Liberal Papers
CHAPTER NINE.................................. 84
   The Radical Paper *Marczius Tizenötödike*
CHAPTER TEN................................... 127
   Other Radical Papers
CHAPTER ELEVEN 157
   The *Munkások Újsága*
CHAPTER TWELVE 196
   Government Papers
CHAPTER THIRTEEN 216
   Kossuth Hírlapja
CHAPTER FOURTEEN........................ 246
   Literary, Professional, and Provincial Papers
CHAPTER FIFTEEN 263
   Papers in Languages Other Than Hungarian

CHAPTER SIXTEEN.............................. 293
    The Early Months of 1849
CHAPTER SEVENTEEN 333
    The Final Phase
EPILOGUE 373

Preface to the Series

The present volume is the twenty-seventh of a series which, when completed, hopes to present a comprehensive survey of the many aspects of War and Society in East Central Europe. The chapters of most of the volumes are selected from papers presented at a series of international, interdisciplinary, scholarly conferences. The present study, however, was solicited for the sake of comprehension.

These volumes deal with the peoples whose homelands lie between the Germans to the west, the Russians to the east and north, and the Mediterranean and Adriatic seas to the south. They constitute a particular civilization, an integral part of Europe, yet substantially different from the West. Within the area there are intriguing variations in language, religion, and government; so, too, are there differences in concepts of national defense, of the characters of the armed forces, and of the ways of waging war. Study of this complex subject demands a multidisciplinary approach; therefore, we have involved scholars from several disciplines, from universities and other scholarly institutions of the USA, Canada, and Western Europe, as well as the East Central European socialist countries.

Our investigation focuses on a comparative survey of military behavior and organization in these various nations and ethnic groups to see what is peculiar to them, what has been socially and culturally determined, and what in their conduct of war was due to circumstance. Besides making a historical survey, we try to define different patterns of military behavior, including the decision-making processes, the attitudes and actions of diverse social classes, and the restraints or lack of them shown in war.

We endeavor to present considerable material on the effects of social, economic, political, and technological changes, and of changes in the sciences and in international relations on the development of doctrines of national defense and practices in military organization, command, strategy, and tactics. We shall also present data on the social origins and mobility of the officer corps and the rank and file, on the differences between the officer corps of the various services, and above all, on the civil-military relationship and the origins of the East Central European brand of militarism. These studies will, we hope, result in a better understanding of the societies, governments, and politics of East Central Europe.

Our methodology takes into account that in the last three decades the study of war and national defense systems has moved away from narrow concern with battles, campaigns, and leaders and has come to concern itself with the evolution of the entire society. In fact, the interdependence of changes in society and changes in warfare and the proposition that military institutions closely reflect the character of the society of which they are a part have come to be accepted by historians, political scientists, sociologists, philosophers, and other students of war and national defense. Recognition of this fact constitutes one of the keystones of our approach to the subject.

Works in Western languages deal adequately with some aspects of the history of these peoples and this area, but with significant omissions. The present work, a study of the press during a particularly crucial period in the history of Hungary, fills a particularly important need in this regard and is, indeed, a pioneering work.

The Editor-in-Chief, of course, has the duty of assuring the comprehensive coverage, cohesion, internal balance, and scholarly standards of the series he has launched. He cheerfully accepts this responsibility and intends this work to be neither a justification nor a condemnation of the policies, attitudes, or activities of any of the nations involved. At the same time, because so many different disciplines, languages, interpretations, and schools of thought are represented, the policy in this and in future volumes was and shall be not to interfere with the contributions of the various participants, but to present them as a sampling of the schools of thought and the standards of scholarship in the many countries to which the contributors belong. As far as the present volume is concerned, the author, of course, is a distinguished Hungarian historian.

The Editor-in-Chief

Acknowledgments

Atlantic Studies on Society in Change conducts research, organizes conferences, and publishes scholarly books on various related social sciences, with substantial concentration on the study of how war affected East Central Europe. On that same subject, it publishes the series "War and Society in East Central Europe," of which the present volume is part. Most of the volumes contain selected papers presented at various conferences of the Program. However, individual scholars are from time to time invited to present complete monographs on important themes that may or may not have been discussed in any of the conferences. The present study is such a solicited study.

The Program has been housed and supported for several years by Brooklyn College of the City University of New York. The National Endowment for the Humanities, the International Research and Exchanges Board, and many other foundations have generously funded various activities of the Program.

The map was prepared by Edward J. Krasnoborski of the United States Military Academy at West Point, New York. The copy editing was done by Barbara Metzger; the bibliographical matter was prepared by Mrs. Miklós Vásárhelyi. Albert A. Nofi, the Assistant Editor of the series, coordinated the preparation of the manuscript for publication. The administrative work of the production process was done by Mrs. Dorothy Meyerson and Maurice Leibenstern.

To all these institutions and persons, I wish to express my most sincere appreciation and thanks.

Highland Lakes, New Jersey
August 20, 1986

Béla K. Király
Editor-in-Chief

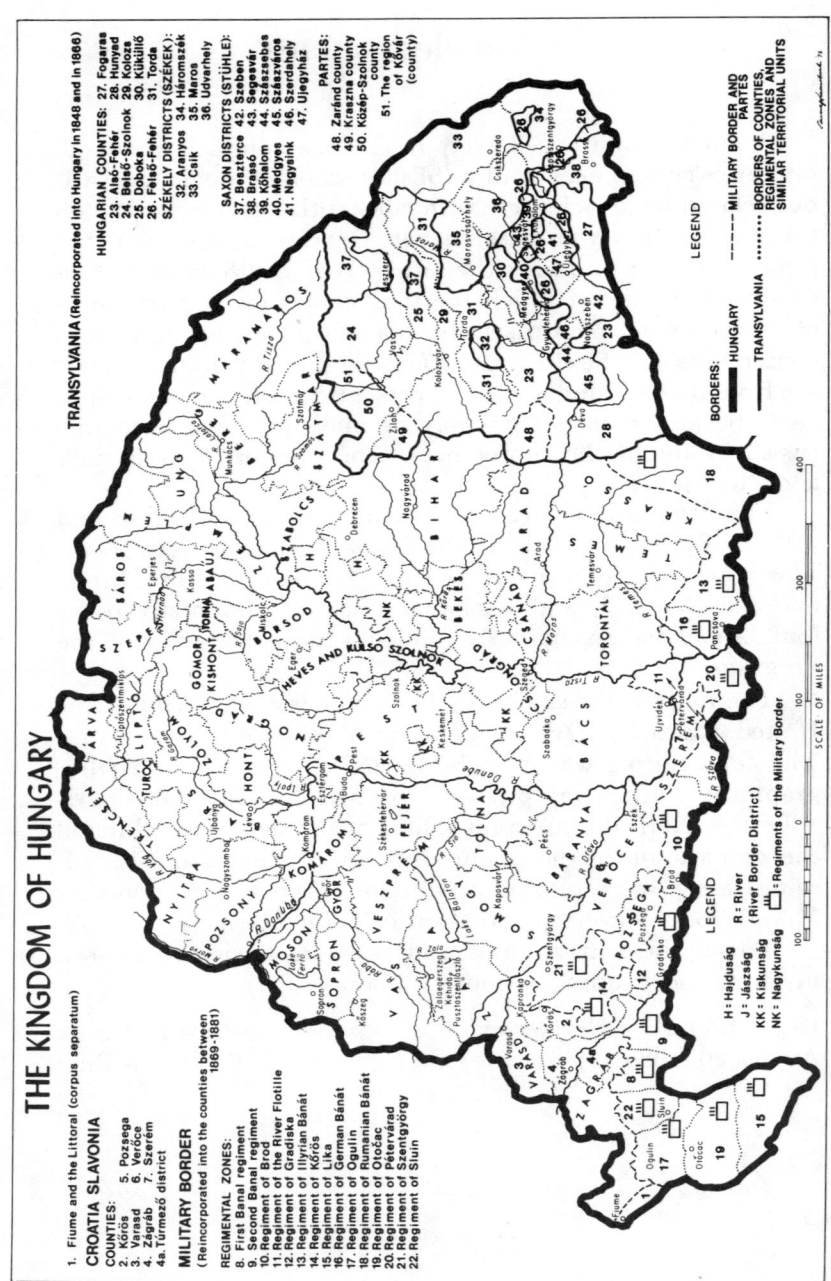

1. Antecedents: The Press before 1848

Beginnings, 1705-1831

The history of the Hungarian press begins in 1705 with the publication, in Latin, of the first issue of *Mercurius Hungaricus* (later *Mercurius Veridicus ex Hungaria*). Its purpose was to keep the public abroad informed on the events of the war of independence (1703-1711) that Prince Ferenc Rákóczi II was leading against the Habsburgs and to counteract the unfavourable impressions being disseminated by the *Wienerisches Diarium* (1703-). *Mercurius* appeared somewhat irregularly. Between 1705 and 1710 only seven issues are known to have been published. The next experiment, *Nova Posoniensia*, was a short-lived weekly (1721-1722) of a different character. Published in Pressburg (Pozsony, Bratislava; Posonium in Latin) by the eminent geographer Mathias Bél, it was used as an aid for teaching Latin and contemporary history at the local Lutheran college. For a time the early representatives of the German press in Hungary, published for the German-speaking citizens of some of the major cities, were of a similarly intermittent and precarious nature. The *Wöchentlich zweimal neu-angekommender Mercurius*, which appeared in Buda from 1730 to 1738 (or perhaps longer), by and large reproduced information taken from the *Wiener Zeitung*. Only in 1764 did the first regularly published journal of a permanent nature appear. Called the *Pressburger Zeitung*, it was to last 165 years, right up until 1929. After 1767 it had for a time a cultural supplement, *Der Freund der Tugend*. The paper's first editor, Karl Gottlieb Windisch, was one of local circle of enlightened intellectuals and later published some short-lived reviews in German as well (*Ungarisches Magazin*, 1781-1788; *Neues Ungarisches Magazin*, 1791-1792).

Pressburg became Hungary's first centre of journalism, although other cities soon had German-language papers of their own (Pest in 1772, Buda in 1786, and Nagyszeben /Hermannstadt, Sibiu/ in Transylvania in 1784). Pressburg, near

Vienna, had been the temporary capital of the country since the time of the Turkish conquest in the sixteenth century. It was important as a political, commercial, and cultural centre, housing government offices and a bourgeoisie and intelligentsia of German, Hungarian, and Slovak origin that generally spoke all three languages and referred to themselves as *Hungari*. Moreover, Pressburg had printers with the required equipment. Papers for German-, Hungarian- (1780), and Slovak-speakers (in Czech, 1783) appeared in succession and for a time existed side by side. It was in Pressburg that the first journal in the Hungarian language, the *Magyar Hírmondó* (Hungarian Messenger) was published from 1780 to 1788 by the enterprising local printer Ferenc Patzkó, who had obtained the right to do so from Maria Theresa.

Although it had had a late start, the Hungarian press developed swiftly. In a relatively short time it covered the long path from simple old-fashioned papers to political journals that sought to influence public opinion and cultural, literary reviews influenced in their conception by the English "moral" weeklies and their German followers. In the fifteen years after 1780 there arose a national press of surprising scope and variety. A slow but steady economic and social evolution in the eighteenth century, the emergence among the privileged nobility of enlightened groups that espoused a certain tendency towards modernization, an expanded reading public and intellectual activity, and the appearance of a new intelligentsia all seem to have assisted in producing the conditions that both permitted and necessitated a regular press. The decree of Joseph II in 1781 (promulgated in Hungary in 1782), although it did not of course introduce freedom of the press in the nineteenth-century liberal sense, did relax censorship considerably and greatly widen the scope for journalism.

Also characteristic of the early press was its fairly close relationship with the Enlightenment and enlightened political ideas. The Enlightenment in the peripheral, less developed areas of Europe, where the bourgeoisie was far less influential, branched out and gave rise to several political trends that in part contradicted one another. The first variant in Hungary, from 1765 on, was the enlightened despotism of the Habsburgs, embracing Josephinism and the reforms it involved. The second arose from the 1770s onwards among some groups of enlightened noblemen who sought to modernize the old system of political representation (the feudal Diet and estates) and to develop the national language and literature. Finally, in about 1785, a third variant appeared. A group consisting of intellectuals and a few noblemen aspired to introduce far-reaching reforms and eliminate all feudal privileges. On their own they did not constitute a serious political force, but they initially supported the system of Joseph II and, after its downfall in 1790, the enlightened "estates" programme. These successive tendencies were reflected in the press of the time, which to some extent shared their lot.

The first Hungarian paper, the *Magyar Hírmondó*, supported the national, cultural, and economic aspirations of the enlightened nobility. It began with 320 subscribers, 171 of them landowners and 93 members of the intelligentsia. The first editor was Mátyás Rát, a young Lutheran pastor of bourgeois origin who had studied theology at Göttingen. Having seen as a pupil of A. L. Schlözer's the importance of the press in Germany, he became on his return a pioneer of Hungarian journalism. In 1786 another Hungarian paper, this one explicitly Josephinist, was launched in Vienna by Sándor Szatsvay, a political journalist with avowed anti-clerical and anti-feudal opinions. His *Magyar Kurír* (Hungarian Courier) played a major part in spreading information about the French Revolution from 1789 onwards, and by 1790 it had twelve hundred subscribers. *Hadi és más nevezetes történetek* (Military and Other Notable Stories) was founded in 1788 by a group of Hungarian aristocrats, again in Vienna. Edited by Demeter Görög and Sámuel Kerekes, two intellectuals in their service, it became the organ for the national programme of the enlightened nobility. For a time the contributor responsible for news on the French Revolution was László Hajnóczy, later to be one of the leaders of the Hungarian Jacobins. Although Vienna had now become the centre of Hungarian journalism, Hungarian papers also appeared in Pest—the *Magyar Merkurius* (Hungarian Mercury, 1788-1789)—and in Nagyszeben—the *Erdélyi Magyar Hírvívő* (Transylvanian Hungarian Messenger, 1790-1791).

However, events took a turn for the worse after 1792. The Habsburg court and the Hungarian nobility were both by then frightened by the radical new developments of the French

Revolution and joined forces to preserve the existing social and political order. When some radical intellectuals tried to organize a Hungarian Jacobin movement, they were arrested and their leaders executed in 1795. Regression had begun. Censorship increased, and whereas eighteen papers were being published in Hungary in 1792, no more than four remained in 1805. The only one in Hungarian was the *Magyar Kurír*, from which Szatsvay had been dismissed as editor as early as 1793. The *Hadi* continued from 1792 as a new *Magyar Hírmondó* but also ceased publication in 1803, having earlier absorbed the *Bétsi Magyar Merkurius* (Viennese Hungarian Mercury), which had been edited since 1793 by Dániel Pánczél.

The development of the early Hungarian reviews followed the same pattern. The first, the *Magyar Museum* (1788-1793), was founded by a literary society in Kassa (Kosice) and became the organ of the national programme. It was edited by the poet János Batsányi. The co-founder was the Josephinist Ferenc Kazinczy, who soon started his own review, *Orpheus* (1789-1790). In Komárom, another local society launched the *Mindenes Gyűjtemény* (Miscellany, 1789-1792), edited by a Calvinist minister educated in Switzerland named József Pétzeli. One contributor to it, Ferenc Kováts, an engineer, went so far on one occasion as to suggest starting a popular journal for simple peasant readers. The first review to serve Pest as a literary centre was *Uránia* (1794-1795), which proved to be as short-lived as József Kármán, the young and very talented writer who edited it.

But the period of political reaction was also one of certain economic and social changes—war boom (for a time), inflation, the growth of Buda and Pest, and a widening of the urban public for reading matter. Slowly, to a degree, and largely in non-political fields, all this helped the press to recover. After some literary reviews in German put out by Lajos Schedius, a professor of aesthetics at the University of Pest (*Literarischer Anzeiger für Ungern*, 1798-1799; *Zeitschrift von und für Ungern*, 1802-1804), permission was given in 1806 for another Hungarian journal to appear in Pest, the *Hazai /és Külföldi/ Tudósítások* (Domestic /and Foreign/ Reports), edited by István Kultsár. Beginning in 1817 it also included a literary supplement, *Hasznos Mulatságok* (Useful Amusements). One sign of growing interest in the modernization of farming was the appearance of the *Nemzeti Gazda* (National Farmer), published between 1814 and 1818 by Ferenc Pethe, who had tried to start a similar venture in 1796. Meanwhile Gábor Döbrentei in Kolozsvár (Cluj-Napoca) edited a literary review called *Erdélyi Múzeum* (Transylvanian Museum, 1814-1818), whose scope extended to history, education, and other subjects. It was followed in Pest in 1817 by the *Tudományos Gyűjtemény* (Scholarly Collection), a paper of a general character biased towards history. The editor was György Fejér, a Roman Catholic priest and historian who became the director of the university library in Pest. It reflected the national views, outmoded and conceived in terms of privilege, of Hungarian noblemen of the day. A measure of change came only in 1828, when the paper was temporarily taken over by the poet Mihály Vörösmarty. More or less similar views were expounded in the *Felső Magyar Országi Minerva* (Upper Hungarian National Minerva), founded in Kassa by Count József Dessewffy in 1825. The last new venture in this period was devoted to literary criticism and aesthetics, *Élet és Literatúra* (Life and Literature), launched by Pál Szemere in 1826.

The Era of the Liberal Reform Movement, 1832-1847

A new chapter opened when a liberal opposition that advocated a new programme of national reform appeared among the politically active section of the nobility. More and more nobles began to sense the economic drawbacks and social dangers, even from their own point of view, of the old feudal system. Models to be followed were found in the liberal countries of the West. Moreover, the absolutist régime of the Habsburgs was so pinned down for a while in Germany and Italy by the international crisis of 1830 that it could not prevent this line of thinking in Hungary from expanding into a political movement. One thing the reform movement needed, of course, was a political press of a kind which had hardly existed in the country since the end of the eighteenth century. In 1832 two initiatives of different natures were made to try and meet the need. The difference between them derived from the multiplicity of variants and trends which existed from the outset within the liberal movement.

The first liberal paper was *Jelenkor* (Present Time), brought into being in January 1832 by the pioneer of the liberal reform movement, Count István Széchenyi (1791-1860), and edited by Mihály Helmeczy. It offered the public something new and soon had over three thousand subscribers. Strict censorship precluded its publishing direct political proposals, but it exerted a major influence merely by describing liberal institutions in more advanced countries. Its supplement, the *Társalkodó* (Conversationalist), was especially prone to using this indirect method and publishing travelogues and other reports from Britain and the United States.

Széchenyi had no doubts about the strength of the Habsburg Monarchy's position internationally and favoured reforms that might strengthen his country without provoking conflict with Vienna, but another, more popular trend in the movement chose to pursue in an updated form the old national policy of "grievances" and oppose the government more or less openly. A political writer of exceptional talent was soon found in Lajos Kossuth (1802-1894), at the time a young provincial lawyer. He undertook in December 1832 to start the *Országgyűlési Tudósítások* (Reports of the Diet), a political paper in manuscript form, circulated as private correspondence and summing up the proceedings of the Diet of 1832-1836 from the opposition point of view. Although the circulation was modest (it had only about thirty subscribers in 1833), this handwritten paper soon assumed real political significance. When it came to a natural end with No. 344 at the close of the Diet in spring 1836, Kossuth decided to continue with the *Törvényhatósági Tudósítások* (Municipal Reports), again "private correspondence" (and so in principle needing no special permission) covering the political debates in the counties (the autonomous local organizations of the nobility). After issuing some fruitless decrees prohibiting the paper, the government had Kossuth arrested in 1837 as one of several unsuccessful attempts to disband the Hungarian liberal movement.

This crisis hampered the development of the political press for a time, but even so the government thought it advisable to start a political paper that would represent its own interests. Called the *Hírnök* (Herald), it appeared in 1837 in Pressburg, edited by József Orosz. Meanwhile indirect ways of spreading new ideas were found by a growing number of cultural reviews.

Various strata in society were influenced by "fashion magazines," mostly literary in character, such as the *Regélő* (Storyteller) and its supplement the *Honművész* (Home Artist, 1833-1841), by *Rajzolatok* (Sketches, 1835-1839), by the *Tudománytár* (Scholarly Magazine), published by the Academy of Sciences (from 1834 onwards), and by popular weeklies of an educational character such as the *Garasos Tár* (Penny Magazine), launched in 1834 by Péter Vajda in Leipzig. The most important venture, the *Athenaeum* (1837-1842), which was jointly edited by the eminent literary critic, József Bajza, the Secretary of the Academy, Ferenc Schedel-Toldy, and Vörösmarty, soon became, with its supplement the *Figyelmező* (Observer), the main representative of liberal ideas, carrying essays, stories, and travel reports about the more advanced countries of the West.

The 1840s began with a kind of temporary reconciliation and witnessed the first really major rise of Hungarian political journalism. Censorship slackened. Kossuth was not only freed but offered with tacit governmental consent the editorship of a paper to be printed and published by Lajos Landerer, with the stipulation that if Kossuth exceeded certain limits he would be relieved of his post. However, the *Pesti Hírlap* (Pest Journal), launched in January 1841, enjoyed such unprecedented success (the number of subscribers rose from an initial sixty to fifty-two hundred in 1844) that for quite some time it was scarcely possible to take any measures against it. It was Hungary's first modern political journal, with regular features, Kossuth's dynamic leaders on the front page, and a more detailed "essay," usually on the same problem, on the back. The staff was an efficient one (for the number of intellectuals living by journalism was rising), and there were many correspondents, recruited among nobles in the various counties. Most of the latter were active later in the Party of Opposition. What Kossuth advocated was gradual, social, liberal reforms designed to "combine the interests" of noblemen, bourgeois, and peasants. He also espoused Hungarian nationalism and soon became one of the leaders of a national opposition that denounced the political and economic subordination of Hungary to Vienna. Széchenyi feared a renewed and more dangerous conflict with the Habsburgs (and with the national minorities). By beginning to polemicize against Kossuth he sacrificed much of his own popularity. But the *Pesti Hírlap*'s main adversary was *Világ* (meaning both "World" and "Light"). It had been started in 1841 as another liberal paper and edited by Péter Vajda but had been taken over by a group of "neo-conservative" aristocrats led by Count Aurél Dessewffy until his death in 1842. In 1844 Kossuth, outmanoeuvred by his own publisher, lost his position with the *Pesti Hírlap* and tried fruitlessly to lay his hands on another paper. The *Pesti Hírlap* remained liberal, however, under the editorship of László Szalay and from 1845 on Antal Csengery, both representative of the most progressive though less nationalist, "centralist" group of opposition reformers. From 1844 its main opponent became the conservative paper reorganized as *Budapesti Híradó* (Budapest Intelligencer), edited by Count Emil Dessewffy, brother of Aurél. Another conservative-clerical adversary of the liberals from 1840 on was the *Nemzeti Újság* (National News), a continuation of Kultsár's old paper. Against this conservative front, it was the modest *Hetilap* (Weekly), a trade paper of the Industrial Protection Association, that Kossuth tried to utilize in 1846-1847, publishing powerful articles and demanding urgent social and political reforms in a continual struggle against censorship.

The reviews of this decade included the *Budapesti Szemle* (Budapest Review), a short-lived but high-quality publication modelled on the *Edinburgh Review* and the *Revue des Deux Mondes* and edited in 1840-1841 by József Eötvös with help from other members of the centralist group of liberals already mentioned. The *Magyar Gazda* (Hungarian Farmer) was launched in 1841 by the Hungarian Economic Society, mostly composed of landowners and followers of Széchenyi, with Lajos Kacskovics and János Török as editors. This was the heyday of the literary fashion magazines, which popularized the new, more "bourgeois" and urbane ways of life of the liberal nobility. The illustrated *Regélő Pesti Divatlap* (The Storytelling Fashion Paper of Pest, 1842-1844) became the *Pesti Divatlap*, edited by János Garay and János Erdélyi and from 1844 on by Imre Vahot and reflecting a national and liberal outlook. *Honderű* (Serene Homeland), edited by Baron Lázár Petrichevich-Horváth from 1843 to 1848, represented the conservative and aristocratic trend and repeatedly attacked the new literature of the "Young Hungary" writers. *Életké-*

pek (Sketches from Life), a liberal and nationalist publication edited in 1843 by Adolf Frankenburg and later by the novelist Mór Jókai, became a forum for modern young writers such as the poet Sándor Petőfi and his circle. Its appeal was mainly to the intelligentsia, the petite bourgeoisie, and townspeople of German origin who were enthusiastic in their support of the Hungarians' cause. In 1847, *Hazánk* (Our Fatherland), a paper edited by the physician Pál Kovács in the provincial city of Győr, became another outlet for the new literature, while the *Magyar Szépirodalmi Szemle* (Hungarian Literary Review) was launched in 1847 by János Erdélyi, Imre Henszlman, and Ferenc Toldy.

Bibliography

The best recent synthesis for this period is György Kókay, ed., *A magyar sajtó története* (History of the Hungarian Press), vol. 1, *1705-1848* (Budapest, 1979). Earlier comprehensive works are Antal Szalády, *A magyar hírlapirodalom statisztikája 1780-1880*, (Statistics of Hungarian Journalism 1780-1880), (Budapest, 1884); József Ferenczy, *A magyar hírlapirodalom története 1780-1867-ig* (History of Hungarian Journalism 1780-1867) (Budapest, 1887); István Kereszty, *A magyar és magyarországi sajtó időrendi áttekintése 1705-1867* (Chronological Survey of the Press in Hungary, 1705-1867) (Budapest, 1916); Béla Dezsényi, *A magyar hírlapirodalom első százada, 1705-1805*, (The First Century of Hungarian Journalism, 1705-1805) (Budapest, 1941); Béla Dezsényi and György Nemes, *A magyar sajtó 250 éve* (250 Years of the Hungarian Press) (Budapest, 1954); György Kókay, *A magyar hírlap- és folyóiratirodalom kezdetei, 1780-1795* (The Beginnings of Hungarian Newspapers and Periodicals, 1780-1795) (Budapest, 1970); József Farkas, ed., *A magyar sajtótörténet irodalmának válogatott bibliográfiája* (Select Bibliography of the Literature on Hungarian Press History) (Budapest, 1972); *A magyar irodalomtörténet bibliográfiája* (Bibliography of the History of Hungarian Literature), vol. 1 /to 1792/ (Bydapest, 1972), vol. 2 /1792-1849/ (Budapest, 1975); Domokos Kosáry, *Művelődés a XVIII. századi Magyarországon* (Culture in Eighteenth-Century Hungary) (Budapest, 1980); idem, "A magyar sajtó megszületése" (Birth of the Hungarian Press), *Magyar Könyvszemle* (MKsz below), 1981, pp. 7-15.

2. Hungary and the European Revolutions

The various regions and countries of mid-nineteenth-century Europe differed widely in degree of socioeconomic development. Less developed conditions and feudalism still prevailed in East Central Europe, including the Habsburg Monarchy and Hungary within it. How, then, could the revolutions of 1848 have broken out almost at the same time, as a single wave over practically the whole continent? What synchronized those revolutions?

First, the various regions and countries were moving in the same main direction, from feudalism to capitalism. In Hungary it is usual to date this preparatory period (which antedates the age of reform) from about 1790, in other words, from the time of France's bourgeois revolution. The age of reform (after 1830) demonstrates particularly well how the examples of the more highly developed countries influenced those following in their footsteps.

Second, the first half of the nineteenth century brought a steady intensification of a variety of internal social and political conflicts within these countries, with their differing levels of development. In France the majority of the prosperous industrial bourgeoisie—not to mention the petite bourgeoisie, behind whom the new working class was preparing to take the historical stage as the next great force—remained excluded from power even after the revolution of July 1830. In Britain a variety of reforms had made it possible on the whole for the various broad strata of the middle class to present a common front against the Chartist movements that emerged among the working class, but in France even the more prosperous members of the bourgeoisie were initially prepared to join other forces in overthrowing the régime of the time. Hungary lacked a powerful bourgeoisie, and so the middle-ranking nobility, slowly acquiring bourgeois attitudes, came, partly as a result of changes in its own socioeconomic conditions and growing awareness of the crisis of feudalism and partly in response to the example of more developed bourgeois countries, to lead the movement, from 1830 on, for social and political reform and to raise the nation from a subordinate political and economic position. In this reform period, one can observe the political, economic, legal, social, and philosophical views of liberalism spreading in Hungary, the radical trend separating from it, and some echo of the new Western socialistic ideas, at times even in the writings of their conservative opponents or in those of liberals who sought to avoid the pitfalls of bourgeois development. Among the main factors determining the policy of the liberal nobility was the internal tension, the potentially explosive antagonism felt by the peasant masses living in feudal serfdom for the privileged, landowning nobility. This antagonism was given no small emphasis in the arguments of those who advocated reform and the forestalling of the dangers. Despite all that distinguished them, the social and political systems of France, Hungary, and the other countries all contained growing antagonisms and approaching crises.

Turning to the third synchronizing factor, the antagonisms were heightened by poor harvests everywhere in the years immediately before 1848. Famine struck in many places, and the economic crisis that emerged helped to produce a revolutionary situation.

The final and most direct factor was the political chain reaction caused by the revolutions themselves. A revolution in one place assisted the others not merely by serving as an encouraging example but by altering the relations of power and laming the old régimes. The first great impetus in 1848 came from the February revolution in France. The second came from the revolution in Vienna that ensued on March 13. The latter's force spread widely, because Habsburg power, embodied in the system of Metternich, weighed at once on the German states, on Italy, and of course on Hungary. Thus when Vienna was shaken the reverberations went out in a number of directions, causing a succession of further movements. This revolutionary chain reaction in Europe gave a new impetus to the slackening reform opposition in Hungary and allowed Hungary to take a similarly revolutionary path to bourgeois national transformation. As concomitants the press won freedom and a liberal press was able to emerge.

3. The Last Feudal Diet and the Press

At the last feudal Diet, which opened in Pressburg in the autumn of 1847, Kossuth's tactic was to avoid issues that might split the opposition nobility and to concentrate on issues that could unite them and set them against the government. On the abolition of feudal privileges, including the big questions of generalization of taxation and redemption of feudal dues, the opposition deputies were not all willing to go the same distance, although even some conservative deputies were prepared to go a little way. On these issues the line between the two parties was less clear than the line that distinguished the government—the system of county administrators appointed by the court—from the advocates of national demands. Thus the subsequent debates in the Diet were centred less on domestic reform than on the growing struggle by Kossuth's supporters to keep the constitutional grievances on the agenda and bring down the existing system of government and on the efforts of the government and its supporters to break the unity of the opposition and split a "moderate" centre party off from it.

How far the Diet got between November 1847 and March 1848 can be reconstructed from the press of the time. It approved a partial generalization of the tax burden. It came close to adopting a motion in principle that would make redemption of feudal obligations compulsory and a concern of the state in cases where the peasantry desired it and paid "complete" compensation, partly in land, but shrank from immediate, general, compulsory redemption and from obliging the state itself to shoulder the payment of the indemnification. It approved a radical amendment of the system of entail (*aviticitas*) but not the full abolition of it. Lastly, it discussed in detail the problem of the royal cities and their suffrage.

With the freedom of the press, which particularly concerns us here, not even that much happened. The subject cropped up immediately on November 16 at the first district session of the lower house in the form of a debate on how greater publicity could be given to the Diet's proceedings. The subject was an old one, but because the role of the political press and the leeway afforded it had been growing, the issue of the press clearly required settling in more general terms. During the debate Kossuth declared, "It is time we took up the issue of the press in full. A free press is the antecedent of everything, and nowhere else in the world is the press in so piteous a position as it is in this country." Kossuth and some others opposed having a special Diet paper, which would take on "the hue of monopoly." He wanted to see "all newspapers freely convey the proceedings of the Diet" and to set up a special committee to draft a press bill. Many opposition deputies agreed, and so did some conservatives such as Pál Somssich, who also believed the press should be free from pre-publication censorship. However, the vote was twenty-five to twenty-four in favour of a special Diet paper, to be bound over with a deposit of 5,000 forints. It was also agreed that a special committee should be set up. It was then decided that until the press issue had been dealt with, the palatine (the highest administrative dignitary in Hungary) should be responsible for seeing that "the proceedings of the Diet can be published by the newspapers without restriction." Certainly the political papers did report developments in the Diet in a fair amount of detail, although not of course without restriction, during the months that followed. In a debate on November 19, János Zarka, the *personalis* (the speaker, the king's personal representative in the lower house), ventured to defend the government by claiming that censorship as an institution was basically sound but censors as individuals made mistakes. This allowed Kossuth to refer to his own experience in speaking against "idea-strangling" censorship and to criticize a procedure aimed solely at making individuals bear the responsibility for the errors of institutions. A committee consisting largely of opposition deputies was set up under the chairmanship of Count István Széchenyi but never really functioned, although we know from Bertalan Szemere that in January 1848 he was working as the committee's secretary on the drafting of a press bill.

Taking all this into account, the opposition leaders might have hoped that this Diet, unlike its predecessor, was taking serious "preliminary steps" in the direction of reform, but they could hardly have hoped that this would be the last feudal Diet at which they would fight their battles. The likelihood was that these "preliminary steps" would fall short of the measures Kossuth and his associates considered urgent. Even though the results outlined above amounted to an advance, the situation they reflected was one in which the nobility's policy of reform was losing momentum and stopping short at inadequate measures. The desire among the opposition for compromise even showed up in Kossuth's struggle against the Vienna régime for national demands. Early in 1848 the government managed to reach a secret agreement with the "moderate" members of the opposition that if the court made a conciliatory written promise to remedy the administrator system and supported the reforms of generalized taxation, redemption of feudal obligations, and the reorganization of the cities, the "moderates" would drop their constitutional grievances and the "agitational matters" which Kossuth had pushed into the forefront—in other words, abandon the constitutional-cum-national struggle. On February 5, 1848, the lower house even voted against Kossuth for the centre party's proposal. By great efforts Kossuth managed to prevent a split in the opposition, but victory continued to elude him. He was voted down again on February 21 by the railway committee of the Diet, which threw out the plan for a line to the Adriatic through Croatia and came out in favour of Széchenyi's central plan for the railways. After that Kossuth himself saw a need to begin negotiating within the government along the lines envisaged by the centre party. As the balance remained temporarily uncertain, he and his adherents scanned the horizon of international politics with growing expectation and noted the appearance of revolutionary forces all over Europe, for the time being in Habsburg-ruled northern Italy in particular.

In the event, the Hungarian opposition was extricated from its predicament by a European revolution that came in two consecutive stages and radically altered the balance of forces in Europe.

The Impact of the Paris Revolution

The first stage began with the revolution in Paris in February 1848, news of which reached Vienna and Pressburg on March 1. On March 3, in accordance with a resolution of the conference of deputies on the previous day, Kossuth submitted his motion on the address to the king "before a vast audience, with the galleries packed to suffocation, amid quivering expectation." It was enthusiastically accepted by the lower house. In a monumental speech Kossuth thrust aside the now superfluous tactic of the grievances: "Let us raise our policy to the level of events." The "true fount" of the troubles, he argued, was to be found in Vienna's bureaucratic, absolutist system of government, which had to be discarded and replaced by a constitutional apparatus before it entangled the Monarchy in a web of direst peril. The goal was constitutional transformation and unification of interests—internal reform. "If we disperse from the Diet without delivering to the people what they so rightfully and justifiably expect of the legislature, who will dare shoulder the responsibility for what ensues?"

Particular care is needed to establish the precise, original meaning of the March 3 motion because Hungarian historians have often assessed it in the light of subsequent developments and on the basis of the demands the delegation of the Diet delivered to Vienna on March 15. The original and the later programme tallied in direction but not in extent. The blurring of the distinctions between them dates back to the middle nobility's contemporary assessment of events. This arose at the Pressburg Diet out of a theory that there had been a magnanimous, voluntary renunciation of noble privileges. The story goes that the Diet of nobles accepted the *entire* programme of bourgeois transformation in Pressburg on March 3, anticipating the revolutionary movements in Vienna and Pest and acting independently of their influence. This is supposed to have encompassed the spheres of national independence (a responsible government for Hungary) and domestic reform of society (abolition of serfdom and generalization of the tax burden) and to have been supplemented on March 14 only by subjects (such as general education and union with Transylvania) that did not require revolutionary pressure for acceptance. In fact, that is not how it happened and under the circumstances could hardly have been so.

All the motion of March 3 called for in terms of domestic reform was *immediate* implementation of what the Diet had agreed to in principle *so far*. It is to this work *previously* completed by the Diet that the following sentence in the motion refers: "We have decided that we shall share, on a basis of generalization of the burden of taxation, those taxes on the populace by which they have so far covered the expenses of the county administration alone and allow the country's new requirements to be covered on a similar basis." This meant the sharing of the burden of the "domestic" tax of the counties and a national fund to which the estates had agreed earlier, *not* acceptance of full generalization of taxation.

Kossuth spoke in the same sense on the issue of the serfs: "We have decided so to effect the dissolution of urbarial relations /a Hungarian Latin term denoting the ensemble of the relationships between serfs and feudal landlords/ as to combine it with compensation." This still fell short of abolishing serfdom with indemnification to be paid by the state; on March 6 (*after* the motion on the address had been passed) the lower house continued its discussion of the problem of redemption in accordance with the earlier positions taken up, and all Kossuth managed to get accepted was the principle that if a feudal tenant had no money to redeem himself, the sum would become a debt: "The urbarial relation would change into one of indebtedness."

More support for the argument comes from the fact that the motion of March 3 failed to mention freedom of the press, which the Diet had not discussed since the committee had been appointed and so could not have come to any decision about. All that happened was that the Diet Youth, the *iurati* (those preparing for legal careers), submitted to the Diet a petition on the subject with several hundred signatures on the same day as the motion on the address was introduced.

As far as administration is concerned, the motion did indeed declare that Hungary needed "a national government independent of all alien interference" and therefore "the transformation of our collegiate system of government into a responsible Hungarian ministry" was "a fundamental prerequisite and essential safeguard for all our reforms." But for the time being the Diet merely urged the monarch to send to take part in the work of the Diet representatives with full power "as members of the Lieutenancy Council" so that the reforms could be seen through speedily. Clearly this would have meant appointing to the Lieutenancy Council new "members," some of them from the opposition, but not the creation of a responsible ministry. Kossuth had originally intended to demand a responsible ministry but found himself unable to do so if he wanted to see the motion passed.

Although Kossuth demanded a constitution for the other Austrian dominions as well, he clearly did *not* consider it realistic or timely on March 3 to place a *full* liberal-national programme before the nobility of the Diet. The events in Paris might have speeded up realization of reform plans already mooted, but they did not suffice to persuade all or the bulk of the nobility of the Diet to advance beyond those plans. This does not, of course, make it less significant that the opposition had now put forward in the name of the whole lower house a demand for a national government, albeit in a transitional form.

At that point, however, during the first stage in the revolutionary chain reaction and while Vienna's position of power was still unshaken, the administration and its adherents managed to deter the aristocracy of the upper house from considering the March 3 motion on the address. In a letter to Széchenyi on March 1, the chancellor, Count György Apponyi, made a veiled but unambiguous threat that assistance would be sought from tsarist Russia if Hungary came up with demands at that time. However, Kossuth, who had already been in touch with the Pest opposition organization known as the Opposition Circle, was expecting the capital to support the struggle in Pressburg with new forces and moves. At a committee meeting of the Opposition Circle on March 4, the radically minded Count László Teleki is known to have responded to an earlier message from Kossuth by proposing that the work of the Diet be expedited with energetic measures aimed at taking advantage of "this important period of unexpected events" to resolve the issues of "freedom of the press and the holding of annual diets in Pest." Just as the committee was discussing what to do, the text of Kossuth's March 3 motion arrived. The committee hastened to embrace the initiatives it contained but thought it necessary to inform the Diet with all speed that it considered the motion incomplete in lacking any reference to freedom of the press. However, the majority of this highly heterogeneous committee was not prepared to take more decisive action. A tougher response was to be expected only from the young radical minority gathered around the poet Sándor Petőfi, which was displaying growing dissatisfaction with this hesitancy and with the motion itself for its failure to mention freedom of the press. Petőfi himself left evidence of this impatience in his poem "Az országgyűléshez" (To the Diet). For the same reason, one young radical member of the committee, Dániel Irányi, went to Pressburg on March 5 to see Kossuth, who thought it would be excellent for petitions to be got up in Pest to try and make the Diet move faster. The Opposition Circle endorsed the plan for petitions on March 9 and went so far as to entrust the drafting of the text for them to another young radical, József Irinyi. This marked the birth of the Twelve Points, which went beyond the March 3 motion not only in their demand for freedom of the press but in their call for equality before the law. Yet they remained within the programme acceptable to the liberal noble reformers and were therefore endorsed by the Opposition Circle on March 13. The Circle did not, however, accept the young radicals' idea that the points should be sent to Pressburg not only as its petition but also in the name of a mass rally to be held on March 19 on Rákos Field, where the people of Pest, already mobilized, might be joined by the provincials and peasants arriving in the city for the St Joseph's Day fair. The Opposition Circle prepared to dissuade the young radicals from doing this at a meeting planned for the afternoon of the following day, March 14. Clearly the liberals and the radicals in the opposition ranks were parting company.

News of these revolutionary preliminaries began to reach Pressburg, where many read Petőfi's poem accusing the Diet of defalcating on freedom of the press. Alarming news was also being spread of peasant movements that were supposed to be springing up in the various parts of the country. But a whole new complexion was put on affairs by the next, decisive turn of events—the revolution in Vienna.

The Impact of the Vienna Revolution

As late as March 13 the palatine returned to Pressburg from Vienna charged with preventing at all costs the passage of the motion on the address to the king by the upper house. No change in that situation was made by the meeting held that day before a large crowd on the promenade in Pressburg by the Diet Youth, who called for the submission of the motion, freedom of the press, and the institution of a government that would be representative of the people. But on March 13 the revolution in Vienna followed the example of Paris and overturned the absolutist régime sustained by censorship and bayonets. The second stage in the revolutionary chain reaction had been reached.

By the time Kossuth announced early on the morning of March 14 to a circular (debating) session of the lower house, excited "to the greatest degree," that "the Metternich ministry has fallen," the balance of forces had totally altered. With a sure hand Kossuth pointed out to the nobility the path open to them after the fall of the government, a path, moreover, which the growth of the revolutionary forces obliged them to follow. "To us falls the formidable task," he told them, "of guiding these movements wisely, and we must make sure the reins remain in our hands, because then we can continue to advance along a constitutional path, but once the reins are jerked from our grasp, God alone knows what the consequences will be." In other words, the Diet should not allow itself to exceed the necessary limit, but it should go to that limit and act immediately.

Kossuth defined the most urgent tasks. First, the palatine should be requested to see that the upper house immediately pass the motion on the address without debate: "I should not like to see the news of the movements in Vienna spread around the country before our motion had been submitted." Immediately after that, it was urgent that a bill on the freedom of the press be drafted. Thirdly, a committee should be created to prepare a proposal "in hours, not in days," to ensure "the defence of internal peace." Thus freedom of the press had now been placed in an extremely important position. "The Viennese already have freedom of the press," Kossuth said by way of justification. "Do we want to subject our Hungarian homeland to a flood of printed matter that is not in the Hungarian language and has been conceived in an alien spirit, or would we rather restore, with necessary circumscriptions, the freedom of the press, to which we have not merely a general, constitutional right but one rooted in positive laws, and which was taken from us only by force and abuse?" The Diet committee concerned "should not spend a long time drafting the law but submit as soon as possible a proposal containing the main principles, lest the freedom of the press be dictated elsewhere instead of here, in the lawful place." The allusion was plainly to the young radicals of Pest and is a sign that Kossuth was informed of what the latter were aiming to do.

The palatine having readily yielded to the request of the delegation that approached him, Kossuth summoned his fellow deputies into continuous session and repeated his proposals on the press and on domestic security, which Zsigmond Bernáth supplemented to general approval by saying it would be better if deputies informed their constituents about developments in a joint report. Then Széchenyi, as chairman of the committee on press affairs, announced that he would "call together" the members on the following day, adding, "I would have done so already if I had not been occupied with the work of various other committees." He said he was still uncertain whether Hungary was "heading for a finer future" or for catastrophe, but he added, "The remedy . . . is in our hands;" the choice had to be made between reform and anarchy. On his part there was "a long-treasured desire to see Hungary turn on its own axis. . . . Our nation's task is to be the basis for constitutional development and the support of the dynasty; now is the time for it to cease being a province and become a motherland." In conclusion he invited the trust of Kossuth, from whom, he said, he had differed up to now only in methods and not in purposes. Móric Szentkirályi then announced that "the bill on redemption has been printed and can be debated at any time." For the time being, however, this and the matter of the cities were laid aside, since "every head and heart in the chamber was filled with the ideas of representation of the people, freedom of the press, and the national guard," as can be read in the detailed eye-witness report in the *Pesti Hírlap* of March 18. József Justh spoke next, saying, "The demand for freedom of the press should be forwarded together with today's message," for "there is no need in this case for lengthy drafting of the law; only two main principles need be stated beforehand: the abolition of prior examination and the establishment of a jury for cases of libel." The radical László Madarász then urged that freedom of the press be declared immediately. He owned himself dissatisfied with Széchenyi's statement, seeing "no further need for lengthy work in committee." All that was needed, he said, was "to proclaim the freedom of the press as the country's sacred possession, shackled only by the political system which has now fallen." The nation should reclaim this "stolen treasure" without delay. "If there is freedom of the press in Austria, why should there not be here? As long as the nation *wishes* to do so, it can effect and ensure it. Let us not allow the moment to slip by; let the committee convene forthwith and without any fancy legislative draftsmanship express the main principles: *freedom of the press*; *jury!*" Dénes Pázmándy agreed that the main principles should be set forth immediately, with their application to be deliberated upon once they had been sanctioned; at this juncture, he felt, use had to be made of the favourable occasion. He considered two important things to have been left out of the motion on the address: *the freedom of the press* and *the jury*. A new message was required, he argued, "in which it is openly stated that the freedom of the press has been accepted." At this point somebody, perhaps Kossuth himself, intervened: "It *is* in the motion on the address." "But it is not in there openly and clearly," Pázmándy replied. "When the motion was prepared the circumstances were different; now it has to be put in clearly." But any kind of new message could clearly cause delay and hindrance, and so Kossuth in winding up the debate explained why he had used "general expressions" at certain points in the motion on the address. In his view freedom of the press had *not* been omitted from the motion: "the general expression that our intellectual interests should be nurtured on the basis of freedom covers freedom of the press as well, and whether more or fewer specifics are attached to these general expressions depends on the will and power of the Diet." Thus "it will suffice for the house to express in the form of a resolution that it understands all these to be embraced." Nor did he think a long process of legislative drafting was required: "the issue of the press is so clear that the law does not need discussing, merely recording." What had to be said, as he saw it, was that freedom of the press was established in Hungary and prior censorship abolished, that press offences would be punished by a jury, and that the penalties would be those found in the penal code proposed by the Diet of 1843-1844. The session eventually concurred with Kossuth's proposals, with the addition that the motion on the address, which had in the mean time been passed by the upper house, should be taken to Vienna the next day by a delegation.

The deputies' joint declaration dated March 14 also contains in the form of a resolution that

> a restricted press cannot remain in this country alongside the neighbouring free press, and so nothing can brook delay less than the restoration of the unannulled and inalienable right of the country to a free press; therefore the drafting of the press law has been left to an authorized committee, that it may proceed as fast as possible, relying in addition on the preparatory studies to be found among the documents of the last Diet.

From Széchenyi's diary one learns that a "press committee meeting" took place at his home that very evening. But the essential thing was that a decision in principle had now been taken.

Interestingly, the deputies' declaration (dated March 14, remember) anticipated, in certain essential points such as the generalization of taxation and the abolition of serfdom, decisions only taken the following morning. At the circular session of the lower house which began at eight in the morning on March 15, Móric Szentkirályi read out a text he had composed "by way of explanation of certain expressions in the motion on the address which was sent to their lordships the aristocracy in consideration of the tasks of the Diet." In this the estates declared that "in referring to the need for the nurturing of intellectual development they also wish the education of the people, the reciprocality of religious rights and the freedom of the press . . . to be literally understood," along with union with Transylvania, and that by the desire for development of the system of representation in a constitutional direction they also wished to express the need for diets to be held annually in Pest.

This all accorded with Kossuth's argument of the previous day that the general expressions in the motion on the address (which rested on the earlier, more modest programme) could be retrospectively invested with the additional demands of the fuller programme that swiftly changing circumstances had made opportune. But one decisive step still to be taken was to face the knotty problems of taxation and redemption of feudal obligations. The revolution in Vienna faced the hesitant nobles with the alarming prospect that the peasants in Hungary might use force and revolutionary methods to free themselves of their feudal constraints and turn against their landlords. As we have seen, the news of the preliminary moves in Pest was interpreted in Pressburg to entail an incipient peasant uprising, whereupon the so-far sluggish apparatus of the feudal Diet suddenly, at the last minute, grew wings. It became apparent that both the motion on the address and the solution of March 6 had been overtaken by circumstances. On the morning of March 15, shortly before the delegation's boat left Pressburg for Vienna, "the lower house, upon the initiative of Lajos Kossuth but principally through an understanding of the great warning uttered by the times, accepted proportionate division in the 'domestic' and war tax and public works, in a word in all burdens upon the people." After several speakers, including Széchenyi, had expressed approval, Szentkirályi "in a few short words put forward his motion that the state would undertake the indemnification of the landowners once problems of urbarial relations had been settled by law. This was received with general approval." Finally, on the initiative of Kossuth, the house gave the city deputies full voting rights and approved the text of the joint statement of the deputies decided upon on the previous day, so that news might spread as quickly as possible of the nobles' having finally overstepped the limits of feudalism and departed for Vienna in the name of the new, bourgeois nation.

The story of the delegation's journey does not need retelling here. Suffice it to say that in Vienna the Council of State held out until late at night on March 16 and only conceded then because the tidings of revolutionary preparations and the behaviour of the Viennese public, which received Kossuth with unparalleled demonstrations of sympathy, made it fear that the revolutionary forces would permanently rob them of Hungary and even storm the Viennese Burg itself with the armed law students of the Hungarian delegation at their head. That fear produced the royal document of March 17 that, with its purposely deficient expressions corrected, formed the basis on which the palatine, already bound by the promise he had given Kossuth and the others, obtained the verbal consent of Ferdinand V and appointed Count Lajos Batthyány Hungary's responsible prime minister.

Bibliography

Mihály Horváth, *Huszonöt év Magyarország történelméből, 1823-1848* (Twenty-Five Years of Hungary's History, 1823-1848), vols. 2 and 3 (Pest, 1868); István Barta, ed., *Kossuth Lajos az utolsó rendi országgyűlésen* (Lajos Kossuth at the Last Feudal Diet) (Budapest, 1951); Domokos Kosáry, "Kossuth Lajos harca" (Lajos Kossuth's Battle), in *Emlékkönyv Kossuth Lajos születésének 150. évfordulójára* (Memorial Volume for the 150th Anniversary of the Birth of Lajos Kossuth), vol. 1 (Budapest, 1952), pp. 1-86.

4. The March Revolution in Pest and the Freedom of the Press

Mention has already been made of the influence that news of the revolutionary preliminaries in Pest, the real centre of the country, had in Pressburg and even in Vienna. But at the time referred to it was still not known in Pressburg or Vienna that in the mean time, early on the morning of March 15, about the time the boat with the delegation from the Hungarian Diet set out for Vienna, the revolution had really broken out in Pest and produced as its first and greatest achievement the freedom of the press.

On the previous day, March 14, fairly heated debate had taken place at the meeting of the Opposition Circle between the liberals and young radicals such as József Irinyi or Pál Vasvári, who insisted on the plan for a mass rally. Eventually the majority followed the suggestion of Pál Nyáry, second *vicecomes* of Pest County, and some other provincial politicians of the liberal nobility that the Twelve Points be sent to Batthyány in Pressburg for him to put to the Diet. The young radicals continued the debate among themselves after the meeting in the Pilvax Café until news reached them there of the revolution in Vienna. Thereupon all were agreed that they had to take a revolutionary course without loss of time and make the Twelve Points public as the resolution of the people of Pest. On the evening of March 14 Petőfi wrote in his diary "Logically the first step and at the same time the first duty of the revolution is to free the press. Tomorrow we must attain the freedom of the press."

In the eyes of the young radical writers, freedom of the press was indeed the foundation and starting point for all other freedoms. Without it the burning political and social issues and the demands for a great transformation could not be publicly expressed. Understandably, then, the very first of the Twelve Points read "We demand abolition of censorship." Only then followed demands for a responsible ministry, equality before the law, generalization of taxation, the abolition of serfdom, and so on.

The reason intellectuals and particularly men of letters made up the vanguard of the revolution was partly the limited development of a Hungarian bourgeoisie and partly the fact that for a long time it had been possible to express revolutionary ideas only indirectly, through literature. But it is worth analysing how and under what circumstances that fairly small literary group usually referred to as the March Youth was able to initiate a revolution of truly historic importance.

This literary group had formed on the eve of 1848 out of small circles of friends. As members one can list about fifty young writers and journalists. Apart from Petőfi and his close friends at the centre, there were like-minded contemporaries of theirs, mainly in Pest but some from the provinces. Most were men of lower-middle-class background whose fathers were bourgeois, minor officials, or in some cases well-to-do peasant burgesses. Hardly any were from noble families, and fewer still had been brought up wealthy. One of the main features they had in common was a radical turn of mind, although this was not universal. Another common feature was their youth: Petőfi and Kálmán Lisznyai were twenty-five, Jókai twenty-three, Gyula Bulyovszky and Pál Vasvári only twenty-one at the time. The oldest were Albert Pálffy, Alajos Degré, and Imre Vahot, who were twenty-eight.

The conditions under which a literary group could be formed and exert influence had largely been produced by the urban development of Budapest. (The name was already being used to denote the three cities of Buda, Pest, and Óbuda.) With a population of a hundred fifty thousand, it was the only really large modern city in the Hungary of that time. It was the seat of the main government offices (*dicasteria*), other offices, and the institutes of higher education. It was the centre economically, particularly commercially, and the centre of culture, literature, and the political press. Pest, with its hundred thousand inhabitants, was naturally the leading city of the three. In March 1848 there were in it nobles, members of the learned professions (*honoratiores*), merchants, artisans and their journeymen, printers, shipyard workers, students, day labourers, plebeian elements, and peasants and traders up for the St Joseph's Day fair ready to react after their own fashion, with alarm or curiosity or as an enthusiastic mass force, to the call of the revolution.

Recent studies of social history have shown that the March Youth should be considered not an isolated phenomenon but the intellectual vanguard of the strata intent on bettering themselves—the petite bourgeoisie in the making. The influence of commodity production and the emergence of a bourgeois frame of mind was not confined to transforming the conditions, lives, and attitudes of the middle nobility that had played the part of a liberal bourgeoisie since the beginning of the age of reform. Their influence extended far more widely, to a variety of strata including rural bourgeois entrepreneurs in the market towns, urban German elements keenly assimilating themselves, and poorer people moving to the towns, particularly the outskirts of Pest, some with ambitions to join the intelligentsia. These shared an interest in eliminating the feudal system and breaking down the barriers to social advancement. Under the conditions in Hungary at the time, they did not represent a force comparable to the nobility, but in a historically critical situation, particularly in more developed and urbanized centres, they could become a significant factor.

Politically they corresponded to the petite bourgeoisie upon which radical, republican endeavours were based in the more developed societies of France and Germany. This petite bourgeoisie in the making exhibited a strong Hungarian nationalism directed against the administration of the Habsburg Monarchy and, in places like Pest, against the better-to-do German bourgeoisie of the guilds. It also sought more democracy, a demand made more immediate by the ordinary man's defencelessness in society. It had little confidence in the nobility's programme of liberalism, which it would have liked to broaden sufficiently to embrace its own aspirations as well. That is how Petőfi, who expressed that radicalism and served as a pattern for the plebeian intellectual, could be so much at ease and find so direct a response among those strata in the various parts of the country, at least until the revolution, while the battle to abolish feudalism was being waged jointly. Soon after that, it became clear that the unity was breaking up, many were calling for a halt, and the ideas of the leader of the March Youth led farther than the petite bourgeoisie and, in part, even the bourgeois revolution wanted to go. But in 1847, before the Diet, when the liberal opposition nobility were playing the leading part in Pest, Petőfi and his writer friends were able to find a temporary mouthpiece in the periodical *Hazánk*, published in the city of Győr, where society had been in the vanguard of bourgeois development since the eighteenth century and so could provide a modest but adequate base for what they were attempting. However, in the spring of 1848, the centre became Pest and the meeting place and political club for the March Youth the Pilvax Café. There they prepared, while analysing the revolutions in France, to take the initiative in the expected revolution. Circumstances gave them the opportunity of playing a truly important role in the revolutionary situation, and that opportunity was truly seized.

On the morning of the great day, a group of about ten persons, including Petőfi, set out from the Pilvax Café in the cold rain, armed with the Twelve Points and with Petőfi's "Nemzeti Dal" (National Song). By the time they had finished their round of university, medical, engineering, and law students, their numbers had swelled to about a thousand. But around ten o'clock, when they arrived outside Landerer and Heckenast's press in Hatvani utca (afterwards renamed Szabad Sajtó utca, "Free Press Street") at the proposal of Petőfi, there was a crowd of about five thousand following them. The proprietor, Lajos Landerer, always knew how to manoeuvre smartly, whether facing government officials or revolutionaries. He had learned of the latter's intentions the previous night and was awaiting them fully prepared with the whole of his staff and sufficient stocks of paper for printing. In answer to the equally well-informed Pest city captain (in charge of law and order), who asked him whether he wanted armed guards in front of the printing office, he is known to have declined, saying that if the crowd were small there would be no need for them and if the crowd were large they would only make matters worse. When Petőfi, Vasvári, and Irinyi, the foreign editor of the *Pesti Hírlap*, along with Jókai, the editor of *Életképek*, which was printed by Landerer, and some others entered the printer's and demanded that the Twelve Points and the National Song be printed, Landerer at first refused as a matter of form, saying that the manuscripts lacked the censor's imprimatur, but then immediately whispered that they should requisition a press. They then walked into the press room, where one of them, probably Irinyi, put his hand on a Columbian iron press and said, "We requisition this press in the people's name and demand that our manuscripts be printed." Landerer, saying he could not oppose force, instructed the foreman, Endre Träger, to comply with the wishes of Petőfi and the others. Five compositors got down to business, and that was how, as *Jelenkor* put it next day, were born "without prior examination the first twins in the legal, clean bed of a Hungarian press uninfected by censorship."

The group then marched to the National Museum, where, learning that the city council was due to meet in the afternoon, they decided, backed by the crowd, to make the councillors accept the Twelve Points too. In the meantime the procession was joined by some liberal opposition nobles such as the county attorney general, Gábor Klauzál, Sámuel Egressy, and Pál Nyáry, men who not long before had been remarking ironically that Petőfi and his companions were playing at revolution. The crowd spilled into the council chamber, "tightly encircling the councillors," the majority of whom showed a lack of enthusiasm when Irinyi read out the Twelve Points. However, the deputy mayor, Lipót Rottenbiller, hastened to greet those present as the first harbingers of spring: "You bring the hope of full liberty, you have knocked the chains off the press, and I fully believe that under your defence this city of ours will be saved from breaches of order." Rottenbiller accepted and signed the Twelve Points on behalf of the city council "as an application addressed to the Diet." The general meeting then decided to set up a revolutionary committee. Four of the March Youth—Dániel Irányi, József Irinyi, Sándor Petőfi, and Pál Vasvári—became members of it. So did three members of the liberal nobility, Sámuel Egressy, Gábor Klauzál, and Pál Nyáry, and several councillors: Máté Gyurkovics, a furrier; Lajos Kacskovics, the city recorder; a noble, a county judge, and a corresponding member of the academy, György Molnár; Lipót Rottenbiller (as chairman); István Staffenberger, a tanner and spokesman of the *electa communitas* in the inner council; and Gáspár Tóth, a tailor and the patron for the first edition of Petőfi's works. Urged on by the crowd, this committee then proceeded to Buda "to call upon the Lieutenancy Council to abolish censorship forthwith" (as Petőfi wrote) and to release Mihály Táncsics, who had been imprisoned for a press offence.

Despite the heavy rain, a huge crowd followed the committee to Buda Castle and into the premises of the Lieutenancy Council. Petőfi's diary reads "The right honourable council blanched and deigned to tremble, and after a five-minute consultation agreed to everything." As the *Pesti Hírlap* wrote on March 17, the chairman of the office announced "that from this moment censorship . . . is officially abolished, and until new press laws providing a system of punishment are brought in, a provisional court will be set up to punish possible offences on the basis of existing law." Pál Nyáry then announced the great news from a window of the palace at about half past five to the cheering crowd, which then marched to Buda prison, freed Táncsics, and drew him over to Pest in a cart.

By that time candles had been lit in the windows of Pest, according to the *Pesti Hírlap* "because something which has been longed for so long by so many, the golden age of the free press, has finally arrived." The house of Landerer and Heckenast was also lit up, and flags were hung from it, while inside there was a bustle among the composing frames. Posters were being prepared in which the committee would inform the people of the capital city next morning about the events of March 15. "We, the fortunate undersigned, are to inform the Hungarian nation officially on behalf of the public of the city of Pest that the reform which in other countries required that the blood of their citizens be shed has been attained in Budapest in twenty-four hours by peaceful and lawful means through lawful agreement." The Lieutenancy Council had decided "to abolish censorship forthwith, and thus the press has been freed of the chains of so many centuries."

Late in the night of March 15 Petőfi enthusiastically wrote in his diary "Today Hungarian freedom has been born because the chains have fallen from the press. Or is there anyone foolish enough to believe that a nation can be free without a free press? Greetings to thee, Hungarian freedom, on the day of thy birth!" Let us do Petőfi justice: this turn of events that almost exactly coincided with the decision of principle by the Diet did indeed mark the beginning of a new, liberal period in the history of the Hungarian press.

On the morning of March 16 the larger of the two banners in the window of the Opposition Circle's premises bore the inscription "Long live freedom of the press!" About 150 workers from three Pest presses marched under a similar banner. From that time on the daily papers went to press without being censored. In the early days some printed on the front page in conspicuous letters "The press is free!" In the next issue of the *Pesti Divatlap*, the editor Imre Vahot published a poem called "Free Press" by Mihály Vörösmarty.

On March 16, after the Pest revolution, the Twelve Points, of which the first demanded freedom of the press, could be sent to Pressburg as a petition that had vastly increased in weight.

Bibliography

Mihály Ács, "Öreg nyomdászok a sajtószabadság első termékéről" (Old Printers on the First Product of Press Freedom), *Vasárnapi Újság* (Sunday Journal) (Budapest), March 15, 1896; Tamás Szana, *A sajtó felszabadulása* (The Freeing of the Press) (Budapest, 1898); Károly Firtinger, *Ötven esztendő a magyarországi könyvnyomtatás múltjából* (Fifty Years of the Past of Book Printing in Hungary) (Budapest, 1900); Ervin Szabó, *Társadalmi és pártharcok a 48-49-es magyar forradalomban* (Social and Party Struggles in the 1848-49 Hungarian Revolution) (Vienna, 1921; 2d ed., Budapest, 1949); Sándor Fekete, *A márciusi fiatalok* (The March Youth) (Budapest, 1950); idem, *Vasvári Pál* (Pál Vasvári) (Budapest, 1951); Sándor Lukácsy, "A márciusi ifjak" (The March Youth), *Valóság* (Reality), 1964, no. 12, pp. 9-20; Aladár Urbán, "A Helytartótanács 1848 március 15-éről" (The Lieutenancy Council on March 15, 1848), *Századok* (Centuries), 1969, and in *A nagy év sodrában: Tanulmányok 1848-ról* (In the Tide of the Great Year: Studies on 1848) (Budapest, 1981), pp. 25-50; Károly Vörös, "Petőfi és a pesti kispolgár" (Petőfi and the Petit Bourgeois of Pest), in *Petőfi és kora* (Petőfi and His Age), ed. S. Lukácsy and I. Varga (Budapest, 1970), pp. 9-57; György Spira, "A nagy nap" (The Great Day), in ibid., pp. 309 ff.; Vera Bácskai, *Pest társadalma és politikai arculata 1848-ban* (The Society and Political Complexion of Pest in 1848), Tanulmányok Budapest Múltjából (Studies of the Past of Budapest), vol. 19 (Budapest, 1972); Aladár Urbán, "A korszerű Petőfi-kép és a költő helye az 1848-49-es eseményekben" (The Modern Image of Petőfi and the Poet's Place in the Events of 1848-49), *Irodalomtörténet* (Literary History /It below/), 1973, and in *A nagy év sodrában*, pp. 273-80; György Spira, *Petőfi napja* (Petőfi's Day) (Budapest, 1978); idem, "A forradalmi ország szíve, 1848-1849" (The Heart of the Revolutionary Country, 1848-1849), in *Budapest története* (History of Budapest), ed. Károly Vörös, vol. 4 (Budapest, 1978), pp. 21-116; Aladár Urbán, "A főváros népe és helyőrsége az 1848 március-áprilisi napokban" (The People and Garrison of the Capital in the Days of March and April 1848), in *A nagy év sodrában*, pp. 51-95.

5. The Press Laws of 1848

The victory of the Pest revolution did not close the subject of liberal press freedom. Before the principle could be enshrined in legal form, a fairly lengthy process in several stages had to be gone through, accompanied by some not inconsiderable clashes.

The first, temporary regulation was a product of the very government that was to be abolished under the new liberal state. The Lieutenancy Council issued a decree on March 16, informed proprietors of printing presses of the fact, and distributed it to the councils of Pest and other cities. In the words of the covering letter, "The inhabitants of the city of Pest have shown signs of unease and exasperation that might . . . if they increased and spread further cause justified fears of disturbances not only in the capital . . . but in the other parts of our country as well."

The first clause of the Lieutenancy Council's temporary regulation, which was to remain in force "until legislation was operative," declared that "the press shall operate freely without prior censorship of any kind." But it went on to prescribe that "for the purpose of exacting due penalties for excesses and abuses by the press" one copy of all printed products of the press, for which the producer was always responsible, had to be sent to the chairman of a twenty-five-member committee appointed for the purpose. If the committee considered the material to constitute an offence against the press laws, the matter would be passed on to the judiciary. In other words, prosecution of press abuses was entrusted to a temporary committee endowed with a jury's power to institute proceedings and to the regular courts. But the decree failed to define what was to be considered as a press offence and omitted to mention one of the chief concomitants of liberal freedom of the press, the security that the papers' publishers had to deposit. The list of committee members in press reports at the time shows that it largely consisted of well-known figures in the liberal opposition nobility. Among them were some adherents of the centralist group and some leading lights among the manufacturing and trading bourgeoisie of Pest.

After that, the issue of the press, along with the whole organization of the new liberal national state, had to be enshrined in law by the Diet in Pressburg. Earlier the last feudal Diet had been taking months to agree on a single paragraph, but under revolutionary circumstances and Kossuth's leadership it was managing to get through important business in a matter of days or hours. On March 18, the day after the return of the delegation from Vienna, it dealt with the generalization of taxation and the abolition of serfdom and church tithes. No small encouragement to haste was provided by fresh news from Pest in which the plans of the March Youth for a people's assembly and the dispatch of new emissaries were translated by the time it reached Pressburg into the beginnings of an uprising by the peasants gathered on Rákos Field. So revolutionary Pest, as emerged later as well, had the strength to spur the liberal nobles on and give Kossuth backing against the reluctance of the right-wing nobles and Vienna. But it clearly did not have the strength to take over the running of the country from the nobility. On this point Pressburg and the leadership of the nobles received firm support from Kossuth himself, who intended Pest to act merely as a useful auxiliary. While warning the nobles who wanted to retreat that "whoever seeks to obstruct this transformation will be trodden underfoot by the nation," he was equally decisive on March 19 when he told the young delegates of the Pest revolution headed by Pál Vasvári that the Diet was not prepared to relinquish leadership and had the strength to trample upon whoever tried to dictate to it.

The internal tensions and contradictions between Pressburg and Pest explain why immediately afterwards, on March 20, the Diet displayed quite unexpected illiberality on the press issue. In this case the influence of Pest tended to stiffen resistance rather than encourage advance. It was primarily the March Youth, the Pest radicals, who saw freedom of the press as their main weapon, and one that they might one day find useful against the liberal nobles as well. This view of freedom of the press as a potential radical weapon against Pressburg was appreciated by the nobles as well, who were alarmed by the revolutionary news from Pest. Having earlier mentioned freedom of the press frequently themselves, they now attempted to render it harmless to them by imposing a financial qualification. In the atmosphere of perplexity and feverish haste the revolution had created, Bertalan Szemere thought it better, at the meeting of the circular session of the lower house that began at five o'clock in the evening on March 20, not to make any positive development of the press bill which had been prepared under the conditions pertaining *before* the March revolution but to introduce it in the form in which it can be read in No. 147 of the Diet Papers, which exacted, in Point 2 of Paragraph 30, an enormous deposit of 20,000 forints for daily papers and 10,000 forints in other cases. At a time when a high-ranking city official earned about 1,000 forints a year, 20,000 forints was a vast sum — enough to buy a smallish mansion in Pest. More remarkably still, the caution money for political papers had earlier been 15,000 forints; Szemere and his supporters had raised it instead of lowering it. Moreover, as Mihály Horváth has pointed out, failure to define press offences clearly was coupled with the imposition of severe penalties for infringing them. According to Horváth's occasionally contestable assessment, the liberal nobles' anxieties were not confined to "incitements by pamphlets" or the "impetuosity" of the press. They also feared that the new freedom might be used by "disguised reaction" and by representatives of national minorities, particularly "Slavic" movements. Thus the legislature tried to prevent "excessive proliferation" of newspapers and "merely sought to abolish censorship rather than actually set the press free." But of the various reasons the main one was undoubtedly the influence of the revolutionary, radical movements. It was a sign of the mood at the time that the circular session, describing it as "temporary in nature," passed the measure relatively quickly without major debate, its example being followed by the plenary session of the lower house at eight o'clock on the same evening. A few deputies such as the conservative János Paczolay of Hont County and Lajos Štúr of Zólyom County, the leading light in the Slovak movement, spoke against the high caution money, but Kossuth himself saw fit to defend it against them. "One must also consider," he said, "that the publishers raise money from the subscribers, and if the free press acts more vigorously there will be a growth in the number of these, whom one cannot leave without any security." Kossuth went so far as to add that "at a later, higher stage of political development only papers that represent specific political parties to a decisive degree will be able to exist, and for these parties it will be very easy to put up a sum even larger than the one now demanded and concentrate themselves around some outstanding talents." So the caution money remained, and the sole concession made was one proposed by Sámuel Bónis that real estate might be mortgaged to the relevant authority in lieu of cash. The *Pesti Hírlap*, whose report only appeared six days later, on March 26, after some perceptible hesitation, noted that "many who did not agree with many parts of the measure thought better of attacking its excessive severity in the present excitable circumstances." In other words, they were obliged by some new circumstance to lay aside their liberal principles. The *Pesti Hírlap* added, "This atmosphere was greatly influenced by certain poems which were printed thoughtlessly and have caused great bitterness to the landowning class, since they are aimed directly at the right of property and incite people to use force. Naturally, such excess of press freedom when it had only just been won cannot fail to cause a reaction." Many have seen this as a reference to Petőfi's poem "A mágnásokhoz" (To the Magnates). However, around this time the poem was only circulating in handwritten copies and had not appeared in print, since the poet himself had burned it not long after it was written, around March 11. Széchenyi is known to have received a copy in a letter from Pest on March 24, and with his wry humour he did not hesitate to quote from it in the upper house and enquire of the "illustrious gentlemen" if their necks were not "itching just a bit." This poem could only have exerted an influence in manuscript. In print it is more likely that one or two of the early products of the radical press in Pest caused the consternation in Pressburg. The subsequent report in the *Pesti Hírlap* seems to have been inaccurate in its details.

But that was not the end of the matter. Revolutionary Pest chimed in.

On its arrival in Pest on the morning of March 22, the press bill caused the utmost indignation in the city that had given birth to the free press hardly a week before. It was first read out before "a numerous audience" in the Pest County Committee of Public Safety. "The exasperation it caused is indescribable," the *Pesti Hírlap* wrote next day. "News of its contents spread like lightning through the city. The dissatisfaction was general." The measure of that dissatisfaction shows up in the comment the far from radical *Pesti Hírlap* appended:

> The members of the legislature do not seem to appreciate the great significance of the movements here. (It would therefore be good if the Diet moved its seat to Pest) before it begins any constitutional organization. The political climate of Pressburg is saturated with the vapours of the overthrown régime. (Moreover,) in many respects this press law would place literature in a worse situation (than the one before March 15.) If it did not include a jury procedure and if one could not draw the consolation that in most cases the nation's love of freedom would not allow that law to be applied, we should be obliged to discard our pens because of the extremely severe penalties awaiting men of letters and the broad and vague interpretation of the offences. In any case our pens are being confiscated by a nation that has not yet provided its writers with sufficient remuneration to allow them to deposit a security of 10,000-20,000 silver forints. (Thereafter) certain major branches of literature will remain a privilege, (merely) the privilege of the merchant princes, (and) the independently minded toilers (of literature) will remain obliged to toil for others' profit.

After a stormy debate the Committee of Public Safety passed a resolution declaring the provisions of this press law to be "merely such as would place mankind's most sacred right of freedom to express ideas on a new footing as oppressive and restrictive as the one before." It went on to protest in more detail that Paragraph 29 would make the press offences punishable from March 20, when the law had not yet been sanctioned or publicly announced—in other words, an attempt was being made to antedate its validity. The resolution described the press offences as indeterminate and found "the size of the prescribed penalties excessively severe and thus disquieting." It also protested against the overly large security, which amounted to nothing other than a surrender "of the matter of the press to one class, the propertied caste," and against the provision that if a fine imposed on the author were not paid it would have to be paid by the press. Finally, the committee declared that it found these provisions entirely unacceptable and considered that if they were sanctioned it would be "a public disaster for intellectual development." It therefore called on the prime minister and the deputies of the county to amend the bill, which would "arouse justifiable misgiving in every thinking citizen of this country." It also referred the matter to the city of Pest.

When the bill was read out again to a meeting that began at three o'clock that afternoon in the council chamber of the Pest city hall, it "aroused extraordinary exasperation," according to the report in the *Pesti Hírlap*. The vast audience, which spilled over to fill "the neighbouring chambers, the lobby, and the staircases leading up . . . loudly demanded" that the bill be burned "even during the reading" of it, in other words, before discussion of it had even begun. Irinyi, Ferenc Pulszky, Petőfi, Irányi, Gábor Egressy, János Farkas, Vasvári, Nyáry, and Klauzál spoke in succession. Some "plainly saw the bill" as retaliation by the nobles in Pressburg for the revolution in Pest. Others deduced from its provisions that the Diet was "not acquainted with the spirit of the new movements." Although Vasvári and Nyáry opposed the move, the document was burned among the crowd in Szabadság tér (Freedom Square) outside the city hall while the speeches were still going on. Ultimately it was decided at Nyáry's suggestion that Pulszky should be sent forthwith as a messenger to Batthyány in Pressburg with a strongly worded demand. The document said, "The legislature has set out to destroy utterly . . . what the population of this city illustriously won by liberating the press on March 15." It called upon the prime minister "to deign to ensure that this unacceptable bill be withdrawn, and at the same time, that until another press law be passed in the spirit of freedom and reform by the true representatives of the people," with minor amendments "the temporary decree . . . of the Lieutenancy Council serve as a regulation. . . . Prime Minister, honoured fellow citizen! The minutes are precious; ensure that action is not taken too late."

When Pulszky left hastily for Pressburg next morning, he was already able to take with him the earliest reactions to the bill by the press in Pest, in particular the previous evening's issue of the radical *Marczius Tizenötödike* (March the Fifteenth), which was the first to protest in print against "this conservatism." It had not, it said, expected a reaction for another two weeks, but "two weeks were not necessary: the conservative tune has been called after twice twenty-four hours." The paper sharply attacked the bill for replacing "the banning and suppression of ideas up to now by the despotic force of terrorism against thinking and ideas." In its fifth issue, on March 23, the paper discerned in the Pressburg bill a design to introduce "a new censorship" whose "liberalism" it described as "a hundred years behind the regulations on the matter made by the Metternich government."

In his memoirs all Pulszky writes of his mission is that once in Pressburg he immediately visited Batthyány, "who himself saw that Szemere had committed an error with his bill," which Pulszky considered "reminiscent of French law current under Louis Philippe." However, it emerges from the press at the time that Pulszky hurriedly returned to Pest on March 25. There printed notices were posted informing the public that he would give a report to a general meeting on that day. "Interest in the subject brought such an innumerable crowd to the city hall that the general meeting had to adjourn into the open air, into Szabadság tér." Pulszky reported that by the time he arrived in Pressburg the bill had already been passed by the upper house, and it was thanks only to Batthyány's personal intervention that the decision was set aside and the bill presented again in an amended form to the circular session. There Szemere himself used "passionate words" in support of the amendments, of which the major one reduced the caution monies to 10,000 and 5,000 forints. The amendments passed both circular and plenary sessions of the lower house unanimously on March 24. The *Pesti Hírlap* reported that the mass meeting, "seeing its demands temporarily satisfied," thereupon gave the Batthyány government "a cordial ovation" and offered a vote of thanks to Pulszky.

One should add that on March 28 the aristocracy of the upper house proposed a few amendments of minor importance which the lower house agreed to in part in a note on March 31, after which the upper house likewise passed the measure. It came up for royal approval on April 7. After the setting aside of objections on one or two matters of detail (such as the size of the property qualification for the jury) by the Hungarian Chancery, still prone to find fault, and by the *Staatskonferenz* in Vienna the law was promulgated with royal assent on April 11, 1848. And that is how Act 18 of 1848 on the freedom of the press came into being.

The first paragraph of the new law laid down that "all may express and freely disseminate their ideas through the medium of the press." Of course a succession of subsequent paragraphs set limits to that freedom. A fine of 500 to 5,000 forints or a prison sentence of six months to six years was to be imposed on anyone who incited to a crime, misdemeanour, or violent breach of the peace, ridiculed public morality or religion, agitated for dissolving the link with the ruling house or amending the constitution by force, insulted the person of the king or members of the dynasty, or libelled authority or private persons. The second section, on judicial proceedings, devoted several paragraphs to jury procedures in press trials, one provision being that the investigating judge had the power to place offending products of the press under lock and key forthwith. The third section dealt with papers that appeared regularly. It was compulsory to register the launching of them with the *vicecomes* or mayor and through him with the ministry. A security of 10,000 forints had to be deposited for daily papers and one of 5,000 forints for papers publishing less frequently. Failure to announce the launch of a paper to the authorities or to deposit the caution money was punishable by a year's imprisonment or a fine of 500 forints. Conviction for a press offence could cause other property of the paper's proprietor, publisher, or editor to be distrained. One copy of each issue had to be lodged with the local authority, on pain of a fine of 200 forints. The fourth section concerned printing presses and "bookselling." Presses too had to be registered. A deposit of 4,000 forints in the capital and 2,000 forints in the provinces had to be made for each press. Failure rendered the proprietor liable to a year's imprisonment or a fine of 2,000 forints. The name and address of the press had to appear in all printed matter, and booksellers could only trade in publications in which these details appeared.

The press law went on to empower the ministry to "effect the establishment of common juries by decree strictly in accordance with the principles of the last Diet's proposal on punitive procedure." This decree in 108 sections was probably drafted by the young assistant clerk István Békey (formerly Drescher), acting on the instructions of László Szalay, who headed the new Department of Legislative Drafting at the Ministry of Justice. It was afterwards corrected both by Szalay and by the minister himself, Ferenc Deák. In view of the urgency of the matter it was completed by April 29 and published in the May 1 and May 2 issues of the *Pesti Hírlap*, which was serving at the time as the official paper. This decree drew, by way of the 1843 proposal, on the principles contained in the French revolutionary code of criminal procedure issued in September 1791.

A few days later, on May 7, the *Pesti Hírlap* published the enacting clause of the press law, issued by Szemere on April 28. The introduction declared that "the press has now become free in this country as well" and that "a free press is one prerequisite for the freedom of the nation." It added, "The press is a real force and a real weapon. In the hands of a shrewd, honest, scrupulous man it brings blessings like the sun; in the hands of an imprudent, false, and reckless man it is a curse like fire. It has therefore been necessary to circumscribe the same with laws that leave the right entire (but) set certain limits on its exercise." Appealing strongly to the conscience of all to adhere to the regulations strictly, Szemere added in the first person in somewhat subjective terms, "I am convinced that although many consider Act 18 of 1848 very strict, there is no belief which cannot be expressed in a way that does not offend against this statute."

Even in its amended, mitigated form, the 1848 press law was criticized right from the start by the radicals. *Marczius Tizenötödike* constantly attacked Szemere, whose first bill "was a stumbling block in the civilized world" (May 13). Mihály Táncsics wrote disparagingly of the common jury decree in the seventh issue (May 14) of the *Munkások Újsága* (Workers' News), enquiring whether the government had no more important business at a time when so much had to be done in the country "than to build a bastion in 108 sections against the peccadilloes of the press." In the report Petőfi was commissioned to prepare by the Radical Circle at the end of June he declared, "We have united so as to achieve true and unconditional freedom of the press free of all caution money," the freedom of the press won on March 15 having been "overthrown by the despotic laws of the assembly of nobles in Pressburg." The Egalitarian Society in a petition on July 30 called on the National Assembly to provide greater freedom of the press, and some members of the Society attempted to draft a new press bill in August.

The flow of sharp criticism was linked with the conflict that in 1848 divided the two main trends in support of bourgeois national transformation in Hungary—the liberalism of the nobility and "petit bourgeois" radicalism. The various radical groups were dissatisfied with the traditional leadership of the nobles—the "politics of the *táblabíró*" (a traditional honorary title awarded by counties for public service)—and made use in their struggle of the press law's shortcomings. For their part, the governing liberals tried, as and when it seemed necessary, to employ the provisions of the press law against their left-wing adversaries. Thus in general terms, condemnation and utilization of the press law became a function of the way internal political power relations evolved within the camp of those intent on transforming Hungary into a new national state.

Let there be no mistake: Petőfi and his group envisaged a new and better press law that would certainly have been far more democratic and advanced than the fairly limited freedom for the press that the liberal nobility had conceded, but one must also stress that the latter constituted a *liberal* freedom of the press none the less. It was one that the nobles, themselves becoming bourgeois and leading the bourgeois transformation, could accept without sacrificing their own interests, and it was one that differed radically from the practice of the feudal system and essentially marked a watershed.

Bibliography

Horváth, *Huszonöt év*; Ferenc Pulszky, *Életem és korom* (My Life and Time), vol. 2 (Budapest, 1880); Ferenc Vargha, "Sajtószabadság" (Freedom of the Press), offprint from *Jogtudományi Közlöny* (Journal of Jurisprudence), 1906; László Feleky, "A szabadságharc és a sajtószabadság" (The War of Independence and Freedom of the Press), *Magyar Figyelő* (Hungarian Observer), April 1912, pp. 112-24; idem, "A 48-iki sajtótörvény és sajtószabadság" (The 1848 Press Law and Freedom of the Press), *Magyar Figyelő*, April 1913, pp. 251-54 (also as an offprint); János Tarnai, "A sajtótörvény keletkezésének története" (The Story of the Creation of the Press Law), in *Sajtójogi dolgozatok* (Press Law Studies) (Budapest, 1913); Szabó, *Társadalmi és pártharcok*; Kamill Sándorfy, *Törvényalkotásunk hőskora* (The Heroic Age in This Country's Legislation) (Budapest, 1935); Árpád Károlyi, *Az 1848-diki pozsonyi törvénycikkek az udvar előtt* (Pozsony Statutes of 1848 before the Court), (Budapest, 1936); Ernő Tamás, "Sajtóperek és sajtórendőri intézkedések 1848-49-ben" (Press Trials and Press Policing Measures in 1848-49), *Politika*, no. 16 (1949); Barta, *Kossuth Lajos az utolsó*; Ödön Both, "Az 1848. évi sajtótörvény létrejötte" (The Creation of the 1848 Press Law), in *Acta Universitatis Szegediensis, Sectio politico-juridica*, vol. 1, no. 4 (Szeged, 1956); Béla Sarlós, *Az 1848/49-es forradalom és szabadságharc büntetőjoga* (The Criminal Law of the 1848-49 Revolution and War of Independence) (Budapest, 1959); Ödön Both, "Küzdelem az esküdtbíráskodás bevezetéséért Magyarországon a reformkorban és az 1848. április 26-i esküdtszéki rendelet" (The Battle to Introduce Trial by Jury in Hungary in the Age of Reform and the Common Jury Regulation of April 26, 1848), in *Acta Universitatis Szegediensis,*

Acta Juridica et Politica (AJP below), vol. 5, no. 1 (Szeged, 1960); Béla Sarlós, "A sajtószabadság és eljárási biztosítékainak fő vonásai" (The Freedom of the Press and the Main Outlines of the Practical Guarantees for It), in *Jogtörténeti tanulmányok* (Studies of Legal History), vol. 2 (Budapest, 1968), pp. 197-202; János Varga, "A dicsőséges nagyurak és a pesti forradalom" (The "Illustrious Gentlemen" and the Pest Revolution), in Lukácsy and Varga, *Petőfi*, pp. 363 ff.; Ödön Both, "Szemere Bertalan sajtórendelete és a vezetése alatt álló minisztérium sajtóügyi tevékenysége 1848-ban" (Bertalan Szemere's Press Decree and the Activities on the Press Issue of His Ministry), *AJP*, vol. 27, no. 4 (Szeged, 1980).

6. The Press and the Political Spectrum

The first attempt to assemble and examine the bibliographical data on the press in 1848-49 was made by the great nineteenth-century bibliographer József Szinnyei. He first published his results, grouped thematically and accompanied by some commentary on literary history, in several installments in the *Vasárnapi Újság* in 1865. He then published them in a more factual form, arranged alphabetically, in the *Magyar Könyvszemle* (Hungarian Book Review). For several reasons his useful pioneer undertaking was no easy task, for the press during that eventful year-and-a-half of revolutionary upswing was marked by many sudden changes and interrupted experiments. Only three to six issues of several papers ever appeared, and of some only the first issue ever saw the light of day. In some instances an advertisement in the press for a particular paper is the sole evidence we have that it existed, if indeed it did.

Although the major papers of 1848, with their fairly large circulations, were more accessible, it was hard subsequently to gather several smaller papers of 1849, which circulated in fewer copies, among a narrower circle, in outlying places or even in a few cases during wanderings from place to place. The scarcity was increased because much material was destroyed, during the period of reprisals and persecutions on the part of the absolutist régime that followed the defeat in the war of independence, by the authorities and police who managed to discover it and by those afraid of being found with it. (It was forbidden to possess revolutionary papers, and one or two copies would have been grounds for arrest.) Unsurprisingly, therefore, the main public collections of the press materials of 1848-49 have remained to varying degrees incomplete. In 1877 János Csontosi even found it necessary to publish special detailed, alphabetical notes on the papers of 1848-49 that he would have liked to obtain for the National Széchényi Library (the largest in Hungary), since they were missing from it. Since then the collection has been greatly augmented, but it still cannot be called complete. After broader general summaries by Antal Szalády (in 1884) and István Kereszty (in 1916), additional, supplementary and amended data were published on several further occasions, mainly in the *Magyar Könyvszemle* and notably from the pen of Alisz Goriupp (in 1925).

According to Szinnyei's summary (in 1877), the press of 1848-49 consisted of 186 newspapers and periodicals published in twenty-six Hungarian and two foreign cities. By language, 86 were in Hungarian, 73 in German, 9 in Slovak, 7 in Serbian, 5 in Romanian, 4 in Croatian, and 2 in French (the last two designed to promote Hungary's cause in Paris). A later attempt at a numerical analysis was made in the centenary year of 1948 by József Fitz, who compiled several tables by region of the country, language of publication, type of periodical, and frequency of publication and even studied the papers of 1848 and 1849 separately. Fitz arrived at totals of 145 papers which had appeared in Hungary (excluding Croatia) in 1848, of which 65 were in Hungarian, and 72 papers which had appeared in 1849, of which 36 were in Hungarian. Most—81 in 1848 and 31 in 1849—appeared in Budapest. Of the other regions, Budapest was followed by Transylvania (27 and 15), the Little Plain (20 and 6), the region beyond the Tisza (6 and 7), the Uplands (6 and 3), the Banat (3 and 4), and the Great Plain (2 and 6). But Fitz himself emphasized that even with relatively accurate information to hand it is not easy to ascertain how many papers there were in each category and in total. Many changed their names, which means they are treated in press bibliographies as two items even though the later may have been solely a continuation of the earlier. Several papers were peripatetic, leaving Pest for Debrecen, returning to Pest, and finally perhaps moving to Szeged or Arad, and this lends uncertainty to the statistics for place of publication. One may add that a numerical total in itself can be misleading. Every modest, old-fashioned local paper or ephemeral little undertaking must feature as just such a separate item as *Kossuth Hírlapja* (Kossuth's Journal) or the *Pesti Hírlap*. Moreover, numerical growth can mask actual decline. If a major paper like the *Budapesti Híradó* gives way after a time to the smaller, less frequently published *Figyelmező*, this does not add to the size of the conservative press, as the bare figures would suggest, but signifies a retreat.

Béla Dezsényi was the first to summarize the press history of the revolution and war of independence in a way that accords with modern requirements. Understandably confining himself to assessing the line of development, he came up with such important statistics as the rise in the number of periodicals appearing in Hungary from 65 in 1847 to 152 in 1848-49 and the fact that the Pest post office was distributing 9,551 copies to subscribers in 1842 and 19,478 in December 1848, at a time when street sales had become significant and the number of provincial papers had grown as well.

The most recent bibliography of the press materials of this period was carefully compiled by Margit Busa in 1957 from the collection in the National Széchényi Library, but where there were gaps she took into account collections in other large Hungarian libraries as well. She used calendar years as the basis and therefore included 1849 papers appearing after the war. Her list contains 227 publications in Hungary (and Croatia) in alphabetical order, with the various supplements to them, the papers imperfectly known only from references, and those of which copies that once existed went astray and can no longer be found. Her useful work provides detailed, encyclopedic information.

But a different organizational principle is required to trace how the press developed, and in this book I shall primarily aim to arrange the data on the history of the press according to political trends, a principle particularly worth following for 1848-49. The press during the revolution and war of independence provided a characteristic reflection of the various political tendencies, which were expressed more sharply and decidedly than ever before, and at the same time actively represented them. Moreover, the press, in its own development, destiny, transformation, bursts of activity, changes in centre of gravity, setbacks, revivals, and ultimate decline, followed and experienced the lively, dramatic turns of political events. One must therefore first trace briefly the main lines of development in the political spectrum before returning to a fuller account of the main papers that reflected them.

The first phase of political development was one in which the range of tendencies and the balance of forces in the Hungarian political press was rapidly transformed under the direct influence of the March 1848 revolution. I shall have to begin the survey with the hitherto predominant conservative papers, with the various signs that they were losing battles, being pushed into the background, and in some cases rapidly readjusting, and with the process whereby the several strong daily papers on which conservatism could rely in March 1848 were reduced by the end of the year to the modest successor of the once so pugnacious *Budapesti Hírado,* the far frailer *Figyelmező*, which appeared only three times a week and after a short while closed down altogether. I shall then turn to the change in the position of the liberal papers in the course of the revolution, in particular to the subsequent career of the *Pesti Hírlap*. As the main organ of the liberal efforts at reform by the nobility, which represented the opposition, the left wing, in relation to the old system of government, the *Pesti Hírlap* had no need to change its standpoint substantially. In the new spectrum it stood, relatively speaking, farther to the right, close to the new government born of the revolution and principally in dispute with the new radical press. But the first phase in the political diagram was not purely or principally marked by a transformation of the previously existing press, for new radical political trends and new papers to go with them broke through the cleft the revolution had opened. Continuing to traverse the spectrum, I shall cover these too.

Right from the start this burgeoning new political press was centred on Pest rather than Pressburg, which remained the seat of government and the Diet until mid-April 1848. Moreover, it differed greatly in character from what had gone before. In its pages a substantial news coverage and information apparatus largely gave way to direct agitation. Circulations were smaller and papers snappier and more active. The long, rolling journalistic periods were replaced by a more immediate, terse "revolutionary" style. There was a change in the social make-up of the journalistic staff, the old leaders of the papers, men with aristocratic or noble, landowning antecedents, giving way in the political press to journalists with petit bourgeois, impoverished noble, intellectual, or even plebeian backgrounds. Moreover, the very first of the new papers that appeared in swift succession represented various shades of the left wing as opposed to the liberalism of the middle nobility that retained the leadership of the country. Therefore, while employing the customary label, it is important to remember that this fairly wide spectrum itself contained the seeds of divergencies of tendency and that within the model of the 1848 bourgeois revolution in Europe the Hungarian variant had some major features of its own.

The Model of the European Revolutions

The European revolutions, with few exceptions, were largely played out in four successive acts.

1. First of all, the opposition forces united to overthrow the existing government. This was a common front that consisted from the outset of various social and political forces. The grande bourgeoisie believed in moderate liberalism, a parliamentary system based on a franchise limited by a property qualification, and constitutional monarchy. The middle and petite bourgeoisie had more radical and democratic goals, believing in "one man, one vote" and the idea of a republic. The principal conflict, however, was not between the various strata of the bourgeoisie but between the bourgeoisie and the new working class emerging in the most developed regions. The working class aimed at true equality, the right to work, and ultimately a transformation of property relations and the capitalist socioeconomic structure.

2. Once the revolution had succeeded, the temporary unity of the opposition front broke up, and internal conflicts reflecting divergent class interests came to the fore. In France, which provides the classic example of the four-act model, the joint revolutionary action of February 1848 produced a coalition government in which the liberal grande bourgeoisie, dissatisfied with having been largely excluded from power up to then, was represented by Alphonse de Lamartine, the petite bourgeoisie by Louis Blanc, and the plebeian masses in a token fashion by a worker by the name of Albert. In this second act, the internal battle between supporters of the national tricolor of the liberals and the proletarian red flag intensified, and in May 1848, after the elections, the right wing in the National Assembly turned decisively against the supporters of a "social republic."

3. The withdrawal of the liberal bourgeoisie from the

common front led to a third act in which radicals and workers, together or separately, attempted to pursue the revolution by force but were beaten back. An armed uprising of Paris workers protested the closure of the "national workshops" and sought to reverse the process of decline in their influence, but their attempt was bloodily suppressed in June 1848. The working class of the German, Austrian, and North Italian regions was far less developed than that of France, but there too the liberal bourgeoisie took fright at the French social struggles and class warfare. When they had to choose, they preferred to sacrifice the revolutionary programme and try to bargain with their old opponents who had previously held power.

4. In the fourth and final act, the chain reaction of international politics served as a brake rather than an aid to the revolution. Counter-revolution and autocracy gained the upper hand, and even the liberal bourgeoisie was pushed aside. Thus in December 1848 the man elected president of the republic in France was Louis Napoléon, who was shortly to become emperor.

Hungary was directly affected by political events in Vienna, where a joint revolutionary action by the grande bourgeoisie, petite bourgeoisie, students, and workers in March 1848 triumphed over feudal absolutism. Then in May 1848 the liberal bourgeoisie went over to the side of imperial power. Later, in October 1848, the workers and students began a new revolutionary action, but eventually they were left alone to face the superior forces of the emperor, even the expected help from the Hungarians being too little and too late. Defeat was followed by absolutism of a new kind.

As we have seen, the liberals and radicals in Hungary came forward in mid-March 1848 at almost the same time as the Viennese and in almost the same direction. In Pressburg, where the Diet was meeting, the liberal nobility took a stand after their own fashion, while in Budapest, the centre of the country, the radical youth took one after theirs. Here too there was tension and discord between the two, but matters never came to a rift or clash between them, mainly because there remained a common external enemy. The central leadership of the Habsburg Monarchy had accepted only with a bad grace, under pressure from the revolutionary situation, the new laws that proclaimed the internal transformation of Hungary and along with it national "independence," although the country was to remain a dominion of the House of Habsburg and within the framework of the Monarchy. From the outset the court considered this too much independence, and after its successes in Italy it set out at the end of the summer of 1848 to win back at least some of its concessions. The Hungarians, on the other hand, were seeking to expand the sphere of national independence they had won in the spring. Prime Minister Count Lajos Batthyány, with Kossuth's support, aimed to extend this independence to a point where a mere personal union remained, particularly because he expected to see a new, unified German national state emerge that Austria would be likely to join in some form or other. Since Hungary would have no such ambition, the link between them would have to be modified and loosened. The radicals for their part sought greater independence still and from the outset considered a conflict with the Habsburgs inevitable. From that supposition stemmed their main criticism of the Batthyány government, which they did not think was preparing for the conflict decisively enough. The result in September 1848 was a crisis, a clash, and then a new hardening of the common front among the forces for the revolution, a new burst of activity, and a war of independence that Austria managed to win only by calling in the tsarist Russian army in 1849, thus gaining massive military superiority.

It was Kossuth, the former leader of the liberal opposition nobility, who succeeded in fusing the country's diverse political tendencies. Thus the Hungarian war of independence became a sequel to the European revolutionary movements which elsewhere had by then died out. As elsewhere, there was a noticeable rightward shift by the liberal nobles on account of the shock caused by the peasant movements, particularly the national minority movements that made use of the discontent of the non-Hungarian peasant movements. But these noblemen's hope of agreement and peace with Austria proved illusory, on the one hand because Austria did not wish to agree and on the other because on April 14, 1849, Kossuth declared Hungary's full independence and the dethronement of the Habsburgs, not least out of a desire to thwart those who favoured negotiation. The final consequence after the defeat in the war of independence was vengeance and arbitrary rule by the Habsburgs.

Hungary's Political Spectrum

Hungarian historians, not without cause, identify in the new lease of life and resumption after the turn of events in September 1848 the principal feature that distinguishes the Hungarian variant of the European revolutionary model. But they usually pay less heed to some other distinguishing marks that make this continuation more comprehensible. They have even tended to explain the events in Hungary using two types of revolutionary model at once, equating what happened in Hungary on the one hand with the simultaneous sequence of European revolutions in 1848 and on the other with the great French Revolution at the end of the eighteenth century. This in itself is justified in several ways so long as a clear distinction is made between the two models. This really was Hungary's first bourgeois revolution, and one in which recourse had to be made to national self-defence against outside attack. But whereas the attempted outside intervention in the first French Revolution caused a swing to the left and a succession of ever more radical régimes culminating in the dictatorship of the Jacobins, the political leadership of the Hungarian nobles, despite its alliance with the radicals in the face of the outward threat, never relinquished control. No other force ever obliged or was in a position to oblige it to do so. Under the relations of power in this country there was an absolute lack of the prerequisites for a Jacobin dictatorship, and it was no mere tactical consideration that prevented such a dictatorship from emerging in the autumn of 1848. One might add that the relative political influence of the nobles' leadership by comparison with the radicals' increased rather than diminished in 1849, although naturally it could not accomplish a Hungarian Thermidor in the field. Alongside and despite the similarities between 1789 and 1848, the differences should be attended to all the more closely because the influence of the parallel itself was not confined to the historical concepts of a later age. Its effect was greater still on people at the time, whose hopes or fears led them to define the efforts, phenomena, and events going on in terms of the earlier French model. Even the cast list and terminology were sometimes borrowed. The differences merit special consideration, first of all because the time that elapsed between 1789 and 1848 brought at once a temporary setback in the shape of the restoration period and progress in terms of deeper thinking about society and the flowering of new, socialistic, Utopian ideas and endeavours. These latter ideas looked beyond bourgeois society and had an influence in Hungary noticeable in the revolutionary espousal of democracy by Petőfi. Secondly, they must be considered because in 1848 new types of events in France—proletarian endeavours, the issue of work organization, the spring uprising of the Paris workers and its failure, and the backtracking by the bourgeoisie—all greatly influenced the way the new ideas and local initiatives of the proletariat were judged in Hungary, a less developed country. Here again one notes signs of the inequality of level of development between the European regions and of the simultaneous influence they nevertheless had on each other.

Despite all the similarities, the socio political forces in Hungary, as the events in September 1848 and the transformation of the revolution into a war of independence show, differed in many respects from those of the four-act revolutionary model. The social programmes of the liberals and the radicals did not diverge enough to prevent them from coalescing in the face of an outside threat to the national achievements of 1848. Hungary's nobility cannot be fully equated with the capitalist grande bourgeoisie of France. The bulk of the former saw no basic danger to their position in their leaders' combining with the radicals at the price of a shift in the internal centre of gravity. And despite the radicals' opposition to the nobility's traditional kind of policy, they were themselves radical principally in national and constitutional rather than in social terms, seeking in the latter scarcely more than had already been won. They believed in a republican form of government, but most did not really desire the universal suffrage that the French petit bourgeois democrats had struggled to gain, most considered the issue of the peasantry basically resolved by the laws of 1848 and the abolition of serfdom, and with few exceptions they distanced themselves from the movements of urban plebeian elements and workers.

In more precise terms one can also discover a variety of shades of opinion or even divergent endeavours among them. The contradictions never became conspicuous only because they never developed to the subsequent stage necessary for them to do so. The vision of the social republic and openness to Jacobinism represented by Petőfi and a handful of others were, as a view of future development, something other and greater than what was espoused even by his few friends and comrades-in-arms among the avant-garde March Youth, not to mention the mass of the petite bourgeoisie and intelligentsia. Nor have I mentioned another category of older men with apparently similar views that amounted to a kind of radicalism for the petty nobility, who, for instance, considered it self-evident that the growing number of political, administrative, military, and other positions in the new national state would be filled by the lower strata of the nobility.

Since the conditions were such that these divergencies never split into separate trends within the press, and since the radical journalists, particularly the March Youth, tended to scatter their forces by writing for several different papers and periodicals, I shall consider the radical papers together, in sequence. Putting first things first, I shall begin with the March Youth's own paper, *Marczius Tizenötödike*, which was started on March 19, 1848, and survived the longest of any of them. Then will come the other, lesser papers, which tried to follow in the footsteps of *Marczius* and represented a range of variant shades of opinion. On April 6 appeared the radical paper *Reform*, the successor to the conservative *Honderű* and apart from its change of political colours an example of how a literary fashion paper might be transformed into a political journal. On April 10 *Die Opposition* was established in Pest. On May 2 came the *Ellenőr* (Examiner) in Kolozsvár and on June 1 the *Radical Lap* (Radical Paper), again in the capital. Unsurprisingly, scholars have noted that the liveliness and excitement of political life produced a plethora of new papers, each attempting to outdo the others in its radical tone. József Ferenczy, who summed up the history of the Hungarian press at the end of the last century, saw this with his conservative-liberal outlook as evidence of a great surge of loud slogans expressing republican "terrorism". But the bare figures have proved misleading on more than one occasion. In fact these undertakings were often short-lived experiments exemplifying the relative weakness of the radical camp. While their metropolitan basis remained, the influence of the March Youth and their paper *Marczius* was magnified for a while, but the other radical undertakings were unable to sustain themselves for long. The *Nép-elem* (People's Element), launched on July 1, survived only till the end of September in spite of absorbing the *Radical Lap* and *Reform* on the way. The *Köztársasági Lapok* (Republican Pages), set up in the autumn of 1848, and the *Jövő* (Future) and *Forradalom* (Revolution) that followed it at the end of the year proved even shorter-lived, although by then the period of unity between the noble leadership and the radicals had begun. Subscriptions confirm this in terms of distribution. Even the chief radical paper, *Marczius Tizenötödike*, had only 733 subscribers. *Reform* had only 110, of whom 87 were in the provinces. The *Nép-elem* after its merger with the two other papers mustered 225 subscribers, while *Die Opposition* had 275. Even adding in the fairly large street sales in Pest, circulations lagged well behind those of the liberal papers. In its period of decline at the end of the year, the *Pesti Hírlap* still had 2,554 subscribers, while the *Pesther Zeitung*, which stood close to the government, had 2,811 and *Kossuth Hírlapja* 4,214.

However, the left wing was not the same thing as the radicals, and if one refrains from viewing the opposing camp with the eyes of the middle nobility of the time, one must also notice an endeavour that in its social programme certainly went beyond what was espoused by the government on the basis of the laws of 1848 and by the radicals, who in this respect did not differ from them markedly. Apart from one or two adherents of the social republic, it was Mihály Táncsics and the paper he founded on April 2, 1848, that represented the real left wing, and to the *Munkások Újsága* and its struggles I shall be devoting a separate chapter, noting the great outcry the true left wing caused in Hungary at that time. This experiment must be considered historically significant even though it proved unable to develop within the balance of domestic forces, was politically isolated and ultimately weak, and was eventually silenced by its opponents. Unlike most of the radicals, Táncsics (and in another way Petőfi) had truly radical and democratic aims for society. Therefore it is hardly correct to follow the common practice of judging political developments in terms of "the Petőfi group" as the kind of united left wing that later writers have sought to posit after the event in the Hungary of 1848, while at the same time weighing up the actual Hungarian achievements of 1848 in terms of revolutionary potentials and postulates conforming to a Jacobin pattern.

The conspicuous new radical colours in the political spectrum of the press were joined in a new stage beginning in the summer of 1848 by the organs of the government to which the revolution had given birth, now settled in the capital as the first responsible Hungarian ministry. Of these the function of an official paper, which the *Pesti Hírlap* had temporarily tried to fill in a separate section, was taken over by the *Közlöny* (Gazette), founded on June 8, 1848, and lasting till the bitter end fourteen months later. The *Közlöny* played an important part in administering the war of independence, but particularly at the beginning it confined itself to publishing official statements, decrees, and notices. It failed to become a political paper that might influence public opinion and provide a programme because the members of the government themselves did not have a united policy at the time it was started. But it was agreed that the people and the peasantry needed informing as quickly as possible about the accomplishments of 1848 and about the limits to those accomplishments. It had to be explained to them what they were and were not entitled to. Grumblers had to be won over, feelings smoothed over, and if possible the influence of Táncsics's paper countered. This purpose was served by a paper the government launched on June 4, 1848, in Hungarian and several other languages, the *Nép Barátja* (People's Friend). A most decided political line was taken from July 1, 1848, by *Kossuth Hírlapja*, whose publisher was given as the government's finance minister but which was from the outset the paper of the opposition within the government, at least for as long as the Batthyány government remained in power. This paper too will be dealt with in a separate chapter. Whereas in the initial period after the liberal freedom of the press had been won there was, as we have seen, a swift expansion of the press (particularly the radical press), the press law now began to act as something of a brake, and that too helped to strengthen the government's position. Regardless of the interest they may have aroused, the smaller undertakings that lacked proper backing could not pay their caution money and were obliged to close down. In August the number of papers stopped growing. Essentially the spectrum which had emerged by then continued during the third period, from the resignation of Batthyány's government and the establishment of the National Defence Commission at the end of September 1848 till the end of the year. The change if any was that the start of the war gave the political press a sharper tone and pushed it towards an increasingly firm anti-Habsburg stance.

One further chapter is required to complete the broad picture of the year 1848. After a survey of the literary and professional press, which became politicized in many respects or at least developed in the main under the influence of the political lines of force, comes an attempt to describe briefly the growth in the provincial press and the situation of the press in languages other than Hungarian. The latter merits attention in relation to the issue of the national minorities and, in the case of the German papers, because the spectrum of opinion among them partially corresponded with that of the Hungarian political press, more than one German-language paper expressly supporting the revolution and war of independence.

So far the press spectrum has been so broad that the major trends, papers, and types of paper have required separate chapters, but in the ensuing period that began on the eve of 1849, when the government and parliament were temporarily obliged to quit Budapest, the range diminished so greatly that one can describe press developments and political debate chronologically in consecutive chapters. Of course the graph still shows some curves. The crisis at the turn of 1848 and 1849 was followed by a measure of growth in the political press in the new centre, Debrecen. In the period after the capital had been recaptured in the spring of 1849, the press for a brief moment prepared for revival and recovery, in other words, for an opportunity to recreate the earlier, broad spectrum in a new version and even develop it further. The hope proved fleeting, for as the first signs of this emerged the capital passed permanently into enemy hands, the government withdrew to Szeged and then to Arad, and soon the war of independence was lost.

Bibliography

József Szinnyei, "Hírlapirodalmunk a 19-i században. 1848 és 1849" (The Hungarian Press in the Nineteenth Century: 1848 and 1849), *Vasárnapi Újság*, 1865, pp. 539, 551, 575, 591, 603, 618, 630, 646, 658, and 674; idem, "*Hírlapirodalmunk 1848— 49-ben*" (The Hungarian Press in 1848-49), offprint from *MKsz*, 1877; Szalády, *A magyar hírlapirodalom statisztikája*; János Váczy, "Hírlapirodalom 1848-49-ben" (The Press in 1848-49), *Magyar Szalon* (Hungarian Salon), April 1886, pp. 577-91; Ferenczy, *A magyar hírlapirodalom története*; Péter Niklai, "Adalékok a szabadságharc hírlapirodalmának bibliográfiájához és egy hozzáfűzött terv" (Contributions to the Bibliography of the Press in the War of Independence with a Plan Appended), *MKsz*, 1913, pp. 188-89; Kereszty, *A magyar és magyarországi időszak sajtó időrendi áttekintése*; Alisz Goriupp, "Adalékok az 1848-49-i hírlapok bibliográfiájához" (Contributions to the Bibliography of the Newspapers of 1848-49), *MKsz*, 1925, pp. 141-45; Ervin Supka, "Ujabb adalékok az 1848/49 évi hírlapirodalom könyvészetéhez" (Fresh Contributions to the Bibliography of the Press in the Year 1848-49), *MKsz*, 1942, pp. 185-88; Ferenc Bay, comp., *1848-49 a korabeli napilapok tükrében* (1848-49 as Reflected in the Contemporary Press) (Budapest, 1943); Béla Dezsényi, *Az időszaki sajtó története a Dunatáj országaiban* (History of the Periodical Press in the Danube Countries) (Budapest, 1947); Jenő Zsoldos, "1848 napisajtója" (The Daily Press of 1848), *Magyar Nyelvőr* (Hungarian Linguistic Guardian, *MNy* below), 1848, pp. 164-66; József Fitz, *A magyar nyomdászat, 1848-1849* (Hungarian Printing, 1848-1849) (Budapest, 1948); Béla Dezsényi, "A magyar hírlapirodalom 1848-49-ben" (The Hungarian Press in 1848-49), *It*, 1949, pp. 105-16; Ernő Éber, "Hírlapirodalmunk a szabadságharc előtt és alatt" (Hungary's Press before and during the War of Independence), ed. Gábor G. Kemény (Budapest); Erzsébet Pozsonyi, "Forradalmi röplapok és gúnyiratok 1848-ban" (Revolutionary Handbills and *radalom és szabadságharc sajtójának ismertetése* (Introduction to the Press of the 1848 Revolution and War of Independence), vol. 1 (Budapest, 1954, duplicated university notes); Margit Busa, "Az 1848-49 évek sajtóbibliográfiája (The Press Bibliography of the Years 1848-49), in *Társadalom és nemzetiség a szabadságharc hadi lapjaiban* (Society and National Affiliation in the Military Newspapers of the War of Independence), Gábor G. Kemény (Budapest, 19); Erzsébet Pozsonyi, "Forradalmi röplapok és gúnyiratok 1848-ban" (Revolutionary Handbills and Lampoons in 1848), *Az Országos Széchényi Könyvtár Évkönyve 1957* (National Széchényi Library Yearbook 1957), pp. 324-61; Sándor Lukácsy, "A sajtó a forradalom és a szabadságharc alatt" (The Press in the Revolution and War of Independence), in *A magyar irodalom története* (History of Hungarian Literature), vol. 3 (Budapest, 1965), pp. 712-15; Aladár Urbán, "Az 1848-as sajtó történetéhez: Okmányok és adatok" (Towards a History of the Press of 1848: Documents and Data), *Irodalomtörténeti Közlemények* (Literary Historical Proceedings, *ItK* below), 1968, pp. 221-31; György Tózsa and György Spira, *Negyvennyolc a kortársak szemével* (Forty-Eight in the Eyes of Contemporaries) (Budapest, n.d./1973/).

7. Conservative Papers in a Period of Change

When the revolution of March 1848 broke out there were six political papers in Hungary and Transylvania: the conservative *Budapesti Híradó*, which supported the governing party; the conservative-clerical *Nemzeti Újság*; *Jelenkor*, which had been founded by Széchenyi but in the mean time had become more or less neutral; the opposition, liberal *Pesti Hírlap*; and in Kolozsvár the stubbornly conservative *Múlt és Jelen* (Past and Present) and its more liberal sparring partner the *Erdélyi Híradó* (Transylvanian Intelligencer). The conservative predominance was such that Kossuth, for lack of a paper of his own, had earlier been obliged on occasion to publish his political articles in the *Hetilap*, the modest bulletin of the Industrial Protection Association, which was on a quite different scale, and to cross swords with the authorities' censors over every one of them.

This conservative predominance was swept away by the revolution. The conservative papers were obliged to retreat and adjust. In one or two cases they went so far as to adopt liberal and even revolutionary colours and cut their political cloth to the mood of the public.

The Nemzeti Újság

The first attempt to change sides was made by the *Nemzeti Újság*, the successor of the *Hazai és Külföldi Tudósítások*, which had been founded in 1806. Still owned by the widow of István Kulcsár, it had appeared under its new title since 1840 and so was the oldest of the six political papers. It appeared four times a week in folio format, printed at the Trattner-Károlyi press. Management was taken over in 1845 by a well-known Pest lawyer and wealthy landowner, Sándor Lipthay (1793-1870), whose family was old established middle nobility and whose father had been a *vicecomes*. Lipthay did not view the paper as a source of income. He was prepared to subsidize it so long as it reflected his political opinions, those of a "new" conservatism more active and up-to-date than the old but no less class-conscious and at the same time strongly Roman Catholic and clerical. Lipthay was the founder and real head of the Gyülde (Meeting Place), a conservative political club. One should add that the paper's *volte-face* was not accomplished or endorsed by Lipthay, who, unable to prevent it, withdrew from the paper at the end of March. His place was taken (formally on April 26, 1848) by János Illucz Oláh (1817-75), who up to then had nominally been editor "under the direction of" Lipthay. Illucz was a literary man of modest talents and noble family. He had begun to study law but from 1843 had edited first the foreign pages and then the press abstracts for the *Nemzeti Újság* under the pen name of Olivér. Later, as editor, he also wrote occasional leading articles, but he remained effectively subordinate. His literary efforts also failed to bring much success. If any notice at all was taken of him by the reforming opposition press, he was mentioned with disdain. Yet it was Illucz who, in the words of a contemporary of his, "went to bed a conservative" on March 15, 1848, "and woke up on the 16th a liberal". Thus, as *Kossuth Hírlapja* later wrote, the *Nemzeti Újság* "denied its former beliefs at the stroke of a wand and became the angriest of liberals." Later still, Mihály Horváth repeated the same opinion: the *Nemzeti Újság*, "which had not lived up to its name at all by so far representing the most extreme wing of the conservatives and clerical interests, now installed itself as the most extravagant supporter of the victorious principles." Certainly the *Nemzeti Újság* was the first paper to appear uncensored on March 16, to carry detailed, colourful reporting of the events in Pest on March 15, and to print the Twelve Points and the National Song. It is hardly surprising that eight hundred copies were sold on the streets in a couple of hours. One should add that this excellent first report, like others that followed of the mass meetings in Pest in March and April, was probably penned by the young Gyula Bulyovszky (1827-83), then twenty-two years old. The son of a Pest County bailiff, Bulyovszky had begun studying law but had already gained a name for himself with his verses, stories, and reviews and was one of the

March Youth who took part in the Pest revolution. In 1847 he joined the staff of *Életképek* and in 1848 moved to the *Nemzeti Újság*, where he became drama critic. His is not the only instance showing that a younger, more progressive generation often lurked behind the conservative façade, waiting for the occasion to step forward. To a degree one might even express this in reverse: the young intelligentsia whose spread has been mentioned had sought protection on occasion and the hope or promise of a livelihood under the shelter of the old régime. It is known that on New Year's Eve 1845 an ornamental album was presented to Lipthay by the conservative Gyülde's sixty young members, headed by the very same Károly Mészáros who was later a prominent member of the Egalitarian Society. Ákos Birányi-Schultz (1816-55), who at this point, after the great turn of events, was writing enthusiastic revolutionary pamphlets and was later to edit a republican paper, had worked not only for the *Pesti Hírlap* and then the *Jelenkor* but also for the *Nemzeti Újság* and the equally conservative *Hírnök* of Pressburg. Károly Majer (1830-90), who as a law student belonged to Pál Vasvári's circle at the University of Pest and was also on the staff of the *Pesti Divatlap*, contributed reports on the Diet in Pressburg to the *Nemzeti Újság*, using the letter "v" as a signature, while working there as a deputy's clerk. Still more striking examples can and will be given. The same precarious social position within the crumbling feudal structure and the occasional consequent instability allowed some of these young men to view their intellectual, journalistic tasks purely as a means of earning their daily bread, while obliging them occasionally and temporarily to attach themselves by more or less weak strands to the old régime. But historically it incorporated into the potential basis for revolution some who had not prepared for the role, and this makes it all the more noteworthy when one finds other young members of the intelligentsia who exhibited this instability little or not at all and who displayed that conscious preparation. One can decide in individual cases whether and when that instability, if any, exceeded the socially accepted limits.

One must consider it natural that men like Bulyovszky should now want to point the *Nemzeti Újság* in their own direction or even appropriate it. Although Illucz was initially permissive on several occasions, he then attempted cautiously to apply the brakes again, from time to time showing his conformist claws or, more precisely, his clerical commitments. Later this dichotomy made the insincerity of the reversal in his views conspicuous and progressively lost the paper the confidence of one side without gaining it the confidence of the other. Of course the editor tried to take advantage of the circumstances. A few days after the great turn of events he condemned all "inane torpor" and opposition to the new order. As other papers did, he placed a slogan on the front page: "Constitution, Nationality, Freedom, Equality!" From May 2 on the paper sported the new title *Nemzeti* (National), with a subtitle "Political Paper", and was printed on László Lukács's new press. From June 1 it appeared daily instead of four times a week. In the mean time it had published on April 6 an article by János Perger, parish priest of Nyíregyháza (and later bishop of Kassa), in which he had begun by saying, "We approve of all that has been occurring in recent days," but continued by trying to defend the primacy of the church's interests: "Let it be clearly understood: world events have embarked on a new path: the church must neither lag behind nor go before them, but under all circumstances keep watch over its own autonomy and the peace of the world." The conservative provincial clergy steadily turned away from the paper that had once represented it, and the subscription soon dropped below eight hundred. Meanwhile József Bajza and Lajos Szeberényi branded Illucz a reactionary and a turncoat for the position he took on religious education and in a less than flattering tone dealt with him in an article in several parts entitled "The Washing of a Weak Head." With growing difficulty the *Nemzeti Újság* managed to survive until the end of the year, when it closed.

The Budapesti Híradó and Figyelmező

The *Budapesti Híradó* had been "under the management" of Count Emil Dessewffy since 1844. It was the paper of the "new" conservatives and of the political line espoused by the chancellor, Count György Apponyi, and so of the régime that had fallen. It too was obliged to recognize as a *fait accompli* the new situation brought about by the revolution, but it did not ape the *Nemzeti Újság* in changing its colours. Although relegated to the background and obliged to make certain changes, it continued to pursue its conservative line faithful to the Habsburgs and passed it on intact to its successor, the *Figyelmező*. For the duration of the Diet all but one or two of the editorial staff moved their offices to Pressburg, where the paper was published and on January 1, 1848, became a daily appearing six times a week. The price of a local subscription for six months was 7 forints and of a postal subscription 9 forints 12 krajcárs. The paper was based in Pressburg at the time of the revolution, and this resulted in the resignation of the editor, József (Kvicsola) Szenvey (1800-57), a translator of Schiller and a corresponding member of the Hungarian Academy of Sciences. On March 18 the editorship was taken over by twenty-nine-year-old Károly Vida (1819-62), who had been born into a Reformed (Calvinist) Church Székely (Transylvanian Hungarian) family of landowners from the Háromszék in eastern Transylvania, studied in Nagyenyed (Aiud), travelled around Western Europe, concerned himself with chemistry and agriculture, worked for the *Erdélyi Híradó* for a time in 1842, and been on the staff of the *Budapesti Híradó* since 1845. He was among the best-educated of the young political commentators in Hungary but also one of the most conservative. He opposed radical efforts at national independence both in terms of the international political concept that the demise of the Habsburg Monarchy would result in Hungary's breaking up or coming under some new kind of subjection and as a true adherent of the dynasty and of the old feudal, historical "constitution" of Hungary. Indeed, as a fervent Hungarian he allowed himself to be carried away by romantic tales of prehistoric adventures, at curious variance with his claims that his political opponents sought to pursue illusions. The paper's new watchword was "Peace among national groups and social classes! Monarchy! Constitutional freedom, order, legality!" This did not in itself conflict in principle with the new laws of 1848, but it betrayed a design to curb them. On one occasion, as we have seen, Kossuth told a delegation of the March Youth to the Diet in Pressburg that if the capital tried to dictate terms the nation was capable of trampling on it. These words of the man the paper had hitherto invariably attacked were reported in the

March 21 issue of the *Budapesti Hírado* in large type with the comment "Kossuth has never expressed public opinion more faithfully." If one adds Vida's hot-tempered, arrogantly self-confident character and his often strongly polemical tone, one can scarcely be surprised at reports that in the climate of opinion at the time he became a real object of hatred. Jókai relates that after a clash with Vida over the administrative system, Irinyi challenged Vida to a duel and shot him in the arm. Several colleagues of his hastened to announce publicly that they did not wish to be identified with him or to cooperate with him. One such was Pál Jancsovics (1817-94), the son of a Lutheran village schoolmaster of noble origin. Jancsovics had exchanged a career in the church and as a teacher for one as secretary to great noblemen and had most recently been the correspondent at the Diet for Dessewffy's paper. In a statement he objected to Vida's blue pencil and then went up to the capital, where Szemere later entrusted him with editing the diary of the National Assembly. The writer Ignác Nagy (1810-54), who till then had been sending biting observations from Pest-Buda to Pressburg about the life and latest doings in the twin cities in the form of a gossip column, resigned as well, saying that "after the full liberation of thought" he now desired "full independence" to present his own ideas. This is a comment that would sound well if one did not know that Nagy, presenting his own ideas, followed up his period of service to the conservatives by entering the service of the absolutist oppressors in the following year.

One should also remark that as a conservative paper the *Budapesti Hírado* followed attentively the phenomena abroad, particularly in France, which presented a threat to "order", including socialistic and communistic endeavours. An article signed Tamás Bizony and entitled "Proletariat" appeared on May 17, 1848. It demonstrated that even from that side it was better under the circumstances to analyse European social problems and changes with the understanding of a humanist: "Whose spirits will not be clouded with sorrow to read of the fate of millions of workers eking out a miserable existence in several European capitals, but particularly in Ireland? And whose countenance will not light up with joy to contemplate (Eugène) Sue's wonderful plan for social reform"? But then comes the continuation: "There is a vast gulf between poetry and life," the welfare of all mankind is "an unattainable desire", and social equality is not merely a chimera but one whose consequence would be a real rebellion against the Creator.

On June 21, just before the new National Assembly met in Pest, the *Budapesti Hírado* expressed the desire for a halt on the path that was being taken:

> The privileged order voluntarily renounced its prerogatives and shared them with the people. Although matters then went farther than even the most extreme members of the opposition had planned, /that/ was induced by the force of circumstances, which did not allow much time for reflection. For better or for worse, that is what occurred. There is no going back any more. /But from the very fact that/ more occurred than the people had even dreamed of it follows that, the gift in question being full and final, we must agree at least for a while on the present position with regard to the broadening of political rights. And that will only be possible if the vast majority of deputies are imbued with this opinion.

One might add that this approach was by no means rare among the nobility at the time of the elections.

The centre of gravity of the press soon returned to the centre of the country, and so on July 1 the *Budapesti Hírado* too returned to the capital that had given it its name. But not long afterwards, on July 17, Vida informed the mayor that the paper would close on the following day, or rather appear again on July 19 as the *Figyelmező*. The new version took a more modest form, appeared only three times a week, and struck perhaps a somewhat more cautious note (although it did not fundamentally contradict itself)—criticizing the government from the right, preaching moderation, opposing the radicals, and championing the monarchy against the tide of republicanism. By then it was the sole surviving right-wing paper. It continued all through the autumn crisis up until December 10, when the National Defence Commission banned it on the grounds that Vida's father had paid the caution money for the *Budapesti Hírado* and not for the *Figyelmező*. Attempts to revive it in 1849 were by then made on the Austrian side.

In Transylvania: *Múlt és Jelen*

In Transylvania a far shorter career was enjoyed by the likewise conservative Kolozsvár paper *Múlt és Jelen*, which had been representing the government's interests since 1841, appearing twice a week with two "appendices" or supplements: *Hon és Külföld* (Home and Abroad) and the *Historiai Kedveskedő* (Historical Pleasantry). The editor and proprietor of the publishing house was Ferenc Szilágyi (1797-1876), a teacher at the Reformed Church College whose opinions became steadily more conservative and loyal to the dynasty in the years before the revolution, in debate with the opposition and with the other, more liberal Kolozsvár paper, the *Erdélyi Híradó*, while frequently complaining about and reporting to the authorities all whom he considered opponents or rivals. As a consequence he became increasingly unpopular, so that eventually, we are told, his paper had a mere two hundred or so subscribers left. But the authorities at the time were still strong, and generous enough to support the paper with a subsidy. Indeed, by slyly mentioning resignation Szilágyi managed to persuade the court in the summer of 1847 to ensure him a salary of 1,000 forints a year on top of the subsidy. He was conspicuous for his tenacious aggressiveness and, even under the old feudal conditions of Transylvania, his niggardly, scheming behaviour but still more, perhaps, for the lack of principle that allowed him to exploit power without scruple whenever the chance was presented. When the turn of events came in spring 1848 he too hastened at first to sport a tricolor rosette. He left the word *Múlt* (Past) out of the title of the paper on April 14, which was superscribed *Jelen, Politikai Lap* (Present, Political Paper) from then on. But an unbridgeable gulf divided him from the local young progressive forces, and deep down he had so little faith in their victory that he shortly began to make advances to the court again. When the youths of Kolozsvár mounted a charivari and demonstration against him, breaking his windows and burning his paper, he thought it better to depart for Vienna. After that the paper appeared for the last time on May 9, and in the same month the chief consistory of the Transylvanian Reformed Church deprived him of his teaching position as well.

The inglorious end of this none too glorious venture was related in 1865 by József Szinnyei in the columns of the *Vasárnapi Újság* in what was the first comprehensive account of the press during the revolution and war of independence. Of *Múlt és Jelen* he writes, "This paper which was wont before the March Days to revile the French revolution later praised the movements in Kolozsvár, whereupon the *Pesti Divatlap* placed its anathema upon it in these words: 'It no longer has a *present* or a *future*, having lost them by its *past.*'" On the change of name the *Pesti Hírlap* commented as follows: "The absolutist-oriented *Múlt és Jelen*, seeking to efface the memory of a past of which it had itself become ashamed, changed into a simple '*Jelen*'. But it did not stand up well to this chameleonic adroitness. '*Jelen*' could not serve the purposes of the revolutionary trend either. So happily it has expired and been buried." After that Szinnyei went on to tell the story of the charivari and to report that Szilágyi had quit Kolozsvár "to avert the danger threatening his person."

But a later reader satisfied with this conclusion will be somewhat amazed to find on leafing further through the old numbers of the *Vasárnapi Újság* that this same Ferenc Szilágyi, to whom all this had happened and about whom all this had been written, who in 1849 had been the lackey of absolutism amid the ruins of his blood-stained country, who had become editor of the collaborating *Magyar Hírlap* (Hungarian Journal), and about whom everyone knew these things, was capable of making an insolent, unmannerly attack on Szinnyei by way of a retort. He accused Szinnyei of being "hostile and malicious" and so quoting "from biased newspapers" and of writing "groundless things counter to the truth." He noted Szinnyei's account of the "brutal and crude" assault, referring to the demonstration, and went on to say that it was quite unjust because he had always served the cause of "justice and constitutional freedom." Moreover, he said, the Unitarian student by the name of Márton Szőcs who had burned the paper had later become a loyal *Beamter* under the absolutist régime. On all these accounts he charged Szinnyei with libel and challenged him to prove his "disparaging assertions." What is indeed extraordinary is not that these insolently nonsensical arguments should have come from Szilágyi but that the *Vasárnapi Újság*, as late as 1865, should have seen fit to publish them in this form. One should add to the account of Szilágyi's doings that in Vienna in the summer of 1848 he wrote a pamphlet at the bidding of court circles under a pseudonym arguing against the unification of Transylvania with Hungary, which he claimed would amount to "a rash experiment in political radicalism" (*Erdély és az unió: Töredék-eszmék Erdélyi Magyar Jánostól* /Transylvania and the Union: Scattered Thoughts from "John the Transylvanian Hungarian"/, 1848). From Vienna he went to Pest, where from July to September 1848 he sent dispatches to the *Wiener Zeitung* as a correspondent under the pseudonym of Ede Kertész. Initially he extolled Kossuth, but on September 14 he wrote of his plunging his country into the maelstrom out of a desire for glory.

Bibliography

Szinnyei, "Hírlapirodalmunk"; Dávid Angyal, "A Figyelmező története, 1849-1850 (The History of the *Monitor,* 1849-1850), *Magyar Bibliofil Szemle* (Hungarian Bibliophile Review), 1925, pp. 113-15; idem, ed., *Falk Miksa és Kecskeméthy Aurél elkobzott levelezése* (The Confiscated Correspondence of Miksa Falk and Aurél Kecskeméthy) (Budapest, 1925); Béla Dezsényi, "Nemzeti Újság, 1840-1848: Nyolc év egy konzervatív hírlap történetéből" (*The National News,* 1840-1848: Eight Years in the History of a Conservative Newspaper), in *Regnum 1940/41* (Budapest, 1941), pp. 313-56, and as an offprint.

8. Liberal Papers

Of the older papers, the *Jelenkor* had been founded in 1832 as a weekly and now appeared four times a week with a weekly supplement, the *Társalkodó*. As Széchenyi's creation it had been at the beginning of the age of reform a pioneer of the new political press, but in recent years it had become steadily blander and attracted dwindling interest.

The Demise of the Jelenkor

The *Jelenkor*'s editor and publisher had been the same from the outset. Mihály Helmeczy (formerly Bierbrauer, 1792-1853) had been one of the Auróra Circle and shown modest literary promise, but now, growing old and with failing eyesight, he had been less and less able to keep pace with developments and performed his duties with decreasing care. As a result, the standard of the paper was declining. Although in principle the *Jelenkor* still adhered to Széchenyi and not infrequently cited his authority, the apathy may well have stemmed largely from the paper's attempt to remain neutral in the heightening struggle between the parties or, one might say, from the way it had retreated from the stormier waters while Széchenyi was battling with Kossuth and in the mean time drawing nearer to the government. But when the revolution led to a change in the front lines and Széchenyi too joined the new responsible Hungarian ministry, the paper was unable to follow the tide of events sufficiently well or to recover its following. After that, things went even worse for the paper than they did for the Trattner-Károlyi press in Pest, which printed it. The man in charge of the latter was István Károlyi, a lawyer in the royal court of appeal who had married into the Trattner business. Around 1840 he had been the first in Hungary to introduce steam power, and for a good while he was the country's leading printer, with five steam and six hand-powered machines and a staff of forty. He was an adherent of Széchenyi and the moderate opposition and principally produced fairly undemonstrative professional and scientific journals. In 1848 he soon lost ground to Landerer, who made such good use of the new demand that for some time there was hardly a product of the press in which Károlyi could be involved. The decline of the *Jelenkor* could not even be stopped when Helmeczy, who remained publisher, was replaced as editor by new blood in the shape of the twenty-nine-year-old Pál Királyi (1818-92). Királyi had been on the staff of the paper as its foreign editor and then its assistant editor since 1845. For a time the young Mór Jókai had worked beside him, for a couple of months as a "writer of novelties" at a salary of 35 forints. Like the *Jelenkor* itself, Királyi supported Széchenyi, whom he had met while attending the 1843-44 Diet as a lawyer's articled clerk. His book *Robot és dézma* (Corvée and Tithes, 1845) had shared the prize in a competition set by Count Kázmér Batthyány and the Hungarian Economic Society with two other studies with similar titles. The events in Pest on March 15 were covered in the *Jelenkor* by Királyi and in the *Társalkodó* reportedly by Ákos Birányi, for it seems that the adherents of the radicalism of the future emerged on this paper as well (some sources also mention cooperation by Józsa Oroszhegyi, later commander of a band of irregulars, and by others). Certainly Királyi too soon left his top position on the paper and later served in the war of independence as an officer in the Hungarian army. On June 3, 1848, Helmeczy informed the mayor of Pest that the editorship was being taken over by József Keresztúry, a lawyer and former junior clerk of the courts in Nyitra County. Once, back in 1839, Keresztúry had been on the staff of the *Athenaeum* and then of the *Regélő* and had written stories and verses. His work on the modification of entailed properties, written for an academic competition, had been awarded a prize and published by the Academy of Sciences. On May 25 he attempted to outline the new programme in the columns of the *Jelenkor*, but ultimately he did not become editor, as the paper closed on June 29, 1848.

After all these, the ranks of the liberal press included two other papers: the more modest and provincial *Erdélyi Híradó* and the far more significant *Pesti Hírlap*.

Liberal Papers in Transylvania

The publisher and editor of the *Erdélyi Híradó* since 1832 had been Sámuel Méhes (1785-1852), a teacher at the Reformed Church College in Kolozsvár. The paper's dry, old-fashioned, abstract character was substantially altered in 1842 when Baron Zsigmond Kemény and Lajos Kovács tried to broach in it the ideas of Hungary's reform movement of the liberal nobility, but not for long, as they were obliged to leave the paper in the following year. Liberalism advanced with more difficulty and less speed in Transylvania than it did in Hungary proper. Later the running of the paper was influenced from above by a patron, Count Domokos Teleki (1810-76), whose views resembled Széchenyi's, although he also contributed to the *Pesti Hírlap*. Now, after the revolution, Méhes was already over sixty, and he had won a seat in the National Assembly. On May 12 he resigned, and on June 1 the editorship was taken over by Ferenc Ocsvay (1819-87), who came from a noble landowning family in Doboka County and had studied law at the Reformed Church College in Kolozsvár. He had been lastingly influenced by his first political experience in 1834, when Miklós Wesselényi had formed an opposition in the Transylvanian Diet. In 1841 Ocsvay became a clerk of the royal court of appeal, but soon, after the departure of Kemény and Kovács, he began performing the editorial duties at the *Erdélyi Híradó* in Méhes's name, for a time in conjunction with Károly Vida. Originally a biweekly, the paper appeared three times a week from March 21, 1848. Under Ocsvay this increased to four times a week, and from July 1 it appeared under a new name, as the *Kolozsvári Híradó* (Kolozsvár Intelligencer). Sámuel Brassai remained the editor of its weekly supplement, the *Vasárnapi Újság*, whose purpose was declared in its subtitle—"For the Dissemination of Publicly Useful Information." A large part of the paper had been taken up earlier by reports of the Transylvanian Diet and later by official announcements and notices, leaving little space for political journalism. Publication of the *Kolozsvári Híradó* came to an end when the city was occupied by the imperial forces in mid-November 1848. Ocsvay was obliged to depart. He served as a Hungarian soldier, but at the end of the year General József Bem's force returned to Kolozsvár, and at Bem's instigation Ocsvay on December 28 founded the *Honvéd* (Soldier), which appeared daily until the defeat.

The Pesti Hírlap

The sole paper to stay essentially the same in a period when the old political press—its staffs, titles, and alignments—changed and various papers altered their colours or closed down was the *Pesti Hírlap*. Since it already espoused liberal national transformation, it had no reason to change allegiance, although its relative position in the political spectrum was altered by the revolution. Hitherto one could have called it relatively left-wing compared with the conservative preponderance. Now, by remaining an adherent of moderate liberalism, it found itself in the centre, and as the radical press advanced, it was relatively to the right of centre, although still representing one of the trends of liberal opinion.

The publishers were the firm of Landerer and Heckenast. Lajos Landerer was a shrewd political operator, as well as a good tradesman and manager, and a prosperous man of the world. He had offered Kossuth the editorship with the sanction of Vienna and had arranged that Kossuth should leave the job in 1844 at Vienna's behest. In a private letter Kossuth had accused Landerer of being in the pay of the Austrian secret police, but in May 1848 it was Landerer whom Kossuth commissioned to set up the Hungarian banknote press. Landerer succeeded so well that he was never subsequently able to climb back onto the political fence and after 1849 was obliged to go into hiding. When he died in 1854 after a long illness, he left the bulk of his ready money to his employees at the press. Landerer's works had new, modern machinery on which several other Hungarian papers besides the *Pesti Hírlap* were printed. On the eve of the revolution he outdid his rival, the more traditionalist Trattner-Károlyi press, both technically and in political flexibility. It was at Landerer's, as we have seen, that the first products of the free press were printed when the great turn of events came.

Even after Kossuth's departure, the *Pesti Hírlap* had remained the paper of Hungary's liberal, reforming opposition, although for a time it lost much of its popularity among noble readers and became the organ of the more moderate wing from the national point of view. In liberal terms, however, it was more progressive and directed by the centralist, "doctrinaire" group. By the eve of the revolution it again had five thousand subscribers and reportedly earned Landerer and Heckenast clear half-yearly profits of 6,000 forints. This was partly because it represented more or less the whole opposition party and partly because of the activities and methods of its young editor, the twenty-six-year-old Antal Csengery (1822-80). Csengery was a member of the centralist circle and a cultivated political journalist well versed in the political life and press conditions of the more developed liberal countries. As an editor he was meticulous and circumspect, paying attention to the tiniest detail. As far as style was concerned, he was in the 1840s among those such as Károly Nagy and particularly József Irinyi who followed foreign examples in seeking to replace the traditional rolling periods favoured by the nobility with the "lighter French style of writing." Csengery's intentions emerge clearly, for instance, from some unpublished notes on style that declare, "One can distinguish in terms of form between a terse style (*style coupé*) and one in periods (*périodique*)." But Csengery was also in touch with the March Youth of his own generation. The various members of the Society of Ten frequently sought him out, even at the offices of the *Pesti Hírlap*. Clearly he and they did not represent the same thing and were not preparing to move in the same direction, but from the point of view of social and political progress members of the centralist group among the liberal opposition like this young journalist were closest to the point at which the young Hungarian radicals were preparing to take over the baton. They were divided by the issue of the revolution, but ultimately it was the centralist group that prepared the ground for the organization of the new state, the responsible Hungarian ministry, and the parliamentary system, opposed by the adherents of the county nobility and the old "*táblabíró* politics." Among the staff of the *Pesti Hírlap* on the eve of the revolution was József Irinyi, one of the March Youth and the composer of the Twelve Points, who had been foreign editor for some years. Another staff member was Dániel Emődy (1819-91), a young Pest lawyer and journalist who took part in the events of March 1848 at the side of Petőfi and Jókai. Also there from 1847 was Albert Pálffy, whom we shall shortly meet again as editor of the main radical paper, *Marczius Tizenötödike*. In a novel Pálffy wrote at the end of the century (*A régi Magyarország utolsó évei* /The Last Years of Old Hungary/, 1894) he gave through the medium of a conversation in the offices of the *Pesti Hírlap* this picture of the "peace-loving centralists"; "Before them indeed were the images of centralization, a parliament elected by the people, a responsible ministry, a free press, equal rights and equitable taxation, but drawing a lesson from experience they reckoned that if all went well for the Hungarians it would be 1950 at the earliest before these things were made flesh, blood, and tangible reality," for in politics as in nature there were to be no leaps and bounds. Pálffy himself, however, made a leap out of the offices of the *Pesti Hírlap* into radicalism.

From the "day of press freedom" at the time of the March revolution the *Pesti Hírlap* renumbered its issues from 1 again, considering that a new era had begun. Shortly afterwards, as noted earlier, it came out against the first draft of the press law, which aroused such an outcry in Pest, and warned the Diet in Pressburg how much the situation had been changed by the revolution. The *Pesti Hírlap* was pleased to note that developments had in effect vindicated the liberal platform it had put forward. It condemned the errors of the bygone régime, although it generally did so in a sober fashion. It stood somewhere between the noblemen of Pressburg and the radicals of Pest, initially showing more inclination to do battle with the reluctant elements of the nobility. On March 30 it attacked the *Nemzeti Újság* for repeatedly referring to the "generosity" of the nobility over taxation: "it appears not to know that the great reforms now won by the nation result not from the nobility's generosity but from the democratic movement which has shaken up the whole of Europe since it began in Paris. Any sacrifice the nobility may have made has not been offered up on the altar of the fatherland; it has been made in its own interest to propitiate the spirit of the people's rights." It also came out against the idea that suffrage was to be general for the nobility but restricted by a property qualification for others. Recalling the loaded sticks that the beslippered nobility had turned on the advocates of generalized taxation in the age of reform, it described the distinction as "scandalous": "What sort of merit has accrued in the past to lesser nobles now unable to meet the low qualification mentioned above that we should consider them worthy of such distinction from the other classes in the country? Or what sort of security do they offer for the future? Behind us is a sad picture of the old world electioneering, before us the pyre of the baleful policy of reaction!" Since the vast majority at the circular session in Pressburg on March 30 gave unreserved support to such a distinction, the paper reproached the "gentleman deputies" on April 7 for having "on this occasion changed into estates of the realm" (in other words, succumbed to noble prejudice), adding, "Since qualifications are set up from the point of view of the people, the bosom of the hitherto privileged class will nurse into fashion *suffrage universel*, with all its perversities and perils." On April 8 the *Pesti Hírlap* published a leading article by Széchenyi, one of the ministers, in which he requested support for the government and expressed a hope that "after a long, mortal sleep" there would now "dawn a glorious day over our so long downtrodden country," although he underlined firmly that the transformation had to be orderly and constitutional. But two days later, on April 10, the paper could not refrain from commenting on Széchenyi's remark in a speech to the Diet that "the generous Hungarian nobility has admitted the people onto the ramparts of rights." The editors' gloss was this: "As far as we know it was the people, inspired by the holy miasma emitted into the air of Europe, who themselves stormed onto those ramparts. This constant adulation ill suits the nobility." Yet basically the *Pesti Hírlap* stood close to the new government, and so it is understandable that when the interior minister Bertalan Szemere began setting up his office in Pest he appealed on April 16 to the editors of the *Pesti Hírlap* to start an official column in their paper "with the object of publishing the governmental regulations and notifications . . . until the official paper of the government can be founded." The editors complied, and started the "official column," which was clearly distinguished in the paper from the "unofficial section." But in fact the paper was not departing from the "official" line when the editorial in the April 23 issue, for instance, put on record that there could be no question of assuming the Austro-Hungarian national debt, for that was also the position at the time of the members of the government, Széchenyi and Deák among them.

Essentially the *Pesti Hírlap* condemned the efforts at land distribution just as the papers to the right and left of it generally did, but it firmly emphasized that the Pressburg Diet had only half done the job of abolishing feudal obligations and that the National Assembly now had to erase the remnants of feudalism. On May 13 it cited the dramatic memories of the revolutionary days and "the work of a few hours that came suddenly" to stress that the immediate abolition of feudal obligations was a condition for survival: "It is enough for us to fight the battle of the races. What will become of us now if we have to fight the battle of the classes as well?" But, it added, one source of much unrest at the time was that no one knew exactly what urbarial lands (the peasant holdings on an estate that figure in the *urbarium*) were. This, it said, "has produced a difficult, disquieting relationship", particularly where the arrangements were incomplete and where

> the landowner demands a plot here, a bit of vineyard there, and a little parcel somewhere else and ducks the meaning of urbarial lands; and the former serfs, on the other hand, not only fail to comprehend that there is a difference between those of them who performed *corvée* and paid tithes and rent and those of them who did the same because long ago a list was drawn up on some basis or other (which in our opinion too is incomprehensible) but also in many cases are attempting to conceal the actual *allodium* that was in their hands at the time the law was published; this is not to mention the cottar and peasant with a part-holding dreaming that the *allodium* or, where there is none, the *constitutivum* of the larger holdings will be divided up and made uniform.

Clearly, it argued, "this situation must be cleared up." The *Pesti Hírlap* declared that certain distinctions made by the law were incomprehensible, and what is more, it was prepared to say that the landowners, even at this juncture, were trying to take advantage of the confusion, while the peasants for their part were trying to retain and even occupy the land.

But the steady alteration in the paper's position in the new political spectrum also appeared in certain staff changes. For a short while Baron Zsigmond Kemény rejoined the staff and on May 9 mocked the Vienna papers for the sympathy they showed for Josip Jelačić, but on May 14 he attacked the radical organizers of a demonstration and charivari in Pest against Lieutenant-General Ignaz Lederer, commander of the imperial troops in Buda. From May 16 he was involved more decisively as co-editor alongside Csengery. Up until the end of the summer one can find eighteen political leaders to which he appended his own name, and at the time he was writing anonymously as well. Meanwhile one staff member to leave was Irinyi, who took up a left-wing position in the National Assembly in Pest, although he dissociated himself from the petty noble version of radicalism espoused by László Madarász and his ilk. On May 16, after Kemény had joined the paper, the editors ranged themselves behind the Batthyány government in a declaration of their programme: "If the ministry cannot strengthen, if obstacles are placed in its path and the majority do not assist it, what else can ensue but turbulence and unstable relations? In this sense and this sense alone the *Pesti Hírlap* will be the government's paper." Apart from defending the achievements of March, the paper supported reconciliation of interests, strengthening of order at home, and the conclusion of the revolution. It refused to publish one of Petőfi's revolutionary articles, increasingly opposed the radicals, and engaged in ever sharper polemics with *Marczius Tizenötödike*. "The revolution, taking the word in its European sense, has now been completed here for the time being," the *Pesti Hírlap* wrote on May 17, 1848. "What can occur after this is the task either of peaceful evolution and perfection or bloody warfare." Turning to the radicals, it said they should "beware not to do a service to reaction." *Marczius* hastened to respond that very afternoon:

> Everywhere in the world there is a certain pseudo-revolutionary party which declares in its sermons as it clambers to power over the corpses of others, "Citizens, the revolution is over...." That is how the July /1830/ French government spoke.... For our part we believe this: one cannot conceive of a more despicable and abhorrently selfish policy in the world than the policy of those who attain power by a revolutionary path and on the following morning call those who bore the brunt on the day of battle turbulent, contemptible, and irksome instruments of partisan strife.

These words, by the way, typify the extent to which the Hungarian journalism of the day was modelled on the French. Hastily responding the next day, the *Pesti Hírlap* described the efforts of its adversary as "underhand politics" which had, in its opinion, "set itself the task of disparaging the ministry." There were "signs of disintegration everywhere" in the country, it went on. "Our people's ideas on property have turned quite topsy-turvy. Classes, lands, and races battle vehemently with each other at a time when we might justifiably have hoped for the opposite, reconciliation of interest. . . . There is peril without and within the country." Thus it considered it time to enlighten the country on the real mood in the capital and on the rootlessness of the radical press. "Where is there even a party that these papers represent? Where in the capital, where throughout the country? Pest wants order. . . . And in the provinces—you would scarcely credit the indignation at this constant clamour. It has but one purpose, to enlist subscribers at any cost." There was no change in this standpoint when on May 19 the *Pesti Hírlap* replied to charges from the right of government weakness against the radicals. The paper said the government could not be accused of lacking energy in matters of the press: since "it remains strictly within the limits of the law . . . since it does not resort to repressive methods (against the newspapers), since it feels itself supported by public opinion in the country, it is unperturbed by the clamour of certain noisy gentlemen." On June 4 Mihály Vörösmarty also asserted in the *Pesti Hírlap* that "intellectual freedom is grounded in the press law," whose shortcomings it would be the task of the National Assembly to remedy. Incidentally, it was his journalism in the *Pesti Hírlap* between May 20 and June 4 that constituted the most important phase of Vörösmarty's part in the events of 1848-49. When the first instalment of his piece "The Days of Transformation" appeared, the editors added a special note: "We are delighted to list among our regular colleagues this friend of ours, who in the days of servitude stirred up and animated the nation with his poems." Supporting the achievements of March, Vörösmarty rejected "all fancies that go beyond the bounds of our established situation." Only thus could they be strong enough to combat the counter-revolutionaries, on the one hand, and those who "villainously attack the sanctity of property," on the other. This he later repeated in an article entitled "A Few Words", in which he defended what had been accomplished and rejected the "bold experimenters" who "*ad novam divisionem* would like to bring a summons against the world," along with the ideas of "inciters and predators" who will, "if we do not keep a watchful eye upon them, serve only to make the ideas of freedom and equality horrific." Vörösmarty sincerely believed in bourgeois equality of rights, but he opposed efforts that went farther and aimed at altering property relations. This accorded fully with the *Pesti Hírlap*'s line, but it soon emerged that Vörösmarty's views did not after all fulfil every desire of the editors. They did not publish his article "The Traditions of Absolutism", and so the relationship broke off. Vörösmarty, we know, became a member of the House of Representatives with the support of Kossuth.

Undoubtedly the *Pesti Hírlap*, with its weighty columns, its painstaking domestic and foreign news service, and its growing strength, exemplified in its appearance daily instead of four times a week from May 27, was the country's most developed political paper with the most subscribers. Its position only became more difficult later because it could not agree (and could hardly have done so) with all the various shades of political opinion that emerged within the government. The *Pesti Hírlap* subscribed to Batthyány's more restrained line and approved less and less of Kossuth's more decisive one. But in the government's interest it did not want to air these internal differences in public, and so it arrived at the solution of endorsing the moves of the government only when it approved of them. This a writer in *Marczius* on June 28 hastened to point out: a paper that supported the government should explain the expediency of the measures taken, whereas the *Pesti Hírlap* was adopting an attitude towards the government of staying silent about what it thought bad about it: "All Europe is in the midst of a revolution, and Hungarian papers are still being edited in comfortable old *táblabíró* style." Essentially the observation was apposite even though the *Pesti Hírlap*, as we have seen, had not originally undertaken to be the government's paper in all things, even though the government had started its own official paper, and even though the main cause of the difficulties lay not in its "comfortable style" but in the growth of political tension.

One can take it as a political gesture that on July 5 the *Pesti Hírlap* was the paper to publish Petőfi's poem "To the National Assembly", in which he refrained for once from expressing republican principles and addressed the representatives as an ally: "For you must now create a homeland too." As the session began the paper again tried to bring the urbarial issue to the fore. On July 11 Zsigmond Kemény wrote that "our agrarian laws are such as to keep tempers at the highest state of excitement." On the people's desires, he considered it "rightful and conducive to our regeneration" that the remnants of feudalism should be abolished. On July 16 Miklós Jósika complained in an article with a rather different tone of the peasants' occupation of the land and demanded energetic action and instruction of the people, to which Kemény responded, "It was mistaken enough that the last Diet failed to go to the final limit in abolishing the remnants of feudalism; by maintaining these, doubts have been maintained in the suspicious people about the landowner's property of another nature." Thus, he said, plain instruction in itself was not enough.

Kemény thought it would be better and wiser in terms of the landowners' self-defence if the urbarial issue were cleared up more fully than it had been in the law of April 1848. We also know from what point of view he found harmony wanting from the workings of government. He would have liked to see Széchenyi, with whom he identified more and more closely, form a political circle, with the help of Lajos Kovács, of the representatives who felt as they did, to see the moderates join forces against the radicals, to see the leaders of the ministry more active, and to see the government party support Batthyány rather than steadily succumbing to the influence of Kossuth's bolder policy. However, his polemics on home policy and attacks on *Marczius*, the *Nép-elem*, and individual radicals such as Mór Perczel tended to be published in the *Pesti Hírlap* without his name, under the mark "-a-". Between July 23 and August 22 one can find six of these. In major, signed leading articles he was more inclined to view the issues of the Habsburg Monarchy, Hungary, and the national minorities from the angle of international policy. In the joint editorial of May 16 which has already been mentioned, it was largely at Kemény's behest that the Slavic danger was cited to endorse an Austrian alliance with the new Germany, although there was insistence on Hungary's independence in the sense embodied in the Pragmatic Sanction. With many other members of the Hungarian liberal nobility, Kemény saw the national liberal movement for German unity as a vehicle for advancing European civilization and modern progress. He hailed the Frankfurt parliament, with which he hoped Hungary might ally itself as a defence against Pan-Slavism. He too considered the movements among Hungary's national minorities as the vanguard of Pan-Slavist efforts to gain power. But concurrently he believed firmly in maintaining the Habsburg Monarchy, among other reasons because he considered that its disintegration would heighten the Pan-Slavist danger. His charge against the new revolution in Vienna on May 15 was that granting universal suffrage would help strengthen the Slavs. He also disapproved of Austria's policy of Italian conquest, since holding onto Lombardy would tie down too many forces and leave fewer to cope with the Slavs' demands. One can go farther: he condemned the machinations of Viennese reaction with such venom not only because he defended the March achievements and the new Hungary but because he saw the Habsburg Monarchy threatened most of all by the ill-tempered stupidity of its own leaders. In five consecutive leading articles beginning on August 13, Kemény attacked this Austrian reaction—Radetzky for succumbing to arrogance again after his success in Italy and Doblhoff and Latour for openly siding with the Croatian and Serbian rebels in the Viennese constituent assembly. "There is every prospect", he wrote, "that the cynicism of the crime will be able to boast of the dissension it has sown among us and the assistance it has rendered to Jelačić."

In a later pamphlet entitled *Forradalom után* (After the Revolution, 1850), in which Kemény decisively argued for the unity of the Habsburg Monarchy and rejected all revolution, he stated among other things that in the autumn of 1848 he had abandoned all debate because of the terrorism of the radicals and withdrawn, considering the situation hopeless. This would seem to be supported by the absence of Kemény's name under any articles in the *Pesti Hírlap* in the new period which began with the September crisis, although he still featured as an editor. But a contemporary critic of that pamphlet, the self-styled "failed diplomat" who wrote *Documentált felelet* (A Documented Response, 1850), asserted with a measure of irony that "around mid-September 1848, when Doblhoff explained the invalidity of the independent Hungarian government by referring to the Pragmatic Sanction, Zsigmond Kemény too was expressing a different policy in his paper." As evidence the author immediately quoted one of the articles signed "-a-" in the *Pesti Hírlap* of September 21, 1848, which content and style indicate was written by Kemény. One can find fifteen articles by Kemény signed in this way between September and December. These all protested bitterly and sharply against the conduct of Jelačić, the hypocritical, pseudo-constitutional measures taken by absolutism, the false charges of reaction, and even the efforts of the Kremsier assembly. These articles show the disillusioned rage of one who sees the dynasty working against itself and reactionary leaders turning the people into republicans. In spite of the fact that still more vehement notes were being struck in the Hungarian press in those days, these articles were unmistakably influenced by the revolutionary atmosphere and the passionate public mood of a nation preparing to defend itself. Therefore it is not surprising that on October 24, 1848, the National Assembly gave Kemény the task of wording the proclamation to be addressed to the people. The proclamation, which denounced the machinations of the court, appeared in the *Pesti Hírlap* of October 31, and its text was recognizably similar to the leader published above the signature "-a-" on October 29. Both rejected the charge of "terrorism" laid against the Hungarian government mainly by Puchner, commander-in-chief of the imperial forces in Transylvania. Both averred that reaction "promised order and delivered servitude." Finally, one can find in the proclamation with only minor changes these two sentences from the leader of October 29: "Since 1789 kings and tyrants have used no other weapon against the freedom of peoples than to frighten them with the purported evils that by their account derive from freedom. To deter the people from it they invariably point to the guillotine, as if it were freedom's inseparable concomitant."

Perhaps Kemény at this time wrote something more or different about national self-defence than he was under later, altered circumstances to acknowledge. But in Debrecen, when real warfare had broken out between Hungary and the power of the Habsburgs, he still tried to represent efforts for agreement and peace in the Hungarian political spectrum. In the mean time he had ceased his editorial work. It would seem that events had overtaken the old *Pesti Hírlap* with its middle-of-the-road, non-committal policy of reconciliation. The number of subscribers fell off. Its sources of foreign news dried up. According to Szeremlei, the government from the autumn onwards "sequestered . . . the Viennese, French, and English papers, and only *Kossuth Hírlapja* at most was lucky enough to get hold of news from abroad. For more than a month the *Pesti Hírlap* began its foreign coverage with this stereotyped phrase: 'The government of this country continually confiscating the foreign papers. . . .'" As early as November 1848 Kemény and Csengery thought it better to leave their top positions on the paper, although at the time their idea was to start another paper instead. Kemény's biographer asserts that in it they were prepared to put their own political line forward even against Kossuth's and that they invited Szemere to join them on the staff because they knew he was opposed to Kossuth's position of power. Szemere, however, while promising cooperation in a reply of December 2 which has come to light, declared himself a believer in a republic, supported the position that the war against the dynasty had to be waged to the bitter end, and branded any negotiation as cowardice. He approved of Csengery's continuing to work in the press field but made it no secret that he disapproved of the *Pesti Hírlap*'s modest, mild tone, since in revolutionary times it behoved the press too to create an outcry. At the invitation of publishers Landerer and Heckenast, Jókai announced in the *Pesti Hírlap* of November 30 that he would be taking over the editorship of the paper in the New Year "with the esteemed collaboration of our fellow citizen Pál Nyáry." On the last day of the year, in the December 31, 1848, number, Csengery and Kemény indeed bade farewell to their readers. The paper's main purpose, they wrote, was to acquaint its readers with political conditions elsewhere in Europe. "Since we live in a century when the peoples of Europe have been or are beginning to be transformed from national fragments into great organizations of state, and we cannot remain insulated from our geographical situation," they considered it necessary "to seek an alliance built upon natural and true interests." But they admitted failing to exert a lasting influence on Hungarian public opinion. "In the days of general enthusiasm . . . the inspired people harkens to the words of inspired men, because these are the moments when, in the words of the Scriptures, man lives by words. These inspirations appear in the Hungarian political press as if in a little *camera obscura*. We read these with great pleasure but to little purpose, and we did not echo them because we could not at the time give shape to the promising dream." The political confession was expressed fairly generally and cautiously, but its essence cannot be misconstrued. Kemény and his group clearly believed that the impetus given by Kossuth could unleash dangerous forces. "In times like these, when the bold phrases of Proudhon and Táncsics are preferred reading to the observations of scholarship", it is all the harder, they said, to influence public opinion, since "opposing relations have poisoned the peaceful revolution." This is how the editors closed the history of the *Pesti Hírlap*'s centralist years: "We can conclude our path as we started upon it four-and-a-half years ago: in a small way with few friends."

The plan, as has been mentioned, was for Jókai to take over as editor in the New Year. But as the issue of January 3, 1849, appeared under Jókai's name, the young editor himself was on his way to Debrecen, where the government and parliament moved along with many others, including Nyáry, Csengery, and Kemény.

Bibliography

Sándor Szilágyi, "Kemény Zs. báró és Csengery" (Baron Zs. Kemény and Csengery), in *A magyar forradalom férfiai* (The Men of the Hungarian Revolution) (Pest, 1850), pp. 339-40; idem, "Brassai, Ocsvay," in *A magyar forradalom*, p. 344; Pál Gyulai, "Emlékbeszéd Csengery Antal fölött" (Commemorative Address for Antal Csengery), *Magyar Tudományos Akadémia Évkönyve* (Yearbook of the Hungarian Academy of Sciences, *MTA Évk* below), vol. 16, no. 7 (1881), pp. 23-27, and in idem, *Emlékbeszédek* (Commemorative Addresses), vol. 1 (Budapest, 1914), pp. 191-224; Ferenc Papp, *Báró Kemény Zsigmond* (Baron Zsigmond Kemény), vol. 1 (Budapest, 1922); László Hofbauer, "Az Erdélyi Híradó története (1827-1848)" (The History of the *Transylvanian Intelligencer* /1827-1848/), *Erdélyi Múzeum* (Transylvanian Museum, 1932, pp. 57-72, and as an offprint; Gábor Halász, "Antal Csengery," *Nyugat* (West), January 1939, pp. 216-20, and idem, *Válogatott írásai* (Selected Writings) (Budapest, 1959), pp. 479-87; Jenő Szentimrei, "A 48-as Erdély irodalma és sajtója" (The Literature and Press of Transylvania in '49), in *Negyvennyolcas Erdély* (Transylvania in '48) (Kolozsvár, 1943), pp. 45-56; Piroska D. Szemző, "Képzőművészetünk és a Pesti Hírlap, 1841-1849" (Hungarian Fine Art and the *Pest Journal*,

1841-1849), *A Magyar Művészettörténeti Munkaközösség Évkönyve* (Yearbook of the Hungarian Art History Partnership), 1951 (Budapest, 1952), pp. 135-37; Gyula Barla, "Kemény Zsigmond 1848-ban, márciustól decemberig" (Zsigmond Kemény in 1848, from March to December), *Studia Litteraria*, 1963, pp. 83-100; János Herepei, "Méhes Sámuel lemondása az 'Erdélyi Híradó' szerkesztéséről" (Sámuel Méhes's Resignation from the Editorship of the *Transylvanian Intelligencer*), *MKsz*, 1966, p. 156; Gyula Barla, *Kemény Zsigmond főbb eszméi 1849 előtt* (The Main Ideas of Zsigmond Kemény before 1849) (Budapest, 1970); Aladár Urbán, "Kiegészítések Vörösmarty életrajzához: A költő 1848-49-es tevékenységéről" (Addenda to the Biography of Vörösmarty: On the Poet's Activity in 1848-49), *It*, 1975, pp. 946-60, and in *A nagy év sodrában*, pp. 408-35; Gábor Erdődy, "A forradalmi magyar kormányzat és sajtóorgánumai a németországi változásokról 1848-ban" (The Hungarian Revolutionary Government and Its Press on the Changes in Germany in 1848), *Századok*, 1977, pp. 463-99.

9. The Radical Paper Marczius Tizenötödike

The new revolutionary press was a child of the capital and, in particular, among the most characteristic and important intellectual offspring of the March Youth. These young members of the intelligentsia by now had become professional writers, journalists, and political commentators and, having worked regularly hitherto on the staffs of the larger liberal or even conservative newspapers and in some cases on fashion papers, now came to the fore and acquired political papers of their own. As they emerged from those constraints, they were the ones who founded most if not all of the succession of new radical papers. Moreover, they each wrote for several papers, tending to dissipate their energies a little, for it is mainly their signatures one finds in the columns of these various undertakings. Literary historians have necessarily noticed and evaluated their journalism, since they contributed to political literature new accomplishments of form as well as new ideas. It was they who made the pointed, terse style whose beginnings we have sought in Irinyi and Csengery's *Pesti Hírlap* so general that one might adopt the apt expression "revolutionary style" applied to it by their contemporary János Erdélyi. In their newspaper articles and pamphlets they domesticated new types of political writing: chronicles of the revolutions and events in Pest and to an extent in Paris and Vienna; political reports (for instance, of Kossuth's recruiting tour of the Great Plain); battlefield dispatches; popular explanations of the bourgeois national transformation, the April laws, and the political programmes; militant, sarcastic *exposés* of the old régime's adherents and their latest activities; and, as a revolutionary variant of the earlier "news" column, the kind of miscellaneous, brief, ironic marginal notes that Jókai in particular began to make familiar under the title "Charivari" in the *Életképek*.

The first, most lasting, and most important component

of the new radical press was *Marczius Tizenötödike*, which bore the date of the Pest revolution as its symbolic name and found its way very speedily into the hands of its readers, appearing first on March 19, 1848, the fifth day of the new freedom of the press. One hardly need add that it appeared without a permit, since it no longer required one under the old law and did not yet need one under the new. Its editor formally registered its appearance at the beginning of May in accordance with the press law which had come into effect in the mean time and deposited the requisite caution money at the same time.

The paper appeared late every afternoon. At first it was printed at the small press in Zöldkert utca (today's Reáltanoda utca) which then still bore the name of the Esztergom printer József Beimel but had long since been taken over by the paper merchant Vazul Kozma. Kozma had reorganized and modernized the antiquated little works, where the employees had been vilely treated, and had hired a new manager, a clever member of the trade from Kecskemét named László Lukács. The post of machinery foreman was filled by the labour leader Sándor Kocsi. Energetic management and low prices meant that in 1848 more papers, nineteen in all, were printed here than anywhere else. Not long after, however, Lukács in partnership with Károly Somogyi struck out on their own and started a press in the Kunewalder building on the site where the natural sciences faculty of Budapest University now stands on Múzeum körút. Using two high-speed presses brought from Vienna, Lukács specialized in printing newspapers, and one of the ones he took with him was *Marczius*, printed on his press from June 21, 1848, onwards.

Printing began in the early afternoon, but fresh news of importance continued to be inserted into the matter already set until the very last moment. Generally speaking this was a new, energetic type of paper, in a quarto format that was smaller than customary and consisted only of a single sheet folded into four pages. It differed greatly from the earlier, more pedestrian papers, which often continued their articles from one issue to the next and were patiently awaited and calmly read by the many provincial subscribers in the village manor houses. *Marczius* principally catered to the avid interest of the urban public in the capital. Even after six months the number of subscribers scarcely exceeded seven hundred, meaning that it lagged far behind the traditional papers. But many copies were sold on the streets of Pest, where for the first time vendors could be heard shouting, "Buy the latest *Marczius!*" The paper sold, said witnesses at the time, like violets in spring. "We often laughed and frequently fumed at this agile little paper," wrote Pulszky, "which even Deák, sitting in front of the kiosk in the square before the theatre with his ice cream, would buy from the lads who noisily sold it while the ink was still wet from the press. This little paper became the organ of the radicals and later became a real power in the land." The paper's bold, sneering tone, unsparing of persons, critical and offensive, seemed to have a startling effect on a country just shaking off its tradition of feudal authoritarianism. Under the name of the paper appeared the motto "No need for *táblabíró* politics." The *táblabíró*, the titular county judge, as the satire with that title written in 1845 for the *Életképek* by József Irinyi bears out, had for years been a symbol and caricature of the fossilized, backward, cumbersome world of the feudal nobility. Thus the motto was a demand for some sort of political departure. Unsurprisingly, the bulk of the provincial nobility, having grown up in the traditions of the counties and gladly bearing the title of *táblabíró*, looked upon this trend of thinking with suspicion and then contemptuous indignation. Later, under the Dual Monarchy, József Ferenczy, the first man to sum up the history of the Hungarian press, could find nothing better to say of *Marczius* than that this paper, "edited cleverly but with much mockery and superficiality," lacked a "lofty journalist spirit" and "a defined political line", since "it neither expressed ideas nor disputed on political principles." In his view this "market-place gazette" was read solely for its "racy complexion".

In fact, the paper did follow a definite political line, which was why there was such an outcry on the other side. Its editor, the initiator of the new kind of press, was the young Albert Pálffy, one of the top revolutionary journalists. In an article outlining the paper's programme he said plainly that it would be the organ of the youth "whose first move has managed to secure freedom of the press." One of the March

The Radical Paper *Marczius Tizenötödike*

Youth and a friend of Petőfi's, Pálffy came to head the radical press.

The Editor and His Staff

Albert Pálffy (1820-97) came from an old but impecunious noble family. He was the son of an official in the salt office in Gyula. The family had borne the same noble predicate "Erdődi" as the powerful Pálffy counts, apparently distant relations, through the mists of the feudal past. But in 1848 he conformed with the revolutionary fashion of the day and ostentatiously wrote his name phonetically as Pálfi to signify his break with that past. The noble contributors to *Marczius* on more than one occasion even spelt the names of aristocrats in the phonetic, "bourgeois" way. This now forgotten custom had clear political significance at the time.

As the simplest course, his parents intended him for the priesthood. After attending schools in Debrecen, Nagybánya (Baia Mare), and Arad, Pálffy in 1887 entered the seminary of János Hám, then bishop of Szatmár (Satu Mare) and later to become notorious as archbishop of Esztergom. For three years Pálffy tried to adjust with growing difficulty, as his interests already tended towards the French language and literature and more enlightened, freer ideas. In 1840 he left and enrolled for a course in law at the royal academy in Nagyvárad (Oradea). Having completed this, he came to Pest in 1842 as a law student, qualifying the following year. But then he turned to literature instead of the law. By the time of the revolution he had published two novels and some twenty stories. The novels were fairly long-winded, complicated, and somewhat unlikely tales, as he himself said later, of "factitious romanticism", for like his young contemporaries he sought a way to imaginative freedom through the French Romantics. In his stories, however, he lit upon an engagingly direct narrative style. Early in 1848 he found a publisher for a volume of stories, although it only appeared later, in 1850, anonymously under the title *Egy földönfutó hátrahagyott novellái* (Posthumous Short Stories of a Fugitive). As a member of the Society of Ten and a close friend of Petőfi's, Pálffy stood higher among young writers than his literary accomplishments alone would have warranted. Jókai later recalled this "handsome, slender, elegant figure as if he stood before me now: he always spoke subtly yet to the point; to his friends' faces he ridiculed their weaknesses, but behind their backs he defended them." His radical views, democratic beliefs, honesty, and sincerity all contributed to Petőfi's acceptance of him as a trusted friend, although they had different characters in many respects. Pálffy paid much attention to formalities and the quiet, orderly discipline of bourgeois social life, preferring to retreat from anything that smacked of sensation. Of course, if one seeks differences of view one can find them among the friendly circle of the March Youth as well. To quote Jókai again, "We were all Frenchmen. We read nothing but Lamartine, Michelet, Louis Blanc, Sue, Victor Hugo, and Béranger." But even those French authors encompassed several different shades of opinion. Petőfi is known to have had portraits on his walls of the great protagonists of the French Revolution: Robespierre, Saint-Just, and Marat. Pálffy's favourite reading, on the other hand, was Lamartine's history of the Girondists. But they were all comrades-in-arms against the old feudal world and the power of the Habsburgs. Pál Gyulai later judged Pálffy to have been "strongly convinced that Austria would take back all Hungary had won, and once it had a little power, try to ditch the Hungarian constitution once and for all. He saw a life-and-death struggle as inevitable. That is why he constantly fanned suspicion and uncertainty, nourished the revolutionary spirit . . . and called for swift action instead of fine words." His paper, "whose line was verified daily by events, grew steadily and exerted an ever greater influence on the public," a process in which his own talents as an editor and a writer played a large part:

> He could repeat his main thesis in a thousand forms, always adding a new stimulus to it. He wrote simply and clearly, without oratorical zeal. . . . He appeared to be more an ingenious, witty conversationalist than a dangerous agitator. But ridicule poured from every line. . . . Yet his mockery was also a species of exposition, his jests dwelling on causes and his sarcasms turning into verdicts. He entertained, enlightened, and excited his readers all at once, without exhausting them.

As a writer he was not really first-rate. He was averse to the role of an orator, particularly to the rhetorical poignancy of the Hungarian nobles, but he came to the forefront of revolutionary journalism as to the manner born, as if he had found his true calling. To achieve this had required no more preparation than he had obtained since 1847, as we have seen, on Csengery's *Pesti Hírlap*, the most liberal paper of the reforming, opposition nobility. From there he jumped straight into the front line of the revolutionary press. He won enthusiastic fans and of course furious opponents by his coherence, valour, republican principles (which appeared early), irony, and direct, unemotional "revolutionary style". The *Divatlap* and later the *Alföldi Lap* (Great Plain Journal) painted him in truly devilish colours:

> If you should see his Mephistophelean visage as he sneeringly gazes, leaning on the corner of the kiosk, at the predatory pages of his paper, and if a fiery glint from the lamplight should fall on the glasses on his nose, which seems about to bite his chin, and if the breeze should ruffle his little pointed beard, your imagination would unfailingly supply the little horns and goat's legs of the damned: he is a veritable demon.

I shall recount later how this young journalist of the bourgeois revolution managed by pursuing his path to clash with his own government in 1849, but it is worth while at this point to take a short look at his subsequent career. In the years after the collapse he lay low in Bihar and Arad Counties. When he returned to Pest in 1853, the amnesty declared in the mean time prevented his being tried, but he was interned for two years in Bohemia. From there he returned home with his wife, the daughter of a prosperous bourgeois family, and tried his luck with literature again. In 1867, as editor of the *Esti Lap* (Evening Journal), he took on the fairly unpopular task of defending the Compromise. As in 1849, one of his main adversaries was Jókai, although the roles were reversed, and the other was Lajos Csernátoni, formerly one of his principal colleagues. But he did not basically deny his old beliefs in liberal progress; he now identified and attacked the aspects of opposition policy he considered to represent outworn views of the nobility and demagogical recalcitrance, exposing the antiquated, *táblabíró* aspects of the policy of Kálmán Tisza and his colleagues to the left of centre. Citizen Pálffy became a modest, upright householder who retained his belief in bourgeois and technical progress in the greedy world of unfolding capitalism. As daytime commissioner of the First Domestic Savings Bank he countersigned the savings books of ordinary men. On one occasion he told Károly Vadnay, "I often wonder longingly if we can reach a stage of contented well-being when there will be proportionally as many small amounts of capital as there are in France."

Apparently it was modesty again that kept him from writing his memoirs. To those who wished him to do so he replied, "A writer of memoirs cannot avoid speaking of his own good self. I, on the other hand, do not make a habit of dealing with myself, least of all when I have a pen in my hand." However, in a novel he wrote shortly before he died (*A régi Magyarország utolsó évei* /The Last Years of Old Hungary/, 1894), he spontaneously described in memoir style the old, pre-revolutionary Pest-Buda and its literary life, a world in which everyone was awaiting the change. In his opinion as an old man, the role after the revolution of the radical youth, including himself, paled into utter insignificance:

> A small opposition to the new régime arose among young people. Seeing the ease with which victory had been attained, some said, "Surely more could have been won at one go!" We who were alive at the time know best that this oppositionism did not bear the mark of earnest. Instead we were inclined to say, "It would be a good idea to frighten the Austrians a little, and let Vienna see what kind of parties there are among the lower orders!" Then they would think better of it and leave the laws of 1848 in peace, for fear that something worse would follow.

This pale memory of the tension at the time shows precisely that the main difference between the radicals of '48 and the liberal nobility was over relations with Vienna, or over how much of the new national leadership was to be shared, for the "lower orders" and their "parties" did not refer in this country to the peasantry or the proletariat or the efforts to take the social achievements farther in their case.

Pálffy did not sign his articles, and it is hard to say exactly what in his paper was written by him. So far no attempt has been made to identify and collect his writings on evidence of style or content, and so it is precisely of the journalistic works of this important revolutionary political commentator that we lack an entirely clear picture. We do know, of course, that he generally wrote the unsigned leaders and that he determined the whole line and style of the paper. Vadnay, who later knew Pálffy personally, reports that he put the name Gedeon Nagy to certain of his humorous, lighter writings.

Nor do we exactly know who several *Marczius* staff members were. All too often they wrote anonymously or pseudonymously. In some cases it was as if it were better that officials of the government not feature as such in the pages of a radical paper. Subsequently we are left to guess who hid behind the various pen names and initials or such grandiloquent, Romantic signatures as *Első osztályú* (First-Rate) *barricadeur* or *Sátán Körme* (Hooves of Satan). Particularly among the many occasional correspondents one find names that may be real, although nothing else is known (at least so far) about them. Into this category fall Bertalan Bucsánszki, who sent reports from Paris, Ferenc Tomor, who submitted several articles republican in tone, and many others.

Of those whose names feature, let us look first at the editor's closest colleagues and friends, the March Youth. One name found under several republican articles is Antal Várady (1819-85), a landed nobleman, lawyer, and friend of Petőfi's. One or two articles appear from Alajos Degré (1819-96), a member of the Society of Ten who shortly afterwards gave up his journalism to become an officer in the Hungarian army; Pál Vasvári (1826-49); Lajos Dobsa (1824-1902), who had lived through the revolution in Paris not long before; and János Vajda (1827-97). Petőfi's name is found under a few poems and statements. Of his young friends, Kálmán Lisznyai (1823-63) and the "mad count" Sándor Teleki (1821-92) appear in the paper, as does Mihály Tompa (1807-68) among the correspondents. All in all, however, one cannot say that the main role was played in any organized way by the March Youth, still less because names like Gyula Bulyovszky, Dániel Irányi, József Irinyi, Mór Jókai, and Károly Sükei are absent. On the other hand, a good number of articles were written by lesser-known young radicals such as Józsa Nyíri (formerly Kandel), whose biographical details and activities are omitted from Szinnyei's *Magyar írói lexikon* (Hungarian Dictionary of Authors), and another long-forgotten writer for the revolutionary press, Viktor

Herczeg, who fell in 1849 as a soldier in the Hungarian army. Also working for the paper was József Oroszhegyi (formerly Szabó, 1822-70), an interesting member of the young radical generation who began as a doctor and became a teacher of poetry at one of the main girls' schools in Pest as well as a journalist. At the end of 1848 he was commissioned by the Egalitarian Society to form a band of irregulars, suffered long years of imprisonment after 1849, and ended up as a chief camp physician in the Turkish army. "He was short in stature, with a pock-marked Kalmuck's face," Jókai recalled. Among the older men to write for the paper was Mór Mérei (1813-58) of Kaposmér, the son of a landowning noble family from Transdanubia who was inclined to adventure. In the 1830s he had worked as a journalist and playwright. In 1848 he became a major in the National Guard; later he was a legal advisor in László Madarász's bureau of police and a factory manager in Manchester, England, where he died. Several articles were contributed to *Marczius* and other radical papers by József Barsi (1810-93), parish priest of Bicske and earlier camp chaplain with the imperial forces in Lombardy, who was the son of a simple schoolmaster from Bars County by the name of Neumann. For these acts of what was considered sedition he was arrested by the Austrians early in 1849 and imprisoned in a fortress until 1856. After 1867, by now a Protestant, he was on the staff of the new Statistical Office. Other older men to write articles for the paper were the anti-clerical, radical pamphleteer János Horárik (1808-64), a friend of Táncsics's, and Gábor Egressy (1808-66), the actor, who was a friend of Petőfi's, later served as government commissioner in Szeged, and returned from exile in Turkey in 1851. Of course, one could list several other more or less occasional contributors, ranging from the progressive teacher and writer of juvenile literature Ferenc Ney (1814-89), who chaired the first general assembly of teachers in 1848, and József Erdélyi (1827-69), a deputy clerk of Heves County, to Gereben Vas, who served the interests of the Batthyány government at the head of the *Nép Barátja* but who latterly, after the turn of events in the autumn, saw fit to supply one or two fairly shrill, jocular articles to the main radical paper. One might recall that on June 5, signing himself "A Retired Lieutenant of Hussars", Artúr Görgey (or, as he styled himself at the time, Görgei) wrote a proposal for the officers' uniform of the new Hungarian army, which he considered should be cheap and serviceable, not ornamental. When the ministry nevertheless prescribed a costly dress uniform with gold braid, his brother's arguments were repeated in a second article by István Görgey. Their appearance in the paper is unsurprising, since both were visitors to the Radical Circle. From all this it emerges, in any case, that the paper represented not some organized political group or party but a trend in which other representatives of Hungarian radicalism ranged themselves behind some of the March Youth.

On April 24, 1848, the first appearance in the pages of *Marczius* was made by Lajos Csernátoni, who soon became the paper's chief columnist and the most energetic, productive, and, one should add, overbearing member of its staff. From time to time he arbitrarily undertook some of the editorial tasks alongside the more reticent Pálffy. Csernátoni (later Csernátony), born Lajos Alsócsernátoni Cseh (1821-1901), was a particularly characteristic example of a very talented, very poor member of the intelligentsia with an unsteady, uninhibited character. Such men emerge not infrequently at the beginning of an era. It is not known precisely how he managed to obtain the deputy's post on the new radical paper, since he belonged neither to the March Youth nor to any other recognized political grouping. He and others alike sought to say as little as possible about the first twenty-seven years of his life. All Szinnyei put in his dictionary of authors, for which he gathered information on contemporaries as far as possible from the subjects themselves, was that Csernátoni came from a noble Transylvanian family, was born in Kolozsvár, where he was a student at the Reformed Church College, also studied law, and "soon entered public life. During the time of the struggle for independence he was Kossuth's secretary and one of the editors of *Marczius 15.*" The swift skipping over the years is understandable in that at the time (1893) Csernátoni was still alive and, as a representative in Parliament and a ruthless journalist with an incisive pen, a formidable adversary it was inadvisable to cross. But his opponents spread the tale that he had served a prison sentence for forgery as a young man. János Pálffy (1804-57), a Transylvanian nobleman who after the union became deputy speaker of the House of Representatives in Pest and then a member of the National Defence Commission as well, in his memoirs in the 1850s expressed contempt for Csernátoni's past, "which he himself did not deny in Debrecen." Pálffy added to the story, in part by relating that later, as an émigré, Csernátoni "was in the pay of the Austrians as their spy in Paris," for which "the Parisian refugees banned him from their midst." One should of course bear in mind that in Debrecen in 1849 Pálffy was among the partisans of peace, one of whose manoeuvres was to attempt to compromise their radical opponents by casting aspersions on them. Later Pulszky, however, mentioned in his memoirs, without giving a name, that the "principal contributor" to *Marczius* "only managed to escape the consequences of his formerly unpleasant contacts with the Viennese criminal courts, but he did not lose the resourcefulness gained in the solitude forced upon him." He soon, said Pulszky, found a path to the Hungarian public, and "in a lively way with little wit and much insolence" chastised "the government for its lassitude, impracticality, and credulity towards the intrigues of the court, discovering and denouncing signs of these here and there with all the greater verve because he particularly enjoyed denunciation." Moreover, there is evidence from Kossuth himself, even though he made use of Csernátoni's enthusiastic and adroit services on several occasions after the critical autumn of 1848. With Egressy and Jókai, Csernátoni accompanied Kossuth on the recruiting tour of the Great Plain at the end of September. The long reports of it he wrote for *Marczius* show that he was capable of enthusiasm as well as denunciation if somebody and something (in this case Kossuth and national defence) were a sufficient attraction for him. In October Kossuth sent him, again with Jókai, on an official mission to Vienna, from where he also sent reports to his paper. At the end of November he became one of the presidential secretaries of the National Defence Commission, working along with others at Kossuth's side. This could hardly have happened if Kossuth had not considered him a talented, useful man and an enthusiastic supporter. But in Debrecen in February 1849, Csernátoni's articles placed Kossuth in an awkward situation, and the latter did not hesitate, in calling on him to resign, to bring up his past again:

The Radical Paper *Marczius Tizenötödike*

> How much fault the world found with me for placing you in this post! They cited your youthful doings, banknote forgery and consequent imprisonment (and they placed evidence of other, more heinous crimes before me too), saying that in my station no place could be found for a conspicuous past such as yours. I held my peace, because I think it sad that people consider that the blunders of youth cannot be atoned for in the course of a man's life. But you have constantly compromised me in a dreadful way.

When Csernátoni hastened to submit his resignation, Kossuth wrote to him in a milder tone: "With your love of your country and your decisive will, I have never denied that you have a whole honourable life before you in which to rehabilitate yourself. A sign of this: that I knew of that youthful blunder and yet held my peace and obliged others to hold theirs as well. . . . With your rare mental capacity you can be of much further use to your country."

The most authoritative statement, however, stems from Csernátoni himself. On February 27, 1849, the *Esti Lapok*, whose editor Jókai had become a political opponent, made the forgery case public, and Csernátoni cleverly thought it best to reveal the story in detail himself. By his account his father, who was a lowly state official, found him a place in Vienna at the Transylvanian court chancery. There he was unable to advance "in the old days of nepotism", but an ill-intentioned relative blackmailed his father by saying he would report his son for theft unless a specific sum were paid. The charge was untrue, but his father paid the sum. The relative, on the other hand, continued to slander him. Embittered by this, he sought oblivion in reckless spending and got himself into debt. Since all his money was gone he did indeed begin drawing Austrian banknotes freehand, and as a consequence served "almost three sorry years" in prison. After his release he resolved to devote his life henceforth to serving his country, and that is what he had done. He continued, "I despise one who would now bring up the blunder in the youthful years of my personal life in order to throw suspicion on my political life or, rather, to wash clean the political wretchedness, apostasy, and reneging I have attacked and exposed." After that he quoted a few appreciative lines from a letter addressed to him by "a great man of this country" — Kossuth. Under the painful circumstances this retort was a clever one, although he passed off as something slightly positive the fact that his crime was "only" a moral, "personal" one, not a political one.

Csernátoni was sent by Kossuth on a mission to France, from where he returned, but after the defeat he escaped again. In 1851 he was sentenced to death in his absence by an Austrian military court. While in exile he wrote articles for the French papers and for papers at home. After the coup d'état by Louis-Napoléon he was obliged to leave France and lived in Britain and for a time in America. In 1860 he played a part on the side of Garibaldi. In 1864 he was a correspondent of the London *Morning Star*, in which capacity he returned to Hungary at the time of the Compromise. Back home he soon became a parliamentary representative, journalist, and supporter of Kálmán Tisza, initially of the left-of-centre party and then of the ruling liberal party.

Of interest in all this is what assists one to understand the personality of this writer at the time and his journalistic activities, for instance, the speed at which he produced his articles. His name (which I write in its 1848 form of Csernátoni, since this was in any case a pen name, not his real one) appeared in almost every issue of *Marczius*, on more than one occasion twice, and he also wrote under pseudonyms. The pseudonym Bence Cserző was his, and since he often began his articles by addressing them to "Berti, my friend!", it is conceivable that we should also consider him to be the author of the articles signed "Republicanus" which began in a similar fashion. He wrote leaders, commentaries, reports, notes, murderous caricatures, and incisive little jokes under the titles "Mimosas" and "Scapegraces". He attacked Vienna, moderates and vacillators at home, the policy of the Batthyány government, and various members of it, such as Lázár Mészáros, Pál Esterházy, and at first the suave Bertalan Szemere. It was not in consistency of revolutionary policy, still less in its social progressiveness, that Csernátoni outdid his editor, Pálffy, for Csernátoni was far more inclined than he to the policy of the nobility. It was in subjective, passionate polemics. What in Pálffy was incisive irony coupled with taste and clear judgement often verged in Csernátoni on personal abuse, unbridled assertiveness, and what Pulszky labelled denunciation. Pálffy found in Csernátoni a highly effective and useful colleague with whom he largely agreed on national policy but one who inevitably put his own mark on the paper, particularly since Pálffy was unwilling or perhaps unable to censor him strictly and from all accounts sometimes left standing things he considered too strong. Then and later, the names and activities of the two men became identified with the paper and the reactions to it. It is high time historians distinguished their individual characteristics.

The Young Radicals and the Government

Marczius represented the revolutionary youth of Pest, at one pole of the new political scene, as against the nobility in Pressburg, at the other, and from the outset it particularly stressed the urgency of the political changing of the guard. According to No. 3, Hungary's was "a monstrous constitution," and on April 5 it described as "an eight-hundred-year-old piece of bungling" the feudal legislature once so highly esteemed: "A nobleman is a bad legislator, the trade does not suit him; only the poor can ply it usefully," since "legislation is work, suitable not for men in golden pelisses but for plain men in blouses" (the phrase by which the French press referred to the workers, the proletarians). Yet it had not even occurred to most of the March Youth that the task of legislation should be handed over to the workers and peasants.

Sándor Lukácsy felt that the March Youth, "characteristically for a group of the intelligentsia, were at home among progressive ideas and slogans but found their bearings with difficulty among the relations between the classes." They "were well able to calculate the stages in a revolution against tyranny," but "their conceptions of the class foundations of power in a democratic form of state were less clear." They thought that as men of reason, cultivation, and progressive thinking they represented the interests of the people and might speak in the people's name; therefore "they omitted to study the actual claims of the classes and came forward in the revolution as spokesmen for some abstract radicalism without relating their policies to any class." They believed that the changes caused by the revolution and the new political freedom were essentially enough to resolve the social problems of the peasantry and the urban working class. They considered the victories won in March in abolishing serfdom to suffice. They were far from any idea of revolutionary satisfaction for the peasantry, whose "excessive" demands they viewed anxiously. The very first number of *Marczius*, on March 19, voiced unease at the "abuses" perpetrated by the peasantry and added to the revolutionary mottoes of liberty, equality, and fraternity calls for order and peace. Next day, on March 20, it was prepared to embrace the slogan of the nobles' "generosity" that the *Pesti Hírlap* repudiated and considered it desirable "to inform the people of this, so that they may join with us in defence of the country." Nor did *Marczius* deal later with the peasantry's problems even to the extent it conceivably might have done without causing a breach with the nobility.

A recoil by the majority of those demanding suffrage marked the statement on March 22 that universal suffrage was "the dearest principle of the radicals", yet "to introduce it without due reflection could kill radicalism itself." At the meeting of the Committee of Public Safety the paper reported on March 27, it emerged that only a handful of people, among them Petőfi and Irányi, were prepared to speak up for a far-reaching extension of the franchise. Even the "Cabetist" Vasvári considered an extension desirable only within limits, with a reduced property qualification, "lest the proletarians should overrun us." Finally they arrived at the view that they would demand "the broadest possible basis" from Pressburg, something which may have gone beyond the nobility's ideas but certainly remained an empty generality.

The young Pest radicals were not strong enough to wrest the leadership from the nobles in Pressburg. Indeed, they did not entirely part company with them and understood that defence of the nation was inconceivable without them, let alone against them. But they did demand *within* the noble leadership a substantial change that would open a path for radical influence, and so on March 25 the paper commented on the formation of the government as follows: "More could not be wished. The radical party in Hungary can hardly count in its ranks anyone over the age of thirty. The ministry is drawn from the aristocracy. It draws its power from the noble class, but it stands only because millions, rather than its own small constituency, rally to it." This is how we must understand matters when the paper on March 28 demanded that the political line should be determined by the Committee of Public Safety rather than by the practitioners of "legislative manufacturing" in Pressburg, where "the *táblabírók* . . . attach themselves to the nobles."

Of course Pressburg did not wish to be led by Pest. But on March 29, when the court ordinance of two days before, in which the separate Hungarian finance and defence ministries were withdrawn and renegotiation of the urbarial law was prescribed, came before the Diet, Kossuth again awaited and received support from Pest, so that Vienna was eventually obliged to back down. At the news revolutionary movements broke out again in Pest on March 30. "After the news had spread," Pálffy wrote in his leader on that day, "groups formed in the streets within minutes, and everywhere was heard, 'They have deceived us in Vienna! Down with German government! Down with the state debt! Long live the national convention!' And in Hungary it was first declared in earnest, 'Long live the republic!'" Let us underline right away that republicanism, which we know from other sources was gaining strength in Pest at this time, was something of a panacea in the eyes of the radicals. It was a concept whose application was seen as in itself capable of curing all society's ills, responsibility for which lay clearly with feudal absolutism and monarchy, or the remnants of them. The same applied to the issue of the national minorities, whose problems now began to appear in the spring of 1848, after the first favourable reception of the revolution, signifying that the various national movements in the country were after some separate, collective recognition and rights that went beyond individual liberty. At this stage the young radicals thought it enough to appeal to speakers of languages other than Hungarian to defend jointly the liberty which had been won. The one study of the policy on the national minorities of the revolutionary left wing in Pest at this time could quote only a single statement in the press, and that was from Pál Királyi, who protested in the liberal paper *Jelenkor* on March 23 against the desires expressed at a meeting of Pest Serbs a couple of days earlier. Noting that the Serbs of the country wished "to represent themselves as a nation", in keeping with the standpoint of the nobility Királyi underlined that in Hungary "there is only one nation, and that is the Hungarian nation." There is a conspicuous lack of palpable reaction in the radical press at this time to the conflicts emerging around the national minorities, especially, for instance, when one remembers some of the later statements in *Marczius*, which marked an advance.

Kossuth, as a member of the government who had several times opposed the guiding role of the capital and defended the county system, was temporarily unpopular with the young radicals as well. According to *Marczius* on April 9, "Lajos Kossuth begins to place himself in a situation that will if continued shortly make him an impossible man. . . . Kossuth does not wish to recognize the Paris of Hungary and would exile himself from a state in which there was centralization. The honoured orator has not considered what he is saying, because if his words are taken literally he will be banishing himself from the civilized world." With a measure of supercilious irony the paper wrote of the government on April 14, at the time it was transferring itself to Pest, "We shall see how the ministry begins. Whether it begins by decreeing a couple of popular pieces of childishness. For example, has the gates freshly painted, appoints a deputation charged with discovering whether a double-headed eagle may perchance have remained in some dark alley. . . . That will be a good thing too, so long as something is done. All we fear is that the ministry will fritter its time away."

On April 17 the paper demanded of the government radicalism "in the European sense", of a kind which "recognizes no extant historical rights and considers only what is useful, wholesome, and profitable from the nation's point of view. . . . Before it there is always a *tabula rasa*." In an unsigned leader on April 20 Pálffy reproached the government for its limited social base: "Our radicalism can certainly not suffer the present ministry to bear the trust of the nation solely *per fictionem*." In vain, he went on, did it consist of the most popular men if its existence depended on the Diet of nobles: "The ministry carries the grave original sin of deriving from the majority of the representatives of one caste. . . . Convene a national assembly, and if you withstand that cleansing fire not a single voice will be raised against you." But under the conditions at the time the government proved the stronger, and once it had moved to Pest it swiftly took power into its own hands. It wound up the Committee of Public Safety, built up a new bureaucratic apparatus (with the young people contributing to an extent at the lower levels), and forced Pest radicalism into retreat. This it could the more easily do because radicalism had advanced beyond both the provincial nobility and the urban bourgeoisie, who were turning against those with the red feathers, and had failed to secure itself a real base among the broad masses. So for a time one tends to find even in the columns of *Marczius* that the only protests are about how the government, instead of employing suitable new men, was trying to whitewash those who, in the words of an article on April 27, "got up at nine as usual on the morning of March 15 as convinced time-servers. At eleven they were struck by the news that the press had been seized. At one they lunched with their doubts. At seven that night they went to bed staunch revolutionaries." On May 9 one reads that "in every appointment it has made so far the ministry has signified its inability to break with the collapsed past." An article subscribed "Lapdacs" (Pill) attacked Klauzál for entrusting the organization of the public health department in the new Ministry of Agriculture and Commerce to the university professor Ignác Stáhly (1787-1849) and his colleague Ignác Sauer (1801-63), in fact a man of bourgeois extraction from Veszprém. One might add that they were good professionals, the latter subsequently being appointed by the National Defence Commission to run the military health service. But the situation soon began to become critical. *Marczius* saw clearly from the outset that the court, the power of the Habsburgs, had made concessions only under duress and would, as soon as it could, use every means possible, even force if necessary, to reestablish its rule over Hungary. It therefore called for preparations, independent defence, troops "organized in the Hungarian spirit", in other words, deeds as soon as possible, and attacked the government for not behaving decisively enough. "Hungary", it wrote on May 1, "is in a state of revolution. If one views our present government from a revolutionary angle one can boldly declare to its face that it fails to answer to its calling or its responsibility." To this one should add, however, that for the government it appeared more seemly to adhere to the forms of legality and if possible not hasten or facilitate the break with Habsburg power, not only from the domestic political and international points of view but precisely because preparations, however effective, would in any case require a fairly long time. By keeping up the appearance of agreement with the court time could be won, and that is not altered by the fact that in September this policy of Batthyány's finally become unsustainable, chiefly because the counter-revolutionary upsurge brought a disadvantageous change in the international balance of forces. Ferenc Deák made a statement characteristic of the government and the liberals on this lack of the means of power in a letter of April 30 in which, referring to the "tendency towards anarchy" represented by, for example, the beginnings of the Croatian and Serbian movements, he wrote,

> And to all this a contribution is being made here in Pest by the loud yet empty declamations of a great number of young and not so young journalists, who speak as if they alone were the whole people and a powerful people to boot; they continually demand energy, power, and strong measures, consider everything too little, find fault, and wilfully forget that energy requires more than loud words for its support, that material force too is required, that of this, sad to say, there is none, and that under present conditions one can hardly create any.

On May 5 *Marczius* inveighed against the fact that the Austrian government and press were in truth "declaring war" on Hungary over the issue of the state debt. Next day, however, it again attacked the government's weakness, saying that "the coming of war with Austria is (as certain as) twice two is four" and that it supported "the young revolutionary party that carries the banner across Europe." On May 8 the lawyer László Bártfay wrote to Count György Károlyi on the new surge of activity by the radical press as follows: "The papers are agitating and distributing news and argument; the daily *Marczius 15* in particular . . . openly advertises revolution as its purpose. The government, however, keeps silent, even though our constitution is monarchical and we should therefore consolidate this situation of ours and without further hitches, let alone woeful scuffles, strive to transform it, because the March bestowers of happiness on the land have already made a breakneck leap." In a leader on May 9 Pálffy's paper argued that if Louis-Philippe were sitting on the throne of France, Germany were not "on the threshold of an overall German republic", and all were going as it should in Hungary, one could not conceive of a policy more honest than the Hungarian ministry's present one. That not being the case, it continued, "we boldly and openly state that the soulless policy the ministry is pursuing places fortitude, independence, and hard-won rights in the gravest danger." The members of the government might be good patriots, it said, but they were behaving like someone who responds when his house has been set fire to in the night by beginning in the most leisurely way to get dressed; the flames were licking at Hungary's borders, and "the ministry should be pursuing a policy so vigorous as to astound the public."

In the same number *Marczius* published the statutes of the March Club, which had been formed on the previous day. Its purpose was "to cause the development of the principles of general liberty according to the Twelve Points and the enactment of the same." By founding the club Petőfi and his group were trying to draw the young radicals into a common framework or unit. They were not fully successful, since there had already emerged a group of extremists that considered the Petőfi group too moderate. Led by Józsa Oroszhegyi, they formed a separate organization called the Club of Democracy, which was also joined by some very recently converted young radicals who had in fact Petőfi's benevolence to thank for the fact that their earlier activities on the opposite side were not held against them. The latter's members played a big part in organizing the demonstrations that now broke out and caused a great stir in the press. *Marczius* reported on May 9 that a charivari had been got up against certain leaders of the former Lieutenancy Council and the Treasury. On the evening of May 10 a crowd of several thousand processed up to the castle to mount a charivari against imperial Lieutenant-General Ignaz Lederer, army commander-in-chief of Buda, who was known to be an exponent of Habsburg rule and against organizing an independent Hungarian army. Here one must add something else, however. On the same day, May 10, the *Pesti Hírlap* announced that the king, as a result of Batthyány's trip to Vienna, had on May 7 signed the order placing the Hungarian military under the command of the Hungarian government, in other words, taking matters out of Lederer's hands. This must have been clear to those organizing the demonstration, who either thought little of this government achievement (just as they set no store by Lederer's military preparations) or considered it correct nonetheless to use this demonstration of public ire to create a crisis that might perhaps lead the government to resign. The facts in any case are that the lines of demonstrators—students and artisans— were met with rifle fire from the soldiers, who had lain in wait for them well in advance. The lessons of the atrocity and of the great public outcry that followed were drawn in an unsigned leader on May 11, perhaps by Pálffy: "Last night in Buda, a few steps from the residence of the king's representative, the blood of civilians flowed." The soldiers, it said, had attacked the young people with "hair-raising barbarity"; news of the bloodshed would "spread like lightning across Europe," and Archduke István, the palatine, would "look to the public like any other genocidal king." It was typical of the ministry's incompetence, the article continued, that although it had sent Mór Perczel, counsellor at the Ministry of the Interior, and Pál Hajnik to the castle on hearing news of the preparations, the imperial officers had paid no heed to them; the government had let the brave youth of the capital "be led to the slaughter" and should therefore resign. "We are not saying," the article went on, "that the ministry has taken action for which it might be arraigned." Nevertheless, it continued, the ministry had done nothing or at most daily demonstrated its incompetence. What use was it that "some of the present ministers are well-educated, learned men" if time had set their learning at naught? "Today there is a new political science," it argued, by this "new national and youthful policy" alone could Hungary be saved.

"Very decided distrust" of the Batthyány government was being declared: "We need men who can act, who are bold and decisive. . . . Let there be an end to the times when it was thought Hungary could not be governed without the ornate names of history." The concrete proposal was that

Pál Nyáry should form a new government: "Let there be agreement with Kossuth." Let Szemere, with his pedantic, outworn phrases, resign; Klauzál too, who knew as much about the concerns of his portfolio as a fish out of water ("a *heyduck* about founding a bell"). "Let Széchenyi retire," having in any case fallen between two stools. Let Ferenc Deák "be content with the laurels he has won" and József Eötvös "retreat to his literature," where great success might still await him.

After this open demand, which did not, however, follow up the call for the advance of Nyáry and agreement with Kossuth by naming any to replace those who were to resign, the article warned again that "our freedom and our constitution will last only as long as the goodwill of our adversaries," and this goodwill "will last only until they believe the moment has come when they can most easily reinstate the old régime." On March 11 the Lederer affair was discussed with passionate indignation by other contributors such as Csernátoni and Degré.

However, this May action against the government by the Pest radicals ended not in success but in defeat. Certainly Lederer fled to Vienna. Nyáry, at the head of a delegation from Pest, obliged the palatine to mount an investigation against the perpetrators of the military atrocities. But the mass meeting on May 12—whose principal motif the article by Pálffy just quoted sought to provide and at which Petőfi remarked, among other things, "I would not trust my country or even my dog to the ministry"—was basically unable to mobilize significant forces, failed to develop into a new, great turn of events, and achieved nothing more serious than the dispatch of delegations to the government. Understandably in the light of the social and political power relations and the leadership of the nobility in the Hungarian revolution, it emerged that at this juncture, after the really great turn of events in March, the plebeian revolutionary Petőfi could no longer exert as a leader of the people a decisive influence on events or on the government's destiny. For his programme he could count on support only from a fairly small and not even homogeneous group of radicals. Broader public opinion was not ready to embrace even republicanism, not to speak of socialist concepts of equality exceeding the bounds of formal, liberal equality of rights. It soon emerged that domestic conditions were not such as to allow the radicals to enter the lists as an independent political factor or party, and therefore they eventually lost out in the spring succession of events, even before the elections had taken place.

Of course *Marczius* continued its great offensive for a while longer. On May 13 it sniped at Szemere. At first the illusion had been fostered that Szemere would represent "the throroughly radical, youthful and national element", but in this he disappointed the radicals. Considering the directions he had given on the press and other matters, Szemere had to be considered "utterly unsuited for the position he holds." At the same time the paper reacted to the protest by the Esztergom chapter "against all illegal moves aimed at the property of the church", which referred to an article in *Marczius* on April 29 setting forth a programme of disestablishment of the church, secularization of church wealth, and use of it for national defence and railway construction. The paper's retort was sharp: "I believe you all know what recalcitrance leads to. In 1793 it led to the guillotine."

But in the May 13 number the first warning sign appeared: a medical bulletin related that Kossuth's alarming state of exhaustion had obliged him to withdraw from everything and leave the capital. In fact Kossuth continued in the mean time to be active, but he wished to keep out of all factionalism, even to the point of distancing himself on May 20 from the radicals. The next sign was that members of the Ministry of the Interior's police department, headed at the time by Mór Perczel, were able with impunity to brand Pálffy and Petőfi in the revolutionary hall—the Pilvax—as traitors to their country. Pálffy refuted this with manly calm: "If you do not like the paper and its manner, the press is free, and on that field, if you please, I am prepared for your attacks." Nor was it long before Nyáry too distanced himself from the radicals. In the May 15 issue he was still being praised wildly as one who "nobly and splendidly speaks up" on the "investigating committee" looking into the Lederer affair and whose "stability and firmness of character assure us that the criminals will not go unpunished." The same article continued the attack on the government and on the Habsburgs, who it said, had been breaking treaties and outwitting the Hungarians for three hundred years. "Radical policy", on the other hand, was to devote "our lives and blood to the evolution of Hungary's independence." Having concluded by pointing out that this "petty ministry" lacked even a "debating gazette", it was able to report in the following issue on May 16 that the *Pesti Hírlap* would henceforth appear as "the *Journal des Débats* of the Hungarian ministry", designed to support the Batthyány government. *Marczius* would gladly do the same, it said, if the government were to show some fortitude, but sadly the latest news on the Serbian invasion demonstrated that "the true national party was right to call night and day for weapons alone."

On May 17 the paper deduced from reports of new revolutionary moves in Vienna that one of the government's main errors was to assume "that the Austrian empire would last for ever." "This is by no means certain," it went on, and so a government was needed that would so conduct itself that "if destiny provides otherwise for Austria, this change will not necessarily cause our downfall as well." On the next day, May 18, the paper emphasized in its very sparse reporting of foreign news how Lamartine had told the French National Assembly on May 5 that Hungary had swept away feudal privileges and "completely separated from Austria." An unsigned article in the same issue reflected with great self-confidence on the question posed by the *Pesti Hírlap* about where the radical party was in the capital and up and down the country. An answer, it claimed, had already been given by "the Hungarian newspaper editors". *Marczius, Reform*, the now "cleansed" *Jelenkor*, and even the *Nemzeti* were all radical, and the paper being prepared by Madarász and his group would be so too. Was the *Pesti Hírlap* alone going to wage war on them all?

Of course this growing attack was not taken passively by the other side. A succession of representations arrived from places ranging from Miskolc to Vas County condemning *Marczius* and affirming trust in the government. The conservative *Budapesti Híradó*, which had now taken heart again, began a series of open attacks on *Marczius*. According to Széchenyi, Batthyány himself, who normally received attacks in the press, "considered mere jobbery", with a superior imperturbability, was contemplating counteraction or even summary justice. But in the end the government surmounted the crisis without resorting to such measures and shortly afterwards found an occasion to strike back at *Marczius*.

The Press Trial

On May 19 the council of ministers met under the chairmanship of the palatine amid great excitement and expectation. Rumours spread that the emperor had left Vienna and a republic had been declared. Towards evening a man came to Pálffy at the paper's offices with news from one of the "ministerial heads of department" that the ministers had proclaimed the archduke, the palatine, as the provisional king. Pálffy, who we know from Jókai would have welcomed such a development at this time, gave credence to the report of the new King István (who shared the name of the founder of the Hungarian state). The paper was already set, and so he placed these sensational sentences in the place of the usual motto under the title of the paper: "Latest—total anarchy in Vienna. Our ministers have proclaimed Palatine István provisional king. Ferdinand in Innsbruck. Let our slogan be: an immediate National Assembly."

But the news in this form was untrue, and publication of it placed the government in a tricky position. Therefore Interior Minister Szemere or, more precisely, the state secretary, János Zoltán, that very evening impounded the paper at the press, apart from the copies already sent out to subscribers. Pálffy then had the incriminating few lines removed, and a new edition was printed and distributed on the streets.

On the following day, May 20, the council of ministers approved Szemere's report of the swift impounding of the paper and instructed the minister of justice to institute proceedings under the regulations on press offences. This move was published in the official columns of the *Pesti Hírlap* on May 21, as a warning to the press and as information and self-justification before the court in Vienna. On this occasion the Pest jury at last came together, and the "public investigation of press abuse", the oft-cited *Marczius* press trial, began.

In the May 20 issue Csernátoni wrote of the government

rather more appreciatively: "We consider that the ministry has outlived its infancy; in its more recent moves we fancy we discern that it has understood the strength of unceasing power and begun to grasp its position. And having discerned this we sense a revival of our faith in it." It is likely, however, that the change of tune resulted less from a climbdown than from the fact that the government had ordered the recruitment of soldiers and begun to create an independent Hungarian army, in other words, objectively to behave in a more decisive way. Pálffy was in any case quite uncowed by the proceedings instituted against his paper. Reacting to the *Pesti Hírlap*'s official pronouncement, he wrote in the issue of May 23, "We believe the ministry will suffer defeat in the trial." On June 6 he published an account of the events of May 19, requesting the bearer of the news to come forward but not repeating that it had been given in the name of Pál Nyáry (the ministerial head of department in question). More recent research has all but established that the trial's purpose, apart from bringing the paper to heel, was to compromise Nyáry, whom the radicals had been pushing to the fore. This immediately makes it easier to understand how Szemere came to act so remarkably quickly. It is still not entirely clear to what extent Nyáry really was the source of the report, but as the move succeeded in prising Nyáry and the radicals apart, there was no longer any need for the proceedings to continue. Later on, when the crisis had taken another turn, the prosecutors (according to *Marczius* on August 15) decided that there were "no grounds for prosecution of the accused." Thus the result was not, as earlier historians have put it, an "acquittal" but a complete withdrawal of the charge.

Pálffy in any case decided on May 20 that the paper had to be defended from the attacks upon it—"the unfounded reports, eccentric suspicions," and "antipathy" appearing in many quarters. By contrast with the earlier optimism about the extent of radicalism, he now stressed the limits of the influence of *Marczius*: "Up to now our paper has been distributing a few hundred copies at most in the provinces," the majority of subscriptions being from individuals not clubs of readers. He particularly objected to the *Budapesti Híradó*'s referring to them "as Robespierreites without scruples". Pálffy refuted this "hardest of charges", considering it equivalent to saying that they had proffered "the banner of terrorism" to the nation. In the same issue he applauded the government's move to invite the monarch to Hungary, for "this alone can save us from oblivion." He gave interesting and ingenious reasons for supporting this monarchist position even though, "if we were entrusted with organizing a country where the necessary factors could immediately be created . . . we would undoubtedly choose the form of government to which nations are the more inclined the more cultivated they are." No reader could have doubted that he referred to a republic. "But", he went on, "the most baneful policy in the world is to seek to skip over the intermediate systems." The king, he said, was popular among the Hungarian people. In this country too, there was "a party" whose "constitutional doctrine contradicts monarchism," after the French pattern. But this was mere theory which "it would be a dire risk" to translate into reality, for the tsar might not even bear with the anarchy in Vienna, and it was "his dearest dream" to annex to himself the northern and southern Slavs right down to the Adriatic, along with Hungary.

The Social and National Issue

Like the reform opposition of the liberal nobility in the early 1840s, the radical youth were inclined to take the concept of the threat of Pan-Slavism as their starting point in explaining the country's international situation and the issue of the national minorities at home. In the May 23 issue Csernátoni warned that "missionaries are fanning the flames of rebellion among the Wallachians (i.e., Romanians) of the two Hungarian homelands" and recommended a German alliance and "the coming of the king among us". Another article on the same day described the appointment of Jelačić as "a challenge". In the face of the Slavic threat trust had to be placed in the Romanians, for among them, the writer declared with noticeably wishful thinking, "one cannot yet perceive a movement that would be a threat from the point of view of the Hungarian issue." The Romanians were "a good and faithful people, with a peaceable, calm, patient, and, despite oppression, honest and upright temperament." The Hungarians "cannot rely so securely upon any other of the nations that dwell here"; one had only to explain to them "what we desire." Of course the young radicals knew of the particularly hard lot of the Romanian serfs under their Transylvanian feudal lords, but they thought, as they did in the case of Hungarian serfs, that the matter would now be resolved by the revolutionary change. They did not think that the demands of the peasantry would exceed the gains made in March, just as they did not think that these demands could win a mass basis among them for separate national aspirations going beyond individual freedoms to encompass collective national recognition. Three days later, on May 26, Csernátoni wrote an article on the eve of the convening of the Transylvanian Diet. He stressed that Transylvania too had need of a union with Hungary: "Let there be but union and five years' peace, and our fatherland will be strong in itself and strong in the face of outside dangers." Another unsigned article returned to the need to win over the "upright, honest, undemanding, good-hearted", yet easily influenced and deluded Transylvanian Romanians with the help of the priests and teachers. A day earlier Csernátoni had outlined the dangers in the intrigues of Vienna and in the machinations of the Slavs, which were designed to halt any closer approach by Vienna to Frankfurt, for they saw "that an Austria annexed to Germany and a young Hungary allied to them will become a power against the Slavic element."

Finally one must note that the March Youth and the radicals as a whole failed to support the workers in their demand for equality before the law that went beyond the achievements of March. Only one or two "Jacobin-inspired" young people were prepared even to accept their assistance for a while. Lajos Dobsa, who gave an eye-witness account of the February revolution in France in the *Pesti Hírlap* on March 29, recounted that the Hungarian workers in Paris hastened to send greetings to the provisional Hungarian government but pointed out that the Twelve Points included not one of the workers' demands—although, he said, they were still awaiting good news from home on this subject, among other matters on the abolition of the guilds. The radical press also began raising this last issue but in doing so tended to demonstrate that it saw the issue of the workers in the light of bourgeois economic liberalism rather than early socialism. In April and May there were movements for higher wages in Pest, but apart, as we shall see, from the

Munkások Újsága, the radical press would have nothing to do with them. As Ervin Szabó put it, "The intelligentsia preferred to relegate the frail embryo of socialist ideas to the background." This tendency showed up more strongly as news arrived of the growing differences between the proletariat and the bourgeoisie in France and of the demonstrations taking place among the workers in Paris. *Marczius* came out against the "infamies" of these demonstrations and against socialist revolution, although it made reference to the idea of "work organization," which Alexandre-Auguste Ledru-Rollin and Louis Blanc had defined after their own fashion and which was for a time accepted with some expectation in Hungary. On May 27 Csernátoni wrote,

> We do not consider the question of work organization an illusion, although we are as unclear about it as the authors of the idea. We consider the initiative, the experiment, to be a splendid one and not an impractical extravagance . . . and we have been cheated. The fight for the idea was solely a weapon for them to gain sympathy for the great working class . . . for them to ensure themselves in the toiling people a vast physical force by whose aid . . . they might snatch the reins of power and themselves become the oppressors of the people over whose oppressed condition they rain perfidious tears.

The whole radical press, including *Marczius* and the Egalitarian Society, distanced itself from "communism" and the June uprising of the Paris workers. To see what this meant in Hungarian practice, one can point to the typical case of the workers' leader and lawyer Edon (or Ede) Keczkés, who was hurriedly arrested by the police for an "inflammatory" speech. Of the divergent assessments of the event one finds in various papers, Csernátoni's in *Marczius* on July 18 was the hardest. According to his account, in Széchenyi Park on the previous day "a lawyer named Kecskés /sic/, so they say, delivered inflammatory speeches." What he had to say was "extremely dangerous in its tendency," describing the government as ill-intentioned and the nobility and bourgeoisie as traitors fattened on the flesh of the people. "A large proportion of the constantly swelling crowd (of day labourers, troublemakers, idlers, and ignoramuses)" applauded. However, when "words were said against this incitement and unmistakable provocation," he was obliged to shut up. "The city police superintendent was informed of the events," and after that the speaker, "who seems to have aspired to the role of Blanqui," was taken into custody. This man, Csernátoni added, had earlier "sought to draw the attention of the public to himself with a placard upon which was written, 'Bread for the people'." Against "such ill-intentioned incitements designed to arouse passions . . . we raise our voice and shall continue to raise it while a drop of blood still flows in our veins."

The March Youth and the radicals as a whole were severely worsted in the elections of June 1848. Beforehand, *Marczius* had indeed written on June 1, "We do not wish to delude ourselves. We know in advance that the purely radical party will remain in a vast minority in the Assembly." But the results were even worse than expected. The only members of the March Youth to gain seats were Dániel Irányi and József Irinyi, along with Sándor Lukács of Győr, who could be counted among them. Petőfi was defeated, and of the machinations used and the opponents he faced he himself wrote in a long statement that he sent to all "editors of honourable principles" and that was published in *Marczius* on June 19. There all can read that he was described as a betrayer of his country and a Muscovite spy. "Never", he said, "have villains so impertinently laid siege to integrity and justice as in this case." The press at the time and later historians estimated that some 36 of the 426 members of the National Assembly belonged to the radical left wing. It was indeed the "dwarf minority" that Kossuth had once angrily called it. But the true left wing was smaller still, in fact insignificant within it, for with the exception of a few such as Táncsics the minority itself consisted of radical noblemen who demanded a firm policy against the power of the Habsburgs and greater results, not radical policies in a social sense. Of course Vasvári was right to remark in the *Életképek* on June 4 that the external threat "demanded unity" and that "in time of danger the force of the nation must not be divided." The trouble was that the vast majority of those on the political stage sought to create that "unity" without allowing any further social gains and by setting aside demands for anything of that kind. An unsigned article in *Marczius* on June 15, for example, said of "the people" that they were "as the people are wont to be:" "they have hardly any conception of anything other than the things that touch upon their daily needs" /and/ "are a quiescent force at the disposal of the one who first harnesses them to his own advantage." Although the author was here referring to the issue of the "Hungarian Vendée," Croatia, the people, in his opinion, were "wont to be" like this. But the paper was all the more decided and eloquent when speaking of national independence. "The Hungarians", it wrote on June 7, "are thoroughly fed up with being a second-class nation." Nor was the common front unbroken on this subject, on which the radical minority battled with the Batthyány government (which it accused of incompetence) and with the majority of the nobles, who supported that government. This majority, according to *Marczius* on July 7, concerned itself with nothing; it did not even register that the Russian army had crossed the River Prut to attack the Romanian movements, although "we have been continually trying to warn the *táblabírók* about the Muscovites since March."

The radical press made repeated efforts to prise Kossuth, of whom it expected most, from the side of the majority and the government. "We are convinced that Kossuth does not agree with the ministry's vacillating and indecisive policy," one can read in *Marczius* on June 30. For a while Kossuth and the radicals confronted each other again in the debates that surrounded the vote on aid for Italy. In the July 8 number Józsa Nyiri alluded to the principle of revolutionary solidarity, quoting Louis Blanc: "All men are brothers, and every revolution is useful to all mankind." Not long after, the same writer accused the government of having bound liberty with its press law, betrayed fraternity by postponing the emancipation of the Jews, and undermined equality by favouring the privileged in the distribution of office. There is no reason to doubt the writer's radicalism, but one rather misses in this attack on the government any reference to the real grievances of the broader strata in society. On July 31 a leading article in *Marczius* reflected on remarks in *Kossuth Hírlapja* on the previous day which it considered to confirm "that there is a very serious split within the ministry": "Kossuth does not feel as the other ministers do," being "convinced that the *táblabíró* politics that is so preponderant in the ministry is not merely incapable of saving the country but constitutes the straightest path to peril." The paper by now was ready to make an open call: "This is the occasion. If Kossuth raises his banner the country will rally around him in a moment," for "it is only Kossuth's name that has so far given sanction to the government's actions." Also typical was the report carried by *Marczius* on the session of the House of Representatives held behind closed doors on August 1. We know that at this session Batthyány requested a week's delay in the hearing on the military bill, saying that it would shortly emerge whether Austria would join the German union, and if it did, there would be an appropriate legal pretext for creating an independent Hungarian army. Naturally *Marczius* could not publish the subject of this debate, but it rejoiced in the fact that Kossuth had opposed government policy: "Kossuth spoke, and one would have thought Hungary's first spokesman was battling against the ministry as the leader of the opposition." It seemed to the writer as if the opposition would see Kossuth again "after a long absence". The majority, he said, had clearly "begun to shrink" and the "right wing become pale and silent", and the ministers, like so many headstrong children, had "turned away from Kossuth." From Petőfi one finds no such expectations of Kossuth, but in a statement in *Marczius* on August 11 he also declared that through the errors of the Batthyány government "we shall suddenly realize we are caught between four instead of two lines of fire. . . . And that is how it will be unless the nation rouses itself as soon as possible and wrests from the hands of the government and its representatives the power which it passed to them in good faith and which those men in part cannot make use of and in part basely misuse." On August 14, *Marczius* made quite a rude attack on the minister of justice, Deák: "You were not seated in your ministerial seats, gentlemen, to let your stomachs grow and to bandy syllogisms." Around the same time Count Lajos Gyulay, member for Hunyad County and in theory if not in political practice a follower of Fourier, expressed his opinion of *Marczius* in his diary: "a strange paper. It vilifies all that is not radical, sometimes amusingly; appearing in the evening, it finds a ready sale on days when events of some import take place. One cannot accept the chap's principles, but nonetheless it is a necessary paper, because without it the ministerial gentlemen would certainly take themselves for granted." *Marczius* primarily expected Kossuth finally to recognize how right the radicals were. "This is the time", Péter Kis wrote in the paper on September 5, "when all men must admit that *Marczius* has been right from the first letter to the last." On the previous day Kossuth had at last announced that the executive had had to resort to weapons appropriate to the danger facing the country and had sent Ödön Beőthy into the army as a government commissioner. Surely, said Kis, if *Marczius* had suggested this a week earlier "they would have shouted with a loud voice, 'Down with the revolution! A commissioner of the Convention for the army!'" But now at last, at least "on one measure the radical party and the ministry have come together." In the "special edition" that *Marczius* issued on September 17, "the day the second responsible Hungarian ministry was formed," Csernátoni followed the example of László Madarász, one of "the most decisive leaders" of the opposition, in expressing support for the reappointment of Batthyány, because although he would not have chosen Batthyány he was convinced of his integrity. But this episode did not last long, and with the critical turn of events in September the policy of the radicals was indeed proved right in that conflict with the power of the Habsburgs became inescapable, Batthyány's policy line failed, and the direction of the defence of the nation fell to the National Defence Commission, in which Kossuth and the radicals at last joined hands.

The Programme of Republicanism and Independence

During the crisis *Marczius* rejected all compromise in passionate terms. "What is happening to us is a vile insult," said a leader on September 26. "Bence Cserző" warned that Austria showed tractability when it felt itself weak; therefore, "again let us not allow time for it to concentrate its strength. If God wishes Hungary to be free, independent, and glorious, it must come to pass this year, when in March the nation made itself worthy of eternal life." And *Marczius* wrote almost movingly, in the same elated tone, of the needy people's willingness for sacrifice and action. Now that Jelačić was approaching closer day by day, one reads on September

21, and "the rich man fears extortion, the householder incendiary bombs . . . the representative loss of his daily allowance . . . the craftsman unpaid labour . . . the task of weeping for the fatherland and freedom that will be lost falls to the poor man, who does not fear for any money or fortune of his in his homeland, but fears for the ground which was wetted with the blood of his forefathers and beyond which there is no place in the world for the Hungarians." But somewhat later, on September 29, it is the turn of the urban poor, in connection with the Lamberg affair: "The greater part of the crowd seemed to belong to the city's poorest class, who people believe will not move without a material incentive to do so. And behold, they are the ones who placed themselves in peril on behalf of freedom, which in any case offers so small a favour to the poor, on behalf of what in their position at any rate is an abstract notion." Those are fine words, but such recognition of self-sacrifice seems to contain something of the idea that the poor man will be prepared to defend this freedom even if he receives no further "favour".

I have already mentioned the enthusiastic reports Csernátoni wrote of Kossuth's recruiting mission. One of them can be found in the issue of October 11, sent from Szeged along with an appeal he had worded to the people of the neighbouring countries. In it there is discussion of the prospects of the new revolutionary uprising in Vienna, particularly of whether the House of Habsburg would exile itself from Austria of its own accord: "King, emperor, and archduke are all one and the same curse on our country. . . . An absolute king is an evil in himself, while a constitutional one, if one looks at his country, is, to say the least, superfluous. . . . Even now the fate of millions depends on the caprice and fidelity of one man. That is the source of the evil; that has to be eradicated and all will be well." This oversimplified explanation of the problems and the panacea for them continued in later issues. "The king is not a king," wrote Gergelyi on the next day, October 12. In the same issue one finds as an encouragement a report from Vienna by H. P. on the new revolution and the hanging of Latour and a letter by "Bence Cserző" from Parndorf Camp, clearly recognizing that the Hungarian side should have used the occasion by taking immediate, decisive action: "The reactionaries were horror-struck and ran wherever their noses led them; with one energetic advance a proportion of the Austrian German community and the army would have flocked to us that could afterwards have brought the others to join forces with us." József Barsi demanded in his article a proclamation "that Hungary from the Carpathians to the Adriatic is one, indivisible, independent, autonomous, fully free" country, although he added "it is a side-issue whether there shall be a kingdom or a presidency, a monarchy or a republic." But after that he briefly reassured readers that the army was republican and would win. Horárik even criticized the National Defence Commission for issuing a proclamation "in the name of king and country" with Kossuth's signature. "We at this moment", he wrote, "have no king"; the country had a "governing directorate" with three members—Kossuth, Nyáry, and Madarász. He added that the press in Hungary "is in practice free" and "will be legally so the moment the clumsy provisional press law is repealed." On October 24 Józsa Nyiri attempted to urge the forces of the nation on to achieve a republic, mentioning it as an advantage that Hungary did not yet have a proletariat, whose demands "can at best be met when Fourier's theories come into effect." In his view this advantage "compensates for the troubles that spring from the various nationalities."

As the Hungarian armed forces were poised on the Austrian border waiting for a decision, the paper weighed up the probable dangers and laid emphasis on the importance of the main base of the March Youth—the capital. "Our most precious treasure is Budapest," it wrote on October 25, "because once it were lost, which might still occur, there would remain only the epilogue to the sad drama of the loss of the country. The advocates of municipal autonomy are greatly enamoured of expressions like 'Pest is not Hungary', but history teaches otherwise." After this insinuation, aimed chiefly at Kossuth, the paper went on: "Pest is as much Hungary as Paris is France or Warsaw Poland. What we have is all in Pest; the rest is only an upright and honest people, without leaders, strength, or support, and once the capital had been lost it would fight only a despondent war against the enemy."

On October 28 the paper finally reported that the army

had advanced towards Austria again, and articles against the dynasty immediately began to proliferate. In answer to the question "Why do the men of Central Europe fear a republic so much?" a writer signing himself "Amerikai" (American) asserted on Hungary's part that "hatred of the murderous dynasty is being distilled into loathing." On the other hand, "Radicalis" (Radical) began a series of articles by saying that Paragraph 1 of Act 3 of 1848 declaring the king's person sacred and inviolable became void beyond certain limits, when "sentence has to be passed on the monarch." If the king treacherously started a civil war and was "a party to murder, robbery, arson, betrayal, perfidy, etc., all capital crimes," it was not enough merely to topple him from his throne; one had to "provide a formidable example for despots, so that they quake in their innermost selves." On October 30 Antal Várady charged the Frankfurt assembly with remaining unwilling to recognize Hungary's independence because of the influence of Archduke John and his associates. László Szalay had only been suffered to remain there, he said, because he "fits in well with that band of doctrinaire, time-serving capons." In his "Republican Letters", Ferenc Tomor warned against making peace with the dynasty in any way, even if "the shoe pinched" it enough for it to show some tractability: "Look at the whole Hungarian press; the republican spirit is growing." In the October 31 number Csernátoni's hopeful dispatch written two days earlier from the camp by the River Fischa related that they were only an hour away from Vienna, and "my dispatch tomorrow will probably be datelined from the general headquarters in Vienna." The leading article declared by way of comment, "There have never been such wonderful moments for the nation as the present," and added, "The Hungarian element at this moment is wholly republican in thinking . . . the country is *de facto* a republic with Kossuth as its president." Then on November 2, "with Hungarian candour", the paper said, "They have certainly thrashed us a bit." One can read in it Csernátoni's report of the battle of Schwechat and the rout of the national guards with their scythes. But, he added, there was no cause for anxiety, as the Hungarian army "needed only a commander and it would be within the walls of Vienna today." It had had such a commander "since yesterday morning in Field Marshal and Commander-in-chief Görgei. May God spare him for us a long while, because Hungarian feeling and honour dwell in his heart and a rare talent for comprehension and a sharp understanding in his head." His manly valour, "eagle eye", and commanding characteristics "make him loved and honoured by the army." In the same number Ferenc Tomor spoke up "in the interest of the republican writers", who were still being threatened with the gallows, since "many people still believe the camarilla will win." However, Kossuth and his comrades would assist and not harass them and provide a chance "for the republican spirit to develop as soon and as well as possible." On November 6 Csernátoni offered the readers cold comfort for the recapture of Vienna by the imperial troops by remarking that the well-to-do, comfort-loving members of the Viennese bourgeoisie were now ruined as well: "the impoverished proletariat has been swelled by some intelligent and educated men." On the same day the paper published an article called "Meditation of a Peasant" to bear witness to the resolute willingness of the people to fight: "We are more ready to die to a man /than to be deprived again/ of our hard-won liberty and our lands earned by the sweat of our brow." The writer went on to say, "We well know that we won our liberty and our lands not from the sickly king or from those damned creatures who now strive to dig the graves of our brothers in the land of their birth, but through the dauntless effort and sufferings of such as Kossuth, Szentkirályi, Nyáry, Pázmándy, and countless others, whom we believe God himself has now charged with the government of our betrayed, forlorn country." Therefore the peasants should be called to arms: "No human power or intrigue can break us, only honourable leaders can make use of our colossal strength."

This article, which in fact contained no reference at all to the grievances and desires of the peasants, served almost as a pretext for one of Csernátoni's pieces in the November 8 issue, in which he demanded the proclamation of a mass draft of the people to meet the attack expected from the Austrians under Prince Alfred Windischgrätz. Another piece on the same day warned Pest rumourmongers that martial law was in force. However, "Radicalis", in his article "The

Policy of the Habsburgs", blamed methods of divide-and-rule for the fact that the other peoples in the country were rising against the Hungarians. On November 11 Csernátoni pronounced in an almost prophetic tone, ""The final victory will not be long delayed," and asserted that the Croatians, Serbs, Saxons, and Romanians would perish for having sided with the Habsburgs against the Hungarians: "How long, oh how long will your blindness last, you sons of Hungary of various races . . . who are nevertheless to unite in the interest of freedom?"

One must add at this point, however, that as far as Transylvania was concerned *Marczius* judged the local aristocracy quite severely, blaming it historically for a great many things and viewing it as far more backward and self-centred than its Hungarian counterpart. By and large, even though progressive men at this time wanted union with Transylvania, it was in their eyes the land of stubborn feudalism and backwardness, nothing other than the bastion of feudal freedom, things which later, after the defeat of the revolution, the regressing Hungarian nobility with its consciousness of history began to discover in it with some nostalgia. It is worth quoting some typical pronouncements in successive issues of *Marczius*. On October 17 an article was contributed by the young Count Miklós Bethlen, hardly eighteen years old at the time, who was soon to be a captain in the Hungarian army, then a writer, and then a journalist and who seems to have rebelled against his own class. Bethlen said that it was a shame that none of the Transylvanian aristocrats had been strung up and demanded that Baron Farkas Wesselényi, for instance, "be declared an outlaw." On October 31 Miklós P. Horváth described Kolozsvár as "a loathsome den of the aristocracy" from whose influence even the bourgeoisie was unable to emancipate itself. Józsa Oroszhegyi on November 11 called Transylvania "the ghastly homestead of treachery, slaughter, fire, and bloody murder," where "the black-and-yellow flag of Wallachian insurrection" flew. But according to an anonymous writer on November 25, "God and man" knew that the Romanians "suffered mortal injury at the hands of the ignoble Transylvanian aristocracy," and the Hungarian government should have stepped forward as a liberator but did not do so: "The

Wallachian people are a faithful people, and whoever sympathizes with them can do what he will with them. We have omitted to enlist the Wallachians in defence of the good cause and abandoned them to evil men." On November 29, the first part of a leading article in several instalments concerned itself with the loss of Transylvania and its dangerous consequences: "Behold, here is the tragic consequence of the *táblabíró* politics of the earlier ministry." Then on November 30 *Marczius* announced that there was no reason to feel sorry for the Transylvanian aristocracy that had fled to Nagyvárad, for it was marked by "putrid pride" and "ridiculous arrogance", living as it did off the proceeds of its past sins.

Meanwhile the paper continued to concern itself principally with national independence and, in the second place, with the proclamation of a republic. On November 16 Csernátoni wrote that if "the proclamation of the republic is put off for the time being," at least "independence and a break and escape from the House of Lorraine /i.e., Habsburg/ should be published," and "the president of independent Hungary" should be entrusted with "the formation of a government." "Republicanus" declared that by "republic" he understood "a democratic republic" and "not some Greek or Roman kind", and he added, "I want something for my country more perfect than the American or French one." It may have been at Kossuth's behest, since Csernátoni was one of his secretaries at the time, that on November 22 *Marczius* revised its opinion of Szemere, whom it had attacked a great deal. Now he was considered "known for his determination and pure democratic principles". A few days later, on November 25, a draft declaration of independence was published in the paper, signed "Bátkai." What principally attracts the attention of a later reader is the optimistic commentary with which the author sought to outline how Europe would receive the move:

> The French—on account of our common cause, I trust—will immediately send an envoy. England, after receiving a little information and seeing that Hungary is more favourable for its manufacturing industry than Austria, which has excluded it, and that there are more favourable opportunities for reciprocal trade with us, will likewise appear among us within a short space of time and be our ally. Germany's manufactur-

ing industry has need of us, and of the provinces on the lower Danube. Turkey will gladly countenance us. The Russians will come last, and follow the lead of the others. The Italians are our friends, and the rest will have no objections.

In other words, nothing else remained "but to take this important step, which will settle our affairs." Familiarity with the intricacies of international affairs hardly seems to have been this writer's strong point. Two days later, on November 27, the paper rejected the proclamation addressed to Europe read out in the House of Representatives that day, describing "the whole thing" as "a ghastly, outworn *táblabíró* response". Europe was waiting, it said, not for this but for a clear answer to the question "Can you drive the treacherous Habsburgs out of every nook and cranny?" If Hungary could "beat the enemy, oblige him to make peace," Europe would "gladly receive us into the great family of nations." In the same number the paper reacted to the report that "an Austrian, Prussian, and Russian alliance had been made" by noting that this "was nothing less than a conspiracy of the kings against the people," against which the peoples had to unite—"the Hungarians with the Germans against the common foe, absolutism, and the basis of it, barbarism." In a leader on November 30 the paper ascribed the fact that the country still lacked an "orderly government provided with all the requirements" to the influence of the cautious "one-foot-in-the-stirrup" policy pursued by Batthyány. But on the following day, if it did not count itself among his supporters, it saw fit to defend Batthyány from the disagreeable and unjust charge made by the *Munkások Újsága* of having imperilled the nation and fled to Vienna. As the crisis approached, passions and expectations rose. Discussing the parties on December 4, Antal Várady threatened the reactionaries at home with the scaffold, and although he did not aspire to establish permanently a "slaughterhouse" like Robespierre's, he thought that at least a similar month and several ropes were needed in Hungary too. On December 15 László Berzenczey was attacked for his ineptitude in Transylvania, while Gábor Vas from Cegléd demanded, "Let us proclaim the republic." On December 19 the paper urged that all forces should hasten towards Győr, while another article joyfully announced that six cannon had been cast in the new foundry, that "with these we shall toll the knell of the habsburgs" /sic/ and "Görgei will be the sexton." Two days later there was reassuring news of victory from Moson, but "Igazmondó Fülöp" (Philip the Soothsayer), writing from Arad, accused Lieutenant-Colonel János Máriássy of cowardice and incompetence, almost of treachery. On the same day, December 21, the paper announced that the Radical Circle would form units of irregulars led by Józsa Oroszhegyi, having been empowered to do so by government commissioner Pál Nyáry. A week later, on December 28, a writer signing himself "K" sought hope in the French presidential election, the final gasp of the revolutionary process, going so far as to suppose that under the leadership of the new head of state with his famous name, Louis-Napoléon, France would assist the cause of liberty all over Europe, for its calling was to "fight the illustrious struggle for liberty. . . . Indeed, the warriors will rise to your betrayed cause, O freedom of Central Europe." A more tangible hope was that "there is our energetic and astute commander, Görgei, there is our brave army, which constantly shows an enthusiasm the history of the world has not known since the camp of the French republicans." And the heightened expectation was sustained to the very last minute that a miracle would happen and Görgei would win, for "there has hardly even been a single occasion on which there was a securer prospect of victory than now." This last *Marczius* wrote in its last issue for a good while, on January 3, 1849, when there was no longer the ghost of a chance that the army, retreating before superior forces and in a critical state, could prevent the enemy from capturing the capital and when the paper itself reported elsewhere that the government and the House of Representatives were moving to Debrecen.

Bibliography

Sándor Szilágyi, "Pálffy es Csernátony" (Pálffy and Csernátony), in *A magyar forradalom*, pp. 342-43; Mór Jókai, "Csernátony Lajos" (Lajos Csernátony), *A Kisfaludy Társaság Évkönyvei: Uj F.* (Yearbooks of the Kisfaludy Society: New Series), 7 (1871-72):255; József Madarász, *Emlékirataim 1831-1881* (My Memoirs, 1831-81) (Budapest, 1883); Albert Pálffy, "Egy lap keletkezése 1848-ban" (The Rise of a Paper in 1848), *Budapesti Hírlap* (Budapest Journal), no. 74 (1884), and *Ország Világ* (Country/World), no. 11 (1884), pp. 170-71; Zoltán Ferenczi, "Petőfi hírlapi cikkei 1848-ból" (Petőfi's 1848 Newspaper Articles), *Petőfi Múzeum*,

1892, pp. 14-17, 30-35, 63-69, and 84-91; Károly Vadnay, "Pálffy Albert emlékezete" (A Recollection of Albert Pálffy), *Budapesti Szemle* (Budapest Review) 94 (1898):355-80; Lajos Hentaller, "Volt-e Csernátony 1848-ban szerkesztő? (Was Csernátony an Editor in 1848?), *Magyarország* (Hungary), March 16, 1898; Rezső Szvacsek-Vári, *Erdődi Pálffy Albert* (Albert Erdődi Pálffy) (Budapest, 1904); Ernő Erdős, *A köztársasági eszme és az 1848/49-iki hírlapok* (The Concept of a Republic and the Newspapers of 1848-49) (Budapest, 1914); Tivadar Rédey, "Köztársasági publicisták 1848-ban" (Republican Journalists in 1848), *Vasárnapi Újság*, no. 52 (1918); Ferenc Szinnyei, *Novella- és regény irodalmunk a szabadságharcig* (Hungarian Short-Story and Novel Writing up to the War of Independence), vol. 2 (Budapest, 1926); András Diószeghy, *Rotáresti Dobsa Lajos* (Lajos Rotáresti Dobsa) (Makó, 1927); Ernő Tamás, "Pálffy Albert és 'Martius Tizenötödike'" (Albert Pálffy and *March the Fifteenth*), *Pesti Hírlap Vasárnapja* (Pest Sunday Journal), March 10, 1935, pp. 4-5; idem, "Az első magyar boulevardlap, a 'Martius Tizenötödike'" (*March the Fifteenth*, the First Sensational Hungarian Paper), *A Sajtó* (The Press), no. 3-4 (1957), pp. 7-10; Gusztáv Heckenast, "A márciusi radikálisok" (The March Radicals), *Valóság*, 1946, no. 10, pp. 1-6; József Waldapfel, "Költők a forradalomban" (Poets in the War of Independence), (Budapest, 1948), pp. 517-59; "Egy újság, amelybe Petőfi nyíltan, Görgey titkon írt: Pálffy Albert és lapja, a Martius Tizenötödike" (A Paper in Which Petőfi Wrote Openly and Görgey Secretly: Albert Pálffy and His Paper, *March the Fifteenth*), *Politika*, no. 28 (1948); Sándor Fekete, "A márciusi ifjak ideológiája" (The Ideology of the March Youth), *Valóság*, 1948, pp. 161-70; idem, *A márciusi fiatalok*; idem, *Vasvári Pál*; György Tordai, *Horárik János* (János Horárik) (Budapest, 1954); Ferenc Terestyéni, "Az újságírás nyelve 1848-ban" (The Language of Journalism in 1848), *MNy*, 1954, pp. 136-42; László Orosz, *Pálffy Albert* (Albert Pálffy) (Gyula, 1960); György Tordai, ed., *Forradalom és papi rend: Cikkgyüjtemény 1848-49 magyar sajtójából* (Revolution and Clerical Order: A Collection of Articles from the Hungarian Press of 1848-49) (Budapest, 1961); Aladár Urbán, "Történeti adalékok egy Petőfi-vers címváltozásaihoz" (Historical Data on the Title Change of a Poem by Petőfi), *ItK*, 1963, pp. 339-42, and in *A nagy év sodrában*, pp. 281-92; Sándor Lukácsy, "Tompa Mihály cikkei a forradalmi sajtóban" (Mihály Tompa's Articles in the Revolutionary Press), *ItK*, 1963, pp. 98-141; György Spira, "Petőfi esküdtszéki tagságáról" (Petőfi's Jury Membership), *ItK*, 1964, pp. 198-203; Lukácsy, "A márciusi ifjak"; idem, "A sajtó a forradalom és a szabadságharc alatt" (The Press in the Revolution and War of Independence) in *A magyar irodalomtörténete*, pp. 691-715; György Tordai, *Az 1848-as március ifjak az egyházról és a vallásról* (The 1848 March Youth on the Church and Religion), ed. Róbert Pogány (Budapest, 1965); Pál Pándi, "Vasvári Pál és az utópista szocializmus: Adalékok és jegyzetek" (Pál Vasvári and Utopian Socialism: Data and Notes), *Valóság*, 1966, no. 3, pp. 82-89; Sándor Lukácsy, "... és piros zászlókkal" (... And with Red Flags), *Kritika*, no. 3 (1968); Aladár Urbán, "Petőfi népgyűlése körül: A költő 1848 májusi közéleti szerepéről" (On Petőfi's People's Assembly: The Poet's Role in Public Life in May 1848), *Kritika*, no. 11 (1969), and in *A nagy év sodrában*, pp. 292-303; György Spira, "A pesti forradalom baloldalának nemzetiségi politikája 1848 márciusában" (The National Minorities Policy of the Left Wing of the Pest Revolution in March 1848), *Magyar Tudomány* (Hungarian Science), 1970, pp. 727-35; Aladár Urbán, "A Március Tizenötödike sajtópere" (The Press Trial of *March the Fifteenth*), in Lukácsy and Varga, *Petőfi*, pp. 485-514, and in *A nagy év sodrában*, pp. 160-208; idem, "Agitáció és kormányválság 1848 májusában" (Agitation and Government Crisis in May 1848), *Történelmi Szemle*

(Historical Review, *TSz* below), 1970, pp. 344-86, and in *A nagy év sodrában*, pp. 209-59; idem, "Petőfi 1848 augusztusában" (Petőfi in August 1848), in *Petőfi tüze* (Petőfi's Fire) (Budapest, 1972), and in *A nagy év sodrában*, pp. 322-57; István Görgey, *1848 júniusától novemberéig* (From June to November 1848), ed. Tamás Katona (Budapest, 1980); Aladár Urbán, "Tíz válságos nap a Batthyány-kormány történetéből, 1848 május 10-május 20" (Ten Critical Days in the History of the Batthyány Government: May 10-20, 1848), in *A nagy év sodrában*, pp. 96-159; idem, "Az 1848-as választások és Petőfi" (The 1848 Elections and Petőfi), ibid., pp. 304-21.

10. Other Radical Papers

"The radical camp," writes the latest contributor to the Hungarian literature, "on the one hand established some excellent traditions of revolutionary journalism but on the other misused its own strength: it dissipated it instead of concentrating it. The radical papers published side by side were all written to a large extent by the same persons, yet they often thwarted each other's intentions and became offensively personal. . . ." This rather apt description leaves unsaid only that the "radical camp" in question was in the process of welding into one camp divergent initiatives representing somewhat different ideas to some extent conveyed by different persons (even if most of the authors did work here, there, and everywhere) and that the various radical papers were in part continuations of one another, what mergers there were between them being really a sign of declining strength.

Reform

The first, most significant, and longest-surviving radical paper, *Marczius Tizenötödike*, came into being, as we have seen, as the organ of the March Youth. In contrast, *Reform*, launched on April 6, was the product of petit bourgeois journalists who right up until the revolution had been the stalwarts of the conservative, reactionary press and ardent foes of Petőfi and his adherents and who only now, in March, experienced a sudden conversion to radicalism that suited, one may add, their voracious ambitions and in essence their social stipulations as well. The editors of *Reform*, Lajos Nádaskay (1816-60) and Gusztáv Zerffi (1820- ?), provide two conspicuous, almost extreme examples of the instability among young members of the intelligentsia mentioned earlier. When they were later blamed quite justifiably by the *Pesti Hírlap* for having worked in the past for the reactionary paper *Honderű*, they indignantly refuted the charge of making a political *volte-face* by saying that they had worked irrespective of politics as literary critics for a literary paper. In fact they had indisputably played a political part while working on *Honderű*. Indeed, *Honderű*'s unequivocal change into a reactionary paper after the end of 1844 had been more the doing of the editor Nádaskay than of the "manager and proprietor" Lázár Petrichevich-Horváth. Nádaskay led the fray against the poetry of Petőfi, or rather against the new type of literature, finding a zealous, unscrupulous tool for doing so in Zerffi. Nádaskay was the son of a village notary from Zemplén County. He had studied at the Sárospatak College, later switching from medical studies to journalism. He was the more calculating of the two, a man who intrigued behind the scenes, being perhaps less an enigmatic figure than, as Ilona T. Erdélyi put it, "simply a rascal." When in 1850 he was released with Petrichevich-Horváth's assistance from prison, where he had been sent as a radical editor, he had no compunction about doing another about-turn and going to work for Ferenc Szilágyi's notorious *Magyar Hírlap*, which supported the absolutist régime.

The other editor, Zerffi, was less a cynical calculator than a hysterical jockeyer for position. His father was a Pest merchant named Áron Hirsch. After a youth somewhat shrouded in mystery he cropped up in the German-language press of Pressburg with some rather quibbling sketches in 1844. Later on, when studying the press in languages other than Hungarian, we shall see how the German press, mainly in Pressburg but partly in Pest, helped in the formation and growing significance of a corps of journalists of Jewish origin whose mother tongue was German but who wrote more and more in Hungarian. Being socially defenceless and at the same time sensitive, they turned against their own religious orthodoxy and joined the Hungarian liberal reform movement, from which they expected newer and better things, among them the emancipation of Hungarian Jewry. Around the liberal *Pressburger Zeitung* in particular there grew up a significant group of this kind, whose members, under now familiar Hungarian names, could be met with later on the Hungarian side in 1848-49 and among the émigrés. Zerffi came from that circle, but unlike the others, who after 1846 strove to popularize the new Hungarian literature in German, he sharply attacked Petőfi in *Honderű*, wrote a series of lampoons on progressive Hungarian literature while working for the conservative *Budapesti Hiradó*, and became a member of the Gyűlde. All this he did after Petőfi had turned down his importunities and efforts to gain attention by praising the poet. His captiousness, of course, cried for a response. In the spring of 1847 Gereben Vas ridiculed the "Writer of Impertinences" in a pamphlet entitled *Irodalmi deres* (Literary Whipping Post) signed "Dániel Harapófogó" (Daniel the Tweezers). Mór Jókai gave him a dressing down too, saying that Zerffi had "turned on the new trend with some low personal remarks" but that the new literature was uncowed by the attack and gave short shrift to such a "slanderer." Meanwhile Zerffi became a main contributor to the German variant of *Honderű, Morgenröthe*, for which he virtually acted as editor. At the end of January 1848 he publicly broke with Petrichevich-Horváth and began working for the Pest *Spiegel*. When the revolution broke out in March, he immediately sided with his old opponents. He hastened to translate Petőfi's National Song into German and waxed enthusiastic in a pamphlet he published over the events in Pest. In the March 18 issue of the *Spiegel* he wrote about freedom of the press and declared personal attacks to be wrong, clearly in self-defence as well. New plans were indicated when Nádaskay (of all people) spoke loudly in Zerffi's defence in *Honderű* on April 2, saying that he was no time-server and going so far as to claim that Zerffi could not be appointed as an editor because his progressive views had earned him a place in Metternich's "black book." Soon the two of them emerged as editors of the radical, opposition *Reform* (from April 6 to August 6). Thereafter Zerffi worked for the likewise radical Pest *Patriot* and in October took over *Der Ungar*, which he edited in a radical spirit.

The opportunism that prompted his conversion to radicalism is obvious, but there may have been some sincerity in it, since it was only from the new, progressive political endeavours that he could hope for social success and the emancipation of the Jews. It may have been such sincerity sheltering behind unbridled pushing that caused Petőfi and the others to forget their personal motives and excuse him for the sake of the cause. Had they not done so Zerffi would have got nowhere either in journalism or as a political organizer, namely, a zealous collaborator with László Madarász in the Egalitarian Society—althought, it is true, Madarász and his circle knew him only in his new guise, since they had little knowledge of the literary feuding that had gone on in the capital. József Madarász himself said he only learned in Debrecen in 1849 who Jókai was. A justified protest at and denunciation of Zerffi by the March Youth would have prevented them from cooperating with him, but in the absence of it Madarász was able to make good use of Zerffi's brisk if fairly superficial abilities. Right at the New Year, Zerffi went to Debrecen, and in the final months he was busy again on editorial work and preoccupied with founding a paper. After he had escaped into exile his lack of scruples surfaced again. Claiming to have been a "private secretary" of Kossuth's, he exploited public interest to publish three volumes in Leipzig of what he entitled Kossuth's collected works, without of course informing the furiously protesting Kossuth or obtaining his leave.

Sometimes it almost seems a shame that the history of the press should also involve dealing with the editors, partly because one inevitably finds oneself writing about persons who would otherwise receive little attention and partly because one is in danger of arousing a certain prejudice and aversion to the paper itself.

In fact *Reform* was basically a professionally edited, good-looking, readable paper. It appeared initially twice a week and from July 1 daily except Mondays in a quarto format giving it more the appearance of a periodical than of a newspaper. The publisher was Gusztáv Emich and the printers the university press. Under the title was the motto, "Liberty, equality, fraternity" and a short summary of the contents. The leader in the first number, entitled "Our Creed," explained the motto, and emphasized in particular, "We place the equality of men not in the quantitative equality of their estates but in the legal and equal relation which we owe to all men as men." Then came an article by Z. (presumably Zerffi) entitled "The Prime Mark of Liberty—Tolerance", which praised the youth, who unlike the philistine German citizens were "receiving Jews in a fraternal way", and also the nobility: "Let us never forget the generosity of our nobility," which had "voluntarily surrendered its rights so as to pass most of them on to you at its expense." Understandably the paper later published several other articles on the position of the Jews, welcoming signs on the one hand of their emancipation and on the other of their assimilation. In the second issue one hears that "our fellow citizen Kunewalder and his whole family exchanged the religion of Moses for the Christian faith" and that this "is only the beginning of a nationwide conversion." Towards the end of April more and more was said about "anti-Jewish agitation" and "devourers of the Jews" among the "philistine German citizens" and about robberies which would have to be severely avenged, for, as the title of a leader on April 30 put it, "Fifty Ropes Are Not the World." Later, on July 11, "Mihály Pecsovics" published a sharp attack on Dániel Irányi for not supporting the cause of Jewish emancipation in the National Assembly. Another recurring topic in the paper was freedom of the press, about which a series of four anonymous articles (perhaps written by Zerffi) appeared between May 9 and 20. Neither Hungary nor Austria had yet realized that "the only true and incorruptible means of defending the people" was by freedom of the press and that both press laws only "scorned press freedom" and were nothing other than "the abolition of prior censorship coupled with the introduction of a far crueller subsequent one."

Quite a few contributors to the paper used pseudonyms or signed their articles with an initial, but a substantial number gave their real names. In the first place there was József Mack, "Imperial and Royal Chief Bombardier of the Ordnance Staff," who taught at the Buda artillery school but had not been promoted for many years because in 1831 he had declined to fire on the rebels in Lemberg (Lvóv) at the time of the Polish insurrection. Here again was an interesting personality full of contradictions: on the one hand a thorough professional knowledge, good organizing abilities, an eagerness to act, and resolute republicanism, and on the other an impetuosity and swashbuckling heedlessness that led him into conflicts. He was one of the organizers of the Hungarian artillery, promoted to major in the autumn of 1848 and lieutenant-colonel in 1849, and his role and hardships at Komárom will be mentioned later when we discuss the military papers. In 1851 he was commissioned by Kossuth to organize the ill-fated conspiracy in the Székelyföld district of eastern Transylvania. In 1848, eager for action, he wrote a succession of articles for *Reform*: a description of the meeting of minds between the soldiers and the people ("A Soldier to the People") on April 20, a proposal for setting up a fifteen-hundred-strong Hungarian artillery battalion written in the form of an open letter to the minister of defence on April 27, ideas "On the Organization of the National Defence Force" in several parts from May 4 onwards, a commentary on the Lederer affair saying that even as an officer he would never have given the order to fire on the unarmed people ("What Would I Have Done on the Bloody Day in Buda?") on May 14, and a treatise on "The Immurement of Pest" on June 4. In all his writings good, useful ideas are mingled with lengthy commonplaces and ample contradictions. Among the others to write in the paper under their own names were Lajos Keresztszeghy, whose suggestion led to the starting of a legal column, György Ferenczi, who wrote about the fairs and guilds of Pest, Pető Orbán, who corresponded from Arad, and László Klesztinszky, who did the same from Kassa. The property qualification was attacked by Lajos Thalabér and by László Újházi, who took issue with the *Pesti Hírlap* on the subject. Károly Vályi wrote on the conference Metternich had once held at Karlsbad (Karlovy Vary), Frigyes Feldinger on "Ideas of Transformation," and Lajos Verebi on education of the people. For us, the most interesting piece of writing came from a lawyer in Békés County, Pál Székács, for in a paper that otherwise ignored the issues of the peasantry he described the grievances of the Békés peasants on June 1, in particular their refusal to serve in the militia while the usufructs (*regalia*) of the sales of meat and drink remained in the hands of the landowners: "The state may take back what it has unjustly granted to certain individuals just as soon as the good of the public requires," he wrote. "I trust that the forthcoming National Assembly will abolish the exclusive exercise by landowners of local monopolies and do so without indemnification, since it has no urbarial character." However, one cannot draw far-reaching conclusions from the exceptional appearance in the same number of a short examination of Auguste Blanqui, "the leading light of the communistic elements, the agitator of the working class of the population of Paris," since on June 18 one can read the same about Lamartine from the same author. On two occasions the paper published full-page art supplements. One was on the unlikely subject of plans for national costumes for priests and the other, on April 23, about "How the Hungarian Academy Makes Use of the Freedom of the Press." The picture, a lithograph by A. P. Walzel, shows figures in plaits (i.e., old-fashioned people) asleep at a table.

Weakest of all were the short, unsigned editorials that dealt occasionally with the country's international position and the question of the national minorities. "Should we be afraid of the Russians?" was the question the paper asked in the second number, on May 9, and immediately answered in the negative, since in that country the state was paralysed by "perfect chaos" due to the unruliness of the great landowners. Its conclusion, "We need only fear states where the people rule," was a rather strange one for a paper that described itself as an ardent believer in democracy. Two months later, on July 9, the news that the Russian troops were advancing, at least on the Romanian principalities, prompted the paper to conclude in its leader, "We must emancipate ourselves in terms of the law of nations." Independence from Austria had to be proclaimed, it argued, and the members of the National Assembly had to "decide that Hungary should henceforth be represented among the world's powers," as if international, diplomatic recognition of Hungary depended solely on what was decided by the parliamentarians of Pest. On the issue of the national minorities the paper espoused an extreme form of the nationalism long traditional among the nobility (April 23), with the difference that it considered county autonomy a direct source of danger from the national minorities, a danger that could come from below, "on the part of the people," if Liptó County, for instance, began conducting its business in Slovak. On May 7 the paper continued its deliberations under the title "Nationality": "This is the Hungarians' own country," where everyone was Hungarian "whether he speaks German, Slovak or any other language." Anyone who "agitates for special rights and national demands" it considered guilty of "a crime against the Hungarian nation" and a traitor.

As the elections approached, the paper conveyed its

"guiding ideas" on "our future National Assembly," attacking the upper house as an institution and the influence of the Hungarian clergy. On June 4 the editors printed a separate "specimen page" of articles putting forward their platform, saying that they were prepared to support the government so long as it did not go against the ideas of liberty but that "the press should be wholly free" and that although "strictly on the side of the monarchy" it would "battle tirelessly for the rights of the people on the broadest possible basis." In a leader headed "Monarchy-Republic" on June 11, it returned to the same subject, saying that one of the new National Assembly's main tasks would be "to establish the form of government." Again the paper stressed that although a republic would in principle be better, it wanted a monarchy, now giving as its sole reason that "the proclamation of a republic would be the swan song of our independence." This monarchy "should be founded on democratic institutions." On June 25 it used strong words to condemn the way Petőfi was defeated as an "underhand" election scandal "infringing every right of man." *Reform* also chastised the governing party's press, which "glories in the sunshine of power" (June 29); it attacked the *Közlöny* as disseminating "no ideas at all" because the ministry did not consider it worth acquainting the people with lofty notions and then the submissive *Pesti Hírlap* and the still more servile *Pesther Zeitung*. On July 29 it gave the *Pesther Zeitung* a special lecture for its attack on the Egalitarian Society. "This paper," it wrote, "has never been an apostle of humanity and has harassed the Jews with notorious impudence. This paper has always served might but never justice, idiocy but never liberty or right." Meanwhile on July 18 it specially mentioned that "the press has not made any advance yet, because what private citizen would feel, when the state itself is in financial straits and all trade is in total slump, like letting 5,000 silver forints lie fallow as unemployed capital at the caprice of the legislature?" In the same issue there was a report on the general meeting on Sunday, July 16, of the Egalitarian Club (since then renamed the Egalitarian Society) and on its statutes. At the meeting stress had been laid on cooperation and there had been quite a debate with delegates from the Democratic Club. Although their union could not be attained, they agreed in distancing themselves from the socialist movements: "We are not communists; to us every man's property is sacred." The statement listed László Madarász as "representative" (i.e., president) and Lajos Nádaskay as "executive" and gave the names of the committee members of the Egalitarian Society as (in this order) Mihály Táncsics, Gusztáv Zerffi, Mór Mérei, Kálmán Lisznyai, József Madarász, Albert Pálffy, Dr. Frigyes Grósz, Károly Mészáros, János Balogh, Zsigmond Rosty, Márton Diósi, Gusztáv Lauka, Kornél Ábrányi, Károly Sükei, and János Bangya. Others present included Julián Chownitz, Ödön Kállay, Vince Perczel, Viktor Herczeg, and Mór Szegfi. The vast majority of those mentioned were working for the press of the time. One should add that on July 2 *Reform* had published the June 26 programme of the Egalitarian Club and that on July 4 it had discussed the Democratic Club formed just two days earlier on Vasvári's initiative, chiding the leaders of the radical youth for not joining the Egalitarian Club instead. Petőfi too is known to have kept aloof for a while. In the August 4 number was an "Appeal" dated July 30 signed by László Madarász and Nádaskay "to Hungarian writers, editor, printers, publishers, and traders in books and to all friends of literature and the free press" calling on them to support the petition made by the Egalitarian Society to the House of Representatives. In this the Society demanded that the current press law be repealed, "the caution monies be abolished for all time," and the press "be released from the constraints imposed by special penal legislation." This statement appeared, by the way, in several radical papers, and so did a statement in the name of the Romanians in which "Zsigmond Pap, Sándor Buda, Euthim Murgu," and others responded to an article by Miklós Jósika in the *Pesti Hírlap* on July 15 accusing the Romanians of being anti-Hungarian and objecting to their elevation to the status of a fourth "nation" of Transylvania. The reply in *Reform* on July 30 said that any "noxious provocation" was Jósika's rather than the Romanians'; for centuries they had shown their devotion to the Hungarians, and their crying out in pain at the injuries inflicted "by the long-standing crimes of the Transylvanian aristocracy" could not be so described. The signatories desired that "the Romanians, in peaceful affinity with the Hungarians, should not be unlawfully repressed" and that "in allowing the exercise of our constitutional rights freely without hindrance, they should allow free and open opportunity for our instruction."

But before the debate could go farther, an "announcement" in the August 5 issue ended by saying it was better that the "divided forces working for a similar purpose" should unite, and so, like the *Radical Lap* a few days before, *Reform* would merge with the *Nép-elem*, which subscribers would receive instead of *Reform* from August 8.

The Ellenőr and the Radical Lap

The *Radical Lap* was founded in Pest on June 1. It was preceeded by the likewise radical Pest paper *Die Opposition*, launched on April 10, which we shall return to later, and by the Kolozsvár *Ellenőr*, launched on May 2. The *Ellenőr* was radical by Transylvanian standards, although it was rather the conservative liberal tastes of József Ferenczy that caused him subsequently to dub it the gathering point for "the coarsest revolutionary outpourings." Be that as it may, it became the spokesman for the youth of Kolozsvár of the same generation as the March Youth, and they tried to strike a similarly decisive note as was struck in *Marczius*. The founder and first editor was László Kőváry (1819-1907). After studying law in Kolozsvár, he became a clerk to the court of appeal in Marosvásárhely (Tîrgu Mureş). It was from reading in the Teleki Library there that he acquired the interest in Transylvanian history that was to occupy him till the end of his life. Articles of his on ethnological, geographical, and historical subjects had been appearing in Transylvanian papers since 1839. After Szemere appointed him in June 1848 as secretary of the statistical bureau being set up, the editorial work was actually done by his co-editor, Dániel Dózsa (1821-89). The publisher was János Tiltsch, a Kolozsvár patrician and bookseller who also supervised the printing until the end of September, hiring the press of the city's Reformed Church College. Partly for that reason he was afterwards imprisoned by the Austrian authorities. The paper came to an end with the arrival in Kolozsvár of the troops of Lieutenant-Colonel Urban, when the Austrians impounded the type set up for the last issues of all the Kolozsvár papers.

Of the two editors of the *Radical Lap* we have already come across Mór Mérei as a member of the *Marczius* staff. The other was Zsigmond Rosty (or Rosti, 1811-75), who doubled as publisher. He came from a family of noble landowners in Fejér County, where he first tried to make a career for himself before turning instead to journalism. His articles in *Hasznos Mulatságok*, the *Jelenkor*, and the *Társalkodó* had mostly been on historical topics. Not long after, he enlisted in the Hungarian army and took part in the capitulation at Komárom as an artillery lieutenant. In an appeal for subscribers to the new paper at the end of May it was emphasized that "in civil law terms we contradict communism and honour property as the foundation stone of human society." During its short life of a month and a half the Pest post office sent out only 255 copies of it a day. It appeared as a folio broadsheet printed by Landerer and Heckenast. Right from the start it was fairly critical of its radical rivals: *Marczius* was called infantile and *Reform* (equally unjustly) extreme. The latter reacted by saying on June 4 that the *Radical*'s editors had no idea what radicalism was, they just mouthed phrases. The *Radical* retorted on June 7 that its partners in debate equated radicalism with the idea of a republic. Replying in turn on June 11, *Reform* declared, "We do not consider that the question of whether there should be a monarchy or a republic has yet arisen in this country." On the one hand, "we have become accustomed to the monarchy;" on the other, "we are convinced of the necessity for it."

Of the staff of the *Radical Lap* special note should be taken of the young Károly Mészáros (1821-9?), a member of a poor noble family who lost his parents early and began, it will be remembered, by supporting the conservative Gyűlde. When he returned from Moson to Pest in May 1848 and saw what embarrassing previous careers the March Youth were prepared to let pass without a word, he hastened to join the extreme radicals and came to be influential among them. This sociopolitical phenomenon has been encountered before. Subsequently, in the spring of 1849 Mészáros became the "historiographer" or war correspondent attached to Perczel's corps. Yet hardly six months after the defeat, in the first phase of the tyranny, he emerged in Ung County as a local judge (*assessor*), providing fresh evidence of his readiness to trim his sails. It is interesting and noteworthy, however, that he was one of the radical journalists to pay more than average attention to the problems of the new bourgeois society and the proletariat and to the lessons to be drawn from the French example. On June 11 he wrote under the title "Workers' Freedom" that "this century, which began with the finest conquests for humanity in the name of justice and right, cannot curtail the freedom to work in the interests of equality and liberty." He went on to provide the motto for economic liberalism: "So down with the guilds, immediately, everywhere!" On June 14 an article entitled "The Working Class" tried to trace the development of the idea of a nation, asserting that "liberalism is a direct ladder to socialism" and demanding the establishment of national workshops after the French example, higher wages, and a fair resolution of the farm labourer question "as a bar to proletarianism." The paper returned to questions of the assessment of equality more fully in its leader on June 16:

> Although we have stated in our programme that we are against communism and support only socialism, several people have taken fright at the latter term as well, and so we see a need to make a clear statement on these two matters. What is communism? Proudhon, the latest exponent of regular communism, answers by positing the basic principle that property is theft . . . in other words all the possessions in the world must be distributed proportionately, and this he calls equality. We use the term equality solely in a legal sense . . . we demand only equality before the law, since we endorse and accept as our own the dictum of Alexandre Dumas: asked what communism is, he replied: "Theft!" Since communism is nothing other than the prayer of a few who would live for nothing, we shall say all the less about it on this occasion, for the Hungarian mind has treated it with suitable contempt and no one has dared espouse it publicly. . . . By socialism we understand nothing other than free association for specific purposes by which the needs of those allied may be supplied more easily and cheaply.

From this, I would add, it is clear that this alliance had nothing to do with the new idea of the right to work or with the experiment, unsuccessful in any case, with "national workshops." The paper went on, "The state cannot rightly be obliged to provide everyone with work; its obligation is to cease all measures that obstruct access to work," for instance, the situation in which "the apprentices in the same town were not free to transfer from one master to another."

The Nép-elem

The *Nép-elem*, with which *Reform* and the *Radical Lap* merged, was launched on July 1. It was a daily, appearing six times a week, but when it closed on September 28 only seventy-four issues had appeared. It was printed as a folio broadsheet by László Lukács and Co. A six-month subscription cost 6 forints delivered to a Budapest address or 8 forints by post to the provinces. The "temporary publishing offices" were at No. 466, Szabadsajtó utca. The paper was edited (and published) by László and József Madarász; after the merger in the interests of "radical democracy" with the *Radical Lap* they were joined by Mór Mérei and Zsigmond Rosty (although the latter remained only until July 29) and the title was lengthened on July 18 to the *Nép-elem, Radical Lap*. An announcement in the August 6 number said that *Reform* would also cease to appear separately and the three papers combine into "a common radically minded, democratically oriented organ." This second merger did not involve any change in the editing or title of the paper, although the staff was again increased.

During the first fortnight of the original *Nép-elem* the bulk of the writing was done by the Madarász brothers. Alongside them there occasionally appeared one or two of their friends, such as Károly Éjszaky of Fejér County and József Kolmár, and pseudonyms such as "Pestifi" (Son of Pest), "Budai" (Buda-ite), and "Vöröstollas" (Red Pen or Red-Feathered). After the merger with the *Radical* the last three were joined by Mór Szegfi, Józsa Oroszhegyi, Zsigmond Rosty, the writer of revolutionary catechisms Viktor Herczeg, and then Pál Szatmáry and, among those sheltering behind pseudonyms, "Polydorus" as the parliamentary correspondent, who may have been Károly Mészáros or possibly Józsa Nyíri. After August 6 one reads, alongside "Pestifi"'s report on the Egalitarian Society and Herczeg's "critical notes" and glosses, László Dorogi's piece on the people's schools, Dániel Oroszlán on the clergy, Pukolai on the Hungarians of Bukovina, Ödön Kállay on the "gardeners' villages" in the south of the country, György Ferenczi on the National Assembly, Zerffi on Austria, Ákos Birányi on military proposals and on Kossuth, and articles by Józsa Nyíri and László Baloghi.

Lipót Lőw, the chief rabbi of Pápa, wrote on "religious ideas" in several instalments, Mór Mérei on the movements in the capital, and a writer signing himself Gróffy on the Pragmatic Sanction and other topics. This list is not complete, but it shows that the bulk of the journalism was supplied by staffs of the two papers merging with the *Nép-elem*, which itself was far less well off in that respect.

The explanation is simple. As the summer began it emerged that radicalism had little support either from voters or from subscribers. Of all the radical papers only *Marczius* remained on a firm footing, and the other papers were obliged to pool their resources. The strongest of them was not the one that could attract the largest staff of intellectuals but the one that could most effectively represent what was, under the circumstances, the strongest tendency—the radicalism of the nobles. The likewise noble, radical leading lights of the *Radical* could not compete in this field with the Madarász brothers, but it was worthwhile assigning them a certain part in the editorial activities. Not so in the case of *Reform*.

László Madarász (1811-1909) and his younger brother and faithful follower József (1814-1915) came from a family of "lesser landowning nobles" in Fejér County, where they led the radical, petty noble wing of the local reforming opposition and in this way entered national politics. Both took law degrees after some impecunious years as students. József went as a *iuratus* and *absentium ablegatus* in 1832 to Pressburg, where the first Reform Diet took place. There, for a small fee, he was one of the copiers of Kossuth's *Országgyülési Tudósítások* and belonged to Lovassy's young circle until more cautious acquaintances advised him to return home. His elder brother László had meanwhile set out on foot without a passport to emigrate to America. He got only as far as Scandinavia, found he was too short for the Swedish army, and returned home. Both these short, spare young men had a resolute tenacity and, particularly in the elder's case, an amazing inner fervour. László, according to his brother, was remarkable for his "quick thinking" and "incisive sarcasm": "The longer the argument was, and the more sharply he was attacked, the more he lashed out. . . . If he became agitated in an argument three veins became visible on his purposeful brow," whereupon "the sparks would fly at his adversary." His first bold entry into politics came in the autumn of 1836 at a general meeting in Fejér County, where he thoroughly upset the governing party, the *comes* and the other great lords, hitherto unused to being contradicted, by refusing to refer to them as honoured or esteemed lords on the grounds of "sovereignty of the people" and "the equality of rights required in constitutional discussions." The doings of the Madarász brothers were even reported in Kossuth's *Törvényhatósági Tudósítások*, and in 1838, during the period of political reprisals, they were charged with treason for having attempted "to incite . . . the needier nobility against the wealthier nobility . . . under the pretext that the former's rights were being infringed." The trial was suspended, however, and throughout the 1840s the brothers continued their skirmishes on behalf of the opposition in Fejér and other Transdanubian counties, among them Tolna, where one person they came in contact with was Mór Perczel, and Somogy, from where László was elected a deputy to the last feudal Diet in autumn 1847. Not having the same success, József broke in disillusionment with the Fejér County opposition and dreamed of emigrating to Switzerland. He was convalescing from a "nervous fever" when he witnessed the turn of events in March. Of course he immediately joined in, initially on the county political scene. At the May general assembly, where the villages where already represented, he untiringly urged the numerous delegation of "citizens" (i.e., peasants) complaining of misappropriations of land and other grievances to keep calm and observe the law and warned them against agitators. Later he was not even prepared to say that the vineyard tithes should be abolished when it was demanded of him in Bicske at the time of the elections by a "pale-faced man" called János Horárik (a real radical) at the head of several hundred people. In June both he and his brother were elected representatives, but in May they had already decided to move to Pest and start a newspaper. Their aim was to win Kossuth over from the government to the radical cause. They had long known him and his family and observed his doings, sometimes with enthusiasm and sometimes with disappointment but always with hope. For the time being, with the radicals reduced to a small minority, there was little likelihood of succeeding, but the Madarász brothers had enough political standing to begin taking into their own hands the organization of the various opposition groups of Pest radicals they were now acwuainted with—nobles and members of the intelligentsia ranging from Nádaskay via Mór Mérei to Pálffy—and gather them into the Egalitarian Society, for which they canvassed for subscriptions on June 26. Five days later their paper, the *Nép-elem*, appeared.

We shall return to the way their political enemies later tried to depict the Madarász brothers as ghastly, diabolic organizers of revolutionary "terrorism," particularly László, whom they also accused of fraudulent dealings. In fact both appear to have been honest, well-meaning, even rather naive men who were able, as long as events allowed, to apply the simple notion of noble radicalism keenly and purposefully but who became confused and almost defenceless once the situation changed. One must note that their paper seems surprisingly primitive, not least because of the cumbersome, painfully faltering, contorted language in which it was written. It was as if the previous, decisive century in the development of literary Hungarian had quite passed it by. After the language revival had come the age of Petőfi, Arany, and Jókai and, one might add, in journalism the age of Kossuth and Pálffy. The better journalism of the time holds the reader's attention to this day, yet the *Nép-elem* was replete with the kind of arbitrary, pedantic expressions and turns of phrase that are so strange as to be scarcely comprehensible without special explanation. The paper's title itself, *Nép-elem*— People's Element—was an attempted Hungarianization of "democracy". Literary historians are wont to comment on the "cumbersome style" of József Madarász, but in my view it was more than a matter of literary ability or disability. In a speech to the House of Representatives on July 10 he used an obscure expression that landed him in an embarrassing position. What he is supposed to have said is that "since the last Diet, intrigue has to a large extent administered the representation to which the country was entrusted." Whereupon Kossuth, who had not been present at that particular moment, hastened to attack him, saying he would not stand for so slanderous a charge and calling him a "disturber of the peace of the country." Yet Madarász had harboured no ill intent, merely spoken ambiguously and in a confused way. There would also seem to be a social problem behind all this. Táncsics, as the self-educated son of a peasant, spoke clearly about the essentials, because he was obliged to expend great effort on acquiring the demanding skills required for subjects that called for disciplined expression if people were to be prepared to discuss them with him at all. A petty nobleman, on the other hand, was able to enter politics through the counties without making this effort. He might then try, if the occasion arose, to analyse the national problems he encountered with means of communication cobble together from what he had brought from home. There is a sign of this in the similar problems confronted by the far more original and talented László Madarász. In the leading article of the first issue his explanation of the rules of bourgeois political democracy and the relations of majority and minority is correct in principle but so laboriously expressed that each sentence has to be read several times.

But despite the many drawbacks, the positive efforts of the editors are apparent, for instance, in the fact that they found space on July 4 and 5 as the National Assembly was beginning for two anonymous articles touching on the problems of the peasantry. One article stressed that defence of the country was more urgent than indemnification of the landowners; one had to express "without disguise the demands of the people" that the contract labourers should owe neither tithes nor corvée and that the usufructs should be "common to all owners of land within the borders" (of the estate) and "the vineyards free." The other was still more reminiscent of Táncsics's attitude and reasoning at the time: "In the petitions of the people one can read of the thousands of illegal acts which have already been committed in the urbarial regulations and dividing up of pasture." A little later, on July 12, László Madarász outlined the position taken by noble radicals. On the one hand he described the landlords who shrank from all further steps as "miserly dwarfs," and on the other he announced, "We wish to incorporate into law compensation by the state for all former landlords of vineyards." Another positive move by the paper was to publish on July 4 the programme adopted by the Egalitarian Society on June 26, 1848, which some think Petőfi framed, although he does not appear among the signatories. More recent research has failed to confirm this, although it has confirmed that the content was acceptable to him. This text again had to frame the common goals in fairly general terms, but none the less, the lively phrases gleam out of the grey pages of the newspaper:

> The ideas of liberty, equality, and fraternity have not been implemented.
> Indeed, the various castes raise their heads more boldly from day to day.
> The freedom of the press won in Pest on March 15 has been frustrated by the tyrannical press laws of the Pressburg assembly of nobles. . . .
> The principle of citizen's equality declared in Pest on March 15 has been betrayed by the property qualification raised by the Pressburg assembly of nobles against all human dignity, and representation of the people in the National Assembly has been frustrated.
> The principle of fraternity declared and realized in Pest on March 15 has been paralysed due to the maintenance by the same noble assembly of the various class categories.
> Thus the fundamental ideas for the reformation of civilized Europe, which the French people proclaimed at the time of the French revolution and we made our own in the revolution of ideas in Pest, liberty, equality, and fraternity, remain only a name and not a reality in this country.
> Since class rule persists to this day, the people continue to subsist as a political proletariat. . . .

The purpose of the Society, therefore, was to facilitate "the vitalizing of liberty, equality, and fraternity . . . by legal means," to achieve "true and unconditional freedom of the press free of all caution monies," and to attain "people's rights uncompromised by any property qualification."

The signatures followed: József Madarász, Imre Medve, Albert Pálfi, Lajos Dobsa, Mór Mérei, Zsigmond Rosti, Lajos Nádaskai, János Ferenczi, Gusztáv Zerffi, Gusztáv Birnbaum, János Eckstein, József Vanczák, Jakab Kulmann, Sándor Dunst, Kálmán Lisznyai, Károly Sükei, Gyula Számwald, Adolf Dux, Dávid Pserhofer, Adolf Müller, Dávid Német, Gusztáv Lauka, Sándor Lipót Pauer.

Thereafter the paper mainly concerned itself with criticism of the government and the issue of national independence, touching less frequently on social matters and then from an angle typical of petty noble radicalism. On July 10 László Madarász saw fit to issue a special appeal that "democrats" should in future address each other by the familiar "you"-form *te*. When on July 15 Károly Éjszaky, writing about representation of the people and criticizing the composition of the National Assembly, happened to describe the petty nobility as "the worst of all classes," the editors hurriedly added a footnote saying, "We do not consider this to be so." On July 18 József Madarász declared in a leader entitled "The People" that equal rights had to be granted before it was too late, because although the people had "irresistibly won the revolution for freedom," they were if dissatisfied "a destructive tide" and a "consuming flame," and if, "being oppressed by cowardice," they betook themselves in the wrong direction they were not worth anything ("the handle of a hatchet"). What the article failed to explain was whether under the circumstances political equality would of itself resolve all the problems of the "people."

The same writer attacked government policy more forcefully on July 21 over the question of assistance to the forces sent by the court against the movements in Italy, a move that "the spirit of Europe" would not tolerate. The next day the paper announced on its front page in bold type that Mór Perczel had resigned his department headship because he could not share in a policy "aimed at oppressing other nations." On the same day, July 22, Józsa Oroszhegyi welcomed the revolution by the Romanians of Wallachia and the fact that neighbours of Hungary's had "shaken off the yoke that strangled their national activity." But he pointed out that their position was perilous and could only be salvaged through energetic moves by other countries. To make them would also be in Hungary's interest, for "if Wallachia falls, our national existence will be faced with its final struggle." He went on to say that it was a mistake to leave the kindly Romanian people of this country open to seditious propaganda, since that meant the country could not rely on them, "for the Hungarians are fairly remiss in displaying sympathy for them." On July 25 Zsigmond Rosty, in an article he called "Mr Kossuth's Conflict with Himself," criticized Kossuth's role in the affairs of military assistance to the Habsburgs in Italy. Two days later "Pestifi" declared that Hungary "laughed to scorn" this kind of "struggle for freedom" by Batthyány, Deák, Kossuth, and their fellows and rejected criticism made by the *Pesti Hírlap*. Meanwhile József Madarász on July 29 urged that the planned colonization of the Lower Danube counties by Hungarians from Transylvania should be extended "right down to the Hungarian coast" and the property of the "Illyrian" (Croatian) leaders confiscated. On August 1 he began publishing a leading article in several parts designed to win Kossuth over. Many, he said, considered Kossuth's policy "ill-defined and inadequate," but he commanded a majority in the National Assembly and was "the spirit of the present government." This did not stop Madarász from using Kossuth's "dreadful budget" as a starting point for a treatise in four long parts on financial affairs beginning on August 6. In the meantime the paper published the Egalitarian Society's petition to the National Assembly on freedom of the press. Among other arguments against the caution money it described it as a breach of "common sense," since it was "a kind of prior penalty" imposed even on those who were not going to offend. It is worth noting a report on August 10 of the August 6 meeting of the Egalitarian Society, from which it emerges that the lawyer Keczkés, whose "seditious" speech and consequent arrest had been described variously and typically in the different papers, had turned to the Egalitarian Society to inform those present of "the circumstances of his incarceration." Keczkés said that during a recruiting speech he had also spoken of the emancipation of the Jews, at which the citizens had grumbled, and then called upon the aristocracy to forego compensation for the feudal privileges they had lost in view of the peril threatening the country, whereupon he had been arrested that night. László Madarász as chairman declared that the matter was worth looking into but that nothing could be done until it had been sufficiently "investigated." A committee was then appointed to do so, but the members of it later concluded that the police could only be faulted for keeping Keczkés in custody too long; his speech "did contain matters which it might have been feared, particularly at that time, would cause serious breaches of the law," and to that extent the committee could not "refrain from endorsing the police's procedure." Horárik was the only one who still attempted to champion Keczkés's cause, but he was obliged to back down when László Madarász intervened firmly from the chair. So the author of the poster "Bread for the

People" could expect no support from a society that bore the label "Egalitarian." One can read in Józsa Nyíri's report of the meeting on August 15 that Táncsics urged the Society to attempt "some notable initiative" to give an "impetus" to the National Assembly—for instance, embracing the demands of the electors of Siklós published in the *Munkások Újsága* and submitting them as a petition. But his proposal only got as far as being incorporated at the request of Madarász among the motions for consideration. Meanwhile József Madarász, in the August 11 issue, wrote in an article entitled "To the Gentlemen of the Left Wing," "They say all the gentlemen on this side wish to be leaders and there is no propensity for agreement among them. Let us delay no longer, let us arise and form ourselves into a party." Historians consider the appeal addressed chiefly to Perczel and Petőfi.

When the crisis of September 1848 came and the Habsburgs openly threatened Hungary with armed force, the paper turned its full attention to the armed conflict, supporting national defence and aligning itself behind Kossuth. They should beware of appearing to posterity, wrote Ákos Birányi on September 13, to have been "cowardly and unworthy of life." On September 16 József Madarász demanded that Kossuth be made governor. On September 19 the paper's front page contained the appeal by Táncsics and Móric Tóth for the Hungarian people to take up arms against Jelačić, "the butcher and genocide"—not to stand aside, and not to believe in him, for "no people or country since the creation of the world has been so shamefully and disloyally treated as we." On the front page on September 20 was the call to arms framed by Petőfi in the name of the Egalitarian Society. Petőfi had withdrawn after his election defeat and taken no part in the Egalitarian Club or the founding of the Egalitarian Society. Nor did he support the opposition policy by which the Madarász brothers sought power in the National Assembly. As he wrote on August 11, he thought the final defeat would follow "unless the people wake up immediately and wrest from the hands of their government and representatives the power the latter in part cannot use and in part abuse." His expectations were inspired by the Jacobins: "a vast revolution" was at hand. No such turn of events after the French model took place in Hungary, but a change did come as the nation undertook the struggle for its own defence. On August 23 the Egalitarian Society decided to draft a proclamation opposing the national defence bill. The proclamation was to be prepared in time for a political banquet on September 8 by a committee of seven, and in this Petőfi was prepared to take part, as it seemed likely to turn into a fairly large extra-parliamentary political campaign.

Some historians see a sign of the weakness of the left in the closure of the *Nép-elem* at that particular juncture, on September 28, a mere three months after it was founded. But how could that be so when the noble radicals had actually achieved their purpose by winning over Kossuth? Surely they were in a stronger position than ever before. In the dramatically tense situation even the circuitousness of Madarász was moderated. The editors themselves explained their decision somewhat later, in the December 4 number of the *Jövő,* as in part because they had found "no material support . . . either in staff or in sympathy" and in part because "under the circumstances of a struggle for the liberation of the people of our country" they could not afford "to expend . . . our talents on publishing the paper." Since they had more colleagues on the staff than when the paper was started and the money had always been tight, the second, almost certainly, must have been the deciding factor. László Madarász was now a member of the National Defence Commission and no longer needed an opposition paper. But the radical members of the intelligentsia who had been concerned with the Madarász brothers' paper were now in a weak position, and they made several attempts to found a paper of their own.

The Köztársasági Lapok and the Jövő

The first new attempt was the *Köztársasági Lapok,* which began on October 11 with the young Ákos Birányi-Schultz as editor. Only twelve issues appeared, at irregular intervals. It was printed in quarto format on the press in the courtyard behind Adolf Müller's bookshop in Uri utca, Pest. The paper was first and foremost an advocate of republicanism. According to the foreword of his *Köztársasági Káté* (Republican Catechism, 1848), Birányi as a believer in the "social republic" also sought to review thoroughly the new social problems of the bourgeois world. In the book he explained that he understood the misery of the proletariat because he himself had "often sweated blood at work." The proletariat was like "a great volcano" whose "fire has been building up for thousands of years, and the later it bursts forth the more dreadful the din and devastation will be." To forestall this he recommended "socialism," by which he understood a republic "in which society not only provides all men with rights through which they may struggle by their own efforts for spiritual and material welfare but itself sees to providing the means for them to do so." These means, after the pattern of the national workshops, were "work organization," "regulation of property," introduction of "appropriate laws," and "association." Birányi distinguished this from "communism," in which "the country's entire property and goods are considered as a public stock of capital in whose income each person shares according to his ability, efforts, and deserts." The latter "demands an impossibly high level of education in man." Sándor Lukácsy has rightly pointed out that with views of this kind Birányi was a rarity among the extreme radicals and even among the March Youth.

The next new undertaking was the *Jövő*, which began on December 1, 1848, as a daily folio broadsheet and came to an end on December 30 at issue no. 25. This too was printed by Adolf Müller, who was later to fall in battle as an officer of the Hungarian army. The subscription for December, delivered to a Budapest address, was 1 forint. The editor, Emil Ábrányi (1820-50), may perhaps have been the young writer to have advanced farthest from his point of departure. From a mansion in Szabolcs County, where he was the son of a well-to-do family of landowners and had, moreover, an extensive library at his disposal, he developed into one of the March Youth. In the 1840s he had spent a good deal of time in Pest on the pretext of studying law but motivated far more by literary and artistic interests. There he had encountered new lines of thinking and made new friends. His writings saw the light of day in the *Honderű* and the *Életképek*. When the March revolution came he was on his estate in Ábrány, from where he sent an open letter to Jókai. Shortly after, he came up to the capital, was appointed a secretary by Szemere, and took part in devising the rules of procedure for the new National Assembly. From the outset he was one of the most active members of the staff of *Kossuth Hírlapja*. Now he finally started a paper of his own, and it deserves attention not least for its progressive social interests, which went beyond the usual constitutional-cum-national radicalism of the nobles. Among the things Ábrányi stressed in the leading article in which he outlined the paper's programme was that "the wounds of the present society can only be treated with social remedies, not with mere political sticking plasters," for "society at present corresponds with neither the reasonable aims nor the rightful desires of the vast majority." Even though the paper was not always able to relate political republicanism proportionately to the demand for social advance, it was perhaps of a higher standard and more noteworthy than any other such venture. The staff was largely drawn from earlier radical papers. Károly Mészáros wrote successive leading articles in a highly radical tone on the war and the urgent need to dethrone the Habsburgs. In later years he made no mention of these at all. In the very first issue Józsa Nyíri began an article in several parts in which he tried to win popularity for the police force which was being set up at the time. The radical pamphleteer Miklós Tölténobserved yi, who had previously tried to start a paper in Vienna, ran a column called "Budapest Mirror." János Horárik too wrote several leaders against "the policy of indecision" and "those of little faith" who thought the power of the Habsburgs invincible. On one occasion, on December 16, he demanded that all should burn their patents of nobility and that the Madarász brothers should set a good example by being the first to do so. On December 27 he argued for "religious equality" and emancipation of the Jews. Károly Kornis and József Kolmár featured in the paper several times. The latter on one occasion accused the Roman Catholic paper *Religio és Nevelés* (Religion and Education) of furthering clerical reaction; Imre Szabó and Antal Sujánszky then attempted a rejoinder on *Religio*'s behalf. Another contributor was József Barsi, the parish priest of Bicske who wrote for so many papers. One pseudonymous writer described constitutional monarchy as neither fish nor fowl ("an iron wheel made of wood"). Another took issue on December 9 with Dénes Pázmándy, the speaker of the National Assembly, for considering efforts to form a republic dangerous and premature and explained that France was paralysed because "the revolution has been transferred into the social sphere and men of property have been obliged by the activities of communism to ally with absolutism." As far as France was concerned, the *Jövő* article argued, "the problem is not communism but the illiberality" of wanting "to leave the great wounds of society unhealed." Communism, it said, was not strengthened by those who sought "to settle the rightful demands of the people" but by those who wanted to sustain the old régime at any price. Apart from the editor, the staff of *Kossuth Hírlapja* was notably represented on the pages of the *Jövő* by Dani Fábián. On December 18 the editor welcomed the Reformed Church minister Imre Révész (1816-81) as a new colleague. Révész, in an article entitled "The Power of Truth in the Struggles of Peoples," said that despite setbacks and obstacles, the advance of freedom could not ultimately be prevented. On December 22 Vilmos Atádi wrote "On the Magyarization of Names," saying that in the present time of crisis name changes too were "yardsticks of zeal" and objecting to the government's wanting to earn 3 forints from each application. In the same number Várkondi, under the title "Kingship and People's Liberty," declared war on the kings, while on the front page appeared poet Gyula Sárosi's translation of the "Song of the Polish Legion."

The *Jövő* took up a resolute position amid the dramatic circumstances of heightened warfare and crisis. All should prepare to defend the country, declared the unsigned leader in the very first number, demanding that once Hungary had won "all alien yokes" be "split asunder and Hungary's full independence" ensue. In the same issue Józsa Nyíri conceded that absolutism still had strong support in Europe and that "the bright days of March have changed into dreary, autumn weather," even in France. But he added, "We should be mistaken to consider that France's present policy . . . will last forever," for "a sizeable proportion of the people do not

favour the path being followed at present." He noted critically
that the "national indecisiveness" of the Hungarians had
contributed, along with the "treachery of the grocer-bour-
geoisie" and the "dissension in the democratic party," to the
fall of Vienna. According to an unsigned article in No. 2,
"Europe can have no other future than confederated republics based upon social democracy." In the same issue the
editors described themselves in a short announcement as "to
some extent socialists." The staff of the *Jövő* was noticeably dissatisfied with the National Defence Commission even
as a partial solution. It wanted dethronement, independence, a new unambiguous political leadership, and a "national governor with royal power" who it considered could
only be Kossuth. On December 5 an unsigned article headed
"Lajos Kossuth" declared that in the countries of Europe
"the events were bigger than the men everywhere except in
Hungary," where Kossuth stood at the head: "We believe
that Hungary's full independence can be safely won only
under the name, banner, and government of Kossuth." It
considered it immaterial whether the new government were
called a ministry or a commission. "Not only do we want
Lajos Kossuth to be the president of this government, we
want his policy to have full and total sway within it." With
the abdication of Ferdinand V, wrote Károly Mészáros on
December 7 the throne had in any case become vacant:
"Let us elect a governor and proclaim an independent Hungary. . . . Long live the Hungarian republic!" The same author
on December 9 argued against those who sought to confine
matters to "a narrow war of self-defence." Their idea was futile, he wrote, "because if the alliance of the greater peoples
of Europe such as the Germans, French, and Italians does
not beat absolutism and the rule of kings, the Hungarians
will share in the dire fall into slavery whatever they themselves may do." In the same number a correspondent from
the provinces included the sentence, "The traitors would
immediately be fewer if one or two of them were hanged,"
to which a footnote was attached: "It cannot be denied.
The printer."

József Madarász had already made one or two contributions, but at this point he began to play a more immediate
part in the work of the paper. Although the *Jövő* went be-

yond the radicalism of the nobles in several respects, the exponents of the latter were likewise dissatisfied with the present state of political leadership. It emerged that a part was also taken in the National Defence Commission by other forces opposed to the noble radicals in alliance with Kossuth. To balance these, József Madarász declared on December 9 that the present "half government, half defence commission" would not do; it had to be reorganized, starting from the premise that in revolutionary times one needed energetic rather than astute men. Continuing his remarks on December 11, Madarász put forward certain proposals for social reform as something of a gesture towards the staff of the *Jövő*. To relieve the misery of the people he proposed that day-labourers and farm servants be exempted from income tax; he also recommended that the state cease to pay or employ the civil servants of the old régime; and finally, discussing Táncsics's principle of equality, he said that progressive, "graded" personal taxation should be introduced. Although he could hardly be said to have grasped the essentials on this, the editors of the *Jövő* were prepared to single out Madarász and welcome him as a regular "working colleague." Then on December 15 Madarász made a call "To the National Defence Commission" to be energetic and investigate how many *táblabíró* had found their way into the ranks of the government commissioners: "Stick to the firm measures the resolution dictates."

On December 16 the paper published a letter from a reader, perhaps a civil servant, saying, "Right is on the side both of the press for pressing for a republic and of the government for not yet thrusting aside the monarchy and proclaiming a republic," since to do so would be needlessly divisive. On December 19 "Barnabás Borona" (Barnabas the Harrow) added a comment on this "double-dealing" stance. He said that the task of the press was on the one hand "to support the moves of the government that are intended to protect the country from its enemies without and within" and on the other "to make monarchy untenable, bring democratic ideas to maturity, and enlighten the people on the advantages of a republican government." The following day Miklós Töltényi, in an article entitled "Political Opinions," stated that continuance within "the sphere of legality" was nothing but a *táblabíró* illusion; it was futile to attach hope to refraining from proclaiming a republic, for either way the country's enemies would threaten them, although "we have nothing to fear from the Russian army outside its own country."

Understandably, growing attention was being paid to the perilous attack by Windischgrätz. On December 14 Horárik reassured readers that Artúr Görgey might be trusted precisely because he was young: "The armed forces and army command, born of revolution, as they are under our Hungarian Görgei," ensured that "for our enemies the ignominy of downfall is inescapable." On December 18 József Kolmár repeated that Hungary would win, for America had won its independence from the British oppressors because "the American people abided by a single thought and decision: to be free or die." "Patriots, to arms!" was the way the rousing appeal on the front page of the December 21 number began. To the news that "Perczel is joining forces with Görgei" the paper added a characteristic comment: "One might say our Görgei has won a curious little *Verstärkung*.... Kossuth is our right eye and he our right hand." The radical intelligentsia would seem to have identified far more closely with Görgey than with the radical nobleman Perczel. On December 22 "Barnabás Borona" reported on the meeting of the Egalitarian Society at which László Madarász resigned as chairman because of another, official assignment. His place was filled temporarily by his younger brother, and it was decided at the same time that permission would be sought to form a force of a thousand irregulars. An unsigned article on December 23 found it necessary to stress that the state had to further the good of the majority and "bring forward this main principle of pure socialism, particularly because, far from splitting the forces allied for the salvation of the country, it would lend new weight to the efforts of the people to save the country at all costs." On December 26 the paper published on its front page Kossuth's great appeal "To the Peoples of Hungary" to mobilize. Táncsics then wrote an interesting comment which expressed his desire to encourage a national conjunction of forces, despite a somewhat ironical title — "The Generosity of the Hungarian Aristocracy." The comment was on the bill on indemnification that László

Palóczy had introduced in the National Assembly on December 23. Of course, Táncsics did not consider indemnification necessary. As the studies submitted a couple of years previously for the competition advertised by Count Kázmér Batthyány had shown, the obligations to perform unpaid labour and contribute tithes were fundamentally detrimental to the landowners as well. "I say what accords with my own opinion and conviction: the peasants have amply served out and paid the compensation over eight hundred years." But, he went on, he had none the less set aside his personal opinion "with an enormous effort" and voted for the measure to assist the cause of internal agreement. From the front page of the December 28 number the sentences again almost cried out: "Life or death! . . . Let the whole population of the capital stand forth!" If they did not wish "to perform unpaid labour and pay tithes" again, "and be the only ones to provide the soldiers," they should arise against the murderous, marauding forces breaking in among them. An article by "Tátrai" declared, "It is impossible to defeat the people, who are conducting a guerrilla war." And the "Budapest Mirror" column captured for all time a memorable scene: "Guerrilla recruiting officers parade through our streets with red flags, to the sound of blaring music; the revolutionary hall is a recruiting station." Shortly afterwards, however, the editor Emil Ábrányi was on his way to Debrecen, where he had to prepare as a government commissioner for the transfer of the National Defence Commission, the ministries, and the National Assembly.

One last ephemeral attempt saw the light of day on December 29, 1848—a specimen number of yet another radical paper, *Forradalom*. This new "political and literary newspaper" had been advertised in *Marczius* on November 6 and was to have begun publication early in 1849, with Imre Hatvani as editor and Ignác Kövér as publisher. For the specimen number, Hatvani (who was later to play an unfortunate part in Hungarian-Romanian relations as the commander of a force of irregulars) was joined by a co-editor, the young literary translator and radical journalist Ernő Magos (alias Grosz). But the specimen number proved to be the last.

Bibliography

Madarász, *Emlékirataim*; Sándor Márki, *Emlékbeszéd Kővári László felett* (Commemorative Address for László Kővári) (Budapest, 1910); Tivadar Rédey, "Köztársasági publicisták 1848-ban" (Republican Journalists in 1848), *Vasárnapi Újság*, December 29, 1918; Klára-Mária Ney, *Ney Ferenc élete és munkássága, 1814-1889* (The Life and Work of Ferenc Ney, 1814-1889) (Budapest, 1943); Tordai, *János Horárik*; Sándor Lukácsy, "Herczeg Viktor: Egy elfelejtett 1848-as publicista" (Viktor Herczeg: A Forgotten Journalist of 1848), *Világosság* (Clarity), no. 3 (1964), pp. 188-90; Csaba Csorba, ed., *Mészáros Károly önéletrajza* (The Autobiography of Károly Mészáros) (Debrecen, 1974); György Spira, "Mészáros Károly önéletrajza előtt" (Considering the Autobiography of Károly Mészáros), *Századok*, 1977, pp. 587-96; Csaba Csorba, "Válasz Spira Györgynek" (Reply to György Spira), ibid., pp. 597-600; Tibor Frank, "Zerffi Gusztáv György, a történetíró" (György Gusztáv Zerffi the Historian), *Századok*, 1978, pp. 497-529.

11. The Munkások Újsága

The second new paper to emerge during the period of the revolution was the *Munkások Újsága*, which began publication on April 2, 1848, almost two weeks after *Marczius Tizenötödike*. Technically it bore still less resemblance than *Marczius* to such broadsheets as the *Pesti Hírlap* or, a little later, *Kossuth Hírlapja*, with their modern display and frequent appearance. Initially it came out only once a week, on Sunday mornings; from August 10 it appeared twice a week. For the seven months right up to September 24, the first series (Nos. 1-33) was presented as a sixteen-page booklet in octavo book format with an old-fashioned single-column make-up. Only after September 29 was it given the look of a periodical, with a quarto format in double columns. To mark the change, new numbering was begun, and it continued up to the twenty-sixth and last number at the end of the year. The fine typography, conspicuous column heads, and attractive layout, thanks to the work of the university press, that marked both the first seven issues (April 2-May 14) and later ones could not compensate for its meagre, even rudimentary character, which was due not least to lack of a financial basis.

Nevertheless, the *Munkások Újsága* was politically and historically significant as a popular political paper essentially different from all the earlier supplements that disseminated popular information and from such experiments in useful entertainment as the *Vasárnapi Újság* (which was in any case aimed more at artisans and the petty nobility). It also differed from the succession of popular papers founded in the months after the March revolution with the idea of using information and written explanation to assuage the discontent of the peasantry, reassure the public, and thwart any efforts towards further social change. This paper of Táncsics's was the only one to do the opposite—to represent the interests and aspirations of broad sections of the common people (principally but not exclusively the peasantry), champion their demands, air the problems left unresolved by the April laws, and set out to develop the achievements of the revolution, although it always urged its readers to be patient and confine themselves to legal methods. Thus it became the only popular paper that managed despite all the obstacles and hindrances facing it to elicit a substantial response from the common people of the villages and market towns. Moreover, Táncsics's paper differed markedly from the radical press in its social programme of completing the democratic development of 1848 and consistently eliminating the remnants of feudalism. Nor did it lag behind the radicals in its national demands and opposition to the Habsburgs; indeed, on occasion it outdid them (and from time to time displayed some naive hyperbole).

The *Munkások Újsága* was the sole Hungarian paper at the time to represent the true left wing, of which a fundamental, principal yardstick must be possession of a social programme beyond national, constitutional radicalism. If it sometimes appears meagre, primitive, and politically powerless by comparison with the other, opposing tendencies, let us not adorn the tale: the entire left wing at the time was just that.

Mihály Táncsics

The paper's publisher and editor, Mihály Táncsics (originally Stancsics, 1799-1884), came from an impoverished Transdanubian family of village serfs and throughout his strenuous life championed the peasantry's cause. By his own account his father was Croatian in origin and his mother Slovak, but he was brought up to be a Hungarian-speaker and an ardent Hungarian. He was successively a shepherd, farm-hand, weaver's apprentice, village artisan, and assistant teacher in small schools. He was almost an adult when he managed with great effort to struggle through the Latin secondary school. He lived as a poor man in squalid circumstances, but he learnt languages, read much and widely, from Rousseau to Cabet, and was a prolific, untiring, varied writer. There were some unusual, unsettled, and odd sides to his self-educated personality and curious career in life. But historically it is less his talents and their distortions that posterity has found so remarkable than the fact that the difficult social conditions from which he had managed to raise himself distorted his talents only to that degree and not in anything essential. Ervin Szabó described him as an "eccentric," yet "one of the most remarkable figures for Hungarian democracy." For decades "he was the only man to carry the cause of the whole people to its ultimate conclusions in principle and in person, and no importunity, prison, misery, or mockery . . . could persuade him to swerve from doing so for a moment." To avoid censorship he published his "citizen's catechism," the *Népkönyv* (People's Book), in Leipzig in 1846. The book, for which he was later imprisoned, made demands for "abolition without compensation" of feudal dues, full equitability of taxation, and universal suffrage, thus going far beyond what the reform opposition among the nobility at the time could call for. Nevertheless, Táncsics supported the reform opposition cause and the national aspirations. Before his imprisonment he went so far as to dedicate to Kossuth another work, *Nép szava isten szava* (The Word of the People is the Word of God), which was to be published only after the revolution, although in it he made a fairly determined attack on the nobility:

> We want redemption /from feudal dues, we want the/ abolition of the corvée and tithes without payment of compensation. . . . Some change must occur, to the right or to the left. This situation will end; either you noblemen or we peasants or both will put an end to it, for it has to end. We shall do what dire need and poverty oblige us to do. The stronger will triumph. This land is our land, for we till it, and if you do not wish to proclaim justice in the law, penury will oblige us to proclaim it ourselves.

It will be remembered that on March 15, 1848, the enthusiastic crowd freed Táncsics from prison and fêted him as a martyr to freedom of the press. For a while he was surrounded by recognition and praise from both the radicals and the new official organizations. On March 21 *Der Ungar* recommended that he edit a popular paper "like that of /the French priest Félicité/ Lamennais" to explain to the peasants "their obligation to keep order and peace". On April 13, Móric Szentkirályi chaired a discussion in Pest on how to "explain to the people the general meaning of the Twelve Points, in particular the origin of the philanthropy behind the laws made by the latest legislature," and eventually decided to found a popular paper, the later *Nép Barátja*; on the committee alongside Petőfi, Vörösmarty, and Nyáry was Táncsics. Szemere requested Táncsics to publish an explanation for the peasants of the new laws, "particularly those which concern the abolition of urbarial ties . . . for the use of former serfs with landholdings." Táncsics later related in his memoirs that this special, officially supported publication never appeared because he did not want to refrain, as Szemere wished him to do, from commenting on the other statutes as well. However, the *Munkások Újsága* in any case began to analyse these laws and in doing so cited Szemere's request. The differences between the government and Táncsics heightened only later when the *Munkások Újsága* began increasingly to voice the dissatisfactions emerging among the peasantry.

In his subsequent work *Életpályám* (My Career), Táncsics to some extent projected this later confrontation back to the earlier time:

> I had conjectured in advance, before the laws were proclaimed or passed, that much would be lacking from them and that what they contained would require a lot of explaining before uneducated men would fully grasp their entirety and understand them well, and so I began preparing to publish a weekly paper entitled the *Munkások Újsága*. I gave this paper of mine this title because the decisive aim I set myself in it was to explain to the less tutored multitude the things they had and would have to know. In the first issue I explained the Twelve Points, which had by then been distributed in every region of the country, and I printed six thousand copies. I myself bought the surplus copies beyond those required for the subscribers /eight hundred/ and distributed them free among the villagers up for the weekly market.

This is indeed what happened, but when one begins to read that first issue one also notices that Táncsics was not yet emphasizing what was lacking in the new laws, how they fell short of his earlier demands, or where they required further development as quickly as possible. Instead he welcomed them with comments that did not really go beyond the position of the radical or even the liberal press described earlier. Understandably, his head too had been turned by the historic developments, the enthusiasm and the expectation.

In the first number (dated April 2) a motto appeared after the name of the paper: "The government exists for the country, and so the nation may always dispose over it." (Six months later this was amended to read "The government and the king exist for country, and not the other way about, the country for the king, and so the nation may always dispose over it.") There followed, under the column heading "Hungary," material on domestic affairs that took up the larger part of the paper. After the first article, in which Táncsics thought it necessary to give specific reasons at rather inordinate length for having changed his name, came what was really the main section of the paper, entitled "Revolution," in which the achievements of March and the political struggles beforehand were analysed. "There are," he said, "no lords or peasants any more, there is no corvée, men are no longer beaten, we are all citizens and brothers with equal rights." He stressed that "the majority of the nobility too" had striven to alter the old situation in which "we peasant workers bore the country's burdens." In other words, the turn of events was the work of the nobility, against their adversaries, including of course Austria, which "considered our miserable situation useful." Having surveyed the Twelve Points, without making any critical observations on them, he went on to compare Hungary's area, population, and other attributes with those of some other European states, concluding that Hungary was quite large and powerful. Of course, Táncsics said, repeating an old desire of his, the king would have to come and live among them, since "the king exists for the country, not the country for the king," although he noted in connection with the Swiss Republic, "The happiness of a country depends not on whether it has a king or a president but on the kind of laws it has and whether they are good or bad." The next article ("Address") was about the use of the pronoun *kend* ("you," a variant familiar form confined almost exclusively to country people), to which Táncsics appears to have attached considerable symbolic importance. More interesting from the point of view of our initial question is the statement that beging "Patriots." Here Táncsics explained to his "fellow worker-citizens" that "our more educated brethren reckon that we still do not understand properly what freedom is." Although "some among us may think freedom lies in pillaging others and damaging others' property," such things "are done only by those so wretched and miserable that they cannot earn their bread by their own efforts." A "true worker" has no need of another's property, and so "from that we consider it despicable of anyone working freely nevertheless to complain of misery." Táncsics seems to have hoped that the new order would at last ensure the poor and the cottars an honest chance to work.

Absent from the first number was the column devoted to reports and correspondence from the provinces that was eventually to become so important, and this feature of the paper remained fairly insignificant for some time. The short foreign column (a mere ten to twenty lines) tended to consist of short comments on one or two selected items of news. In the first number, under the title "Italy," the paper adds to the news of Lombardy-Venice's secession from Austria, "It was certainly infuriating how the rulers, princes, and governments went over the heads of nations and countries as if they were abandoned wildernesses and the people in them grazing cattle." Finally, Táncsics told his readers that one could subscribe to the paper at the post office or through "our bookselling fellow citizen" Mihály Magyar of Pest, who had also provided security until the caution money prescribed could be deposited. In the second issue he added that booksellers Gusztáv Emich and Adolf Müller would also handle subscriptions. The subscription for the nine months of the year remaining was 2 silver forints in Budapest and 3 by post to the provinces. A single copy cost 8 krajcárs.

The tone was the same in the second issue (April 9). Táncsics announced that his *Népkönyv* and *Hunnia függetlensége* (Independence of Hunnia) were being issued in a new, cheap edition, and he quoted some quite long passages from the latter to the effect that Hungary had always been independent and that there was no bond whatever between it and Austria. He then continued his article on modes of address, in which, among other matters, he appealed to workers employed abroad to return home. The main article in the third issue (April 16) objected to Hungary's undertaking a proportional share of the state debt: "For, fellow worker-citizens, would we not be the least sensible people in the world if we took on the debt of another country, and of all countries, moreover, the one that has robbed us of all our fat and sucked our blood"? More importantly, he rejected the idea because the Austrians could no longer defeat the Hungarians, since "we former peasants and nobles have merged into one and become equal and thus strong." And the new, united nation was none the weaker if this equality, as Táncsics put it in an article of that title, meant only that "each of us has a perfectly equal right to a livelihood," although men differed otherwise in their wealth, etc. The paper went on to take issue with an otherwise well-intentioned pamphlet on the Twelve Points published by Frigyes Gömöry for arguing as if the liberation were ascribable to the mercy of the king, the Diet having abolished the corvée and tithes by his command. In fact, "the nobility abolished them voluntarily out of goodwill and love of justice." To the third issue Táncsics (exceptionally) attached a political supplement: a piece of writing covering two sheets by Lajos Keresztszeghy (Szabó) entitled "The Transformation of the Hungarian Land."

Unsurprisingly, the radical paper *Reform* gave a very appreciative report of the *Munkások Újsága* on April 15, as a paper that could favourably influence the people, allowing them to "experience" the liberty now won and "if necessary defend it." *Reform* wrote, "A man whose ardent patriotism, sense of justice, and frank words not long ago . . . landed him in jail is now openly and freely addressing his message to the people. . . . Since his release this fellow citizen of ours has launched a paper on behalf of the workers." The spirit of this paper was in *Reform*'s view a tribute to the man "who suffered as a martyr for the liberty of the people." Táncsics's newspaper

> does not depend on recommendation, since it recommends itself . . . it is written in such popular and simple language that all whom nature has blessed with common sense will understand it, and by inspiring and strengthening them it will sway the hearts and minds of the people. . . . The task of the working class now is to read the paper conscientiously and from it gain mental strength and power, that they may be worthy of the freedom attained and won and capable of enjoying it and in time of peril defending it.

Therefore, *Reform* continued, it would be a good idea if the towns and villages were to obtain large numbers of copies, distribute them free among the poor, and on holidays have them read aloud for the illiterate.

Táncsics for his part wrote appreciatively of the young radicals. In the very first issue he stressed the significant role played by Petőfi and his companions. Later he described them as "the nation's most ardent men," to whom "particular thanks should be given for the splendid change, salutary to all good citizens, which has taken place in this country." He ascribed the role the young members of intelligentsia were able to play partly to the fact that "many of the children of our peasant brethren," after acquiring higher education, had found a living in the capital. However, Táncsics and the young radicals did not stand, either then or later, for precisely the same things. They were of different generations—Táncsics was now approaching fifty, and despite his indefatigability this was a big difference. Most of all they held divergent views of society and only partly parallel aims. There were certain signs of all this from the outset. Táncsics wrote that even before he set up his paper, "in the very first days of freedom," he tried to publish an article on the new edition of *Népkönyv* and *Hunnia függetlensége*, for obvious reasons, in *Marczius*, but his manuscript "was mislaid at the editorial office, so they told me." After that, he went on, "I had no intention of submitting other articles" to the paper. Therefore it was in the *Pesti Divatlap* that he published a piece in which he advocated admitting the Jews as opposed to the German citizens into the militia. Disregarding these small details, however, Táncsics did not wish initially to presume either the radicals or the government ill-intentioned. When in the fourth issue (on April 23) he had to react to a host of complaints indicating that the post office was delivering his paper rather inadequately, he hastened to reassure his subscribers and urge them to be patient. He had, he said, been to the Buda postal administration personally so that the paper "might be distributed by post like other journals, particularly since this was not being done gratis." When he was told that the ministry would have to issue an instruction to this effect, he sent in an application, even though in principle he did not think it was necessary to do anything of the kind. Indeed, he paid a personal call on ministers Kossuth, Szemere, and Klauzál to

The *Munkások Újsága*

request "that they kindly give instructions to the post office about the possibility of distributing and accepting subscriptions for my paper, and this they promised, it being in any case their duty as a government to do so." Táncsics also expressed a hope that for his paper (since it only appeared once a week) some reduction would be made in the customary postal fee and urged readers to "distribute the paper as much as possible," for if it had two thousand subscribers, it would be possible to lower the price next year.

In the same number Táncsics, under the title "Acts," explained that the Diet had made only the urbarial lands the property of the former serfs. He warned against those who were stirring up the people to demand that the lands that had never been urbarial be distributed free as well:

> /Whoever/ lays his hands on these will have transgressed the law and as such deserve a harsh punishment, because property is sacred and violation of it forbidden under any pretext. . . . Many have said that there are deceivers going up and down the country trying to incite us former serfs against the former landlords. /But people/ do not know our goodwill /if/ they imagine of us that we will be roused against the very people who harkened so honourably to the call of the times, who showed a due sense of justice towards us in abolishing the corvée and tithes. . . . everywhere else this had to be obtained by bloodshed. /In this country, however,/ the upright nobleman did it voluntarily and voluntarily surrendered his privileges. /Certainly/ there may have been some among them who did not do so with a good grace, but nevertheless they did it, because the justice of public opinion obliged them to concede. Such people were exceptions, and taking the class of the nobility as a whole, it did everything it did out of the promptings of its soul, and for that it shall have its reward, a great reward.

On the other hand, this emphatically loyal statement about the generosity of the nobility, which the *Pesti Hírlap* classified as legend, was at once a prelude to and a conscious counterbalance for the first complaint brought by Táncsics's paper, about the "sad occurrence" in which a Torontál County landlord (or rather his bailiff) continued to demand the corvée from his former serfs and claimed for himself a piece of land that the peasants had reclaimed from flooding. To this Táncsics hastened to add, "I hereby call on all among you, my fellow workers, who know of any kind of abuse or illegality" to send a report of it, "and if it is well grounded I shall readily publish it at any time." This, he said, would "deter frail and evil men from crime" and would also be "a great and useful service to the government," whose "prime responsibility is to uphold the laws."

The Development of Táncsics's Programme

It was precisely because the *Munkások Újsága* became the spokesman for increasingly widespread peasant dissatisfaction around the country that it began to take a line that steadily diverged from that of the radical and liberal papers. With growing force the inadequacies (and in part the inadequate application) of the April 1848 legislation and the problems of feudal remnants, abuses, injustices from earlier partitioning of pasture, non-urbarial lands, contractual serfs, and landless cottars began to mount up, and in some places where there was no hope of a solution from above these were expressed in arbitrary actions by the peasants. One must say emphatically that Táncsics never by a single word encouraged arbitrary use of force instead of legal measures, nor could any sentence of his have been so construed by his readers. He urged them to be patient and to take their troubles to the tribunals prescribed, to the government and then to the National Assembly, staying within the bounds of legality. But by publicizing the complaints, embracing the peasants' cause, and advising and encouraging them, his paper became the vehicle for the interests of a wide range in society, particularly because the programme that eventually emerged from the various individual cases aimed at the complete abolition of the remnants of feudalism and the investigation of unjust enclosures of pasture and seizures of land, in other words, the further development of the 1848 reforms. Henceforward Táncsics increasingly saw the situation as he later described it in his autobiography: Whereas "in general it was said at this time that from now on we have equal rights and have merged into one great united people and nation," this (although not long before he himself had written something rather similar) "was a deceit, a piece of self-deception," because among other impositions the vineyard tithes and a number of usufructs remained in the possession of "the formerly privileged class." Therefore, he said, "I had the great task in my newspaper of battling against the maintenance of these." In the sixth issue of the *Munkások Újsága* on May 7 he wrote, "There is nothing more important now than to clear up the urbarial issues."

The paper in the mean time concerned itself with other problems as well, principally with the latest intrigues by Vienna and the former dignitaries. The writing in part was done by colleagues of Táncsics's. In the fifth issue (April 30), Lajos Kenézi, an assistant Lutheran minister from Gyula who later became a chaplain in the army, reported that the *Munkások Újsága* had a growing number of country subscribers, but people should try to obtain it in other places and if need be "let two or three people get together in company." He urged them to write to the paper as well, for "you too are free to write in this journal," and give their opinions, for "you too can make laws." In the same number Sándor Márton addressed an open letter to the students of Reformed Church colleges in Transylvania, for whom he ordered the *Magyar Gazda* and a year's subscription to the *Munkások Újsága*, recommending "diligent use of it." Also in that number Károly Hunyadi began an article in several parts headed "Freedom and the Law." Among his assertions was that "a republic is the most perfect of all forms of society to date, because it provides the broadest basis for justice." In the second part he called for the convening of the National Assembly with all speed, finding "no one entirely satisfied" with the April laws and judging that since the public interest demanded "that the National Assembly put others in the place of these laws," it was necessary to elect the kind of representatives "who can and will rectify matters radically." So decided a desire in this particular paper deserves noting even if the writer would seem to have been dissatisfied with the results so far on political and constitutional rather than social grounds. Here Táncsics wrote somewhat naively of the national minorities that apart from "a few beguilable and eccentric" young men, none among them showed "a mood of opposition" to the Hungarians apart from the German citizenry of the capital. He wrote on the affair of the demonstration against Lederer and of the problems of Budapest, giving it that name because "at the next parliament the two cities will merge into one city." He published the "appeal" of Reformed Church minister István Cserki to the youth, the physicians, and the electors to take good care whom they sent to the National Assembly, then a piece by Lajos Szeberényi against religious pilgrimages, a poem by the printer Lajos Dienes, and a "proposal" by engineer Samu Nagy about the University of Pest. He added a comment to the official communiqué in the *Pesti Hírlap* on press offences, enquiring rather scathingly whether the government had no more urgent business than to concern itself with such matters and whether the minister of justice seriously imagined "that the danger will derive from the press." But among all kinds of other matters the paper always returned to its main motif: remnants of feudalism, the battle against the injustices suffered by the peasantry, and the idea that the people could be expected to defend the country only if their social grievances were remedied. "Every sober man perceives," Táncsics wrote, for example, in the eighth issue on May 21, "that these two things—the militia and the corvée—would not go together. Anyone who is still obliged to do corvée is not a free citizen, will not take up arms, and will not join the militia."

But Táncsics included more than the peasantry in the category of "workers." He meant, to use today's phrase, "working people" and included those whom we see as forerunners of the working class. In the spring of 1848 these were already playing a certain part in the movement in Pest. Táncsics did not view them from afar, as he had himself been an artisan's apprentice. On his wanderings abroad in the economically more developed cities and centres of industry from Germany to London Táncsics felt at home among the Hungarian workers employed there. At his suggestion those in Paris had formed a "regular Hungarian society," although they had got together earlier still and ordered "Hungarian newspapers." It is not surprising, then, that Táncsics again espoused their interests. "My paper is published in the interest of the great class of workers," he wrote on May 7 in the sixth issue, "and so I know it is my duty to publish the petition which the bookprinting workers of Budapest have submitted to the ministry." And there indeed one can read the application made by the printers of Pest on April 30, 1848, in which their requests include a ten-hour working day, recognition of elected shop stewards, and above all higher wages, "because we workers provide the press proprietors with their entire profit." Later, when writing his autobiographical *Életpályám*, Táncsics no longer remembered all the details correctly and related that it was when he had given better wages to the printers in the little press he had bought that others had been encouraged and turned to him for backing and mediation with the minister:

> I spoke about their cause in the *Munkások Újsága*; my intervention in their interest was crowned with success, for Gábor Klauzál, the minister of industry and commerce, called the printers and their assistants together for a meeting which was held in the chamber of the city hall. Being present there too on behalf of the printing workers, I spoke in their favour, and as a result it was decided to improve their wages. . . . The wealthy press proprietors became my enemies, but the entire body of workers honoured me with the ceremonial title "father of the printing workers" out of gratitude.

In fact, the printers of Pest had gone into action after the printers of Pressburg, following the example of colleagues in Prague and Brno, had called upon them in a letter of April 23 to try and improve their own lot by demonstrating and establishing international connections. In spring 1848, a compositor's weekly wage with an eleven-hour working day was 6 silver forints at the university press and usually 7 at private presses, sums which were being eroded by inflation. The encouragement could hardly have come from Táncsics's press, since it began operating only later and did not produce its first product until May 21. Nevertheless, Táncsics did support the printers' movement, preparing calculations for them based on the budget of his own paper, helping them to express their applications in good Hungarian, and attending the talks which produced somewhat more favourable rates. The printers issued a statement of gratitude to Táncsics, among other things for having been "an honest friend of the people who cooperates wherever it is a matter of alleviating the sufferings of the proletariat." In the light of this it is hard to understand how Dezső Nemes a couple of decades ago could have considered that Táncsics "may have viewed the workers' movements benevolently, but he did so from outside, did not attempt to develop them," and gave no news of the majority of them because he was afraid of any independent political intervention by the workers, of public disturbance's spreading and spilling over to the village people as well. In fact there is no sign that Táncsics had any such fears. He supported the workers with the best will in the world, but he realized that under the circumstances their problems carried less weight than the peasantry's. Moreover, in an industrially backward Hungary just emerging from feudalism, the workers were still unorganized as a class. They could not intervene as an independent political force as their colleagues in Paris had done, and they cannot retrospectively be judged by the significance of later developments and labour movements. The curious logic by which accusations of failing to help the workers are made against the one editor who was prepared to support them in his paper betrays a dogmatic perception of history quite divorced from the reality of the time.

To demonstrate the breadth of Táncsics's concept of the "workers" and show that he did not intend his paper solely for the peasants, I shall quote a statement in the June 4 number:

> Some people have said this newspaper is purely for the villagers, in other words, the villagers who till the land, because some short-sighted people consider only farm workers as workers, but I understand by "workers" all who live by what they earn themselves, by the sweat of their brows, and so artisans, of course, form a notable part of the great class of workers. Also belonging to the class are those who create highly craftsmanlike, prodigious artefacts, those who are distinguished by the name "artist".

Táncsics bought his modest little press or, rather, galley press from István Dobrossy (1810-53), a Pest lawyer who had secretly printed Kölcsey's diary on it before the revolution. Dobrossy also concerned himself with translating literature and drama and made literary contributions to the *Társalkodó* and the *Pesti Divatlap*, defending Petőfi, for instance, in 1845. In 1843 he had published a book on shorthand, and he had prepared reports on the Diet proceedings for Kossuth. What is most important about him, however, is that he had voluntarily undertaken Táncsics's defence free of charge and then become a member of his paper's staff. Táncsics thought it would be cheaper to produce his paper and other works of his on his own press, with a staff of two compositors and a printer. It was in any case costing 37 silver forints 54 krajcárs to prepare three thousand copies of each issue of the *Munkások Újsága*. (In the first quarter three thousand was the regular print run, far more than the number of subscribers.) Very little remained after that of the money brought in by subscriptions. Táncsics sold no advertising—he only drew his readers' attention to his own works or those of persons who shared his principles. He had no capitalist to support him. The state subsidy and reduction in postal charges went only to his rival, the *Nép Barátja*. Judging from the repeated complaints, moreover, the problems with postal delivery continued.

At any rate, Táncsics prepared Nos. 8-15, from May 21 to July 9, on his own small press. In No. 8 he hopefully assured his readers that it would in future be possible to subscribe for 1 forint a quarter, but the undertaking did not go well. Later Táncsics complained that his assistants had cheated him, since he did not understand the printing trade, but the real problem was that, along with all proprietors of presses in Pest, he now had to pay a deposit of either 4,000 forints in ready money or mortgage property worth 8,000 forints in addition to the 5,000-forint caution money he already owed. This was more than he possessed. When the mayor of Pest, at the instigation of Szemere, warned him to pay the caution money, Táncsics was obliged to say that the two small houses he owned in the Józsefváros district of the capital were only worth 2,000 forints, "nor can I find a guarantor or one who would pay the sum in cash." But he noted that since his printing house consisted of only one press, he could print only his own works and paper on it, and having already assumed responsibility for these as editor and publisher he considered a deposit for the press superfluous. Whereupon Rottenbiller, the deputy mayor, went so far after the council meeting on June 14, 1848, as to seek new instructions from Szemere as to whether, since Táncsics "cannot supply the desired deposit either in cash . . . or in mortgage guarantees," his press should "really be closed or not." As Szemere stuck by the rule book, Táncsics was obliged to part with his galley press. Under the headline "Free Press," he wrote as follows in the June 25 issue of his paper: "I bought a press and on it I print this paper of mine entitled the

Munkások Újsága; I bought it in the hope that I would thereby be able to sell my paper more cheaply to my poor, penniless fellow citizens in the villages, and also in the hope that I might be able to gather the required deposit of 4,000 silver forints with the help of some good person or other, but I was wrong." He added he would not rest until the stupid press law on the basis of which the caution money was demanded of him had been "finally repealed." Beginning with No. 16, dated July 16, 1848, the paper was printed on Vazul Kozma's press.

Some radical papers made use of the affair of the Táncsics press in their attacks on the press law and the government. On July 29, *Reform* described as barbarous the proceedings against Táncsics, adding that in its opinion similar treatment would soon be meted out to other journalists without money; the government, which had one official (the *Közlöny*) and one semi-official (*Kossuth Hírlapja*) paper at its disposal, would find itself in a monopoly situation, for it would achieve a position in which "there will be no open control on the affairs of state" or, in other words, "the force that is one of the main guarantees of liberty will be paralysed." *Der Ungar* noted that the press had been taken from the very Táncsics whom the people of Pest had freed from prison at the time of the revolution and whose sole comfort would be that it was by legal means that he would starve as well, if it came to that.

Meanwhile some signs of the development of the *Munkások Újsága* could be seen in the steady growth in the number of its staff and of its correspondents, who ultimately numbered about fifty. They were principally drawn from the rank and file of the intelligentsia: schoolteachers, Protestant ministers, and lawyers were to be found among them, as were village mayors and "citizens" from all parts of the country. From Szeged came enthusiastic lines reporting that a lawyer by the name of Mihály Tóth, who himself "originated from the farm labouring class" and whom people had at one time wanted to put in prison as a demagogue, had been elected chief magistrate (No. 9). Dani Hamar (Dániel Hamary) attacked the monastic orders (No. 10). Dobrossy contributed a two-part article (Nos. 11 and 12) entitled "The Old and New System of Government" after the ideas of

Thomas Paine. Later Móric Tót, a frequent contributor, wrote on the issue of church property and the lawyer Imre Kocsiss on "The Just Ordering of Social Relations" (No. 15), while another lawyer, Károly Bulcsú, sent in some rousing verses. These men and others mentioned earlier were shortly joined, particularly towards the autumn, by a number of new ones: József Barsi, István Gyüszü, Pál Igaz, Dénes Kemeneczky, Mózes Lóki, Sándor Nagy, Imre Osgyán, Márton Pap, Dániel Szabó (a primary schoolteacher from Piskolt who was interested in state reform of schools), István Talabér, István Tóth (who sent a report on the parliamentary election in Putnok), Imre Tüzkű, and several obvious pseudonyms such as "Vas Borona" (Iron Harrow), "Kancsuka" (Knout), and "Vasvilla" (Pitchfork). We know from *Életpályám* that Imre Osváth, the Reformed Church minister of Kötegyán who provided refuge for Táncsics for a time after the defeat, was also among the contributors to the paper. Historians have wondered whether apart from the known writers this comparatively broad network of contributors was not partly a fiction—whether one should not seek Táncsics's authorship in some of the articles signed in other names. This question cannot really be resolved through stylistic analysis because Táncsics in any case reworded much of the correspondence he received. But one must consider it likely that the concrete complaints received from the villages described real events with real actors, even though Táncsics may have contributed to expressing them or perhaps prompted their writing. The paper's political significance, from the period of the elections and the first National Assembly onwards, was provided precisely by these letters and reports and by the conclusions and proposals Táncsics drew from them.

On June 4, in No. 10, Táncsics called for the right of all to vote without a property qualification and for the election of representatives who supported a Hungarian army, nationalization of church property, state salaries for teachers and Protestant ministers, abolition of the upper house, etc. In the same issue a correspondent from Bihar County complained that a local landlord wanted to take more than half the villagers' land on the grounds that it was held not as urbarial land but on a contractual basis: "We would not take away the land of the lords for the world, and we are accustomed to being patient, but we will not willingly let our land go either." Of course, Táncsics knew that the law called for the transfer to peasant ownership of only the urbarial lands, but for that very reason he said of all kinds of contractual lands in an article in the same issue entitled "An Urbarial Issue, Yet Not an Urbarial Issue," that the imminent National Assembly must consider as "one of its chief, indeed I am fully convinced . . . prime, obligations to abolish entirely all urbarial liabilities, because otherwise such lands will serve as a cause of eternal contention, whereas the country has no greater need than for peace and agreement." "Whoever now proposed that lands of this kind should remain in their situation so far," he continued, "would be proposing civil war and trampling upon equality." However, Táncsics swiftly reassured his "fellow citizens" that everything could now be arranged by legal means, "all that has remained will be arranged, all kinds of tithe and corvée will end." He added to this hope, in what was clearly a pious fraud, that "this would already have happened at the last Diet . . . but for the great haste, since the splendid events of March made the legislators hasten to disperse precipitately; in other words, what needs must happen was not omitted deliberately, it was just that the hon. estates of the realm forgot it." One can certainly not describe these words as an encouragement or incitement to lawlessness. Undoubtedly they were aimed at taking the achievements of the spring farther by legal means. Two weeks later, on June 18 in No. 12, Táncsics summarized his proposed legislation in sixteen points, among which universal suffrage as a consequence of equality, progressive taxation, and several less essential subjects could be found. The peasantry would have been most interested in the ninth, tenth, and eleventh points, which concerned full abolition of urbarial ties and the setting of the amount of compensation to be paid at not too high a level (in the country's interests), a revision of the earlier prejudicial partition of the pastures and arable, and the abolition of the nobles' usufructs and local monopolies. Táncsics demanded supervision of the partitioning precisely on the grounds of the oft-mentioned sanctity of property: "If property is declared to be sacred, the property of the community must be sacred too, and so communal pasture that it was improper to have occupied under the pretext of regulation or for some other purpose must be reoccupied; for there are indeed plenty of former serfs, and they have great need of this land." Táncsics held that the investigations should be carried out in each electoral constituency by elected tribunals of eleven members each, within two months in cases of compensation and three in cases of enclosure. This was not "incitement" but merely a proposal to be put before the National Assembly. But the landowners understood what an avalanche would be let loose by a retrospective revision of this kind. On June 10, in the thirteenth issue, there was a report from Bihar again of growing "unrest and dissatisfaction." Of this "one principal cause is that many of the noble lords still cannot abandon the inhuman behaviour they have used for so long against the poor former serfs." Another cause was "that the partitioning of pasture and the reallocations of the fields are not being conducted justly." A third was "that the men of property and wealth do hardly anything towards joining the militia. . . . But the dissatisfaction stems most of all from the retrograde way in which the urbarial issue is being arranged."

It was precisely the ever greater and more threatening peasant dissatisfaction that made the *Munkások Újsága*, as the mouthpiece or even the instigator of the complaints, appear increasingly dangerous to the landowners and their adherents, so much so that they became inclined to see Táncsics, who warned about the phenomenon, as responsible for its existence. The initially friendly or at least condescending attitude to Táncsics became one of suspicion and rage. The first signs of this change appeared in the feigned objectivity of a report in the June 24 number of the conservative *Budapesti Híradó*. "I know Táncsics is a man ready to do anything for his well-meaning, eager, oppressed fellow men, and I admire him for it," one reads in an article signed Tamás Bizony. "But as is often the case with characters of that kind, a deal of prejudice, one-sidedness, narrow-mindedness, and infatuation comes his way. Táncsics has not avoided this. . . . So it is hardly surprising if his counsels often do more harm than good." Luckily, the writer added, the Hungarian people were indolent and his agitation did not influence them much. Later the hatred became more open, coupled with an attempt to mock Táncsics's "eccentric" characteristics and hold him up to ridicule as a half-educated, half-crazy figure whose irresponsible agitation might yet make him dangerous. In fact Táncsics acted least like a self-taught eccentric and best displayed himself in his realistic, serious style as a discerning analyst of social matters when he was dealing in his paper with the concerns of the peasantry.

Táncsics was inclined to overestimate the influence of his writings somewhat, but later, in his memoirs, he rightly cut down to size the exaggerated estimates of the "members of the gentlemanly, educated class" that his paper had a circulation of ten to fifteen thousand and that he could therefore direct the masses at will. In fact, he wrote, the majority of the former serfs, living hard lives and brought up without the necessary education, "could not even read, and those who could did not read newspapers, they read devotional books, songbooks, and trashy stories; the number of my subscribers approached without exceeding nine hundred." Nevertheless, he went on, everything was tried against him from obstructing postal distribution to trumping up charges against his person, claiming for instance that through the rustic "you"-form *kend* he was trying to drag the people back into barbarism instead of educating them. Thus "considering my forlorn circumstances I marvelled not that the subscribers to the *Munkások Újsága* did not proliferate more but that their number rose as high as it did."

In the fourteenth issue on July 2 one can read no fewer than nine letters of complaint from the villages, including several in Somogy County (Nagybajom, Csákány, and others), and alongside them a strongly worded protest from Táncsics to the ministers that the post office was now clearly hindering the distribution of the paper for political reasons: "The postmaster at Siklós is turning the worker-citizens away by saying he has no time at present to accept subscriptions; at that the poor working men go away. But putting their work aside a second time they go down to him, and he again puts them off, saying they should come another time. Provocation! At Kecskemét the postmaster will in no wise accept a subscription to my paper because, he says, he has had instructions not to." In the same issue Táncsics also denounced the "duplicity and villainy" by which "the dear man of the people, Petőfi, was defeated" in the elections. As we know, Táncsics became the member for the Siklós constituency with a programme that can be said to have left him isolated even within the small group of the radicals, who had come off so badly in the elections. On the afternoon of that same day, July 2, after the first formal session of the National Assembly, there was a meeting in the county hall at the instigation of Pál Nyáry of a group of representatives who were prepared to support the cause of dealing with the remnants of feudalism. The meeting agreed that the vineyard tithe should be abolished, with compensation to be paid. Táncsics went farther than this, waiving tactical considerations to propose that only the landowners with incomes under 3,000 forints a year should receive compensation and again urging a retrospective enquiry into unjust enclosures. As the *Munkások Újsága* reported afterwards on July 16 (No. 15), his words were received even by the opposition with great displeasure. Táncsics argued that "pastures and fields which have been enclosed in the last twenty years by the former landowners or their bailiffs by force, by military power, by threats, by intimidation, by deceit, and under any pretext whatever shall be handed back, and local judges shall be elected by the whole people in every constituency to accomplish this." As Táncsics wrote later in his memoirs, the reason for the outcry was that "the greater part of the representatives consisted of landowners," and from them derived the "undeserved, unjust accusation" that he had attacked "the sanctity of property."

A week later, on July 19, Táncsics summarized his desires in the sixteenth issue of the *Munkások Újsága* under the title "My Political Creed": the achievements of March had to be taken farther, full equality of rights ensured, all remnants of feudal relations abolished, indemnification paid only to landowners whose income stemmed solely from tithes and corvée, and illegally appropriated pastures and fields returned to the peasants. The estates of rebels and those who had turned against the national cause had to be divided among the soldiers and cottars, church property sold, priests given state salaries, and the press law repealed. On July 23 the semi-official *Pesther Zeitung* attacked Táncsics by saying that people thought he was mad and laughed at him. On the same day, in No. 17 of his paper, Táncsics saw fit to return to his proposal of July 2, which had aroused so much opposition, and to the charge that he had thereby attacked the sanctity of property: "If the sanctity of property is injured when the state takes away without compensation the tithe gathered by the rich man," he wrote, "the sanctity of property is injured in the same manner" when the state taxes the poor instead of the rich. "Before that, the legislators of the noble class had *unjustly* taken away the property of the non-noble poor and used it to discharge their own share of the taxes; now the whole people (in the interest of the poorer people in particular) may *justly* desire to compensate by denying compensation for tithes. In that there is no injury done to the sanctity of property, simply reciprocation and nothing else." This explanation was if possible less capable still of reassuring and winning over the legislators, of whom a majority were "of the noble class" into the bargain, whether they belonged to the "moderate" majority or the "radical" minority, for one could by the same logic cast doubt on the legitimacy of any kind of compensation. Certainly one can establish from his argument that Táncsics's ideas were beginning to lean towards abolition of serfdom without compensation, a Hungarian version of the French revolutionary solution.

Essentially this issue isolated Táncsics in the National Assembly, even though on the national issue he formed a common front with the radicals as a member of the opposition to the Batthyány government. In the eighteenth issue of the *Munkások Újsága* (July 30) he sharply censured the ministry for being too tractable towards Vienna and not daring to act energetically and argued that "things are not going well" in the National Assembly. Quoting Kossuth's memorable statement, he added that "one should not have desired to suppress so violently . . . the minority" to which "I too have the good fortune to belong." Finally he reported how each member had voted on aid for the Austrian side in Italy. "The question was, shall we or shall we not assist Austria against the Italians? We who said that the way Austria concluded the war it had unjustly declared on the Italians was not our affair were a mere thirty-six in number."

Among the members of the "dwarf minority" it is worth

noting particularly the relations between Táncsics and the Madarász brothers. According to *Életpályám* József Madarász had once been Táncsics's "schoolfellow and friend," with whom he had spent a couple of days in Cece in 1847 during his period in hiding, although not even at that time did the two see eye to eye on everything. Indeed, Madarász tried to talk him out of some of his objectives, with less success, no doubt, than he subsequently claimed in his memoirs. However, the *Munkások Újsága* on May 7 recommended to its readers' attention the paper *Nép-elem*, which would be appearing in July. It belonged to the Madarász brothers, who "have been proving ever since the time they were active at the county level in public affairs that they wish to continue devoting all their talents to struggling in the interest of the people." Although, as we have seen, the Madarász brothers were not prepared to support the peasant demands at the time of the elections, they took their places alongside Táncsics in the Egalitarian Society which was formed after preliminary negotiations on July 23. Táncsics later recalled in his memoirs that he could not agree with the members on everything: "Our society should have been purely democratic, but it did not become so completely." Expecting the members "to act fully in accordance with the principle of equality," he was disappointed, and in hardly six months László Madarász himself was introducing measures against the *Munkások Újsága*. In the nineteenth issue on August 6 Táncsics also wrote quite cordially about the radical paper *Marczius*, saying that although "it is a very scathing paper" and "many are angry with it," "it is well loved except by those who have been thoroughly chastised by it." Károly Bulcsú's poem "Don't Harm the Italians" in the same issue accorded as much with the desires of the radicals as did Móric Tót's assertion that the Batthyány government was incapable of saving the country. Another common factor was that Táncsics shared the radical desire to prise Kossuth away from the government and win him for the opposition:

> Kossuth is struggling within himself. He can no longer agree with the other ministers. Whenever he is roused it emerges that he feels himself to be one of us, the minority, but then once again, when they are arguing in the cabinet meeting his fellow ministers vote him down, because the majority decides. Citizen-minister, we ask you for the honour of

> your country, respond, do not hesitate, resign, stand at the head of the small minority which in your passion you wanted to trample down, admit your error, and your action will be crowned with praise.

This, let us remember, was all in accordance with the radical line, and Táncsics approvingly reflected on what the *Kossuth Hírlapja* had written on August 2 about abolishing the feudal remnants: "I am glad indeed that other papers have begun to profess what we have long considered of the utmost importance." However, the essential difference at once shows up clearly, again in the August 6 number, in an article entitled "Budapest Scene" written by the lawyer Imre Kocsiss about Ede Keczkés's speech in Széchenyi Park and his subsequent arrest. *Marczius*, it will be recalled, spoke of incitement and provocation and endorsed the action of the police, but the *Munkások Újsága* gave a somewhat different version of the story (saying that in a recruiting speech against the Serbs Keczkés had attacked the National Assembly for negligence and described the mighty and the rich as traitors) and protested his arrest: "There is something amiss with the country, for those who a few months ago were making stronger protests than this against the injustices of the previous government now disregard the legal system and summarily lock up without any investigation a patriot who has always been freedom's man for his overzealous patriotism." Táncsics himself added in a note that this was really not a good policy. In the same August 6 issue Táncsics found it necessary to reflect on the charge of insanity levelled at him by his foes on the grounds that in the National Assembly he wore a plain linen coat like a militiaman and rather than delivering a speech simply spoke his mind. In fact the fabrication could be attributed to the fact that he "spoke in the interest" of the peasants. Still in the same number, Móric Tót spurned the attack by the *Budapesti Hírmondó*'s successor, the *Figyelmező*, since this paper "is always scribbling against Hungarian freedom, independence, and felicity."

In the twentieth issue early in August Táncsics announced that the paper would in future appear twice a week, on Sundays and Thursdays, while the subscription rate would remain the same. No. 21 on August 13 contained a critical letter from one Antal Vas, whom some scholars have sought to identify with a rival, Gereben Vas. The letter said that the paper contained not only platitudes but falsehoods, with the result that there was something between the lines "which cannot be read since it has not been written, but only explained in this way, and that is what causes amazement"; it was thus, said Vas, that rumours spread that Táncsics was a troublemaker. This of course gave Táncsics the opportunity to reply in a sober fashion: "I do not want to be believed blindly, nor do I want to be praised; I simply say what I consider is just, for the benefit of the whole people. . . . Bear in mind what you feel is good in many utterances. If anyone should express his ideas on why he feels one thing is good and another bad, or rather what he feels is good and what bad, send it in right away to my paper; I shall be glad to print it so that once we have enlightened one another the better argument may win."

In the same issue of August 13 he published a remarkably long letter from his Siklós constituents by which he sought to draw the attention of the National Assembly to the tense public mood and the urgency of action. "You have promised us a great deal," they told Táncsics,

> but of that great deal, as we can see from your own paper, nothing will yet come. For a month the representatives (if only those seated there were but people's representatives!) have been together, yet they have done nothing but require us to provide soldiers and pay up; so far they have said nothing about why we should provide soldiers and why we should pay up. People say the country is in danger. But of whose country it is, of what we who are Hungary's peoples may call our own, of what emoluments we may share in, of these things you seem to avoid speaking. Our impression is that you mean to deceive us again—let us defend the country, and then we shall see. . . . The Croatians in Zagreb did not act like this; they first made promises to the people. . . . We cannot believe in you until we see ourselves insured.

Among the conditions whose insurance would make the people ready to go to war, they said, were abolition without any compensation of all dues to landlords and rights of usufruct and the return of the lands taken away from the peasantry. "For more than a hundred years we have been paying fodder tax for the army that we did not owe, in addition to the corvée and tithe; this already comes to 700 million, and are we now to pay more millions for redemption? Instead, let the Muscovites come and eradicate the tyrant lords of Hungary."

The latter, the correspondents complained, "even say that all the land in Hungary is theirs, earned by arms and bloodshed. So what is ours? Did not we, or our forefathers, serve as soldiers at the same time"? In the last paragraph the warning is repeated: "Enact these things without fail at this National Assembly, because we will not be pacified until you do an we will not gladly shed our blood for nothing. It in Kossuth's words the *insurrectio* (nobles' obligation to provide military service) is now extended to all, let property likewise be extended, lest the Hungarian aristocracy dig its own grave."

From *Életpályám* we know that about sixty villages in the Siklós constituency alone sent Táncsics complaints about enclosures unjustly made in the past. But this particular text at this particular time must have been intended by Táncsics as tactical support for the bill on reallocating the pastures that he put before the National Assembly, publishing the text in the twenty-third issue of the *Munkások Újsága* on August 20. It would provide for the repeal of the first clause of Act 10 of 1848, which declared that earlier partitionings and agreements were inviolable: "In all communities where the enclosure of the pastures clearly and undeniably took place by compulsion and force to the detriment of the inhabitants of the village there shall take place a new division and a just allocation." Táncsics now wanted to extend the revision right back to Maria Theresa's Urbarial Patent of 1767. But again from *Életpályám* we know that his proposal was hooted down and derided by the representatives, who shouted that this was no time for something like this, when the country had to be saved.

Suppression of the Paper

The Munkások Újsága on August 31 (No. 26) gave a list of the representatives who had voted against placing the whole army on a Hungarian footing forthwith. Departing from its usual style, it published a woodcut cartoon in the text after an original in the *Charivari* showing a "Hungarian soldier standing on a German footing" wearing a braided Hungarian jacket above knee breeches and slippers. Right after this Táncsics placed the title "Press Trial" and reported a rumour: "It is whispered in the city that they want to institute a press trial against me."

The grain of truth in the news was that on August 26 the Ministry of Justice had indeed instructed the Pest city court, or its prosecutor, to institute proceedings against the *Munkások Újsága*. In addition, the palatine on August 29 had sent notice to Deák, the minister of justice, enclosing copies of two papers in which passages marked, he said, "contain things which can hardly be reconciled with freedom of the press within the meaning of the press law." Would Deák say "whether these have been reported to you as press offences and whether any consequent legal procedures and measures for punishment have been taken"? One of the articles objected to was in *Marczius* and the other in the August 24 issue (No. 24) of the *Munkások Újsága*. In the latter Móric Tót had included in his piece entitled "Good God, What Have We Come To?" the following: "Money is for the defence of the country, and the poor men are handing over their last fillérs, but the great lords, the palatine, and the king are giving nothing." Deák passed the notice on to his state secretary, who reported that the *Marczius* article objected to could not be considered a press offence but that proceedings would be initiated against the *Munkások Újsága* "through a censure by legal process." But the matter was removed from the agenda by the great turn of events and the departure of the palatine. On the file containing the draft reply was inscribed, "Dispatch of this letter was omitted due to the changes that intervened, and it is to be placed in the archives."

But a wider and more dangerous action against Táncsics's paper was initiated from outside the government. On September 4 Zemplén County sent a petition to Szemere against the *Munkások Újsága* as a paper "very dangerous in these present times of transformation and one that tramples damagingly upon property." Such "pernicious, infectious weeds," it said, had to be uprooted before it was too late, and since it would take too long to do so through a regular press trial, the interior minister should "waive this" and summarily close down this paper which "endangers domestic peace and the security of property." Nor would the "common people" then remain without a press, it continued, as "they may read the *Nép Barátja* for their edification." The instigator of the action by Zemplén County was one of its representatives in the National Assembly, Gábor Kazinczy. As a young man he had been a progressive reformer, a leading opposition figure, and a friend of Vörösmarty's and Wesselényi's, a man indeed to whom Petőfi in the autumn of 1847 had written a poetic letter as to a colleague and kindred spirit. But of Táncsics and his paper Kazinczy was to prove one of the most resolute adversaries.

"In view of the urgency of the matter," Zemplén County did not even wait for the interior minister to act. Its petition was circulated to the other counties, causing an avalanche of similar petitions from counties all over the country, from Vas and Sopron through Szepes and Bereg right over to Transylvania. Each county referred to Zemplén's example, and most called with similar energy for steps to be taken against the *Munkások Újsága*. At most they differed only on the means for banning it. Bereg, for instance, rejected Zemplén's suggestion as running counter to freedom of the press, but even Bereg requested Szemere "to deign to act in accordance with the current laws if the editor of this paper should exhibit his overly zealous and liberal tendencies more zealously still and thereby cause a breach of the peace." On September 14 Fejér County dealt with the issue at a general meeting: "To our knowledge people do not subscribe much to this weed (*lap*) or, more precisely, burdock (*lapu*) of a paper, but some have to our knowledge come, for sometimes a few are sent here and there gratis to taint the air in our county; to this end we shall write to the ministry about banning the said paper." In this way the joint action by quite a large proportion of the landed nobility began to grow, making use of the traditional machinery of the county system, and to elicit a reaction, partly through the official *Közlöny*, which published the county resolutions one by one as official documents.

The nobility at the time were so much a force to be reckoned with that Kossuth, as we know, saw a need to place the issue of indemnification on the National Assembly agenda on September 13, during the crisis, so that the nobility might "feel inclined to defend the country in this great peril," although two days later, on the 15th, a decision was reached to abolish the weightiest remnant of feudalism, the vineyard tithe.

Táncsics, for his part, on September 14 in the thirtieth

issue of his paper, encouraged his followers to defend the country, lay aside their grievances, and bring about a national rallying of domestic forces and strongly objected to the charge that the *Munkások Újsága* was responsible for the peasants' not hastening to join the militia. He had always said, he wrote, that the men of property had to show the way, but now that the country was in danger the old injuries had to be set aside. He warned his followers against the enemy, which was encouraging them "by deceit and incitement" to "seize this, that, and the other from the former landlords." Of course, "all you want is to receive back legally and justly what you have long possessed but . . . had taken from you by guile and force." At this juncture, however, he went on,

> I ask you in the name of God and of our sacred homeland to leave off . . . the kind of wrangles many are making, saying "I will not do this or this until that and that have been seen to." My friends, all things cannot be done at once, but one day they will be done one by one; first of all we must put our enemy, our common enemy to shame and make him a laughing-stock, because if we, former landlords and former serfs, now quarrel amongst ourselves, it will be grist for the mill of our common enemy, and he is indeed striving hard by every means to encourage that very thing.

In the next number, on September 17, Táncsics under the title "Who Is a Good Patriot"? rebuffed an attack by the *Nemzeti Újság*: "Watch out for yourself, you who were the pliable, stunted, blind tool of Metternich's wicked policy aimed at ruining this country. Did you think that had been forgotten"? But at the same time he had to reflect on the charge of *Kossuth Hírlapja* that he wanted "to foist absurd principles on the people." "We believe," wrote Táncsics, "that you do not like the principle and notion of equality, that to you it is an absurdity."

The *Munkások Újsága* of September 24 (No. 33) gave first place to a call to the Hungarian people, issued by the Egalitarian Society and bearing Petőfi's signature, to take up arms against Jelačić. From the correspondents' reports it emerged that Táncsics's followers, clergymen and teachers, were the ones who were calling on the people to defend the country, although not always with success. In a report dated September 6, the Reformed Church minister of Szaporca said that he had "gathered the people together to persuade them to take up arms," but they had roundly declared that they would not fight against Jelačić and the king and the lords wanted to deceive them and had done nothing in the National Assembly on their behalf. All this, coupled with Táncsics's open sympathy with the country's cause, served as evidence that the peasant reluctance resulted from spontaneous dissatisfaction rather than being aroused by the *Munkások Újsága*. In the same issue encouragement for Táncsics came from "Vas Borona," who wished that "the bolt of truth" would strike down those who called Táncsics mad.

The same pattern of defence, counter-attack, and national rallying marked the first number of the paper in its new, larger quarto format, dated September 29. In Táncsics's interest it repeated what had been said at the very beginning: that the Hungarian nobility had behaved very worthily in voluntarily sharing its rights with the people, "which the nobility has not done of its own free will anywhere in any other country." It reassured its readers: "Give the lie by your deeds to those who say you have not understood, have not been enthusiastic about the country, and have not hastened to defend it." Then it immediately turned to Gábor Kazinczy by name and to the action begun against the paper. "One could hardly credit how much my fellow representative Gábor Kazinczy has against the *Munkások Újsága*. Since the sessions began he has picked a quarrel with me on several occasions for ruining the people with my paper; on the other hand, he has announced what luck it is that in the area he represents, in other words, Zemplén County, no one reads it, and he wishes that it were not read anywhere."

The succession of protests from the counties had not ended when the Ministry of the Interior passed the matter over on September 25 to the Ministry of Justice, saying that "this seditious and dangerous paper from the point of view of public morale and the safety of property" had to be banned, particularly because as far as they knew "measures had also been taken earlier by the Ministry of Justice under the press laws because of false statements in earlier issues." It listed the articles in the *Munkások Újsága* that were "an incitement to disorderliness and immoderation." But amid the current crisis the Ministry of Justice preferred not to hurry its response, and Táncsics was able to continue his work undisturbed for the time being. On October 3 (No. 2) he declared that a governor should be elected from among the ministers, since the king had proved himself a lawbreaker; full powers should be invested in someone like Kossuth, "who enjoys the full confidence of the people." Táncsics had offprints made of the article and distributed them personally. Between October 13 and November 3 (Nos. 5, 6, and 11) he included a long article in four parts entitled "Republic," arguing that a king was detrimental even if he chanced personally to be better than other kings and that the desires of free citizens could only be fulfilled by a republic, which offered Hungary the only means of taking its place among the great nations of Europe. In the October 13 number one finds the second and last illustration published in the *Munkások Újsága*, an unsigned lithograph with the title "The Pragmatic Sanction." It showed a scroll and a crown thrown onto a burning torch, and Táncsics attached the following explanation: "The Pragmatic Sanction and the crown are cast into the fire; that is all. These two must be burned in this way or otherwise destroyed or we shall never find happiness." He added that the crown should at the very least be locked away in a museum so that it would never again be placed on the head of an Austrian emperor. The Hungarian people needed a governor, in the person of Kossuth.

However, in No. 6 on October 17, at the very time of peasant demonstrations at Mezőberény and Orosháza in Békés County, he again published, under the signature "Workers," a strongly worded letter clearly stating the authors did not intend the peasant demands to be set aside once and for all. The writers of the letter were receiving one call to arms after another, but "if Kossuth himself were to come to us with his eloquence, it is certain that he would hardly be able to recruit as many among us as in Cegléd, Kőrös, or Kecskemét. At this you will say we are insensitive and bad patriots. We recognize that we are so." Were the people, they went on, who had not even counted as a nation, as Hungarian, now to be expected to defend the country against Vienna, the Croatians, and the Serbs? At least the estates of the traitors to the country might have been divided among them:

> So should we spill our blood that those who are the real betrayers of their country . . . if with God's help we clear the country of the enemy and there is peace, that those fine fellows will wing their way home and be able to say, "But that was mine . . . it remains mine henceforward. . . ." Do you see why we feel no enthusiasm for the uprising and for your appeals so far? We shall indeed rise up, not to your call but because we really cannot allow the Hungarian race to be wiped out; but if God allows our cause to be brought to a fortunate conclusion, then we shall settle accounts in Kossuth's fashion.

This last observation may have been a kind of reference to a phrase Kossuth used in an appeal to the Hungarian soldiers: First we have to win, "and then we shall settle accounts with the traitors." Táncsics and his adherents cherished visible hopes of Kossuth in their struggle with the reluctant elements of the nobility and in defending themselves against Kazinczy's charge.

On October 31 (No. 10) a Veszprém correspondent expressed the class struggle between noble and peasant in very sharp terms. If the several million cottars would not take up arms, he wrote, the country would be lost, but the poor were asking why they should defend the lands of the "patentees" (owners of patents of nobility) and where they were going to get the land they needed to support their families. "These are the kinds of questions we shall put afterwards, patentees! Tremble, you delvers into darkness, may the day of justice come"! The formerly privileged hated Táncsics too, the writer continued: "They hate and loathe you in the villages controlled by the nobility; they would like to imprison you again and then hang you: they say you stir the peasants up against the patentees because you are a peasant yourself."

Meanwhile Táncsics sought to encourage peasant correspondents from a wider sphere than before, with such success that the correspondence columns began to grow into the paper's principal feature:

> I well know that among my village brethren, particularly among the farm labourers and poorer artisans, there are one or two in every community who are more ardent in the cause of the country and the village than the others; they would like to rebuke the abuses, errors, and crimes they notice around them because they sense that this is the duty of all men; they would like to speak up for truth or all their innocently suffering fellow men, but they do not know how to do so or dare not commit themselves in writing because they think it requires some great scholar-

> ship for a man to write to a newspaper. . . . One who dares not enter the water will never learn to swim, and so let anyone who wants to inform the newspaper editor of some notable matter in the community do so bravely. All you have to do is to set down the matter itself, the bare truth, in a few lines and you will scarcely notice how you get the knack of writing in practice.

This encouragement and one might say experiment coupled with methodological advice in expanding the network of local, peasant correspondents was something quite new in the history of Hungary, but at the same time it expanded and reinforced the chorus of peasant demands and invited conflict with the radical and non-radical nobles who had come together in the new leadership. In the "Announcements" columns of *Kossuth Hírlapja* on November 10 even Táncsics's erstwhile friend, the commoner and enlightener of the people János Horárik, thought the time ripe to attack him for what Horárik considered an incriminating article: "You are a leader of the people, and that is a rare good fortune. But the role involves a grave responsibility not to corrupt the people, stir them up by bad example, or corrupt them by improper advice, because in that case a curse be on your head and a curse be on your ashes too"!

In the mean time the Ministry of Justice at last took up the matter of the submissions made against the *Munkások Újsága* by the counties. State Secretary Kálmán Ghyczy himself wrote in his report dated November 24 that "several press offences have been committed in the past and more recently" by the *Munkások Újsága,* but he considered that under the present circumstances any press trial could end in a very dubious result, and since this was a sensitive political matter he requested instructions from the National Defence Commission:

> I do not believe it timely to institute or pursue press trials at all, and so I do not at present consider that the desire of the aforementioned counties can be complied with, there being in any case no place for banning newspapers by political measures. Since according to the ministerial regulation governing the trial of press offences not only the jurors but also the trial judges and prosecutors are elected in local government areas without any government influence at all, there is no more independent jury in Europe than Hungary's, and so one cannot, particularly at this moment, in any way predict the results of any proceedings that might be instituted.

From this request it emerges that no report had arrived at the ministry from the persons concerned on "the result of proceedings taken" previously against the *Munkások Újsága*; "nor in more recent times were circumstances such that further moves might have been made in this matter by the ministry." From this it is clear that the terms of the 1848 press law, which were so heavily criticized, did after all prevent any arbitrary, forcible action by the government if they were adhered to as strictly as they were by the temperate, cautious liberal nobleman Ghyczy. In fact Kossuth endorsed Ghyczy's opinion that it was needless to arouse a political stir, particularly if the result were so doubtful. On the file can be read this decision: "The Commission shares the view of the state secretary for judicial affairs."

Thus Táncsics had won time again. On November 28 (No. 17) he addressed a call to the workers of the Pest armaments factory. He stressed the great importance of their work and the fact that they merited the same acknowledgement as those who fought on the battlefield. At the same time he urged them to lay their grievances aside for the duration of the struggle. "If you do not provide weapons /the soldiers/ cannot win. My friends, forget the indignities and unpleasantnesses hitherto, for you know that various kinds of intrigues have gone on in the army as well, but our heroic brothers have not lost heart because of them." But Táncsics did not confine himself to fine words. On December 5 he summed up under the title "Proposals" what ought to be done to mobilize the country's defence and put first on the list that the wages of the arms factory workers should be raised along with the pay of the troops. He then repeated the most important tasks in order to win over the peasantry: the legislature should declare that "all kind of local monopoly rights /*regalia*/ belong to the whole community and the usufructs from them shall be devoted to the community's expenses; all contractual services shall cease forever without compensation." Turning to the legislators "in the name of God and our country," he urged them not to "pinch pennies when it is a matter of establishing our country's greatness and our nation's exaltation."

In his memoirs Táncsics related how he tried to solve permanently the increasingly urgent problem of the caution money for the paper, which he thought had been solved by the guarantee from the bookseller Mihály Magyar. He hastily entered into an agreement with the printers László Lukács and Co., who took over the printing of the *Munkások Újsága* on December 1, whereby the latter undertook to put down the deposit and pay all the expenses for 1849 for one-third of the subscription income. Táncsics advertised in *Marczius* on November 27 and *Kossuth Hírlapja* on December 3 that the paper, secured in this way, would in 1849 appear three times a week, in quarto format, covering three half-sheets, the subscription costing 2 forints 24 krajcárs for half a year. Clearly he counted on the *Munkások Újsága*'s strengthening and expanding in the coming year.

Even in his subsequent autobiography one can sense the astonishment as he wrote how not long afterwards, on December 14, Kossuth attacked him in the House of Representatives, unmistakably if not by name. Speaking on the events around Kassa, the assault by Count Franz Schlick and J. M. Hurbán, and the issue of indemnification, he said, according to the official report.

> All conflicts of interest must now end, and anyone who is a patriot must join in the task of saving the country; I declare as a consequence that it is a disservice to the country, and if I were a suspicious man I would suspect alliance with the camarilla, but I do not wish to suspect anyone, but rather, I say it is a disservice to the country for any individual citizen or any of the various classes of the people to occasion conflicts of interest. (General approval.) This is all *querelle domestique* which can be resolved afterwards; now the country must be defended! Anyone who urges others against the nobility, the aristocracy or anyone else is an enemy of his country, or to say the least, does not know what he is doing! (That's right!) For we now need strength, and to stir up the people with paltry matters of pasture or anything does nothing for the people but detract from the strength which is needed for the task of saving the country.

According to Táncsics, when Kossuth alluded to the pasturage question a number of deputies began shouting Táncsics's name. "I was astounded," he wrote, "how Kossuth could have strayed onto that at that particular time; I thought one of my fellow opposition deputies might have set him against me just before his speech," since the issue of pasture had been mentioned a while back, right at the beginning of the National Assembly. It is of course likely that by mentioning pasture Kossuth merely wanted to bring home that he now considered all these questions secondary and that on the subject of stirring up the people the stress was on "anything." In Ervin Szabó's view Kossuth's censure was provoked by Táncsics's proposals of December 5, quoted already. But if one seeks an immediate cause, one could presume that Kossuth had in his hand at that time the statement by Antal Hunkár, government commissioner for Veszprém County, which he had sent him, as chairman of the National Defence Commission, on December 3 in connection with Táncsics. According to the report, somebody had shouted to people coming out of church in Balatonfőkajár that there would be no peace in the country until the lords had been exterminated. A few days later the people had threatened to assault the district administrator, who was recruiting for the army. Hunkár had immediately hauled four of them before a summary court, but they had defended themselves by saying they had taken the remarks about the lords from Táncsics's paper. On these grounds Hunkár judged the paper dangerous in that it "rouses and leads into discontent" the very masses "upon which we can best rely now," thus playing into the hands of the camarilla. Therefore, he argued that "in some good way a barrier had to be erected" against the *Munkások Újsága*.

Let us set aside the fact that Hunkár demanded action against the paper not by quoting from actual writings in it but by citing its (supposed) influence. The essence was that the rage of the nobles against Táncsics now found its opportunity, grounds, or pretext to take action against the *Munkások Újsága*, effectively and, one can add, at a government level. In No. 23 on December 19 Táncsics was still confidently writing, "There is great power in us, in the millions; this will all be yours if only you know how to handle it"! With equal confidence he published the greetings of a correspondent from Ács: "God bless Mihály Táncsics, the God of the people called you to this walk of life, and may you have good fortune in it. The guilty alone fear the pages of the free press as the devil fears incense; only the tyrant fears the enlightenment of the people." But in fact the scale had tipped. When the *Munkások Újsága* attacked the idle, card-playing representatives and their neglect of their duties in the twenty-fourth issue on December 22, the edition was seized. Táncsics at any rate wrote after the event in his autobiography, "For that they denounced me to Kossuth and confiscated that number of my paper, contending that I spoke as if I were supporting a proclamation issued by Ferdinand, emperor and king. Kossuth summoned me and told me to my face that if I were not Táncsics he would deliver me into the hands of the law."

Although Táncsics put his memoirs to paper some time after the event, there is little reason to suppose that he would be mistaken in his record of so critical an occurrence as a personal interview of this kind with Kossuth himself. However, from another source we know of another (or yet another) discussion of this kind. When Hunkár's report came before the members of the National Defence Commission, they wanted in ther initial anger to publish it in the *Közlöny* and brand Táncsics's activity as damaging. Kossuth would not allow this and instead passed the report on in the Commission's name to László Madarász, who headed the police bureau, saying that he should "summon Táncsics to him and convey to him that this is damaging activity, adding that on the next such occasion the government will indict him as an agitator who obstructs the defence of freedom and the country's independence in the interest of the camarilla." From the endorsement on the fair copy of the file it emerges that on December 26 Táncsics was indeed summoned: "Táncsics being here and recognizing the ill effects of his past deeds, will not give cause for anything of the kind in the future." (Signed) "Madarász."

The two warnings, one from the celebrated Kossuth and the other from Táncsics's former radical comrade-in-arms Madarász, only threatened Táncsics personally in the future, if the behaviour objected to were repeated, and still did not formally hinder the continuation of the paper. The hindrance, however, came from another direction. In the last but one issue of the *Munkások Újsága* (No. 25) on December 26, 1848, Táncsics included a fairly ironical article entitled "Long Live Freedom of the Press and Gréfl, the Pest Judge." From the article it emerges that the judge had fined him 500 silver forints for failing to deposit the caution money for his paper with the city authorities and obliged him on pain of further punishment to publish the verdict. In obeying this instruction Táncsics indignantly commented that they were making him publish something like this at a time when the imperial army had invaded the country and there were other, more important matters to report to the people. Then he added sarcastically that he nevertheless "owed thanks" to the Pest judge, for he might, he had been informed, have received a jail sentence of up to a year on top of the fine, all because he had expressed his convictions to readers in the paper. But the Pest city authorities, having imposed the penalty, had immediately made arrangements for the paper to be banned, so that in fact the final number should not have been allowed to appear. The National Defence Commission informed the city that although it did not wish to interfere with the move to ban the paper, the appearance of the twenty-sixth and final number of the *Munkások Újsága* should not be prevented. Looking back later on the closure of his paper, Táncsics did not allude to the city of Pest as the executive body, instead recording, "The *Munkások Újsága* was banned at the end of the year by László Madarász."

Even in the last issue Táncsics wrote that he would find room in 1849 for a number of articles not so far published. "Next year, if possible, we shall do more."

It was not possible. The career of the *Munkások Újsága* had ended, and editing the paper was to be the main count against Táncsics when a sentence of death was passed on him *in contumaciam* by the imperial military courts. The fact that Táncsics too followed the government and legislature to Debrecen on the eve of the New Year and that a number of other papers closed of their own accord at this juncture has tended to obscure the other fact that the *Munkások Újsága* was closed by the Hungarian government just before Windischgrätz entered the capital. The sadly dissonant final note, farewell or justification, came in a gross attack on the "mad" Táncsics by Gereben Vas in *Kossuth Hírlapja* on December 28. He had, Vas asserted, either wittingly or out of obstinacy played into the hands of reaction. He was responsible for the people's failure to rush to the country's defence. On the subject of private property he had explained to the people that "thine is mine." He had agitated against the lords. He had behaved with freedom of the press like a monkey with a razor setting about shaving the cat. If he were to ponder coolly what he had written in the paper he would stop beating his breast and beat his head against the wall: "Táncsics, you /kend/ are mad indeed."

And that ended the story of the only paper in 1848 that was truly left-wing in the social sense.

Bibliography

Mihály Táncsics, *Életpálya vagy emlékiratok* (Career or Memoirs) (Pest, 1873); István Iványi, "Zemplén megye körlevele Táncsics Mihály ellen" (The Zemplén County Circular against Mihály Táncsics), *Figyelő* 19 (1885): 394-95; Mihály Révész, "A magyar szocialista előidőkből: A Munkások Újsága" (The Early Times of Hungarian Socialism: The *Workers' News*), *Szocializmus*, no. 5 (1908), pp. 204-18; Mihály Táncsics, *Életpályám* (My Career), ed. László Szeremlei (Kolozsvár, 1943); György Bölöni, *Hallja kend Táncsics* (Harken to Táncsics) (Budapest, 1946); András Babics, "Táncsics Mihály követté jelölése az 1848/49. évi országgyűlésre" (Mihály Táncsics's Nomination for Representative to the National Assembly of 1848-49), in *Dunántúli Tudományos Gyűjtemény* (Transdanubian Scientific Collection), vol. 1 (Pécs, 1947); Gyula Mérei, *Munkásmozgalmak 1848-49-ben* (Workers' Movements in 1848-49) (Budapest, 1947); Mihály Révész, *Táncsics Mihály és kora, 1799-1857* (Mihály Táncsics and His Age, 1799-1857), vols. 1 and 2 (Budapest, 1948); Győző Ember, "Magyar parasztmozgalmak 1848-ban" (Hungarian Peasant Movements in 1848), in *Forradalom és szabadságharc*, pp. 189-265; Dezső Nemes, "A munkásság az 1848-49-es forradalomban" (The Workers in the 1848-49 Revolution), in *Forradalom és szabadságharc*, pp. 267-314; Mihály Táncsics, *Életpályám* (My Career), ed. János Czibor (Budapest, 1949); Piroska D. Szemző, "Táncsics Mihály 48-as Lapja, a *Munkások Újsága*" (Mihály Táncsics's Paper in '48: The *Workers' News*), *It*, 1952, pp. 481-509; Béla Sarlós, "A pesti munkásság forradalmi harca és programja 1848-ban" (The Revolutionary Struggle and Programme of the Pest Workers in 1848), *Századok*, 1955, pp. 78-96; Tibor Erényi and Gábor G. Kemény, "Revendications ouvrières et presse progressiste 1848-1849", in *La Presse ouvrière, 1819-1850* (Paris, 1966), pp. 299-312; Ilona Illés, *Munkások Újsága (1848), Forradalom (1849), Arany Trombita (1869): Repertórium* (The *Workers' News* /1848/, *Revolution* /1849/, and *Golden Trumpet* /1869/: Index) (Budapest, 1973); György Spira, "1848 nagyhete Pesten" (Holy Week, 1848, in Pest), *Századok*, 1974, pp. 323-69.

12. Government Papers

For a long time the Batthyány government, which had itself emerged from the revolution and managed the affairs of the new constitutional monarchy, had no publication of its own whatever. By and large arguments were being put forward from the right by the conservative press in Pressburg and from the left by the radical press in Pest until mid-April. Then, as we have seen, the interior minister, Bertalan Szemere, asked the liberal *Pesti Hírlap*, whose line was closest to the government's, at least to publish the official decrees in a separate section, for unless this were done the new state apparatus could scarcely function. János Pálffy remarked in his memoirs that the government "should have established a powerful organ of the press, which had started to become powerful." No attempt was made by the government to do anything of the kind. Several people commented that deep down Batthyány despised journalists and believed that opinions should be left to develop freely without guidance. On the other hand, when he found the abuse from *Marczius Tizenötödike* too much to put up with, he is supposed to have toyed for a while with the idea of taking Gábor Kazinczy's advice and combatting the radical press with a mouthpiece of his own, an "Anti-*Marczius*" of some kind that Albert Pákh, who was receiving medical treatment abroad at the time, would have been summoned home to edit. Nothing came of it, but in the mean time the "official" section of the *Pesti Hírlap* could clearly be considered only a temporary, emergency solution. Szemere swiftly issued an invitation to subscribe to a projected official gazette, announcing in the name of the government that "all its proceedings belong before the tribunal of public scrutiny" and "a need therefore arises for a journalistic organ that can keep it in constant touch with the nation." As early as April 26, the *Pesti Hírlap* reported that Szemere had asked József Bajza to "prepare a plan for the official *Közlöny*." Bajza had already attracted considerable literary and political attention in the age of reform, for instance, as a leading light on the *Athenaeum*, and later (in 1847) as editor of the opposition publication the *Ellenőr*, which was compiled abroad. The invitation signified that at this stage Szemere was still thinking of launching a government political paper, not a mere repository for decrees. Bajza did in fact prepare a plan, with the help of Ferenc Toldy. The "official" part of the paper was to have contained decrees and official announcements and the "unofficial" part other communications. These would have included "justifications of the measures taken by the government or individual ministers," "assessments, treatments of public affairs," and reports on parliamentary and other domestic affairs and on foreign affairs. Bajza too was unwilling to forego political debate in the paper. In terms of French equivalents, his paper would have been both a *Moniteur* and a *Journal des Débats* explaining government policy and striving to gain it acceptance; in Austrian terms it would have played the part of an *Österreichischer Beobachter* as well as a *Wiener Zeitung*. The plan came to nothing, less because Bajza eventually declined the task and a couple of weeks later accepted instead the editorship of *Kossuth Hírlapja*, which obviously suited him far better, than the reverse—neither Bajza nor Gábor Kazinczy, who was asked subsequently, wanted to undertake the official paper because under the circumstances the project could only be accomplished in a less exacting form. Eventually the editorship went to a thirty-five-year-old Transylvanian born in Szászváros (Drastie), Adolf Gyurmán (1813-69), who had studied law, become a journalist on the staff of the *Hazai és Külföldi Tudósítások* and *Jelenkor*, served as foreign editor of the *Pesti Hírlap*, and written a radical pamphlet. Because he burned his diaries and correspondence before he died and no biography of him came to be written, one can only outline how his political opinions developed from 1848, when he was close to radicalism, up to 1867, when he became a firm believer in the Compromise. Szinnyei described him as "one of the most authoritative Hungarian political commentators," crediting him with encyclopedic knowledge. In 1849 he was appointed a ministerial counsellor. After the defeat he followed Kossuth first to Turkey and then in 1851 to America. There he wrote articles and briefly edited a paper in German, but by then he had incurred Kossuth's displeasure. He cropped up again in 1854 in London, making a living by giving language lessons and writing occasionally for the *Times*. On returning home in 1863, he spent two years as foreign editor of the *Pesti Napló* (Pest Diary) and finally became a staff member of the *Budapesti Közlöny* (Budapest Gazette). Gyurmán was a liberal democrat but, to continue quoting Szinnyei, "a foe of all fancies and exaggerated ideas." Lajos Szeberényi, who in 1849 worked with Gyurmán on the *Közlöny*, described him as "a middle-aged man of quick wits, nimble mind, and swift pen" whose "wit was coupled with whimsy." He would flounce into the office in the afternoon, "fret and fume, vent his rage in curses," and then "a few minutes later become jovial again and give rein to his sparkling sense of humour."

The Közlöny

By the second half of May 1848, when Gyurmán rushed to get the paper started and assemble a staff for it, the earlier conception of it had changed. No longer to be a state-supported venture of one of the private publishers, the *Közlöny* came into being expressly as a state publication produced, like other official printed matter, on the university press in Buda Castle under the professional guidance of overseer Lipót Krüner. Krüner's staff and the editor were employees of the Ministry of the Interior, in other words, civil servants paid by the state. Gyurmán, who received a salary of 2,000 forints, had five assistant editors, mostly members of the intelligentsia who were political adherents and personal acquaintances of Szemere's. One was Károly Berecz (1821-1901), twenty-seven years old at the time, the son of a landowner who was town clerk of Rimaszombat (Rimavská Sobota). During the Diet of 1843-44 he had been the youth spokesman when a torchlight musical procession had been held in Szemere's honour. The twenty-three-year-old poet József Lévay (1825-1918), in contrast, came from a poverty-stricken noble family from Borsod County. At the last feudal Diet he had been *iuratus* to Szemere. The other assistant editors, who in the ministry were ranked as junior clerks, were the thirty-three-year-old László Kelmenfy, who had begun life in Nagyvárad and become a journalist and playwright in Pest-Buda, István Tóth, and Károly Kiripolszky. As proofreaders one finds the names of Gyula Jakabffy, Dániel Somlyai, and János Rizdorfer and as distributors those of János Szabó and György Büky, while preparation of parliamentary reports fell to István Friebeisz and Pál Jáncsovics. This was the staff with which the *Közlöny* began publication on June 8, 1848, as a broadsheet daily in folio format. It continued to appear regularly till the very end of the war of independence, following the seat of government across the country.

The first and most important section of the *Közlöny* published the decrees. Previously the counties and cities had received these from the government authorities as separate publications, and at first they found it strange to have to leaf through the official paper looking for them. To these were added other announcements of an official nature. The second section contained reports of domestic affairs, which were supposed to be, if not "official," then "historically accurate." At the end of May Szemere sent a circular to county *vicecomites* and city mayors ordering them to appoint municipal correspondents for the paper, but this news-gathering apparatus was slow to develop. By mid-summer there were still only seventy-nine correspondents, most of them men long concerned with local affairs. Obviously the official county correspondents represented the interests of the county nobility, although their political complexions varied. The editors of the *Közlöny* collated these texts and toned down what seemed too conservative or too radical in them so as to accord with government policy. Nevertheless, there were instances of protest by the opposing party in one county or another and demands for correction. As far as possible the editor refrained from encouraging debates of this kind, because, as he wrote on July 18, "We do not consider there is time or place for journalistic squabbles in these grave times and because we do not feel at all inclined to turn the *Közlöny* into an arena for passions." Reports in the *Közlöny* were usually blander than similar dispatches in other papers, although there was fairly regular reporting of events. By and large the paper came down against the conservatives, but the peasant movements were censured too. Stenographers were used for the parliamentary reports, which were detailed and if possible included all the speeches delivered, so that the paper had to be increased in length to accommodate them. It was suggested that the *Közlöny*'s coverage might serve as the official record of the proceedings, but for that purpose the text was not invariably faultless.

The foreign pages varied in extent but often went into a fair amount of detail, particularly on events in other countries of the Habsburg Monarchy, Germany, and France. Formerly a foreign editor himself, Gyurmán did the work efficiently but as a rule confined himself to translating or paraphrasing the foreign news without comment, betraying only in his news selection a sympathy with movements for liberty everywhere. No official statements on foreign policy could be found in the paper, for the members of the government, from Batthyány through Széchenyi to Kossuth or Szemere, differed to varying degrees on international relations.

The function of the *Közlöny* was important in the administration of the state and even in the war effort, but Éva V. Windisch has rightly pointed out that it was notable for "an aloofness from the task of political guidance and an absence of articles shedding light on the government's policy at home and abroad." There was an absence of the "assessments" and "justifications" of ministerial measures that had featured in Bajza's plan. Clearly this was because political opinions within the government soon diverged to an extent that precluded the official government paper from advancing a detailed political programme. Only a paper that confined itself to publishing decrees could act as a common denominator; otherwise it risked heightening the disagreements between ministers. At least in the early months before the autumn crisis the *Közlöny* was largely a vehicle for the government's administrative communications, and political discussion with any content and value was eliminated as far as possible. A half-measure of this kind was dictated by political circumstances, even though that very limitation prevented the paper from achieving what was expected of it and one minister, Kossuth, concluded that it was necessary for him to establish a separate political newspaper of his own. "The official paper," Defence Minister Lázár Mészáros wrote later in his memoirs, "was as boring as could be, perhaps even more boring than the *Wiener Zeitung*. The ministry would have liked to have established a more appetizing paper that expressed public opinion, but it did not succeed, and so the *Oppositió*s and the *Marcziu*ses could boldly continue their charivari."

The *Közlöny* took shape under the guidance of Szemere, who as interior minister was largely able to keep it in his own hands. He informed local authorities of the paper's establishment in a circular: "Since the government will render its decrees public in the *Közlöny* and they will take effect upon appearing therein, ordering of the same is declared compulsory . . . for every local authority, county, district, and royal city." Depending on population, circumstances, and postal conditions, smaller communities might order the paper collectively or as a district instead of individually.

In effect a subscription to the *Közlöny* was compulsory for local authorities, counties, cities, towns, and Hungarian-speaking villages. However, to continue quoting Szemere's instructions, "where the villages are not Hungarian-speaking, the paper itself will not be sent; on the one hand the local authorities will make sure that the official decrees are distributed in its area in translation, and on the other they will be sent, at least in extract, in papers in other languages already in existence or due to appear as a result of my measures and instructions."

Szemere's efforts to this end will be covered in a later chapter, but the issue itself is worth noting. As we shall see in the case of the *Nép Barátja*, the government was prepared to publish, in other languages spoken in the country, papers designed to calm the peasantry, but it was seemingly not prepared to do the same on a higher level in the case of its official paper, as if that would have amounted to the collective recognition of the national minorities that we know it shrank from giving. In the case of German-speakers, there was partial compensation from April onwards, when the *Pesther Zeitung* began publishing decrees under the column head "Offizielle Rubrik". But Kismarton (Eisenstadt), for instance, complained on July 27 that the *Közlöny* was not fulfilling its purpose for the town's German-speaking population and requested the interior minister to appoint a German paper "which will enjoy to the highest degree official authority and authenticity and so be fully suited to the purpose desired." The government kept speakers of Slovak, Serbian, Romanian, and other languages even less well informed. On July 4 the town of Bazin (Pezinok) requested that the decrees at least should be sent in German and Slovak translation. Turóc and Liptó Counties asked for translation in Slovak and Vas County in Croatian and Wendish (Slovenian). This the Ministry of the Interior (and the government) refused to undertake, passing the job of translating decrees on to the counties and cities. In so multilingual a country as Hungary at the time, this would hardly have sufficed to keep the minorities informed under normal conditions of peace and was less adequate still in a period of revolution and growing political, social, and national tensions. Julián Chownitz, who edited the radical German-language paper *Opposition*, was quite right in looking back on the history of the Hungarian revolution (in *Geschichte der ungarischen Revolution in den Jahren 1848 und 1849* /Stuttgart, 1849/) to fault the government for not having published an official paper in German, Slovak, Romanian, and so on, to further its own success. In this way, he wrote, the minorities had been left uninformed on what the government was doing. Indeed, the inadequacies and errors of the government's policy towards the national minorities are painfully apparent in such omissions, by which it effectively abstained from employing a major political means of convincing and informing people.

During these months the *Közlöny* had three to four thousand subscribers. Some two hundred other copies were distributed free to ministries and to other papers, and the total print run was forty-five hundred. A subscription till the end of the year cost 7 forints delivered in the capital and 8 forints by post in the provinces. At Szemere's request, Klauzál, the minister of commercial affairs, exempted public authorities from paying the registration and postal fees, and so private subscribers were paying more for the paper. Nor was it only the other papers that the post office delivered belatedly and inefficiently (for political reasons, those concerned suspected); judging from the many complaints from the provinces, the same fate befell the official paper. Moreover, many communities would receive the decrees late in any case where the post came only twice a week. Zala County, for instance, suggested that the decrees might be publicized by having the clergy read them out in church on Sundays and feast days before or after the service or having the parish clerk do so before the entrance to the church. Behind a protest from Zemplén County there was a clash with the noble, feudal traditions of the counties. The authorities there wrote on June 2, before the *Közlöny* had been launched, objecting to the government's communicating its decrees directly to the villages and not through the county authorities. "The people," they claimed, lacked "the intelligence, the participation in public affairs, and the desire . . . to make the effort to read or take note" of the decrees, and so they would not put them into practice either. Moreover (and this was the essential point), the counties' powers would be infringed "if our villages were to receive the decrees of the government directly, from a source other than the county," and the practice would concurrently "loosen the tie and end the relation which exists between the overall county authority and the villages from the administrative point of view, a relation which should be sustained, not loosened, particularly in the present times of danger." Zemplén considered it proper for the *Közlöny* to be sent to the *vicecomes* and magistrates, who would arrange matters in relation to the villages.

The *Radical Lap* objected that the *Közlöny*, along with the *Pesti Hírlap* and the *Pesther Zeitung*, was monopolizing publication of official statements, thus gaining an unfair advantage. Did the minister of the interior "consider as a monopoly the decrees which given certain conditions and fees might be divided out"? Of course the minister denied this rather curious charge. According to *Marczius* on June 13 it was unlikely that the *Közlöny* would "express the foreign policy of the ministry" (i.e., the government), but it would be disloyalty on the government's part to allow the *Közlöny* to compete with other papers by using the resources of power and the budget: "The official paper can only be considered as an official record that simply and clearly expresses in writing the state of the country." During the summer the *Közlöny* branched out into war dispatches and news, in which it naturally presented the government's actions in a favourable light. On July 26 *Marczius* reacted sharply—"The public should not go wild about the *Közlöny*, for the official paper is just like the *Wiener Zeitung*, in which the Austrians were constantly beating the Italians"—but had in the end to retreat nevertheless.

The September crisis and the formation of the National Defence Commission brought some change in the character of the *Közlöny*. On the one hand, there was a growth in the number of correspondents as the village clerks and the soldiers sent in their lines of patriotic enthusiasm; on the other, Gyurmán attempted to rectify the want of interest through the columns of foreign news. On October 2 the paper sharply attacked the new, anti-Hungarian editor of the *Allgemeine Österreichische Zeitung* and on October 10 criticized the *Wiener Zeitung*, "every number" of which "is full of the most odious and unprincipled aspersions on our affairs." On October 11 it condemned the policy of the camarilla and on the next day described the "splendid events" of the latest revolution in Vienna. On October 24, discussing the October 16 and 17 ordinances of Ferdinand V, it conspicuously opposed the policy of the Habsburgs, declaring, "The ruling house is the camarilla's captive," "The time for the final battle is nigh," and "The military might of absolutism has declared war in the name of the king on the peoples, on liberty, and on human and civil rights." On November 3 Gyurmán went farther still, writing that the camarilla was trying to keep foreign newspapers out of Hungary to prevent the Hungarians from learning of the great battles taking place abroad, in which peoples were rising in rebellion against despots and defeating them. "These struggles," he added, "can end in only one way: the princes will dig a grave for the peoples and fall into it themselves." The moral was that the Hungarian people had to struggle as the other peoples of Europe were. However, as a piece of anti-dynastic, anti-monarchical writing that went beyond the policy of the National Defence Commission, this statement was considered too strong by the Ministry of the Interior, which called the editor of the *Közlöny* to order: "Since we currently live under monarchical forms of government, the official government should not publish anything that wholly conflicts with the forms of government that pertain." The ministry went so far as to note that "for some time the *Közlöny*, particularly in its foreign section, has been taking a stance that departs both from the sober attitude expected of an official paper and from the forms under which we live. Wherefore the editor is warned that henceforth he should bar similar articles from the government's official paper." For some time after that, more decided expressions of political opinion vanished again from the *Közlöny*, and as foreign news scarcely came its way any more and the domestic reports grew fewer, it published little of note except the many orders of a military nature.

Meanwhile there had been some staff changes, and some problems of financial management had arisen. János Szabó had resigned as publisher at the end of July, and Gyurmán had done his job as well until a new publisher, Györyg Büky, was found. Of the assistant editors, Kiripolszky and Berecz left at the end of October. To replace the latter, one of the proofreaders, Jakabffy, was promoted at Gyurmán's suggestion, while a lawyer called József Máday took Jakabffy's place. From October the paper also had a correspondent "accredited to the National Defence Commission." The other assistant editorship was filled by Károly Karlsay, but he resigned in December.

Since more documentary evidence has survived on the *Közlöny* than on other papers, proportionally more is known of its managerial problems. It emerges that the paper's office was lax about distribution and kept its books in a disorderly fashion. After several reminders, all the Ministry of the Interior managed to obtain were some questionable accounts at the end of November. Gyurmán protested that he had no time for such tasks, for which a separate cashier should have been employed. The ministry set up a committee of investigation which concluded that "the account books have not been kept in accordance with the regulations." The Ministry of Finance then sent the assistant auditor János Appell to put matters to rights. It was discovered that although the paper had by then over four thousand subscribers, the majority of the subscription fees had never been received. Since September the ministry had been paying for the printing direct, and the editor was quite unable to account for a total of 1,139 forints. Gyurmán may not have been much more disorganized than other editors, but this being a state concern he had to do battle with stern, meticulous ministerial controllers, reared on Austrian bureaucracy. Once Gyurmán had made good the missing money, he probably received some backing from Szemere or Kossuth. In the future he was relieved of doing the accounts and a cashier, József Gamel, was appointed. Not least, the purpose of the exercise was for the paper to fulfil its function to a higher standard, in a more active way, and with fewer printing errors. The National Defence Commission also warned the university press to take more care, as worn, blurred type was common in the paper. The only incurable problems were with postal distribution, and since there was a war, these became worse still. "I cannot omit to mention," Gyurmán wrote to the Ministry of the Interior, "that on the basis of five months' experience and the countless complaints made to me I can boldly say that there may well be no other example in the whole civilized world of the disorganization to be found in our post office, and not even the official organ of the government is safe from the system practised by the post office in the case of newspapers." On December 27 *Marczius* commented sarcastically that although Fót was only two hours' walk from Pest the *Közlöny* often arrived there eleven days late; yet this "will surprise no one, since every community that receives the *Közlöny* is totally convinced of the official thoroughly republican, instantaneous precision of the paper's deeply respected editor."

Little change was yet promised in the programme outlined in the paper on November 30, when a call was made for the renewal of subscriptions: "In outward appearance, content, and extent, the paper will remain as it has been. Its chief task will be to place swiftly before the public the official decrees and actions of the government and inform its readers of the true state of affairs through trustworthy domestic and foreign reports." Since the National Defence Commission could not be described as politically united either, the *Közlöny* still had to refrain from taking a clear position, although its role and significance grew with the outbreak of the war of independence when it became the only medium through which the country and the army could keep in touch with the measures the government was taking. Indeed, from December the government arranged for every infantry battalion to receive three copies of the *Közlöny* and every cavalry battalion two. During December Kossuth managed to concentrate major matters in his own hands and deal with them through the presidential office, circumscribing the authority of the National Defence Commission's members. At the same time he took over political direction of the official paper, for Szemere had received new duties as a government commissioner in Upper Hungary. The *Közlöny* struck a new note when it published Kossuth's call concerning the militia on December 17 and his decree of December 19 on the general levy on the people. The great appeal on the latter subject, which appeared in the paper on December 25, sharply attacked the Habsburg monarch and urged defence of the revolutionary achievements. Kossuth consciously and confidently set about employing the *Közlöny* as a means of rallying and mobilizing the public. He signed and added comments to the war reports published. It was Kossuth, along with Miklós Jósika, various members of the National Defence Commission, and people on his own personal staff, who phrased the decrees and reports. The paper's "unofficial" section altered as well. In a two-part article on December 19 and 20, counsellor Pál Szőnyi refuted the attack on the Ministry of Education made from a clerical standpoint by *Religio és Nevelés*. On December 20 the paper published Petőfi's "Csatadal" (Battle of Song) and letter to the House of Representatives.

When the National Defence Commission removed to Debrecen at the time of Windischgrätz's advance, it of course took its official paper with it. On December 31 László Madarász ordered the editorial staff of the *Közlöny* to travel immediately to Debrecen via Szolnok: "We expect of your patriotism prompt fulfilment of this order." Since Gyurmán had already left Budapest in haste, "leaving no arrangements or instructions for the editorial staff behind him," László Kelmenfy arranged matters on his behalf. He told the manager of the university press to "arrange about the *Közlöny*'s type and printing presses and everything needed for printing it" in such a way that "along with the printing staff they should depart without hindrance for Debrecen tomorrow morning." As for the printing staff, half of it, the eight unmarried printers who happened to be on duty at the time, along with four mechanics and the equipment required, did indeed set out for Debrecen.

The Nép Barátja

The "popular paper" entitled the *Nép Barátja* was also a government publication, launched on June 4, 1848, as an "official" variant of a type of paper then coming into favour. A desire to enlighten the people on the great changes was apparent on all sides, but the ends in view varied depending on who wanted to influence the people and in what direction, whom the paper merely wanted to inform and whom activate or appease. Later on, Táncsics too was explaining matters to the people, and, from an opposite point of departure, so were certain church papers.

On April 14 the *Pesti Hírlap* reported that on the previous two days first the city committee and then the county committee "had concerned themselves principally with the question of how one might explain to the people the meaning in general of the Pest Twelve Points" and the origin of the generosity which "the last legislature had made law." At the meetings "there was talk of a popular paper" as well, and the question arose of "who would provide assistance in publishing it." The Pest tailor Gáspár Tóth offered to subscribe for a hundred copies himself and gathered a total of thirty-four hundred signatures of subscribers among the citizens of Pest on the following day. A committee was appointed with Petőfi, Vörösmarty, Sükei, Táncsics, Nyáry, and Elek Fényes among its members. Landerer offered to see to the technical preparations. Eventually it was decided to ask the ministry to agree that the post office should distribute the paper free.

Petőfi wrote on May 5 to the poet János Arany in Nagyszalonta (Salonta) that the committee on the popular paper had met on the previous day. The paper was to be published by the Pest County Central Committee and in languages other than Hungarian as well. Petőfi had recommended Arany as the Hungarian editor, and, he reported, "I did not have to repeat my recommendation, as the whole committee agreed." He urged his friend to come quickly to Pest and take up the position, which would carry a salary of about 3,000 forints a year.

Arany gave an account of subsequent developments in some private notes:

> I went up to Pest as a consequence of the letter, but as I did not consider that the matter looked permanent I did not want to place my family at risk . . . and simply sought to withdraw and leave the editorship to Gereben Vas, who likewise aspired to the post. But Petőfi convinced me that even if I stayed in Salonta I should not part company from the paper. I signed a contract with Gereben Vas whereby he would be the actual editor but my name would be included as associate editor, and the net income would be divided between us. In the end the net income accruing to me reached 1,200 forints. . . and a large part of this was lost /to me because it was paid/ in Hungarian banknotes.

And that is how the name of Arany came to appear in the paper as associate editor next to that of Gereben Vas, who as "responsible" editor actually managed the paper, in the event quite differently from the way Arany would have wished. Vas, or, to give him his real name, József Radákovits (1823-68), was the son of a bailiff on a nobleman's estate. After rather stormy years at school he used the matriculation certificate of a friend with a similar name and completed a law course in Győr. There he became a lawyer and was known at the time as a lively, red-faced young man, something of a local wag with literary ambitions as well. His main qualification for the post of editor was that right after the March revolution he had started a kind of popular paper in Győr called *Öreg ABC vén emberek számára* (Great ABC for Old People). He had written it weekly himself, bringing out four issues in all, in quarto format. (The first and only edition of a similar publication was edited in Győr by Imre Kozma at about the same time, although the exact date is not known. It even anticipated the government paper in its title, *Népbarát* /Friend of the People/, to which was added the subtitle "or an Explanation of How We Should Understand the New Changes.") On March 24 the Győr paper *Hazánk* wrote,

> Gereben Vas, one of the most outstanding champions in our city militia, is not just a clever lawyer; he has written the people a great ABC in which he explains to them in very clear, popular language the most notable point in the transformation of this country. Last Friday the first booklet of this went on sale at the price of two garas and enjoyed an incredible sale. In particular, almost every village peasant up for the weekly fair took one home with him. . . . Realizing the timeliness of this work, Antal Bay,

the county chief justice, immediately ordered a thousand copies to distribute among his serfs and other village people.

The undertaking broke off after No. 4 because Vas went up to Pest, where he was appointed to edit the *Nép Barátja*, possibly at Kossuth's behest. The government, which was now installed in Pest, took up the initiative and encouraged it, particularly because Táncsics in the mean time had begun publishing and distributing his paper, whose influence the government wished to counter.

The "subscription prospectus" that Vas worded and published for the new paper made clear the style and policy with which he was preparing to perform his task:

> We wish a lucky good day to each and every one of ye. . . . Behold, dear brethren! You have hitherto heard various tidings in the form that some gossiping old woman has picked it up at the end of the village . . . but it would be good to know something of the country's affairs. . . . The gentlemen of Pest have been reflecting on this a great deal . . . and so it has been decided to start a paper for our village brethren, its name being *Nép Barátja*. The paper will talk of the world in which there was still no freedom or equality, in which we went out to perform unpaid labour and we alone paid the taxes! But we shall also tell of what is now free and in what we are now equal, and how we can take advantage of that, lest we greedily fall upon everything, for as a horse gobbles up what he's given, so a lot is a lot to a man.

The comparison, one might add, was not a particularly tasteful or flattering one.

From June 4 the paper appeared every Sunday in quarto format. The subscription for the rest of the year was 7 forints 30 krajcárs. An exceptionally large number of the first issue was printed. The Ministry of Education bought six hundred copies to distribute to the elders in the poorer villages for them to read out to those who could not afford a paper. Towards the end of the year the Pest post office was sending out 2,710 copies of each issue. Initially the "Pest Central Committee" appeared as publisher, but from June 16 Vas assumed this function as well. The government decided to publish the *Nép Barátja* in four other languages widely spoken in the country. Of these the Slovak edition *Prjat'el Ludu*, with Lukács Maczai (or Mácsai) as responsible editor and László Szeberinyi (or Szeberényi) as associate editor, proved the longest-lasting, for it continued for a while into the following year. The *Pučki Priatelj*, in Croatian, edited by Iván Bujanovics, lasted until December 7, and the *Ancien Poporului*, in Romanian, edited by Zsigmond Papp (or Pop), appeared from June 15 until November 30. The German-language *Der Volksfreund*, edited by Sándor Czigler, ceased publication as early as October 6.

Perhaps as a memorial to the initial high hopes of the paper, the *Nép Barátja* also published verses by Petőfi, Arany, Tompa, Garay, Lévay, János Vajda, and Gyula Sárosy from time to time, but these did not set the standard for the paper as a whole. Since it was a government paper, it is not in itself surprising that the rather scarce political articles set out to explain the justice of the existing situation and mollify the village people, although it warned them, with arguments so puerile as to constitute a disparagement of its readers, of the dangers from the land redistributors and other demagogues. In its pedantic, patronizing, boorish, lecturing style and attitude there was indeed an element of disdain and condescension. It hardly ever acknowledged the justice of the peasants' grievances and complaints. In No. 10, for instance, it wished the worst on some inhabitants of Öttevény who were prepared to provide soldiers only if the landowning count provided as many as the number of half-holdings his estate represented. No. 11 included articles in a folksy style on freedom of the press and on the National Assembly; it explained the national colours and the country's coat of arms and tried to arouse enthusiasm for the militia, while making sarcastic remarks about the opposition, which for its part expressed open disgust at the paper's bowing and scraping. Eventually the committee in Pest began to regret having helped bring the paper into being. "The most time-serving paper in all the land," Petőfi called it in a letter to Arany. Petőfi is known to have intended his poem "Hány hét a világ" (How Many Weeks Has the World) for the *Nép Barátja*, but Vas refused to publish it and so it appeared as a leaflet at the end of August. Vas saw Táncsics as his main foe, however, largely because a correspondent from Szabolcs explained in the *Munkások Újsága* on August 13 why the peasants did not like the *Nép Barátja*. The reason, he wrote, was that "it belittles them" and "uses superfluous words, as if they would not understand any other kind of speech," and that it published more verses than news. Táncsics continued the criticism by remarking that the *Nép Barátja*, this curious paper, spoke to its villager friends as if they were not quite right in the head, as if they were all "blithering idiots." A paper like that, he suggested, would hardly make them any the wiser, yet the education minister recommended it and even distributed free copies. Vas reacted angrily to the criticism in the August 27 number of his paper. He took Táncsics to task, considering that he was only quarrelling with him over their shared profession, journalism. The task of journalists now was "to remove the scales from the eyes of people who have been kept in blindness for centuries by premeditated villainy." One had to write for them in an explanatory style because there were millions in their ranks who in fact were still children.

Although Arany's name appeared formally in the number in which Vas put forward that point of view, he expressed basically similar objections to the *Nép Barátja* himself. In letters to Petőfi he found fault on several occasions, saying he felt ashamed to have his name in it and receive money without doing any work for something in which he had no practical say whatever. "This was not the kind of popular paper of which I dared not accept the editorship. . . . If there is one thing I regret in my life it is letting the editorship of the popular paper slip out of my hands. . . . I have never swallowed a bitterer pill than this. I should like to withdraw my name from the editorship but it is too late; I am implicated. I must bear the honoured title of an embezzler." Vas, he said, stood before the people like a schoolmaster before his pupils: his "You know what, brethren"? would be followed by lengthy explanations of each word, as if the people were stupid, and instead of news half-baked wisecracks and moral dicta. All of this, he continued, covered one small printer's sheet a week printed with big headlines, wide margins, and the largest of capital letters, spaced wide, and every piece of correspondence included, to cover the pages somehow. Arany went on to say that he had really wanted to elevate the people with a political and literary paper differing from others only in that its subject-matter and language would have been understandable to them. A paper of this kind, he said, should have been headed by political leading articles that would introduce legislation and political events in simple, clear language without stooping to familiarity. And if the truth were written, whether it was good or bad, there was no need to fear it would do harm to the people. In Arany's view "the basic outlines of all political matters are of concern to the people, because the people are no longer a *misera plebs contribuens* but a governing, legislating power; so the people must be familiar with political affairs and follow them with constant interest." All that needed adding, he argued, was enough explanation to allow a man of common sense to understand it; there was no need to assume, as the *Nép Barátja* did, that the people were dim-witted. From experience Arany wrote that many farm labourers "consider themselves belittled by the crazily explanatory style of the paper." He had heard people say, "This, mate, is just like a child reading out of a book of dreams; there's nothing sensible about the country in it at all. One should respect the seriousness of the people, lest they take this constant hail-fellow-well-met for mockery and grow angry." Vas was in error, he continued, to hide things from the people or even distort the truth:

> The trouble with our people is that we have always kept secrets from them. We have not imparted the true state of affairs, and so we have not allowed public sentiment to develop. The public has no opinion and never will have while the policy of the country can only be followed by a few pedants, those known as the intelligentsia. But once the people have circulating among them a paper that establishes a practice of truthfully reporting the political events of the day, patriotism will flare up in their indestructible souls and they will no longer need driving with sticks to defend the country.

One must agree with Arany's exigence, although considering the circumstances he seems to have erred on the side of stricture. The *Nép Barátja* was probably not so bad as one would suppose from what he said, although it gave a rather low-standard representation of the government's policy. By doing so it robbed itself of a chance to influence a broad new potential public even to the extent that the policy itself would have allowed. Deficiencies were noticed by others as well. In an article entitled "The Civil Life of Our People" in *Kossuth Hírlapja* on September 14, Imre Révész declared in passing that although the *Nép Barátja* was sounder than Táncsics's paper with its preposterous notions, it left much to be desired:

its make-up was defective, the type too large, and the lines too widely spaced, and too much room was taken up by the poetry, even though one should really not have been grudging space or effort to the people at that time. He also pointed to the meagre influence that it and the popular papers in general exerted: "In the district where I live they are not read by a hundredth part of the people; and I do not think things are different elsewhere." The National Defence Commission, and Nyáry in particular, tried to remedy this deficiency by instructing the parish clerks to "read out" the paper "to the people on Sundays and feast days" so that "realizing the country's misfortune they may not be taken in by sly inciters to disaffection."

The *Nép Barátja* is known to have received every support from above. The government excused Vas from lodging the caution money prescribed by the press law or, rather, transferred the obligation to the city and county of Pest. It allowed the paper to be distributed post-free and arranged that every village council order a copy. Yet it was able to exert an only limited influence. Be that as it may, the paper and its editor faithfully followed the government to Debrecen.

Bibliography

Sándor Szilágyi, "Közlöny és Népbarát" (The *Gazette* and the *People's Friend*), in *A magyar forradalom*, pp. 338-39; Viktor Szokoly, ed., *Mészáros Lázár emlékiratai* (Memoirs of Lázár Mészáros), vol. 1 (Pest, 1867); Lajos Falaky, "Szeberényi Lajos" (Lajos Szeberényi), *Figyelő*, February 1877, pp. 275-81; Béla Váli, "Vas Gereben—Radákovits József" (Gereben Vas—József Radákovics), *Egyetemes Philologiai Közlöny* (General Philological Gazette), 1883, pp. 536-58 and 738-60; idem, "Egy hírlap története 1848-ban" (The Story of a Newspaper in 1848), *Nemzet* (Nation), 1883, nos. 38-40; Béla Révész, "A legelső magyar néplap és Arany János" (The Very First Hungarian Popular Paper and János Arany), *Magyar Paedogogiai Szemle* (Hungarian Educational Review), 1883, no. 2, pp. 43-47; János Arany, *Hátrahagyott iratai és levelezése* (Posthumous Writings and Correspondence), vol. 2 (Budapest, 1888); Andor Szeberényi, "A szabadságharc kormányának hivatalos lapja" (The Official Paper of the Government in the War of Independence), *Aradi Közlöny* (Arad Gazette), 1889, no. 72; Károly Berecz, *A régi "Fiatal Magyarország"* (The "Young Hungary" of Old) (Budapest, 1898); Béla Iványi, Albert Gárdonyi, and Elemér Czakó, *A Királyi Magyar Egyetemi Nyomda története, 1577-1927* (History of the Royal Hungarian University Press, 1577-1927) (Budapest, 1927); Gábor Tolnai, "Arany János ismeretlen fogalmazványa" (An Unknown Draft by János Arany), *It*, 1945, pp. 44-47; Ernő Tamás, "Egy néplap 1848-ból: A 'Nép Barátja'" (A Popular Paper from 1848: The *People's Friend*), *Kis Újság* (Little Newspaper), November 25, 1951; Győző Ember, "Kossuth Lajos a Honvédelmi Bizottmány élén" (Lajos Kossuth at the Head of the National Defence Commission), in *Emlékkönyv Kossuth Lajos*, pp. 175-285; Éva V. Windisch, *Közlöny 1848-1849: A forradalom és szabadságharc hivatalos lapjának története* (The *Gazette* 1848-1849: The Story of the Official Paper of the Revolution and War of Independence), Értekezések a történeti tudományok köréből (Treatises in the Sphere of Historical Studies), new series, no. 8 (Budapest, 1958); Erdődi, "A forradalmi magyar kormányzat".

13. Kossuth Hírlapja

The divergent trends and shades of opinion in the Batthyány government could not, as we have seen, be accommodated within a single political paper. Nor could each possess a paper of its own. Széchenyi was left without one after the *Jelenkor* closed down, and Eötvös could rely only to a certain extent on the *Pesti Hírlap*. Kossuth was alone in managing to start a new paper, moreover one that rapidly came to the fore. Kossuth served in the government as minister of finance, but on several issues and to a growing degree he held different opinions from his colleagues. The differences found expression in his paper, which may therefore be described as representing an opposition within the government.

It was perfectly natural that the chance should have been seized by Kossuth, who had opened a new chapter in the history of the political press in Hungary as editor of the *Pesti Hírlap* and after losing the job had made vain efforts to gain a new paper. He did so not merely "to have a publication in case he should quit his ministerial position one day," as he occasionally put it, or merely, as Béla Dezsényi suggests in his study, "to place the new responsible government under pressure from progressive public opinion by means of his own publication, as he had earlier done to the petty nobility." The tactical considerations all found a place in the overall platform that his paper continued to support after the fall of the Batthyány government: to rally the national forces on as broad a basis as possible behind the development, independence, and defence of the new bourgeois, national Hungary. Certainly no one could vie with Kossuth in doing so. When he chose the title for *Kossuth Hírlapja* he was quite clear in his own mind what his name represented and virtually symbolized.

Kossuth began preparing to launch the paper as soon as the government moved to Pest. One Viennese paper, the *Wanderer*, knew of his plans as early as May 10, and on May 15 Kossuth complied with the press law by giving notice to the mayor of Pest that he intended to publish *Kossuth Hírlapja*. At the same time he enquired if a certificate for the stock he held in the Pest savings bank could be accepted as a deposit. It could not, and on June 24 he was obliged to deposit the caution money in cash. On May 17 he had released a prospectus in which his aims were set out in greater detail. At the end of the Diet he had told his friends he would make another attempt "to sway public opinion through the periodical press." "The course of my policy," he went on, "will never change under any circumstances, for this course is the course of justice, people's rights, national self-rule, and national freedom. My paper will be the advocate of this course." He stressed, with an eye among others to the radical youth, that this was a juncture at which "we need order, fellow citizens, order that is faithful to freedom and provides shelter under which we can consolidate the new conditions." He also stressed that the majority of the nation was "monarchical in sentiment"; the paper would therefore foster fidelity to the king,

> and there will come a time when my prediction that it is on the age-old hills of Buda that the kingly throne resting on people's liberty is firmer than anywhere else will be corroborated before the world. . . . In relation to foreign countries my paper will be an advocate of national self-rule. It is for us to display the maturity that will make alliance with us in the interest of civilization valued and sought after; and my paper will be the one to win the Hungarian name recognition as an important factor in the balance of Western freedom and Western civilization and make its hand of friendship accepted, as we shall gladly accept the hand of friendship and respect the rights of all peoples just as we demand respect for the rights of our nation. . . . With Austria there will be candid, amicable understanding, on a basis, if it is willing, of mutual rights, mutual independence, and mutual equality of interest.

There was no cause, he said, to lay at the door of the Austrian people the insulting tone adopted by certain Austrian papers: "The German element is the element of civilization; I shall gladly ally myself with it, but I will not sacrifice the self-rule of my nation, the rights of my nation, or the freedom of my nation to any alliance." At home he demanded "free development alongside the Hungarians . . . for all ethnic groups" but "elevation over the Hungarians for none. . . . The ill-intentioned vainly accuse me of desiring to suppress the inhabitants of this country who speak other languages;

my whole life belies the charge; but I shall indeed oppose eternally all attempts to make Hungary a German, a Slavic, an Illyrian /Croatian/, or a Serbian country or to carve it up into such provinces. . . ."

Kossuth specially emphasized that his paper would also concern itself with international relations and foreign policy. A good deal of light on his motives and methods of organization in this respect is shed by a confidential letter he wrote on June 7 to Ferenc Pulszky, who at the time looked after the affairs of the Hungarian "Foreign Ministry," more precisely the "ministry around the monarch" in Vienna, as a state secretary alongside or rather in place of Prince Pál Esterházy. In the letter Kossuth began by saying that the king should come to Buda, which should be the centre of the Monarchy, for "we must direct the diplomacy of the empire." He went on to detail all the things he would like to ask Pulszky to arrange on behalf of *Kossuth Hírlapja*, which would "need to take on a great importance in Hungarian politics." One thing to arrange was that he, like Lajos Batthyány, should receive the Viennese papers and the foreign papers from Vienna more quickly than he could by post. Pulszky was to sign on two Vienna correspondents. One of them, at a salary of 20-25 forints a month, might be Adolf Frankenburg, who at the time was working at the Hungarian Foreign Ministry as a translator and registrar. The other, again "from the sphere of our Foreign Ministry," might be István Wargha, "assuming that he has occasion to be initiated into your diplomatic relationships." For two or three reports a week he might receive 400 forints a year, and also see about ordering the papers right away. (At the time of the Industrial Protection Association, Wargha had been one of those Kossuth had trusted, and the association had sent him abroad on its behalf.) Kossuth went on to say that someone in the office of Pulszky's father-in-law, who was a Viennese banker, might send the paper commercial news. Then he put a harder, less usual question: whether the French and the British and perhaps the Prussian envoys might be persuaded "to send *brevi manu* to Wargha any news they may receive from home of a kind that from their point of view it would be good, or at least not inopportune, to convey unofficially to us." Apart from that, Pulszky should try to find persons on the staffs of the Austrian legations in Paris and London who might each "be given the idea that we shall gain more influence in diplomacy day by day and be able to reward his services" and induced "to send direct to me or through you to me reports that would not conflict with his position." Finally, Kossuth requested Pulszky to send him a leading article "on foreign affairs" as quickly as possible.

Kossuth saw his paper as an initiator and repository of the future policy—and especially the independent foreign policy—of Hungary. To him it was self-evident, therefore, that the staff of the Hungarian Foreign Ministry should be at his disposal in building up his network of correspondents and that these members of the ministry staff should report their own official business for the paper. Here the lines became blurred not merely between his functions as finance minister and as the proprietor of a noticeably oppositionist paper. On June 7 he also wrote of the future to Dénes Pázmándy, who at the time was in Frankfurt with László Szalay as a Hungarian delegate to the German Assembly. Mention was again made of removing the court to Buda, of the idea that "we must direct Austrian diplomacy," and of the assumption that if Austria in the narrower sense acceded to a unified Germany the problem of diplomatic recognition of Hungary would be resolved as well. And again he added a personal request: that Szalay send the paper a weekly report (for Pázmándy, having been nominated as a candidate for speaker of the National Assembly, was already preparing to return home) and gather "as many correspondents as possible among the supporters of our cause," Germans and "if possible Britons, Frenchmen, and others as well."

The Editorial Staff

In the prospectus Kossuth had announced, "Since my official commitments prevent me from editing my paper, Mr József Bajza has kindly undertaken the responsible editorship, but my constant contacts with the paper will not be confined to the relations of proprietorship." Kossuth indeed concerned himself with the paper a great deal. He wrote several articles, usually signed but sometimes anonymously, particularly if he wanted to express personal opinions which did not fully accord with his official position. To a greater or lesser extent he suggested the major political articles or at least the line that they took, and on occasion he looked over or even corrected writings and reports by others. Nevertheless, the role of József Bajza (1804-58) was far from nominal. He was one of the pioneers of literary criticism and journalism in the best tradition of liberalism among Hungary's middle nobility and had been so since the 1830s, not least as one of the editors of the *Athenaeum*. His close ties with the Opposition Party and Kossuth are apparent in the fact that in 1847 he edited the *Ellenőr*, a political handbook or collection of articles on opposition policy published abroad. Understandably, Kossuth chose to entrust his paper to someone with whom he agreed politically and someone whose name and reputation guaranteed that the paper would maintain a suitable standard and authority in putting this policy forward. As for Bajza, he had been trying to get his hands on a political paper for some time. Therefore he gladly accepted Kossuth's offer and presumably because of that prior commitment turned down the editorship of the *Közlöny* when it was offered to him by Szemere. He turned out to be an excellent, meticulous, cool, and tactful political editor but an energetic one prepared for debate and polemics if need be. He played no small part in ensuring that *Kossuth Hírlapja* performed its important role as a shaper of public opinion to so high a standard. Ferenc Toldy, who had once been the third of a triumvirate at the *Athenaeum* with Bajza and Vörösmarty and in 1848 was left far behind or even swerved away from Bajza politically, spoke later, in a memorial address, of Bajza's role at *Kossuth Hírlapja* with regret, almost with disapproval: "In the second half of that fateful year he was so taken up with the running of the paper that apart from hindrance of his work he did not even get round to writing articles, and the period passed in self-sacrifice, devoid of appreciation." The remark is less than surprising, however, in that Toldy disapproved of the paper itself, along with the policy it espoused and other phenomena of that "fateful" year.

Bajza was able to maintain an unclouded relationship with Kossuth, both in the running of the paper and in public. Beforehand, in the *Pesti Hírlap* on June 14, Bajza found it necessary to state that "Kossuth's paper is not an official paper, but a wholly private undertaking; the *Közlöny*, on the other hand, is the official paper of the government, and so a subscriber to the *Közlöny* will read quite different things from those the *Kossuth Hírlapja* will contain, for there will not be the slightest connection between them." But in the eyes of the public, "the fact," as Pulszky put it, "that there is another semi-official paper besides the *Közlöny*, one that is not the ministry's, merely one of the ministers', has served as disquieting evidence that there is no unity in the government and that at least two different trends exist within it." During July it became increasingly apparent that *Kossuth Hírlapja* was taking a political line that differed from or ran counter to the government's on certain major issues. Several people remarked on this, and in response Bajza placed the following loyal statement in the July 17 number as "Information concerning the Editing of the Paper": "To prevent any misunderstanding I consider it necessary to state that although Minister Lajos Kossuth is the proprietor of the paper he is not concurrently its editor, and consequently he is in no wise responsible either for the whole content or for specific articles, of which he has no prior knowledge." To him could be attributed, Bajza continued, "only the articles signed with his name"; should anyone have any observation to make he should turn to the editor, who bore full responsibility for the paper. A couple of days later, in No. 21, Bajza announced personally that if it were up to him he would not provide a single soldier to serve against the Italians.

Kossuth Hírlapja began publication on July 1, 1848, on the eve of the day the new National Assembly convened. It appeared every day except Monday on four large sheets set in three columns, printed on Vazul Kozma's press. A total of 157 issues appeared up until December 31, 1848. A half-yearly subscription cost 8 forints delivered to a Budapest address and 10 forints by post to the provinces. Its content, its comprehensive news service, and not least the significance of its political line gave it pride of place among the papers during the revolution and war of independence. *Marczius Tizenötödike* may have been livelier and spicier and the social programme put forward by the *Munkások Újsága* more thoroughgoing and novel, but neither paper could offer the breadth of information that the public by that time expected and neither managed to attract as many subscribers and readers. No small contribution to the paper's success was made by the policy and popularity of Kossuth and the response he elicited. It is therefore understandable that in circulation the paper should have overtaken all its rivals, with the possible exception of the *Közlöny*. In December 1848 the print run was over 5,000, of which 4,214 were sent to provincial subscribers from the main post office in Pest and the remainder sold locally in the capital.

Bajza took over the mantle of the old *Pesti Hírlap*, but using the scope offered by freedom of the press and following in part the example of *Marczius*, he raised the whole venture onto a higher plane. If one compares the paper with its rivals and considers the response elicited, one is forced to consider as unjust opportunism Sándor Szilágyi's fastidious remarks in 1850 that the paper "lacked the colour of life—it was faint and moribund" and that "like a patient taking his medicine, one reads it with reluctance."

Moreover, *Kossuth Hírlapja* had a larger staff than any other paper, estimated at fifty to sixty persons including provincial correspondents. Curiously enough, the first name that needs mentioning is Adolf Gyurmán, the editor of the *Közlöny*. Originally it had been intended that he head the foreign section, but Bajza told Kossuth on June 19 that there were "so few leader writers offering their services that we shall ultimately be obliged to employ him as a permanent leader writer instead, at the regular fee agreed upon." Another member of the staff was Emil Ábrányi, whom we have met already as editor of the radical *Jövő*. Then there was Pál Matisz, born in Komárom, thirty years old at the time, a lawyer in Pest, a friend of Petőfi's, and a translator of Victor Hugo and Shakespeare who himself dabbled in poetry. There was the poet János Garay (1812-53), who at about this time received the chair of Hungarian language and literature at the University of Pest and who worked on the paper as an assistant editor in August and September. The business side was handled first by István Dobrossy, a lawyer, stenographer, and journalist, and then by two men—Ferenc Stuller (?1806-74), a lawyer and secretary successively to the kindergarten association and then to Kossuth, and Antal Vörös, a long-time trusted adherent of Kossuth's.

At the head of the first column would be one or sometimes two successive leading articles outlining a political position or line of policy, either with a title or, following the custom of the time, with the date where the title would normally be. These leaders were sometimes signed but often anonymous or signed only with initials. Gyurmán, for instance, never signed his articles. Of the various writers of them, Kossuth was the one who signed the most leading articles. Handwritten notes by Antal Vörös that are not entirely accurate record that forty-six articles were by Kossuth, but missing from that list, for instance, is "Summary of the Finance Minister's Report on the Nation's Financial Affairs," which appeared in four parts in Nos. 50-53. From more recent research there appear to have been forty-nine articles by Kossuth, of which almost half appeared under his name or bear unmistakable signs of his authorship and fourteen were unsigned. However, the latest edition of Kossuth's complete works includes some articles signed "F. Sz." and "L. Sz." whose authorship would seem to be questionable, since Frigyes Szarvady, for instance, also signed himself "F. Sz." on occasion.

Ruled off at the foot of the front page was a feature entitled "Feuilleton," initially run for a short while by Ferenc Toldy. The feuilleton in the first issue introduced the famous work by the Hungarophile French author Auguste de Gérando on the "*esprit public*" and political thought of Hungary (*De l'esprit public en Hongrie depuis la Révolution française,* /Paris, 1848/) and went on to devote a few lines to the subject of fine art. The second issue had an exhaustive piece of analysis entitled "The Rise of the Latest Republic in France." Nos. 4-5 had a two-part political essay called "World National Movements in 1848" by Emil Ábrányi, who argued, "Not even the power of the Russians with their several hundred thousand troops will be able to foil the efforts of the peoples for freedom and brotherhood." In any case, "the Russian invasion will necessarily bring about a fraternal alliance among the nations of Europe." On July 11 (in No. 9) Károly Szabó used the feuilleton feature to call for "A Hungarian Name for the Hungarian Regiments," while Pál Hunfalvy issued an appeal "To the Members of the House of Representatives." On August 12 Gusztáv Szontagh drew readers' attention to the importance of having "Hungarian words of command" in the army. Shortly afterwards the feuilleton form was abandoned as a feature. Belles lettres found their way into *Kossuth Hírlapja* on only two occasions; János Garay's poem "Unió" (Union) appeared in No. 7 and Czuczor's "Riadó" (Alert) in No. 149.

Before the remaining sections of the paper came a short résumé of the main decrees that had been published in the *Közlöny*. Then came detailed parliamentary reports, followed by lively news and comments entitled "The Capital's News," compiled in the autumn months by Károly Szathmáry and not infrequently including some political allusions. In the very first issue there was a veiled hint that Kossuth did not entirely identify with the government and was thinking of resigning. The report, one reads, that the minister of finance had "already resigned" was false, but "his steadily worsening state of health can hardly fail to force a withdrawal from the ministry /i.e., government/ upon him." The next section of the paper was devoted to lengthy dispatches and reports from all parts of the country on county and local authority affairs, and in later months, as a new section of the paper, came the war reports. Quite a few of the correspondents had transferred from the *Pesti Hírlap*, including Pál Major of Moson, János Ludvigh (1812-70), the district recorder of the Szepes towns, who was the National Assembly representative for Igló (Spišská Nová Ves), János Besze, and Zsigmond Beöthy, who had been writing stories, verses, plays, and political articles of various kinds since the latter half of the 1830s and in 1848 became an assistant clerk at the Ministry of Education. Also among the correspondents were Károly Samarjay (1821-94) from Torontál, who was a friend of Jókai's, and Miklós Krizbai, more correctly Miklós Krizbai Dezső, from Kolozsvár, who had previously worked for the *Erdélyi Híradó* and was later appointed public prosecutor by the Hungarian government. After the defeat the Austrian authorities condemned Krizbai to nineteen years' imprisonment, from which he emerged mentally deranged. *Kossuth Hírlapja* received reports on the affairs of the Transylvanian Saxons from Lajos Bruz.

It is worthwhile to take special note of the foreign coverage in the paper, which gave fuller, more influential, and higher-standard reports on conditions, political endeavours, and turns of events in other countries than any of the other papers. It paid close attention to events in Europe, providing documentation which helped satisfy the demand often voiced by leader writers that Hungary have a say in foreign policy and the development of international relations. It gave particularly painstaking reports of what was going on in France. No. 8, for instance, contained an account of the suppression of the workers' uprising in Paris. Although the uprising was condemned, the paper added that "the afterpains of the rebellion, which has luckily been suppressed, will cause suffering to the republic for some time to come," wrote with horror of the carnage and the desperate fighting, in which even ten-year-old children took part, and warned the government at home of the lessons to be drawn from this and the importance of resolving the social question. In the August 6 number, the Paris correspondent, who signed his dispatches "G," praised Lamartine as a man who had protected France from foreign wars and the "storm of red revolution" and "declares himself in favour of the kind of prudently progressive and moderate republic that the good citizens have desired." He went on to ask, "Who in Europe now remembers the Crémieux, Louis Blancs, and Alberts"? In the September 1 number the same writer contributed a leading article entitled "The Foreign Policy of the French Republic." His interpretation of Lamartine's policy was that France had at first been prepared to assist the Italians to liberate themselves but was now less willing to do so because Charles Albert had been reluctant to take it up on the offer. In the foreign section on October 12, however, there was an instructive warning: "Anyone who thinks that a republican system of government suffices to ensure the happiness of France and doubts the need to do more to improve the lot of the poor or smooth over the sharp conflicts between the rich and the propertyless has grievously erred." If "the democratic republic is not willing to satisfy the rightful demands of these people, it is on the brink of disturbances that may be even bloodier than those hitherto." In the same number there was a well-informed account of political events in the French provinces. Then came a report from England of how the *Morning Chronicle* had written appreciatively of the

Hungarian political leaders and the efforts to attain national independence, disapproving only of Hungarian repression of the Slavs. Also on October 12 there was an article called "Certain Romanian Schemers and the *National*" relating that the September 30 number of the *National* in Paris had reported the receipt of comments on an article about the Hungarian-Croatian affair from several Romanians who were still trying to present Jelačić as a hero of the liberation struggle against the Hungarians. Instead of publishing these the *National* had only criticized them in reply, from which the Hungarian commentator concluded that a huge contradiction could be observed "between the words of ardent patriotism used by certain representatives of Romanian origin and the deeds of the vast majority of our fellow citizens of Romanian origin." On December 10 it was reported in the foreign section that a great press debate had broken out in Paris in mid-November between the *Journal des Débats*, which supported the cause of Austrian centralization and reliance on the Slavs, and the *National*, which defended Hungary even against the threats of Windischgrätz. As we have seen, *Kossuth Hírlapja* was receiving detailed reports on events in Vienna with the help of Pulszky and his associates. However, during the last year of the war, when open warfare broke out, the sources of foreign news gradually dried up.

At the bottom of the last page of the paper were advertisements. Auctions, the Danube Steam Navigation Co., the Applied Art Gallery, and the latest books were advertised. Papers invited subscribers, and a dentist sought new patients. There was even an advertisement for "five new kinds of cigar" which the dealer had named after such leading politicians as Batthyány, Kossuth, and Szemere.

The Main Political Topics

To trace the paper's political development chronologically through its main leading articles one should begin with the first policy statements contributed by Kossuth. At the beginning of issue No. 1 on July 1, Kossuth, "By Way of Introduction," stressed among other things that it was not "a matter of personal interest" for the members of the Hungarian ministry to remain in office and outlined the shortcomings he saw in himself as an office-holder. In the same number he contributed two shorter, unsigned comments, one on the Serbian agreement and the other on the return of Széchenyi and Eötvös from a visit to the court of the palatine. In the latter piece he described the arrival of the king in Buda as "very likely." On the next day, in No. 2, he sketched the government's policy towards the Croatians under the head line "The Illyrian Revolt." If it were true, Kossuth said, that the Zagreb provincial council had responded to news of the June 10 manifesto against Jelačić by forming a provisional government and preparing to send agents into Italy to recall the Croatian soldiers there, the Hungarians should return home too; Radetzky's troops would then "scatter" and "the disintegration of the Austrian monarchy would become irreversible." Vienna should, he said, have listened to the Hungarians; "the loss of Italy was a certainty months ago," but at the time compensation would still have been given for it. There was, Kossuth said, only one last way of saving the empire: "Let the dynasty place itself openly and candidly in the arms of the Hungarians" and the king come to Buda. On July 3 there was another leader signed by Kossuth, this one on the tasks ahead of the National Assembly. Expression, he said, had to be given to the nation's decision to defend its independence and liberty" come hell or high water. . . . If we do not prepare, we shall be attacked." In his view, the reason for the revolt in Zagreb, the Serbian attack on the south of the country, and the Austrian attempt (mentioned also in the Viennese papers) to take back control of the finance and defence portfolios was that the Hungarians were known by their foes to be unprepared and short of money and arms. For the same reason "the Austrian deputies in Frankfurt are entertaining hopes of cutting up our country and merging us into a federation in which we would be equal in our weakness with the others." He saw this "federal" idea of the Austrians', under which Hungary would be divided up on an ethnic basis, as an attempt to parry the clause in the draft German constitution put forward in Frankfurt stipulating that princes who joined the new German state, including the Austrian emperor, could retain non-German provinces only if the link were altered to one of personal union, an idea Vienna found unattractive. Kossuth ended by saying that the Hungarians, although they did not want war, did not want "the peace of servitude either." The preparations Hungary was making "do not merely concern the Croatian revolt; this preparation is a means of averting all dangers." On July 4 came Kossuth's fourth leader, this one, entitled "Our Relations with Austria," unsigned. Its point of departure was the chance that the parliament in Vienna might agree to annex the Croatians, who were breaking away from Hungary. In that case, he wrote, "we may live to see, despite the protests of our lord king, the men of reaction declaring war on the king of Hungary in the name of the emperor of Austria." Were the scheme to succeed the outcome was predictable: "We should see an Austrian empire stretching in a thin slice from Prague to Varasd (Varaždin). . . . Above would be a Slavic monarchy, a satrapy under the northern Colossus; in the middle Vienna, either as a free republican city or as a border town of the German empire. And the Austrian ruling house would lose its throne." But there was one other chance of salvation: "In these days of peril God has appointed Buda the permanent seat of the Austrian house. If our lord king will accept this, his throne at Buda will rise to be the imperial seat of a great empire." In the same number Kossuth commented in an unsigned article on the news that the Austrian government wished to abandon its neutrality. This was ridiculous, said Kossuth, as the relations between Austria and Hungary were regulated by the Pragmatic Sanction. But "if Austria renounces its alliance with us, we shall renounce our alliance with it, and if we need an alliance at all we shall seek one elsewhere and in all probability find one." In a piece entitled "Love and Equality" on July 5, Kossuth dealt with the position of the Monarchy and the attempt at counter-revolution, which was stirring peoples up against one another: Hungary "has not disturbed the Monarchy, which is progressing towards disintegration," for "we have rejoiced at the prospect of Austria's uniting with the great German nation and believed that a nation of such perfect humanity and high cultivation can only exert a good influence on the destiny of the world." In Vienna, on the other hand, he saw forces that were instigating hatred and war, and he argued that instead of remaining "a parasite body living off the fat of the countries it oppressed" Vienna should become "a working member that wins strength and increase from the great German homeland." Bohemia he considered a country to which "we can never grudge freedom" because of its "historical foundation and consciousness of nationhood and viability," but he criticized it for its "insatiable desires," pointing out that it had "rejected the German alliance to which it belongs, quarrelled instead of cooperated with Austria, and preached hatred and fanaticism against Hungary." It was the Croatian leaders who hated Hungary most of all, he went on, because "we stand in the way of the establishment of a vast Slavic empire." They were deceiving the people, he said, and in fact sought servitude, being "slaves to Muscovite influence and only temporarily the Viennese old régime's faithful tools" and supporters of the latter's desire to handle defence and financial affairs from Vienna. Clearly Kossuth was most preoccupied with the likely consequences of the German unity that appeared to be emerging. One result would have been the affiliation of the German provinces under the Habsburg Monarchy, or rather the provinces that belonged to the German *Bund*, with the new German state, causing a change in the relations between Austria and Hungary that would provide more room for Hungary to manoeuvre independently in foreign affairs and international policy. Kossuth's next article, which was unsigned, appeared on July 6 under the title "The Hungarian, Russian, and Wallachian Issue." In it he turned his attention to the matter of "life and death" that lurked among the complexities of south-eastern Europe. He argued that Russia was "exercising a protectorate" in Wallachia. Austria, whose "calling it would be" to counteract that, was actually "an open servant of the Russians." Moreover, the revolution attempted by the Romanian boyars in March had failed. "Can the Hungarians annul this influence, and if so, how? They might indeed if they had a legation in Constantinople" and the legation succeeded in "persuading the Turkish court to entrust the handling of its Wallachian affairs to the Hungarian consul there." In that case "no law or decree could be ratified in Wallachia without the influence of the Hungarian consul." Out of that situation it would be desirable to bring about a Hungarian-Romanian "confederation." In other words, the role of the now weakened Turkey against the power of the tsars would be taken over by Hungary through diplomatic representation—no mean undertaking! In another unsigned article on the next day, July 7, Kossuth continued with some reflections on the news of the Romanian revolution in Wallachia on June 23. The revolution's objective was to unite the two Romanian principalities and shake off Russian and Turkish colonialism. The Hungarians, Kossuth said, were sympathetic towards this objective, but "the two poor lands" (Hungary and Romania) were without armed forces, had an oppressed peasantry, lacked strength, and had only an "orphan" freedom, for they waited in vain for assistance from Germany or Austria. The Romanians might well be opposed to the Hungarians, he reminded readers, because to them the Hungarians meant Austria and "the inhuman laws of Transylvania" and because many Romanians lived in Hungary and had to be warned to keep the peace and kept under observation militarily as well. "But we shall do all that we can for our neighbours by diplomatic means," he said, "so as to guard them from Russian interference." For instance, Hungary might intervene with the sultan on their behalf. Thus by remedying "the offences of the past," Hungary might not be unsuccessful in extending them a helping hand, for "the sultan, the Germans, and the Wallachians" were Hungary's natural allies. The Hungarians were receiving refugees hospitably, he pointed out; "our sympathy would demand more from us, as would the interests of our own security," but at this juncture "we are not masters of our time."

Meanwhile other authors appeared in the paper, sometimes using their own names, as Ábrányi did when on July 8 he explained to the Slavs that the Hungarians "wish to consider them as brothers and share liberty and justice with them but wish to see the primacy of their nationhood secured." But in the early period Kossuth continued to contribute a large number of articles. On July 10 he released and commented upon a letter from the Vienna correspondent V. (perhaps István Wargha) about the downfall of the Pillersdorf government and along with it, he hoped, its ill-fated policy. On the next day he commented, again anonymously, on a report in the *Prager Zeitung* of a call from the Slavic congress in Prague. The summons, he said, spoke of freedom and of no desire for conquest, but if that were the case why did it "count in" certain counties of Hungary "as an additional part of the greater Slavia envisaged"? And why was there "this constant flirtation with the power of the Muscovites"? Clearly, he said, the purpose was not to give liberty to the peoples but to extend power "over as many countries in civilized Europe as possible."

The relations between the Viennese court and the Slavs were analysed in an unsigned article entitled "Possibilities," which was written either by Kossuth, as historians have assumed, or at least under his influence. With mild irony it said that the Hungarians were following Vienna's course "with sympathetic concern . . . for the happiness that will derive if it links itself as closely as possible with the German union." However, it went on, Vienna had failed to grasp the essence of the Slavic movements, the fact that the efforts in Prague and Zagreb had the self-same purpose: "to penetrate from the Black Sea right into the heart of Germany, paying no heed to Hungary's rights and independence, and to conquer this part of the world for the wildest intolerance and tyranny." If the Slavs promised "to set up the Slavic empire" under Vienna's leadership, they were "bluffing." Were the German union "to transfer its sessions to Vienna," he suggested, it would provide support against the Slavs, but if the Austrian leaders "managed to poison the German union with ambition for conquest . . . the vast population of the German land, which is now friendly, might press upon us with its full force." Germany's interest, he went on, was to create unity, which the ambitions of the Austrian reactionaries could only endanger: "We strongly believe that this German union will be wise enough to see, and just enough so to combine that in the triumph of its unification it does not omit to respect the independence of Hungary, as a country in whose interest it is to be a faithful neighbour and ally."

It is usual to follow Antal Vörös in attributing an unsigned article on "Our Foreign Affairs" to Kossuth. This is an important piece because it was the first to propose amending the 1848 laws to provide more freedom for manoeuvre in Hungarian foreign policy. Kossuth certainly approved of and supported this idea, but it is doubtful that he could actually have formulated a concept to which the editor of his own paper attached a note describing it as inadequate. If that is the case, it can only be seen as a rather complex piece of manoeuvring to which Kossuth is unlikely to have resorted. The article stated that "the edifice of the independent governance of Hungary . . . has not been completed" by Act 3 of 1848; Clause 13, on foreign affairs, "will sooner or later occasion conflicts with Austria and among ourselves." It was proposed that "we hasten to remedy" this deficiency "while we have the chance to do so." The country did not, it said, in fact have a foreign ministry: "Over there in the east the foreign ministry officials in Russian pay still sit; there sit the petty Metternichs," while the Hungarian agents, "whom our ministry does not omit to employ, cannot be provided with diplomatic positions." This the writer viewed as dangerous because "our march" to the brink "is made by others" and "yet we cannot shake these others from our necks, because they are strangers and because they are attached to our collars by the law," which is "deficient, obscure, and bad." To correct the situation, he argued, the Hungarians had to take action "against the power which is our natural foe" and seek "our natural friends, the countries made such by their geographical and political positions: the Swedes, the Turks, and the fragmented nations of the lower Danube." The clause had to be amended so that the Hungarian Foreign Ministry (in Vienna) would assign to posts important for national defence Hungarian diplomats "who will be constantly around the person of his excellency the ambassador and in all matters which are the common or several concerns of this country and the hereditary provinces constantly and responsibly represent the independent ministry of this country." To this last remark the editor added the comment, "Too little. Unity and agreement if possible, but a weight of its own in any event." It would seem likelier that the remark, and not the ambiguous proposal, was made by Kossuth.

An unsigned article on July 23 headed "German Incitements" reported that the *Deutsche Zeitung* had declared against the union with Transylvania and was complaining about oppression of the Hungarian Germans. On July 26 Miklós Wesselényi wrote on "How a Peace in Accordance with Our Honour May be Implemented," concluding that there was a need for military and financial preparations. On the following day Dani Fábián, a Reformed Church minister of Kézdivásárhely (Tîrgu Secuiesc) who had been contributing frequently to the *Regélő*, the *Társalkodó*, and the Transylvanian papers since the 1830s and was now a "Székely (Transylvanian Hungarian) representative" in the National Assembly, wrote on Székely affairs and patriotism. On July 29, Lajos Szeberényi (1820-75) attacked "certain agitators among the Slovaks of Hungary" and their "Pan-Slavist" castles in the air. Szeberényi, a Pest lawyer and journalist who had also studied Lutheran theology, figured frequently in *Kossuth Hírlapja*, signing himself with his full name or just "Sz-i. L." On July 30 Kossuth returned to the subject of the relations between Austria and the German Assembly, saying that the country would not bargain over its independence with reactionaries who made threats against it. "I have taken an oath as a minister," he wrote. "According to this oath my conscience tells me—this is what to think, this is the only permissible way to think. If they think otherwise where they take measures at a higher level than the ministries (which I do not believe is the case at all), all well and good—then I will of course cease to be a minister. But a Hungarian citizen—that I shall remain." In Deák's opinion *Kossuth Hírlapja* was preparing the ground for a resolution proposed in the House of Representatives on August 3 by Nyáry: that Austria should not count on assistance from Hungary if it were involved in war with the imperial government in Frankfurt over the question of German unity. On August 6 the council of ministers heard an objection by the palatine to Kossuth's leading articles as not representing the government's position. Archduke István called on Kossuth to give up writing articles, but Kossuth replied that the newspaper was his own private affair and immediately offered his resignation, which the palatine dared not accept. For a while at any rate, Kossuth wrote no further articles, unless one assumes that the writings of various lengths and occasional leaders that appeared after August 10 under the initials F. Sz. were his. Meanwhile, on August 5, an article signed "L. B-y" reflected in a fairly forceful tone on the latest attacks by the *Österreichische Allgemeine Zeitung* and the intrigues of the camarilla: "Never again shall we be a colony of Austria's!

Rather than that we are prepared to stand up like men and do battle for our independence."

It is worth noting especially some articles contributed towards the end of August by István Szokolay (1822-1904), a Pest lawyer, journalist, and nobleman, the author of a book published in 1846 on the guilds and industrial freedom, and a member of the staff of the centralist *Pesti Hírlap*. Szokolay wrote in favour of abolishing vineyard tithes, usufructs, and remnants of feudalism in general. In an article on August 18 he said the lot of cottars had not been substantially improved by the laws of 1848, which "exuded a noticeable stench of aristocracy." One proposal he made was that residual lands be divided up among the landless peasants. Imre Révész (1826-81), a young Reformed Church minister and *praeceptor* of the college at Debrecen, wrote on August 17 about Pan-Slavism, quoting a Berlin scholar's opinion that there were various kinds of Slavs. On August 24 Lajos Szeberényi discussed the "Serbian Proclamation" to the Slovaks of Bácska and the Bánát, which he considered grasping at straws. On August 25 János Dobos (1804-87) of Pécel, another Reformed Church minister, wrote under the title "What Are the People Doing and Thinking"? about the reluctance of the inhabitants of non-Hungarian villages around Pest to join the militia. On the one hand, he blamed this on colonization by foreigners in the past, since "the garbage cart of the damnable settlement . . . emptied in this district"; on the other, he warned of the dissatisfaction over the deficiencies in the abolition of serfdom, which was being exploited by reactionaries opposing the recruiting drive. On August 26 János Pálffy, a Transylvanian representative who was later to be a member of the National Defence Commission and one of the Debrecen peace party, enthusiastically urged the patriots of Transylvania to pursue the struggle and protect Transylvania's union with Hungary (although he did so in a tone that remained faithful to the dynasty) and spurned any feelings of nostalgia for separate Transylvanian government. In his view the Transylvanians could scarcely look back with much pride even "on the age of our national princes." Even in those days the lead had more than once been taken by "petty tyrants" and "knavish minions." Later Pálffy wrote against the efforts at a breakaway by the Saxons of Nagyszeben too. A similar position on the issue of Transylvania was taken on August 27 by László Kőváry, who asked, "Is the Mere Shadow of a Political Government Required in Transylvania"? and answered no. Transylvanian separatism, he said, was "an unhappy idea" both now and in the past: "Was the land of Transylvania, while it governed itself separately, not a constant setting for the dissensions of oligarchs? While we were under Turkish protection the ridiculous little pashas who as princes were a mockery wove their intrigues against each other on the field of battle, and since we have come under German protection the petty tyrants do the same behind the curtains of the camarilla." One might add that this appraisal came from a Transylvanian who had made a painstaking study of Transylvanian history. On the same day, August 27, Lipót Lőw, the rabbi of Pápa, said in an article headed "The Hungarians and the Germans" that although some Viennese certainly did not like the Hungarians, the better part of the German nation appreciated Hungary and saw it as a "natural bulwark against Russia." On August 31 came a leading article by J. G. and J. A., describing themselves as "Romanian representatives," entitled "A Few Words to the Romanian People." They explained that it would be "ingratitude" to claim official, local-authority rights for the Romanian language, since that would endanger the unity of the country and lead to a perfect Babel. On September 3, the eve of the crisis, László Nagy contradicted Viennese assertions by saying that it was certainly possible to have "two ministries in the Monarchy," for the Hungarians had earlier known themselves to be an "autonomous, independent nation" and the present independent Hungarian government was therefore to be considered "solely a concomitant of our constitution" and not an acquisition "born of revolution."

The September 6 number contained Vörösmarty's reply, entitled "On the Hungarian Army, to Petőfi," to an attack on him by the latter in a poem that had appeared in the *Életképek*. Vörösmarty declared that the majority had in fact voted for expanding the existing regiments. To react in a way "more petulant than necessary" was fruitless. "In any case, I do not think this little war of words need destroy the good relationship between us. The press is there so that we may write in it. Petőfi has expressed his opinion of me, and now

I shall express mine. He considers me a culpable politician, I him a very feeble and reckless one." The editor added a note saying that the majority, at that time of urgent need, had acted correctly in trying to strengthen the existing regiments with recruits as quickly as possible; therefore it was neither prudent or patriotic to attack the government and the majority on this subject and so turn the people against the army. Around this time Károly Szathmáry devoted several articles to the question of the Serbs and their demands, stressing that it was not oppression but subversion of them by Austrian reaction that had caused them to take up arms. The Hungarians for their part, he said, were prepared to offer them an olive branch and indeed recognize that a Serbian nation also dwelt in the country. On September 7 Márton Diósi refuted the attacks on the Hungarians made "under a veil of democracy" by the *Österreichische Allgemeine Zeitung* in Vienna. On the same day came the first dissertation on foreign policy in *Kossuth Hírlapja* by Imre Sz., probably Imre Szabad (Frereych or Freireich), of whom the reference works say only that he was a teacher of English in Pest who wrote for the *Életképek*, although he featured fairly frequently in Kossuth's paper towards the end of the year as a writer of leading articles. Szabad is known to have become a ministerial official in 1848 and done military service in 1849. After the surrender at Komárom he was a teacher in London and Edinburgh. He joined Garibaldi's legion and then gained the rank of colonel on the side of the North in the American Civil War. In this article (headed "Let Us Look Around") he predicted that after the conflict a "diplomatic compromise" with Austria "would unfailingly follow," but this in itself would not provide enough of a guarantee. He suggested that the Hungarians "familiarize civilized Europe with the internal structure of our conditions": this "accord will offer us the best of occasions for introducing ourselves to the world. Let us settle our affairs with Austria, but in the presence of the envoys from London, Paris, and Frankfurt." Here again the subject was some kind of move towards attaining diplomatic recognition for Hungary partly in the form of foreign guarantees of a type once sought by the old feudal Hungarian politicians. On September 9 a writer signing himself "S." contributed an article called "Our Position and Our

Politicians" that sharply attacked the line taken by the radical *Nép-elem* and those who had initiated the September 8 resolutions of the Egalitarian Society, arguing that they were "employing every means to bring down the present government." Behind this one can perceive an indirect warning from Kossuth that he disapproved of the extra-parliamentary activities. On September 12 Wesselényi spoke up again, on this occasion to defend Széchenyi, who had been taken off to the lunatic asylum at Döbling, from aspersions cast by *Marczius Tizenötödike*: "I consider a low slanderer . . . anyone who dares assert that Széchenyi would have been capable of deserting the cause of his country at any time, least of all in the hour of danger, or of fleeing from peril, or particularly makes the trumped-up charge of sinking to reprehensible and shameful support for dastardly reaction." Later, on November 7, Wesselényi wrote from Freywaldau to defend himself against similar charges by *Marczius*.

The Crisis of Autumn 1848

The great turn of events was signalled by Kossuth's "Announcement" on the front page on September 14: "From this day forth I am no longer a minister. From this day forth my hands are no longer tied by the bonds of ministerial comradeship." After a week's rest, he said, "I shall profess myself a journalist, a newspaperman again, and alongside the editorship of Mr József Bajza I shall conduct my paper myself. . . . From next week the reader will find the spirit of my policy and continued studies of mine on these pages." But of course Kossuth did not simply become a journalist again. In fact, as head of the National Defence Commission, he took an even more important part than before in the preparations for the struggle. Yet he did, as Mihály Horváth put it, begin "a series of articles, some addressed to the nation and some to the armed forces; written in flaming words, they left a trail of fire behind them and awakened enhanced enthusiasm in the minds of men." Articles by other writers continued to feature as well. On September 15 Károly Szathmáry held out hope of victory. On September 17 Károly Szabó urged "military training" for the younger generation, while the Romanian János Drágos, in an article headed "The Romanians," explained why it was more correct to speak of the Romanians than of the Wallachians and reassured readers that there was no need to fear any desire to separate from Hungary. On the other hand, he argued that "the assimilation operation . . . of zealous Hungarian citizens" was provoking feelings of distress and that it would be right to recognize the Romanians legally as a nation. But all this, along with the news coverage and correspondents' reports, paled before Kossuth's vast and dramatic utterances and proclamations summoning the nation to war. On September 19 Kossuth predicted that "the incursion of Jelačić . . . will be followed by the liberation of Hungary" and proclaimed a mass uprising: "To arms, whoever is a man, while the women dig a horrific grave between Veszprém and Fejérvár /Székesfehérvár/ to bury either Hungary's honour or the adversary." In the same number, Kossuth contributed an article called "My Resignation and What Ensued" on the turning point and the events leading up to it, saying that "in five months" there had "never been a moment . . . when I could be satisfied with myself." According to the September 20 number, "Even in the breasts of the most faithful men fidelity and reverence towards the monarchy have been more shaken by the monstrous experiences of the last two months than the greatest enemy of the king was able to shake them over many years." On September 22 Kossuth addressed an ardent appeal "To the Hungarian Soldiers," which according to an editorial note also appeared as a separate leaflet: "To arms, all who have Hungarian souls! Let us win and then settle accounts with the traitors"! After that came a rousing article by Ábrányi. A separate leaflet was also made of a soul-stirring appeal to the Hungarian people by Kossuth which appeared in the paper on September 24: "So to arms, you poor, forsaken, yet brave Hungarian people"! This was Kossuth's last article before he departed the same day on his recruiting tour of the Great Plain; he appeared in the paper again only in November, after his visit to the upper Danube camp, apart from his farewell speech in the House of Representatives, which Bajza published on September 26. Other writers took over, among them Pál Hunfalvy. He was later to be one of the peace party in Debrecen, but on September 28 he brought all his historical knowledge and analytical ability to bear in attacking "the Austrian camarilla." Having detailed the "devilish intrigues" against Hungary ever since 1526, he contributed a five-part article between October 3 and October 15 entitled "A Few Critical Observations on Viennese Policy," which made a no less sharp attack on its political villainies. József Kolmár, a friend of Petőfi's who had at one time been an assistant editor of the *Életképek* and at the last feudal Diet had served as proofreader for the *Országgyűlési Napló* (Journal of the Diet), now belonged to the staff of *Kossuth Hírlapja*, having been invited to do so by Bajza. On September 29 he contributed a call to arms that maintained the trappings of fidelity to the dynasty, entitling it "For Our Country and Our King." In the same issue there was a report from Gábor Egressy on Kossuth's tour of the Great Plain and the uprising of the people. On September 30 Anasztáz Theodorovics supplied a leading article in which he warned the Serbs that by abetting "Austrian tyranny" they were opposing the cause of freedom; the writer added a note saying that his piece had originally been intended for the Serbian paper in Pest, but he had realized it would be "incompatible with the spirit" of that paper. On October 5 and 6 József Barsi addressed "The Prelates of Hungary," remarking that they absented themselves when it came to furthering the nation's cause. During October there were leading articles almost every day from Ábrányi, signed with his initials, calling the people to arms, arousing enthusiasm, and considering the likely destiny of the Viennese revolution. Szathmáry too spoke out against "The Policy of the Camarilla." Among the advertisements was one for a series of pamphlets he was starting, with the title "The Three-Hundred-Year-Long Efforts of the Austrian Ruling House to Oppress the Hungarian People." On October 10 the principal place was taken by a report from V. on the latest revolution and the day that "conferred honour on the Austrian people." In the same number K. N. (perhaps Károly Nehéz) said that the Viennese cabinet had not managed "to topple this country over into anarchy or force it into open revolution, which in Hungary could only be social." Moreover, he said, the people now possessed political rights. If the Monarchy, on the other hand, obstructed national development, it "would directly force the nation into /declaring/ a republic." K. N. contributed several other articles in the weeks following. For instance, on October 20 he said, "May Heaven save us from Anglo-French intervention," arguing that the British and French had talked about the Italians without doing anything for them, the Cavaignac government was pursuing a miserly and purblind policy, and "this perverse and selfish French policy is mediating in order to suppress the revolutions." On October 22 Ábrányi reflected that if there were a battle near Vienna, where Hungary's forces were, "the past, whose name was royal absolutism, military tyranny, and aristocratic arrogance," would do battle "against the future, whose name is people's liberty, national independence, and civil equality." In the same number Szabad contributed an article on the Viennese papers and Szathmáry one on the Transylvanian Romanians. Barsi addressed a few words "To Hungary's Great Aristocrats," remarking on the grim part they had played in Hungarian history, while recognizing some "praiseworthy exceptions" and "white ravens among the ungrateful hordes of cuckoos." Afterwards *vicecomes* Balázs Szőllősy, a former member of the staff of the *Athenaeum*, reported from Máramarossziget (Sighetul Marmaţiei) that the Hungarian hussars wanted to return home from Galicia. On October 29 the paper published a report from V. in Vienna, written on the morning of October 23, that Messenhauser was hoping that the Hungarians would approach and that "the fate of Europe is being decided during these days." However, on November 3 Szathmáry argued that the withdrawal from the vicinity of Vienna did not amount to a Hungarian defeat. On the following day T. devoted a leader to the slanders by the "yellow-and-black papers," which were purporting to discover rebellion, anarchy, and terrorism. Pál Balogh began an article in several instalments by saying that because "the stubborn maintenance of the tyrannical régime over three long centuries" had left the nation in ignorance, there was a need for enlightenment and good proclamations. On November 7, Sz. examined the question of the Transylvanian Romanians, while Ákos Birányi, one of the March Youth, reported on the formation on the Bocskai corps. In an article headed "Polish Affair" on November 10, Imre Zsarnay said that the traditional Hungarian sympathy for the Poles should not decrease because, when it came down to it, the Polish representatives in the Viennese National Assembly had also voted against receiving the Hungarian delegation; although the Poles were Slavs, they were not Pan-Slavists. On November 14 Ábrányi reminded readers that this was now "a battle of life and death for the Hungarian people" and that "the loss of our freedom" would mark "the end of everything we have and of the prosperity of all." On the following day, November 15, came the first article by Kossuth since the end of September, concerned with the exposure of the "Vienna-Olmütz (Olomouc) Den of Crime." After that it was again foreign policy matters that came to the fore and indeed became subjects of debate in the columns of *Kossuth Hírlapja*. Szabad put forward the argument on November 16 that "only the indifference shown by the diplomacy of Europe has made possible the treacheries committed against Hungary by the House of Habsburg. We are left to our own devices, and knowing that, we must bravely pit ourselves against the soulless sleuths of the dynasty." On the next day, November 17, Hunfalvy began a fairly long leader in instalments entitled "Policy," in which he was clearly referring to the radicals when he described how "certain men are fidgety about the National Assembly's not having declared Hungary's independence." To do so, he said, would first and foremost be superfluous, because as things were there was an "independent, responsible Hungarian ministry" at the head of the country in the legal sense. "Nor should anyone think," he went on, in reply to the arguments of the radicals, "that the foreign powers will only recognize us as a sovereign country if we make a declaration of some kind or other." In his opinion the matter did not depend on a declaration; if the Hungarians beat those attacking them, they could make their declaration, but if they did not, a declaration would be "adding folly to misfortune." In the continuation of the article on November 24 Hunfalvy said, "European foreign policy does not recognize peoples or their inalienable rights; it only recognizes the governments that rule over them. Against this our mind and emotions rebel; we believed it would change, but sadly we realize it has not." Hunfalvy then reviewed the development of international policy and the predominance of the eighteenth-century principle of a European balance of power. He concluded, with no small insight, that the Frankfurt assembly would not create a unified Germany, that German unity would be brought about by the "iron rod of Prussia," and that France and Britain would side with Austria, the Habsburg Monarchy. "We are justly defending ourselves against unjust attack. . . . We must fight a life-and-death struggle and prepare ourselves to the utmost so that our just demands may be recognized as reasonable, for Europe has no place for the weak." Szabad took issue with Hunfalvy's arguments on November 28. In a leading article entitled "Foreign Policy" he asserted that the system of balance of power was over, that "the break-up of the House of Habsburg is inevitable," and that although "the declaration of our independence may perhaps win allies for Austria, it will certainly win them for us." The anti-dynastic tendency of the paper grew appreciably stronger during the final month of the year. In the mean time, on November 25, Barsi had demanded in an article entitled "Let Us Act" that the government do more about teaching Hungarian to those of non-Hungarian extraction. He suggested that the best way would be for "one or two kindergartens to be opened in every non-Hungarian community." To the November 30 and December 1 issues L-s F-y contributed an article in two parts entitled "To the Doubters" in which he condemned those who were cowed, informing them that one "cannot bargain with tyrants" and that the "three-hundred-year-old Habsburg yoke" could not be borne any longer. On December 5 Kossuth supplied an unsigned article arguing that the elevation to the throne of Francis Joseph, who was preparing to suppress the so-called Hungarian revolt, had disregarded Hungary in a shameful and ridiculous way. "Our army and all officials," he continued, "are freed of their allegiance to Ferdinand V. No allegiance of any kind is owed to anyone any more," but all the more was it therefore owed "to the nation and to the constitution". The Hungarians, he said, were "not vassals," "not an absolute monarchy," and could not be treated like a flock of sheep; "let the National Assembly seek a governor." This anonymous article went noticeably farther than the "official" text that Kossuth sent as a guide for the proclamation by László Csányi and Görgey published on December 10. On December 6 Kossuth's last article was published in the paper, declaring "There Is No

King," Francis Joseph being no concern of Hungarians'. On December 10 Béla Dezső warned in a leader that if the Hungarians did not assist Transylvania, Hungary too would run into trouble. Two days later Szabad cited the example of the great French Revolution to prove that in difficulties one could win through a popular uprising, taking steps against the Vendée and legislating energetically: "Constant rigour and steadfast energy, which the historians call terrorism because of certain private trespasses, were what freed the French nation, swimming in a sea of troubles." As the crisis deepened, Bajza decisively refuted an unfounded charge Zerffi had made in the columns of *Der Ungar* purporting to discover anti-Semitism in *Kossuth Hírlapja*. Zerffi, he said, had "written many foolish things" but had now gone to extremes. Zerffi had suggested that "sheltering behind the name of our greatest man" could not save Bajza from hearing the truth. Bajza's superior response was this: "During my writing career I have already heard so-called truths from my adversaries, without anyone's once being able to show that I needed to shelter behind the name of another. I have encountered greater heroes in this truth-telling business than you, Mr Zerffi, and I have always found a goose quill a sufficient weapon with which to defend myself." Somewhat later Szeberényi and Bajza had a sharp bout of polemics with János Illucz Oláh, the former editor of that "unbearably odious time-serving paper," one bone of contention being that the *Nemzeti*, while under his control, had described as illegal and a piece of treachery a government decree by which "religious education" in the Pest grammar school was to be "a subject for private tuition and not a school subject." But all in all, the battle against Viennese policy steadily squeezed everything else into the background. On December 16, Szabó, under the title "The Latest Phases of Illyrianism," identified and attacked the duplicity and underhand operation of this policy and the part played in it personally by that "blood-sucking woman" the Archduchess Sofia. In a continuation of the article on December 19, Szabó quoted the *Agramer Zeitung* as saying that the insurrectionists in Budapest would now have to follow those in Vienna in atoning for the death of Latour: "Kossuth, Perczel, Madarász, and many others must share the fate of Blum and Messenhauser." Meanwhile, on December 17 the paper replied in a leading article headed "Magyar" to what it identified as lies in the *Journal des Österreichischen Lloyds*. Szabad, who was one of the most frequent contributors during the final weeks, returned on December 19 to the subject of international politics with rather more optimism than before: "Who can express doubts, saying that the long-promised armed intervention by France can be postponed much longer"? On December 22 the same writer quoted some lines of Byron in English and drew a parallel with the American war of independence against Britain. In the same issue M. declared that "the intrigues of our enemies only hasten and strengthen our development," for "the emergence of republicanism . . . has been assisted by the intrigues of the camarilla." It was also in the December 22 number that there appeared the "Notice" of the National Defence Commission to "the organs of the periodical press" that they should handle the news of the war carefully or risk aiding the enemy: "The government, which honours the principle of press freedom, will not gladly resort to repressive measures against the press; but it warns the press that one careless word may often do more harm than a whole plan of betrayal, and the government therefore cannot tolerate that the press should do harm to the country out of carelessness." The last two issues at the end of the month carried an unsigned, two-part leading article headed "A Few Words on the Handling of the Press." Austria, it said, was trying to oppress the Hungarians, but they should not be afraid: "Let the press roar in the ear of the people the undeniable truth that if the people has a will and if its millions are inspired by a single idea, there is no power on earth that can withstand it." The article took exception to the fact that some, such as the radicals, ignored this essential task and, "considering declarations to be factors of special effect, constantly urge us to make a declaration: to declare independence." However, one of the things that Bajza warned in a few observations on the article made in an editorial note was that the press, "because of the general conjunction and merger into one party, should not close its eyes to reactionary movements."

Leafing through these six months of material one immediately notices what a widespread and varied body of contributors *Kossuth Hírlapja* possessed. One could list others as well, for instance, István Gorove (1819-81), the economist, landowner, and liberal politician, the poet Mihály Tompa (1817-68), older men like Sámuel Fabriczy (1791-1858) of the Szepes region, who had been on the staff of the *Jelenkor*, members of the March Youth such as Gyula Bulyovszky, the Pest professor of medicine János Balassa, and others ranging from future members of the peace party to Count László Teleki. The only names one misses from paper are those of the Madarász brothers, the radicals who stood close to them, the majority of the contributors to *Reform* and the *Nép-elem*, and, let us add, Táncsics. The broad influence of *Kossuth Hírlapja* is reflected in an abortive attempt in December 1848 by the Austrians to hoodwink the Székely inhabitants of the Háromszék by distributing forged copies of it. Kossuth's paper was the most powerful weapon of all the publications at the time of the political preparations for the war of independence and the defence of the nation.

Bibliography

Sándor Szilágyi, "Bajza," in *A magyar forradalom*, p. 339; József Ferenczy, *Garay János* (János Garay), (Budapest, 1883); Árpád Károlyi, *Németújvári gróf Batthyány Lajos első magyar miniszterelnök főbenjáró pöre* (Trial for a Capital Offence of Count Lajos Batthyány of Németújvár, the First Hungarian Prime Minister), vols. 1 and 2 (Budapest, 1932); József Szücsi (Bajza), *Bajza József* (József Bajza (Budapest, 1914); István Barta, ed., *Kossuth Lajos az Országos Honvédelmi Bizottmány élén*, vol. 1, *1848 szept.-dec.* (Lajos Kossuth at the Head of the National Defence Commission, vol. 1, September-December 1848) (Budapest, 1952); Dezső Tóth, "Bajza József" (József Bajza), *It*, 1954, pp. 121-35; Béla Dezsényi and Gábor Salacz, "Két ismeretlen Bajza-levél Kossuth Lajoshoz" (Two Unknown Letters of Bajza's to Lajos Kossuth) *ItK*, 1954, pp. 93-97; Béla Dezsényi, "Kossuth, a forradalmi publicista" (Kossuth, the Revolutionary Journalist), *It*, 1953, pp. 5-63; István Sinkovics, ed., *Kossuth Lajos cz első magyar felelős minisztériumban, 1848 április-szeptember* (Lajos Kossuth in the First Responsible Hungarian Ministry, April-September 1848) (Budapest, 1957).

14. Literary, Professional, and Provincial Papers

With the vigorous development of the political press that followed the revolution, the literary and other periodicals were either pushed somewhat into the background or became strongly politicized themselves. But one should add that the fashion papers that played a literary role in the 1840s had even before the revolution represented various tendencies of a political nature. None of this was altered by the fact that the growing corps of professional journalists, most of them impecunious members of the intelligentsia who lived by their profession, often worked concurrently for papers with quite varied approaches.

Literary Fashion Papers

The biggest change of all took place in the "literary, artistic, and fashion paper" *Honderű*. It had begun in 1843 as a well-intentioned and successful weekly with an attractive layout, printed at the university press. Among the contributors were Vörösmarty, Miklós Szemere, János Garay, and Miklós Jósika and of the younger generation Kálmán Lisznyay, Alajos Degré, and even Pál Vasvári. Lázár Petrichevich-Horváth (1807-51), who started it, was a Transylvanian aristocrat, the well-educated son of an army officer, who had more ambition than perception, managerial skill, or knowledge of his fellow men and allowed his staff, headed by Lajos Nádaskay as editor, to turn the paper into a forum for literary and political reaction and a defender of the old order through its attacks on young Hungarian writers and Petőfi in person. Thus it was Nádaskay, with his quibbling salon jokes, who went down in Hungary's literary history as the negative figure others might as well have been cast as. Meanwhile Petrichevich-Horváth's enthusiasm was curbed by the paper's declining popularity and rising losses, and he considered handing over the right of publication to Gusztáv Emich in mid-1848. But the March revolution intervened, and the Nádaskay who had hitherto been the evil genius of *Honderű* now hastened to climb on the revolutionary bandwagon. On March 18, he gave an enthusiastic account of the Pest revolution, published the National Song, and saw to it that the paper henceforward appeared with the heading "Peace, liberty, concord, serene homeland, liberty, equality, fraternity." Whereas earlier in *Honderű* Imre Medve (alias Péter Tatár) had confidently sidelined those who had "allowed themselves to be deluded" by the work of "Mr Cabet," *Honderű* after the great turn of events cut off a series entitled "Letter from a Proletarian," saying that the articles had "like the *táblabírók*, been too late with their ideas of reform; time has passed them by." Medve went on to appeal to his "fellow citizens" to consider "the cause of the despised, neglected, scorned proletariat as your own." On April 2 Nádaskay announced that the paper would cease publication, and not long after, as we have seen, he started the radical paper *Reform* with his colleague Zerffi. For a while Petrichevich-Horváth tried to continue *Honderű*'s German version, *Morgenröthe*, and even asked the palatine for a loan of 2,000 forints. Finally he chose to take one of his frequent trips abroad, this time to the Holy Land.

Unlike the conservative *Honderű*, the *Pesti Divatlap*, a weekly which had been appearing since 1844, served the cause of the opposition among the nobility. It became so popular among the "middle orders," the rural middle and petty nobility and the intelligentsia of noble origin, that its circulation topped three thousand. Imre Vahot (1820-79), the publisher and editor, is considered to have been a fairly typical bourgeois periodical proprietor who on more than one occasion revealed himself as having a petty, business mentality and an eye for the main chance. Not unexpectedly, he tried to use Petőfi, who was an assistant editor for a while, as something of a living advertisement. Nevertheless, he supported the policy of the noble reform movement, particularly the policy of Kossuth, who was a relative of his, to the end. He espoused the cause of national independence and its feudal traditions enthusiastically and those of the Hungarian language and Magyarization if possible more enthusiastically still, but he showed far less interest in social problems. Unsurprisingly, Petőfi and his group soon outgrew this liberal line of the nobility and indeed turned against it, although certain members of the younger generation remained on the staff. One such was Gusztáv Remellay (1819-66), the son of an official in the Szolnok salt depot, who not long after became a colonel and judge of the military court in Görgey's camp and then suffered long years of imprisonment. Another was István Kléh (1825-1913), who wrote an eye-witness account of the March revolution in Pest. Vahot and his associates eagerly took up the outward "national" forms such as dress and dance. The *Divatlap*, like *Honderű* and *Életképek*, often carried fashion plates as a supplement. Most of these were engraved in copper or steel by Domokos Perlaszka, following Paris models. Unfortunately they were often cut out of the paper by readers (presumably female in the main) at the time, with the result that copies of these periodicals have come down to us incomplete. However, in 1848 the long-neglected woodcut started to come back into fashion, and woodcuts could be placed within the text.

From the beginning of 1848 the *Divatlap* was already expressing its political sympathies more forcefully. The first number of the year included a portrait of Kossuth as a supplement and contained detailed reports on events at the Diet. Later there was a long article on the March revolution and the winning of freedom of the press, and the National Song was published as well. More and more often issues began with expressly political leading articles by Vahot, with titles such as "Equality before the Law" and "National Army." Then followed a column by József Kolmár in which he summed up the events in the final stages of the Diet in Pressburg. From July 5 the paper took the new title of *Budapesti Divatlap*, a "social, literary, and artistic gazette," and appeared in a larger, quarto format. Vahot changed his printers as well. The earlier firm of Beimel, which had been bought by Lukács, lost the contract to Rudolf Eisenfels, who had left Kozma to start a press in Három korona utca, in the Lipótváros district of Pest, where he printed a succession of revolutionary publications so eagerly that in 1849 Windischgrätz consigned him to prison in chains. From July 5 there also appeared a twice-weekly supplement called the *Nemzetőr* (Militiaman) that could be ordered separately. It intended to publish what "interests the militiamen and friends of our society, literature, and art." On September 10 the *Nemzetőr* published some lines by "A Volunteer" attacking Petőfi for allowing his sword to rust during the time of the battles in the south and championing Vörösmarty against Petőfi's poem attacking him, since the former "as a legislator voted with the majority on the subject of setting up the army at the honourable and prudent instigation of Kossuth, and not with the Madarászes, who rush against everything like blinded flies."

By this time the *Divatlap* had fallen behind its main rival, *Életképek*, the publication of the radical youth. In a column entitled "Newspaper Skirmisher" Vahot took issue with *Életképek*, taunting the young writers for fleeing from fashion towards "more precipitous ideas of advance." When Vasvári wrote in *Életképek* (No. 24) that the March Youth had "played a guiding, leading role in the history of the transformation of our country," Vahot swiftly dubbed this an illusion, along with the idea that the Pest revolution had had any effect on the Diet in Pressburg. This, he said, was "the officiousness of a vain leader, conceit, boastful display in borrowed feathers," Vasvári thinking he was Lamartine. The *Divatlap* continued to follow the line of the nobility until the paper came to an end on December 24, 1848.

Életképek started in 1843. Its initiator, Adolf Frankenburg (1811-84), was an enterprising journalist who wrote well, although he coupled the job with an official post on the Lieutenancy Council. Since he came from a bourgeois family of Hungarian Germans, he was divorced from the outlook and prejudices of the nobility. He tried to popularize the ideas of the new, bourgeois Hungary among the urban bourgeoisie, which was becoming Magyarized, and among commoners in the professions. He hastened to offer the paper to Petőfi and his group when the Society of Ten turned against Vahot. In 1847 the government not fortuitously transferred him to Vienna, but he managed to retain the right to publish the paper while handing over the editorship to Jókai, who relied on Albert Pálffy and Károly Berecz as assistant editors and had Sükei, Vasvári, Petőfi, and early in 1848 Arany among his contributors. After the March revolution, which was reported for the paper by Jókai and Gábor Egressy, *Életképek* too adopted the triple slogan on its title page but with a unique and conscious alteration of the sequence: "Equality, liberty, fraternity." The subtitle became "Word of the People," although Jókai omitted this again from May 21. The "Innovations" column announced that with the abolition of noble ranks, names would henceforward be written differently—Dezsőfi instead of Dessewffy, for instance. "Our line," one can read in the March 23 issue, "has been proclaimed under the open sky, and we shall retain it in the field of the free press. To protect all that is oppressed, to pursue all that is tyrannical. . . . That is our motto." The number of political articles and news items rose, even in the lively "Feuilleton" column. From April 30 Petőfi's name appeared beside Jókai's on the title page, as associate editor. Thus *Életképek* became the second organ of the March Youth, after *Marczius Tizenötödike*, or perhaps the true one, but it was at the same time an instance of the divisions among them. The editorial tasks continued to be performed by Jókai, whose various writings, articles, and notes in the "Charivari" section of the paper showed more and more clearly that he was distancing himself from March radicalism. Petőfi was restrained only by his contract from leaving the paper altogether. In the April 2 and April 9 numbers Jókai was still concerning himself with "The Details of the World-Famous Conspiracy Trial of the Martinovics," evoking the memory of the Republican Catechism of 1794. But on May 18 he wrote about "the great mass of tillers of the soil" with marked disillusionment:

> We deceived ourselves for a long time. We thought we had a people. But we have not. While we still had a people, it was the nobility. To the great mass of tillers of the soil the word "home country" was unknown. And it still is. For liberty they are thankful to the next man but not to their country. If you ask them to rise up to defend their country from the Muscovites, they burst into tears and cry that they would rather do unpaid labour service and starve. . . . They loathe men in black coats and will not believe them. They do not understand the national colours, and to them the law is not law unless adorned with the imperial seal of the double-headed eagle. They will not bear arms on our behalf, they will not trust in our words, they will not assist us in our plans.

On the other hand, the radicalism and republicanism of Petőfi were far in advance of the average reader. Sensing this tension at the time of the elections, Petőfi himself saw a need in the June 11 number to admit the right of the monarchy to exist under the conditions that prevailed in the country, while maintaining his opinion in principle:

> As for my poem addressed to the kings, which is the main cause of my unpopularity, it was the first open word of republicanism uttered in Hungary, and those who believe it was also the last are infinitely mistaken. Monarchy in Europe is coming to an end. . . . Once an idea becomes accepted in the world, one can sooner destroy the world than eradicate that idea from it. Such now is the idea of a republic. . . . However, the monarchy still has a future in this country, indeed there is an inescapable need for it nowadays, and so I have not proclaimed a republic, I have not agitated for the idea (as people claim I have), I have only broached it, so that people may become accustomed to it. To do more than that would have been sheer madness, and I have been compelled to do this much, at personal sacrifice, only by my love of the country and of mankind.

In the same article he pinpointed his position in relation to the government as well: "By saying as I did that I did not trust the ministry, I did not wish to drive them out; I wished to spur them on . . . to behave so that they might enjoy general trust and affection. A coachman cracks his whip not to make his horses fall between the shafts, but to make them go faster." Petőfi had originally intended this article, dated May 27, for the *Pesti Hírlap*, but in the end Zsigmond Kemény had rejected it.

The columns of *Életképek* continued to feature lively, colourful dispatches. For instance, reports from Vienna came from its correspondent Gábor Pap right up until October and then also from Jókai, who had been commissioned to go there with Csernátoni by Kossuth. But the paper showed growing signs of decline. The number of subscribers had been around fifteen hundred in March, but a couple of months later it was under a thousand. Petőfi's last appearance of any note in *Életképek* was on November 26, with his poem "Tiszteljétek a közkatonákat" (Salute the Rank and File), saying how much the soldiers were sacrificing for their country, even though "they only exchange one misery for another." Towards the end of the year, when Petőfi had distanced himself from the paper and the editorial work, it was almost symbolic that Sándor Szilágyi, ever adroit and busy positioning himself, was taken on as an assistant. "With the last number of these pages," Jókai wrote in farewell in December 1848, "my editorship's time is up. If the God of my country had not placed greater cares upon me I should never have divorced myself from this field of activity. . . . With my departure from it, the paper will not change, in fact I believe it will become better." In fact, the end of the year brought the end of *Életképek* as well.

Alongside these papers was a fourth that should be mentioned. *Hazánk* was published in Győr by the grocer Richárd Noisser three times a week as a folio broadsheet, the printers being the Streibig press. Originally, as a "commercial and literary paper," it had not concerned itself with politics, but the fact that from 1847, with the cooperation of the liberal opposition physician Pál Kovács as editor, it provided a forum for the young writers, particularly Petőfi, gave it a specific, indirect political colouring. Moreover, the Lieutenancy Council notified the Győr censor in January 1848 that "inclusion of any blatantly political or governmental comments, news, reports, or witticism, in other words, those definitely forbidden in the paper's draft, are banned on pain of losing its licence." Of course the revolution changed the situation. From April 6 *Hazánk* appeared with a new subtitle: "Political and Literary Gazette." Ferenc Nagy, the twenty-year-old son of a Győr corn chandler, shortly to be a Hungarian soldier, signing himself with his noble predicate "Eöttevényi," wrote on April 20 desiring "the liberation of the working class . . . from the tyranny of their employers," in other words, "the safeguarding of the workers by the country from the private masters," although for the time being he demanded only public works for the "unemployed" poor. From July 1 the paper continued under the new name of the *Győri Hírlap* (Győr Journal), and on August 10 it unexpectedly closed down. Although Kovács opposed radicalism, he allowed space on principle to all expressions of opinion, including an article by János Pompéry (1819-87) that sharply attacked the Győr militia or, indirectly, local citizens prepared to take up arms against revolutionary plebeian elements but far less willing to do so against the power of the Habsburgs. The article aroused local indignation that bordered on violence, and so Kovács, having fled to Pest, announced on August 15 in *Kossuth Hírlapja* that the paper was closing because Győr "has almost tangibly shown that it has no conception of freedom of the press."

At this point one should mention finally the revolutionary comic paper *Charivari*, edited by Gusztáv Lauka (1818-1902), one of the March Youth. It was the first of its type in the country's history, using humour as a weapon against the political efforts of the conservatives. After a specimen copy had been distributed on June 15, it began to appear twice a week in Pest from July 1 in folio format, with the subtitle "Dongó" (Bumblebee). Appearing alongside Lauka as publisher was Miklós Szerelmei (Szeremley or Lieb, 1803-75), a graphic artist who had started life as an officer in the imperial corps of engineers but preferred to roam around the world. He had been on the barricades in Paris in 1830, then learnt lithography, cropped up in America, England, and Scandinavia, and eventually opened a lithographic press in Pest in 1845. He drew the cartoons for the *Charivari*, after the manner of Daumier. He served as a Hungarian lieutenant-colonel during the war of independence and afterwards emigrated to London. The paper had a modest circulation. A mere eighty-two copies were forwarded by the Pest post office. It ceased publication hardly three months later, on September 21. In his words of farewell the editor's explanation was that "since the bulk of our writers have been sent off to camp," there was not enough copy. He himself was occupied with official tasks (as clerk to the National Defence Commission), and of course he did not have enough money.

Professional and Educational Papers

To some extent the influence of politics was also felt in the professional press. For instance, the *Academiai Értesítő* (Academic Bulletin), edited by Ferenc Toldy, which appeared monthly until the revolution of March 1848, failed to appear again until the summer of 1850. On March 18 the *Pesti Hírlap* commented on Toldy's conduct in another context, considering it conspicuous that "in the apartment of the Academy of Sciences, where inscriptions and transparencies were wont to appear on all other occasions for illumination, now there was nothing at all when the freedom of the press was to be celebrated. To our knowledge these inscriptions are usually ordered by the secretary. How come they have now been omitted"? However, the *Orvosi Tár* (Medical

Magazine), edited by Pál Bugát and Ferenc Flór, appeared regularly every week right up until December 25. Bugát is known to have become the national chief physician and for that lost his university chair during the subsequent period of Austrian absolutism. From August 15 to September 15, 1848, and perhaps longer, a biweekly *Gyógyszerészi Hírlap* (Pharmacological Journal) was edited by Adolf Ferenc Láng in Nyitra (Nitra). Another new periodical to start up in Pest seems only to have got so far as a first, undated number. This was *Magyarföld és Népei Eredeti Képekben* (Hungary and its Peoples in Original Pictures), edited by Imre Vahot, with the subtitle "Geographical, Ethnographical, Statistical, and Historical Periodical." Under editor Elek Fényes, the modest *Hetilap* of the Industrial Protection Association, which Kossuth had attempted not long before to use as a political organ of the opposition with his vast articles, now became in fact what its subtitle promised, "A Periodical of Encyclopedic Content Devoting Special Attention to the Economy, Manufacturing, and Commerce," but as such it ceased publication on April 28. The Hungarian Agricultural Society's *Magyar Gazda* appeared irregularly until March 12, 1848, after which it came out twice a week in quarto format, edited by the Society's extremely moderate, almost conservative secretary János Török (1807-74). On April 23 it called on its landowning readers to recommend ways of calculating urbarial dues and compensating for them. The eleven detailed replies received were published between April 30 and June 14. According to the June 15 number, however, Török was obliged in a speech to his Cegléd electors to declare his support for abolishing the usufructs. In practice the paper ceased publication on September 21, although after a long gap one further number appeared on December 7. On July 1 a lawyer named Lőrinc Tóth (1814-1903) who had represented Breznóbánya (Brezno nad Hronom) in the last feudal Diet and then become a counsellor to the head of a department in the new Ministry of Justice is known to have started a professional legal paper called *Törvényhozási és Törvénykezési Lapok* (Legislative and Judicial Papers), which was printed and published twice a week by Landerer and Heckenast, but no one knows how long it survived and no copies of it have been found. A decree from the minister of religious and educational affairs, Baron József Eötvös, dated July 25, 1848, shows that he planned a publication to be known as the *Nevelési Szemle* (Educational Review). It was to follow the example of François Guizot's paper in France and raise standards among teachers. The launch planned for January 1, 1849, never took place. Educational affairs were left largely in the hands of the religious press. A Roman Catholic periodical in this field was *Religio és Nevelés*, which was edited twice a week in Pest by Károly Somogyi (1811-88) and then from July 2 by János Danielik, after which the positions it put forward drew frequent criticism from the radical press. It also had a weekly supplement called *Egyházi Literatúrai Lap* (Church Literary Journal), but after a number of gaps of various lengths it ceased to appear altogether on June 25. Somogyi, by the way, was a partner in László Lukács's printing house and later one of the canons of Esztergom and a corresponding member of the Academy of Sciences. He ultimately perpetuated his name by presenting his valuable library to the city of Szeged. Among his colleagues was István Majer (1813-93), a Catholic priest, copperplate engraver, and teacher at the archiepiscopal institute for the training of master craftsmen, who contributed landscapes and articles to several papers, among other subjects on the public elementary schools. On the other hand, there was the *Protestáns Egyházi és Iskolai Lap* (Protestant Church and School Journal), which had been appearing since 1842. The editors were József Székács (1809-76), a poet and Lutheran bishop, and Pál Török (1808-83), a bishop of the Reformed Church. It was printed in quarto format by Landerer and Heckenast and was a weekly until July 2, after which it came out twice a week. The paper gave an enthusiastic welcome to the achievements of March 1848, including freedom of the press, and also published a poem on the subject entitled "Ima" (Prayer). In the last number, on December 31, 1848, the editors declared that all special interests had to be silent in the face of the peril that threatened the country. Their words of farewell enjoined all to unite in defence of the nation. However, one secular educational publication is known of as well. *Nevelési Emléklapok* (Educational Mementoes) was started in 1846 to mark the centenary of Pestalozzi's birth by Lajos Tavasy (formerly Teichengräber, 1814-77), the principal of the Pest Lutheran School, who came from the Szepesség. It appeared at six-monthly intervals in octavo format, printed by Trattner-Károlyi; six such booklets have survived. While we are on the subject let us mention, exceptionally in this chapter, a paper in German. The *Eltern Zeitung* was brought out monthly by Károly Seltenreich (1813-55), also from the Szepesség and the proprietor of an academy for girls in Pest, and József Fischer (?1794-1887), principal of the Pest School of Commerce. Finally, there was a little professional paper on librarianship entitled *Honi Irodalmi Hírdető* (Domestic Literary Advertiser). It was published monthly in octavo format by Eggenberger and Son of Kecskeméti utca, Pest, the publishers for the Academy and the Kisfaludi Society.

Papers intended to disseminate knowledge in a popular way had once been fashionable, but by this period they survived only in Kolozsvár. The *Erdélyi Híradó* had a weekly supplement called the *Vasárnapi Újság* "for the dissemination of publicly useful information," edited by the polymath and teacher Sámuel Brassai (1800-97). Then there was the *Természetbarát* (Friend of Nature), from July 2 known as the *Ipar- és Természetbarát* (Friend of Industry and Nature), which was edited by Áron Berde, for a time in conjunction with Brassai. Both papers ceased publication in mid-October 1848. However, a new kind of venture, if not always with the same purpose, was represented by the various "popular papers." One such was the *Nép Barátja* already mentioned, and prior to that the *Öreg ABC vén emberek számára*, likewise edited by Gereben Vas and resembling a pamphlet, only four issues of which appeared in Győr from March 24. In Pest a total of six issues appeared between May 2 and 19, 1848, of a publication styled the *Közügyvéd* (Public Advocate), according to its subtitle "A Charitable Popular Paper for Founding a Humanitarian Society." The publisher was Adolf Müller and the editor Ferenc Jósa, a lawyer. József Eötvös had been one of the persons from whom Jósa had requested support, but the venture failed. On July 3 József Santkó, secretary of the "Good and Cheap Book Publishing Society," which had been started with a Roman Catholic bias under the chairmanship of Count István Károlyi, informed the mayor of Pest that the society had decided to launch a *Katolikus Nép-*

lap (Catholic Popular Paper) to be edited by Imre Szabó, a university professor of theology. It first appeared on July 6 in quarto format, printed by Lukács and Somogyi, and continued to come out weekly until December 28 and then with some interruptions through to the autumn of the following year. One might add that the Catholics and Protestants each published a German-language popular paper. *Der Katholische Christ* was edited by János Nogáll and József Krotky from May 7 to December 24, 1848, and *Der Evangelische Christ* by György Bauhofer from March 25 to October 15.

The Provincial Press

With the local advertising papers, which appeared in Hungarian in Pest, Miskolc, Kassa, Debrecen, Arad, and Kolozsvár, one arrives at the subject of the provincial press. With 102 papers in Pest and 5 in Buda, making 107 in all, the press in the new capital far outstripped that of the other cities numerically, Kolozsvár coming a poor second with 15 Hungarian-language papers, followed by the old capital of Pressburg with 13 if one includes the German and Slovak papers. In fact only one of Budapest's papers was in Hungarian, the conservative *Budapesti Híradó*, which survived until July 1. But numerous other places had 2, 4, 6, or even 8 papers, and literary historians have rightly described 1848 as a boom year for the provincial press. The Győr papers have already been discussed. In Kassa, where hitherto there had only been the *Kassa-Eperjesi Értesítő* (Kassa-Eperjes /Prešov/ Bulletin) in Hungarian and German, the first Hungarian illustrated weekly, the *Ábrázolt Folyóirat* (Illustrated Periodical), began to appear in January 1848 after a long period of preparation. From March 25 its name changed to the *Képesújság* (Picture News), and it reappeared on August 5 after a short gap as the *Mulattató* (Diverting) *Képesújság*, continuing until December 9 in large folio format complete with a supplement called the *Értesítő* (Bulletin). The title changes were probably connected with the fact that the editor and publisher, Károly Werfer, the owner of a printing press, initially included political reports as well. When some real estate of his was not accepted in lieu of the deposit required for a political paper, he had to confine himself to entertainment after all. The title changes may also have been connected with a change of editorship on August 5, when János Tichi and later Ferenc Tichi took over. Until the summer of 1848 the leading articles were written by Pál Hunfalvy and his younger brother János. Keeping its readers posted week by week on recent events, the paper published a total of 196 pictures during the year, most of them reproduced from foreign publications. The Paris *Illustration* was a popular source; the captions would be translated from the French by a retired lieutenant, József Staut. But around 40 original pieces by Hungarian graphic artists were included as well, some of them engraved by Werfer himself. The most talented artist on the staff was István Majer, a Catholic priest as well as an illustrator. Majer, who provided about 10 original woodcuts for the paper, has been mentioned already in connection with *Religio és Nevelés*. Understandably, the pictures published were woodcuts, as these were cheaper and easier to position. When a Pest critic objected to this, Werfer pointed out, "In this country original steel or copper engravings cannot be provided for a couple of hundred subscribers." The paper had to close down in December 1848 when Schlick's imperial forces arrived in Kassa. Under orders from the Austrians, Werfer was obliged to set up a camp printing press, but after Schlick had been driven out again he put this press at the disposal of the Hungarian government in Debrecen and with the rank of full lieutenant supervised the operation of it himself, following the main Hungarian camp from place to place.

In Debrecen Károly Balla had been publishing since 1843 a weekly *Debreczen-Nagyváradi Értesítő* (Debrecen-Nagyvárad Bulletin) confined to "articles on sales, purchases, leasing, and the like," but on July 2, 1848, the first truly political paper was started. The *Alföldi Hírlap* emphasized that "the national will and opinion can only be known if every district possesses its own gazette." The new paper's publisher was Lajos Telegdi Kovách, a local bookseller, and the editors were Telegdi, whose pen name was Ottó Csatári, and József Szanka. It appeared twice a week and then, from the end of January 1849, three times a week in folio format, right up until August 2, 1849. A local subscription for six months originally cost 2 forints 40 krajcárs and a postal subscription

3 forints 30 krajcárs. The cost of preparing an issue of five hundred copies was about 15 silver forints. Like the *Értesítő,* it was printed on Debrecen's city press, whose works manager, Endre Tóth, had persuaded the council to buy new iron presses and obtain new type from Prague.

At Arad, where there likewise existed an *Aradi Hírdető* (Arad Advertiser) appearing in Hungarian and German editions, a weekly called *Arad* was started on July 1, 1848, with the subtitle "Political and Literary Gazette." The editor was Pető Bangó, and publication continued until December 23, 1848. The paper was printed in quarto format by the local printer József Schmidt, who was subsequently imprisoned by the Austrians.

The *Miskolczi Értesítő* (Miskolc Bulletin) was already in its eighth year by 1848. Edited and published by József Lichtenstein and Ferdinánd Furmann and set on the press of Lajos Tóth, it appeared as a weekly advertiser, but after the revolution, from March 23, it began to provide political news and leading articles as well. It emerges from a report by Borsod County on May 11, 1848, how it was prevented by the press law from developing into a political paper: it had at first "intervened in debate on political subjects," but unable to put down the caution money required of a political paper it had later undertaken not to concern itself with political themes. However, fate decreed that Szemere, the very man in the government who had applied the press law so strictly, should be the one who later developed it for a time into a political paper. As government commissioner for Upper Hungary, Szemere established himself at the end of 1848 in Miskolc and needed a paper in which to publish his ordinances and other documents. Thus on December 22, under the editorship of Aurél Okruczky, the *Értesítő* temporarily, only until December 27, became a daily paper and the "official" gazette of the government commissioner. It published alongside some rousing speeches the poem "Riadó" (Alarm) by Gergely Czuczor.

In Pécs the editor of the local *Fünfkirchner Zeitung*, which began publication in German in the spring of 1848, was Ernő Adolf Neuwirth, a cultivated, liberal journalist from Verőce (Virovitica) who sympathized with the cause of the Hungarian revolution. From May 31 a Hungarian supplement, the

Pécsi Tárogató (Pécs Clarinet), was published as well. Some researchers consider it to have continued right through until September, although only two issues have so far come to light. The paper is known in any case to have dealt so severely with the members of the city council who were opposed to the March revolution that on June 16 the local chief prosecutor received instructions to institute proceedings under the press law. On June 25 Pál Angyal noted sarcastically in the *Pesti Hírlap* that the mayor of Pécs had forbidden the printing of the *Tárogató* out of "pure devotion to the freedom of the press."

In August 1848 publication began in Szeged of a paper called *Alföldi Csaták* (Battles on the Great Plain), a "Periodical containing War Reports" which appeared irregularly until December. The editor and publisher was Mihály Szabó. Other experiments followed in 1849. Finally, a weekly paper called the *Honunk állapota* (State of the Country) began appearing in Szabadka (Subotica) on November 3, 1848, with Ferenc Szép as editor. The paper, whose purpose was declared to be "enlightenment of the people," was printed in quarto format until January 5, 1849, by the printer Károly Bittermann, who had moved there from Óbuda. Several other experiments followed.

Understandably, the geographical distribution and changing centre of gravity of the press at this time depended on the political and military developments in the revolution and war of independence. Pressburg, once so important a centre of printing in the country and the cradle of the Hungarian and Hungarian-German press, became less and less significant during 1848. This was partly because of the great burst of activity in Budapest, the new capital and centre of the revolution, and partly because Pressburg was occupied early on in the war by imperial forces, which never lost the city again. After the fall of Budapest, Debrecen became the centre of the press for a time, until the move back to the capital began after the victorious spring campaign. Hardly had this been completed before there was a great retreat to the south-east through Szeged, and that likewise left its mark on the press.

Bibliography

Gyula Vahot, ed., *Vahot Imre Emlékiratai* (Memoirs of Imre Vahot), vols. 1 and 2 (Budapest, 1880); János Váczy, "Az első magyar élclap" (The First Hungarian Comic Paper), *Ország Világ*, no. 7 (1887), pp. 104-5; Virgil Koltai, *Dr. Kovács Pál élete és működése* (Life and Activities of Dr Pál Kovács) (Győr, 1889); Gyula Csernátoni, "Vonatkozások Petőfire a 'Charivari'-ban" (References to Petőfi in the *Charivari*), *Petőfi Múzeum*, 1891, pp. 141-44; Zoltán Ferenczi, "Petőfi hírlapi cikkei 1848-ból" (Petőfi's Newspaper Articles of 1848), *Petőfi Múzeum*, 1892, pp. 14-17, 30-35, 63-69, and 84-91; István Berkeszi, *A temesvári könyvnyomdászat és hírlapirodalom története* (History of Book Printing and the Press in Temesvár /Timişoara/ (Temesvár, 1900); Tamás Vécsey, "Tóth Lőrinc emlékezete" (In Memory of Lőrinc Tóth), MTA Emlékbeszédek (Hungarian Academy of Sciences Commemorative Addresses), no. 11 (Budapest, 1903); Kálmán Stiller, *Vahot Imre* (Imre Vahot) (Eger, 1912); Ernő Kiss, *Szemere Bertalan* (Bertalan Szemere) (Kolozsvár, 1912); Asztrik Kovács, "A legrégibb magyar élclapról" (On the Oldest Hungarian Comic Paper), *MNy*, 1913, pp. 19-21; Lajos Kemény, "A kassai könyvnyomtatás történetéhez az 1848-49-es szabadságharc korából" (History of Book Printing in Kassa at the Time of the 1848-49 War of Independence) *MKsz*, 1914, pp. 263-67; Pál Pitroff, *A győri sajtó története* (History of the Press in Győr) (Győr, 1915); Károly Máté, *A sajtó története Pécsett és Baranyában* (History of the Press in Pécs and Baranya County) (Pécs, 1934); Zoltán Nagy, *A magyar litográfia története a XIX. században* (History of Hungarian Lithography in the Nineteenth Century) (Budapest, 1934); Gyula Szentirányi, "Szerelmey Miklós" (Miklós Szerelmey), in *Petrovics Elek Emlékkönyv* (Elek Petrovics Memorial Volume) (Budapest, 1934); László Horváth, *Petrichevich-Horváth Lázár élete és munkássága* (Life and Activities of Lázár Petrichevich-Horváth) (Budapest, 1937); Béla Dezsényi, "Az első magyar képes hetilap: A kassai Ábrázolt Folyóirat története" (The First Hungarian Pictorial Weekly: History of the *Illustrated Periodical* of Kassa), *MKsz*, 1940, pp. 17-35 and as an offprint; B/éla D/ezsényi/, "Hová lettek a régi divatlapok műmellékletei"? (What Has Become of the Art Supplements of the Old Fashion Papers?). *MKsz*, 1942, pp. 333-34; Béla Dezsényi, "Egy felvidéki hetilap két elfeledett cikkírója" (Two Forgotten Writers of Articles in an Upper Hungarian Weekly), *It*, 1943, pp. 175-77; Adorján Morlin, "A magyar nyelvű élclapok első évtizedei, 1848-1868" (The First Decades of the Hungarian-Language Comic Papers, 1848-1868), *MKsz*, 1943, pp. 166-83 and 383-406; Teréz Gerszi, "Daumier és az első magyar élclap" (Daumier and the First Hungarian Comic Paper), *Művészettörténeti Értesítő* (Art Historical Bulletin), 1953, pp. 138-44; Ferenc Hernády, "Pécs sajtója 1848-ban" (The Pécs Press in 1848), *Dunántúli Napló* (Transdanubian Journal), March 15, 1958; idem, "A Pécsi Tárogató két száma" (The Two Copies of the *Pécs Clarinet*), *MKsz*, 1958, pp. 67-73; idem, "A Pressfreie Flugblätter első száma" (The First Number of the *Pressfreie Flugblätter*), *MKsz*, 1959, pp. 363-66; Pál Pándi, ed., *Petőfi összes prózai művei és levelezése* (Petőfi's Complete Prose Works and Correspondence) (Budapest, 1960); András Hegedüs, "Petőfi és a győri 'Hazánk'" (Petőfi and the Győr (*Our Fatherland*), in *Tanulmányok Petőfiről* (Studies on Petőfi), ed. Pál Pándi and D. Toth (Budapest, 1962), pp. 349-95; András Martinkó, "Hogyan szünt meg a győri 'Hazánk'" (How the Győr *Our Fatherland* Closed Down), *It*, 1966, pp. 381-83; Béla Dezsényi, "A Honderű válsága 1847-ben" (The Crisis at *Serene Homeland* in 1847), *MKsz*, 1966, pp. 152-56; Imre Lengyel, "Az Alföldi Hírlap 1848-ban: Adatok egy vidéki hírlap társadalmi szerepének vizsgálatához" (The *Great Plain News* in 1848: Notes towards an Investigation of the Role in Society of a Provincial Paper), *A Debreceni Kossuth Lajos Tudományegyetem Könyvtárának Évkönyve* (Yearbook of the Library of the Lajos Kossuth University of Sciences in Debrecen) 5 (1966): 135-80; Zoltán Sárközi, "Bruz Lajos, 1807-1856" (Lajos Bruz, 1807-1856), *TSz*, 1967, pp. 343-55; László Szekeres, "Jókai, az 1848-as Életképek szerkesztője" (Jókai, the Editor of the 1848 *Sketches from Life*), in *Jókai Mór, Cikkek- és beszédek* (Mór Jókai, Articles and Speeches), vol. 2 (Budapest, 1967), pp. 408-507; László Molnár, "Das Pester Modeblatt (Pesti Divatlap) und das ungarische Kunstgewerbe", *Annalis Universitatis Budapestiensis, Sectio Historica*, 11 (1970):251-68; Anna Tamás, *Az Életképek (1846-1848)* (The *Sketches from Life* /1846-1848/) (Budapest, 1970); András Martinkó, "Petőfi útja a győri Hazánkhoz" (Petőfi's Path to the Győr *Our Fatherland*), in Lukácsy and Varga, *Petőfi*, pp. 81-142; Ilona T. Erdélyi, "Honderű, 1843-1848" (*Serene Homeland*, 1843-1848), in *A magyar sajtó története* (History of the Hungarian Press), ed. György Kókay, vol. 1 (Budapest, 1979), pp. 608-18.

15. Papers in Languages Other Than Hungarian

Hungary was a multilingual country, and there were papers in languages other than Hungarian that covered the same lines of political thinking and introduced some of the same journalists. The Hungarian revolution and the efforts of the March Youth were to some extent represented as well by some new papers in German that came into being at this time, and to that extent the political struggles of the Hungarian revolution spread beyond the bounds of the press in Hungarian.

The German Papers

With the possible exception of the papers designed for the Transylvanian Saxons, the German press in Hungary did not serve a developing, separate "nation" within the country. The public it catered for was largely a German urban bourgeoisie in the process of assimilation, including some German-speaking Jews.

From the 1830s onwards, an increasing number of journalists writing for the German press in Hungary were Jews of Austrian, Czech, or Hungarian background who wrote in German and had been reared on the new ideology of Young Germany. In time many subscribed to the Hungarian reform movement. A large number congregated in Pressburg around the oldest established paper in the country, the *(Städtische) Pressburger Zeitung* (founded in 1764), and its supplement, *Pannonia*. The management had been taken over in 1841 by the young Adolf Neustadt, a man of liberal opinions who came from a family of Prague Jews. Among the group were some young journalists who soon began to write in Hungarian as well, Magyarize their names, and adhere to a modernization that conflicted with the orthodoxy of their own religion. One such was Frigyes Szarvady (Hirsch, 1822-82), a young lawyer who reemerged later in Paris at Teleki's side and as one of the press organizers among the émigré supporters of Kossuth. Another was Adolf Dux (1822-81), the son of a Pressburg trader, who translated poems of Petőfi's for papers in Vienna and in 1848 had verses and literary translations published in the Pest *Morgenröthe*. So too were Ferenc Karl, who was later a Hungarian army officer using the name Fülöp Korn and played a part in exile, and Ignác Eichorn (1825-75), later known as Ede Horn, likewise prominent in exile and continuing to be so back in Hungary after 1867. These men aligned themselves with the Hungarian reform movement, hoping it would provide, among other things, equality before the law for Hungarian Jewry. A rather different path from the same starting point was chosen by Gusztáv Zerffi (Hirsch), who has been encountered already as an opponent of Petőfi's and of the new Hungarian literature. The man who wrote the report for the paper on the important decisions taken by the Diet on March 14, 1848, was Joseph Weyl, a German Jewish journalist of Viennese extraction who was on the staff of *Pannonia* and went on to write light, humorous sketches. On March 16 *Pannonia* appeared uncensored, and that morning an assembly in the Pressburg concert hall welcomed the freedom of the press. A *Volkskomité* was formed with Weyl, János Bangya, Lajos Kuthy, and Gereben Vas among its members. On March 17 the *Pressburger Zeitung* reported the results of the journey to Vienna by the delegation of the Hungarian Diet and the establishment in Pest of the Committee of Public Safety. On March 19 Dux gave an enthusiastic summary of the events in Pest on March 15, while Neustadt hailed the freedom of the press. But at that juncture there were anti-Semitic stirrings among the German bourgeoisie of Pressburg. The city council sacked Neustadt, who left for Prague on March 21. The following day the editorship was taken over by János Bangya (1817-68), the son of a noble Pressburg family who for a time had been a member of the Hungarian noble household guard, had then run an agency office, and had been working as a journalist since 1846. Later, in exile in England, he was thought by Marx and Engels, probably not without cause, to be an agent of the Austrians. At this point, however, he was the first person against whom proceedings were taken under the new press law, on the grounds that he had "ventured to abuse and libel the legally established military corps with the basest libellous expressions and gibes," although he was eventually acquitted by a jury on June 23. From the beginning of July the *Pressburger Zeitung* also had a Viennese supplement called the *Österreichische Konstitutionelle Deutsche Zeitung*, largely edited by the Viennese citizen Heinrich Löw, who is thought to have been the *Pressburger Zeitung*'s proprietor. At the beginning of July 1848 the Pressburg paper split in two. The city council, dissatisfied with Bangya's work, contracted out publication to Károly Wiegand, and on July 1 Sándor Pusztay was appointed editor. At the same time a new radically inclined paper with the similar title of *Pressburger Deutsche Zeitung* came into being, with a supplement called *Hungaria*, and of these János Bangya became editor. For a while the two Pressburg papers were published in parallel, but at the end of August Bangya's came to an end. At about the same time there was an end to a kind of series of pamphlets which had been appearing once a month since the beginning of the summer, edited by Lajos John, a former censor with the Lieutenancy Council, and published by József Landes. These bore the laborious title *Briefe eines Ungaren an seinen Freund Michl an der Donau, dem Rhein, der Spree, der Elbe und Ostsee*. Of these, however, I have been unable to peruse even the first, of which a copy is known to exist. In addition, John wrote a pamphlet recommending that a "German opposition paper" be started (*Vorschlag zu einem deutschen Oppositions-Journal für Ungarns Zustände, 1848*). By the autumn the press in Pressburg was taking its orders from the staff of the imperial army.

The German-language press in Budapest ranged over a wider spectrum and consisted of more papers, particularly as the influence of the revolution itself raised the number, although several were short-lived and of a good many hardly the title is known.

Of the older papers, the *Pesther Zeitung* was edited first by Ede Glatz and then from June 1 to October 5 by Albert Hugo. It was published by Landerer and Heckenast in folio format four times a week and from July 1 daily. From May 14 to July 13 it had a supplement called the *Volks-Tribune* that appeared at irregular intervals. After the March revolution the paper announced in large type that "the press is free at last," and it became almost the official German daily for the government in power at any time. It served Batthyány's ministry, the National Defence Commission, in 1849 Windischgrätz and the Austrians, then Kossuth, and after that Haynau, with the excuse that an official organ was always needed. Soon the advantages of such a position were being sought by other German-language papers as well. The feuilleton section of the *Pesther Zeitung* was run by the Austrian poet and journalist Heinrich Ritter von Levitschnigg, who after the defeat of the Hungarians in the war of independence assembled a series of portraits of the Hungarians who had figured largely in the recent past (*Kossuth und seine Bannerschaft*: *Silhouetten aus dem Nachmärz in Ungarn* /Pest, 1850/).

In January 1848 a daily called *Morgenröthe* (from May 2 *Ungarns Morgenröthe*) was started. It was in fact the German-language equivalent of the loyalist *Honderű* and was likewise published by Lázár Petrichevich-Horváth. Originally it was a fashion paper, describing itself as a "Tageblatt für Kunst, Literatur and Sociales Leben," but from March 21 onwards its new interest in politics was proclaimed in the subtitle "Politisch-belletristische Zeitung." On May 1 Petrichevich-Horváth requested the Hungarian government to make the paper an official bulletin, since the publishers of the *Pesther Zeitung* had monopolized the situation long enough under the old régime. It would be desirable, he wrote, "for Hungary's interests to be represented to our neighbours of German extraction and to Germans abroad by a German-language paper that was imbued with Hungarian patriotism, order, and love of one's country," although the main purpose he had in mind, of course, was to raise the number of subscriptions. Working alongside Petrichevich-Horváth as associate editor from April 9 was Izidor Heller (1816-75), a man born in Prague who had led an adventurous life and latterly been working for *Der Ungar*. Supposedly he was obliged to leave the country in May because of the attacks he had made on the policies of the Batthyány government and Kossuth. The same Heller appeared as editor of *Der Zeitgeist: Illustriertes Blatt*, of which seven numbers are supposed to have appeared in Pest in 1848. His place on the *Pesther Zeitung* was taken on May 27 by the young Gusztáv Körtvélyi (Birnbaum) and then from June 1 by Johann Janotyckh v.

Adlerstein, the Bohemian husband of the proprietor of a Pest academy for girls. He was a soldier, music teacher, and journalist and attacked Hungarian political endeavours so sharply that he was for a time imprisoned. Later the Austrian authorities were glad to provide him with a job in the police. During 1848 he issued several leaflets, including one against Pál Nyáry (*Das Sedlnitzky'sche Censurgericht in Pest*). Subsequently he compiled a chronicle and collection of documents on the Hungarian revolution.

However, on April 10, 1848, a new radically minded German paper called *Die Opposition* was set up to oppose conservative or openly counter-revolutionary efforts of that kind. *Die Opposition* was the first to interpret the ideas of the March revolution for the bourgeois public of Pest, most of whom still preferred to read German, as they had done hitherto in conservative or at most liberal papers. Thus the new venture at once resolved a matter which had been aired among the March Youth, whether *Marczius Tizenötödike* should not be published in German as well. The specimen issue of *Die Opposition* on April 9 declared straightaway that it considered *Marczius* the best paper in Pest, since it pointed out what the "policy of the future" could be like. "We wish to stay faithful to our revolution," it said, and "build the edifice of state that was planned in the Twelve Points." But rather than becoming a duplicate of *Marczius* it built up an image of its own. Indeed, on such issues as the workers and the national minorities it took a more progressive position than the Hungarian radical papers. The editor, Julián Chownitz (or Chowanetz, 1814-?), was the son of an imperial officer and born in Érsekújvár (Nové Zámky). In the course of an eventful life he had been a journalist in several places in Germany and had there published several pieces on Hungarian subjects. On receiving news of the March revolution he had come to Pest and soon reached agreement with Müller's bookshop in Szervita tér, which undertook publication and put up the caution money. The venture had remarkable success, in which a part was played by the energy of its editor and by the colourful local reports it published on so many subjects. On the first day five hundred copies were sold, but by mid-May they were apparently printing about five thousand, often in several editions. When sensational events took place special numbers were issued, while the more interesting articles were reprinted as leaflets. Sometimes there was a virtual scramble for copies, particularly as the paper thoroughly understood the techniques of effective street sales and was bought out of curiosity by many who were not radicals. In the meantime, the paper grew in size and strengthened in content. Originally it was printed in small octavo on the Trattner-Károlyi press. From May 10 it appeared in quarto and from May 29 in folio format. The staff grew as well. An old Pest friend of Chownitz's, Eduard Eisler, became editorial secretary. Frequent contributors included Mór Zsengery (a member of the Radical Circle who signed himself "Democrat," "D.," "M. Zs.," or "Zs."), Gusztáv Remellay or "A Mogyoróssy" (a medical student), Gusztáv Zerffi (using the initials G. Z.), and several provincial correspondents such as János Bangya in Pressburg (who signed himself "B"). The paper was considered worth attacking as well; the secretary of the Pest German Club, Ignaz Beyse, attacked it (and was attacked by it), even though he had earlier tried to wheedle his way onto its staff. It was not long before Beyse was writing a separate leaflet against the "threefold renegade" Chownitz (*Die Opposition...*, 1848). There is no doubt, however, about the number of people who resorted to the paper with their letters and problems, particularly petty officials, artisans, and poorer members of the intelligentsia. On May 4 and 10 the paper wrote with some sympathy about the movements among the bakers' apprentices and others in that trade; on May 12 it published the printers' statements of their intention to strike; on June 17 and July 1 statements from the bricklayers' apprentices appeared, while the June 8 issue reported that the Jewish workers of Sámuel Goldberger's blue-dyeing works in Óbuda had sent the editors the forints they had gathered in a collection among themselves for the defence of the country.

Chownitz followed the Hungarian radicals in demanding a more energetic policy, but he did not follow them with resolve and commitment when the confrontation really occurred. He had so little faith in the success of the revolutionary resistance that on hearing the news of Jelačić's approach he fled to Vienna on September 25 for fear of reprisals, although he used the temporary pretext that he would make propaganda there for the Hungarian cause. He remained editor in name, but in his new, smaller Viennese paper, which also bore the title *Opposition*, he objected on September 28 to the Pest paper's writing under his name about the killing of Count Ferenc Lamberg "almost with approval." When the new wave of revolution came he moved on to Prague, from where he issued a statement that he had not written a line in the Pest paper after September 25 and that there was absolutely no justification for placing his name in it as editor. From October 10 D. Schuller joined *Die Opposition* as associate editor and from October 22 as full editor, which he remained until the final number at the end of the year. Of Chownitz it is perhaps worth adding that in Germany in later years he compiled several works on the justice and cause of the deposing of the Hungarian king and on the history of the Hungarian revolution.

On May 1, 1848, a new German paper appeared. Initially it was called *Neue Politische Ofner-Pesther Zeitung* and from July 1 the *Allgemeine Pest-Ofner Zeitung*. It appeared in folio format initially three times and from July 1 four times a week. It had a twice-weekly quarto-format supplement entitled *Gemeinnützige Blätter zur Belehrung und Unterhaltung*. József Jánisch (or Janscha), who edited the paper until December 31, had originally been a teacher in Vas County. From 1835 to 1845 he had already edited a Pest-Buda German paper, and he now sought to take advantage of the new interest in the press. This fairly colourless paper was set on the oldest and by now smallest press in the capital, that of Márton Bagó, which stood at the Buda end of the Chain Bridge, had previously issued pulp literature and calendars, and now switched to newspapers for the local German citizenry.

The Pest paper *Der Ungar*, which had been appearing since 1842, counted as a fashion paper, as its subtitle "Zeitschriftliches Organ für ungarisches Interesse, Kunst, Eleganz, Literatur, Theater und Mode" suggested. However, its supplement, the *Wegweiser*, also covered economic and commercial subjects. The founder and editor of the paper was Hermann Klein (later known as János Kilényi, 1805-89), who came from a wealthy, cultivated family of Jewish traders from Miskolc. He cautiously tried to place his paper at the service of Hungarian national liberalism and among other activities occupied himself with translating works by Széchenyi, Jósika, and Eötvös into German. Two writers who featured on the paper were Karl Beck (1818-79), who was the son of a Baja merchant, a notable German poet, and a friend of Nikolaus Lenau's, and the young Miksa Falk (1828-1908), likewise the son of an impoverished merchant family, who was later to become one of Hungary's best-known journalists. From March 17, 1848, the paper carried a series of reports by Márton Diósy on the revolutionary developments in Pest. But certain elements among the German bourgeoisie seem to have done all they could to oppose Klein and his paper. From an announcement in the *Pesti Hírlap* on May 7 it appears that a petition to the government was got up against him, and when it had no success the petitioners called on the citizens of Buda and Pest to commit themselves, by signing papers which had been distributed in various places, not to support this "gossip paper" or even frequent coffee-houses where the "filthy paper" was delivered. In June Klein apparently had some difficulty in depositing the caution money, but he managed to hold his own until the turn of political events in the autumn. On September 12 *Kossuth Hírlapja* wrote that the editor of *Der Ungar,* who was now preparing to resign, had "supported the Hungarian interest faithfully when it was somewhat more awkward to do so" than it was by then. From October 1 the paper was taken over from Klein and continued till the end of the year by Gusztáv Zerffi, who took János Bangya on as assistant editor. The subtitle became "Allgemeine Zeitung für Politik und Belletristik." Among the contributors one finds János Horárik, who wrote most of the leading articles. In one entitled "Austria and the Ruling House" on October 20 Horárik wrote of revolutionary Vienna, "We can now see the punishment for imperfection as the real misery emerges. Around the city are the bloody, wild, and servile battalions of tyranny. In the city is a host of the treacherous and cowardly, despair among the populace, and but one ray of hope for the salvation of Austria: the enthusiasm for freedom among the intelligentsia and industry" (by which he meant the workers). The November 14 number contained Horárik's speech to the electorate, in which he spoke of his revolutionary training abroad in the

German craft unions and of his ideas about society. On one occasion, on December 3, Zerffi even took issue with *Kossuth Hírlapja* when he thought he had detected anti-Semitism in it. The charge, however, was, as we have seen, forcefully rejected on December 12 by Bajza, who said it was purely "out of a desire to inform the honest Israelites" that he took on Zerffi, whom "the month of March persuaded out of the pro-Habsburg sentiments of the infamous *Honderű* and the still more infamous Lázár P. Horváth."

In opposition to this radicalized paper there immediately arose, on October 3, another German-language paper that considered itself a "true" continuation of *Der Ungar. Der Wahre Ungar,* as it styled itself, was subtitled "Zeitschriftliches Organ für politische und sociale Interessen." The editor was Zsigmond Saphir (1801-66), cousin of the Viennese humorist and editor. Saphir, born in Lovasberény, belonged to the older generation of Jewish-German journalists and had begun his career as a doctor. *Der Wahre Ungar* came to an end on December 31, but Saphir himself stayed on in Pest and before long was happily acting as an editor again, this time of the old-established Buda German fashion paper *Der Spiegel,* which he had taken over from a relative of his, Sámuel Rosenthal, in the autumn of 1848. A supplement to this, while it was still edited by Rosenthal, was the *Pesther Handlungszeitung,* which survived until June 18. Another was *Der Schmetterling* until June 29, and after its demise *Der Telegraph,* subtitled "Volksblatt für Politik und Tagesinteressen," appeared somewhat irregularly twice or three times a week between July 2 and September 29. Saphir's *Spiegel,* by the way, ceased publication between November 29 and December 13, 1848, and again from December 20 until January 20, 1849. This circumstance, coupled with its "moderate" stance and not least the influence of Saphir's relatives in Vienna, explains how he was able to work in Pest after the Austrian occupation. The drama reviews for *Der Spiegel* were written by the young Károly Hoffmann (1828-82), originally from Pressburg. Later Hoffmann was sentenced to two years' imprisonment by the Austrian military courts for translating a patriotic Hungarian poem, but he subsequently became a notable journalist in Vienna.

On June 1, 1848, a new radical German paper called *Der*

Patriot: *Neues Politisches Abendblatt* appeared. It was published by the Pest bookseller Adolf Müller, at first in quarto and then in folio format. The editor until it ceased publication on August 31 was Ludwig Wysber, who had heralded the revolutionary spring of 1848 in enthusiastic pamphlets but soon proved a turncoat and a charlatan. Not long afterwards he published in Vienna his "satirical" reminiscences of Hungary (*Lebensbilder aus Ungarn*: *Satyrische Zeitgemälde /1850/*), in which he chose to express particular personal animosity towards radical journalists who had formerly been his rivals.

Not all the German papers that appeared in the capital at this time can be described, because not all are known to us, but of those that are, one can mention chronologically *Das Junge Ungarn*, a radically inclined paper that began under the editorship of Ökonom Naum, for a while in conjunction with Antal Gazda. It appeared twice a week and from May 23 every day but in the summer closed down, or rather appeared on July 20 as a mere "leaflet" entitled *Der 20-ste Juli: Ein Flugblatt*. Between April 15 and September 26, 1848, the aforementioned Ignác Eichorn's weekly *Der ungarische Israelit* campaigned for progressive internal reform among Hungarian Jewry. *Concordia* is also supposed to have appeared in the spring, but no copies can now be found. Nothing further is known of two papers edited by M. Steinitz, *Die Volksstimme* in the summer of 1848 and *Constitution des Thierreiches*, or of a publication resembling a newspaper that appeared in August under the title *Politisch-Satirische Vogelfrei Blätter*. There was the *Közlöny* (Gazette) *des Teufels*, which appeared in September 1848 as "the official paper of Hell" under the editorship of "Asmodeus," who may have been Hermann Höchell, a printer of German extraction, in view of the fact that from July 1, as an employee of the Sándor Czéh printing press, Höchell published a "monthly" in Magyaróvár called *Der emancipirte Satanas* as a series of twelve pamphlets. The *Constitutionelles Tageblatt*, edited by Fülöp Weil and printed by Márton Bagó, appeared daily from October 1 to December 30 along with a supplement called the *Pesther Figaro*. Finally, two publications, booklets or newspapers, were printed by Rudolf Eisenfels in November: *Die erste Epistel der Ungarn an die Wiener* and the *Blätter vom Baume der Erkenntnis*. There is evidence that publications resembling newspapers called *Pestvárosi Tudósítások* (Pest City Reports) / *Berichte vom Rathaus* and *Legújabb a Városháznál* (The Latest at City Hall)/ *Neuestes am Rathaus* appeared on December 14 and December 21 in Hungarian and German, the editors of the latter being Kocsiss and Á. Kaan. József Fitz reports that Ede März, a compositor at the Kozma press, was subsequently sentenced to two years' labour on the fortifications for having poked fun at the imperial army in his comic paper (or collection?) *Der Grosse Spatzen Sammlung*. But in the case of the last it is not even certain whether it appeared in 1848 or in the following year.

To this list must be added the provincial press. In Pécs a progressive paper called the *Pressfreie Flugblätter* was started on April 5, not long after the March revolution. It continued after May 12 as the *Fünfkirchner Zeitung*. Its motto was "Für Freiheit, Volk und Vaterland", and the editor, Ernő Adolf Neuwirth, was an enthusiastic, rather eccentric republican and Hungarian patriot who has already been mentioned in connection with the paper's supplement in Hungarian. After the press law had come into effect, Neuwirth made it known to the authorities that, wishing to continue publishing his *Fünfkirchner Zeitung*, a paper "in an entirely Hungarian spirit," he would deposit the caution money by June 11. This appears not to have gone as smoothly or swiftly as he had hoped, but the paper continued appearing until the end of September, complete with sharp attacks on the Viennese camarilla. At that point Neuwirth was obliged to flee before the forces of Jelačić, after which he emerged on the staff of the radical press in Vienna during the days of the October revolution. Among the charges later preferred against Batthyány was one of supplying money to Neuwirth for purposes of press propaganda. After the fall of Vienna Neuwirth went to Pest, where the radical papers began at the end of December to advertise a new venture called the *Südungarische Grenzbote*, which Neuwirth planned to start on January 1, 1849. Research has shown, however, that he was captured by the Austrians at the beginning of 1849 and sentenced to fifteen years' imprisonment in Olmütz, where he eventually lost his mind.

In Kassa there was a German version of the local advertising paper, called the *Kundschaftsblatt*, and a German version is also known of the Hungarian illustrated paper. The *Oberungarische Illustrierte Zeitung*, using the same pictures, appeared from April 7 until the end of the year, edited first by J. Schmelz and from July 1 by Domokos Stolz and published by the Werfer press. On August 5 a new paper appeared from the same publisher, also edited by Stolz. Its title was *Pecsovics* (Time-server): *Ein Blatt für das Volk ohne Politik*, but right after the first number appeared it was banned by the city, according to the mayor's proclamation because it appeared "without any prior notification," because in spite of its title it concerned itself with politics, and because no caution money had been deposited for it.

In Arad the local *Kundschaftsblatt* was joined from July 1, 1848, by a new free-thinking weekly called *Der Patriot*, a "Politisch-belletristisches Sonntags-Blatt" published by the Schmidt press. Until it ceased publication on October 8 it was edited by a Pápa-born teacher in the Arad Jewish school named Lipót Jeitteles (1812-87). As a result he was afterwards imprisoned, sharing a cell for a time with Lajos Beniczky.

In Temesvár there was a German weekly even before the revolution, the *Temesvarer Wochenblatt für nützliche Unterhaltung und heimatliche Interessen*. Along with its supplement, the *Anzeiger*, it was published by József Beichel's press and edited by the lawyer son of a clerk in the town, Mór Stockinger (later known as Sulyok, 1821-78), in company with Dávid Wachtel. It continued under those editors until October 10 (or formally until October 28), when the commander of the garrison at the head of imperial troops turned against the "Hungarian rebels." The paper itself, accommodating itself to changing circumstances, survived right up until June 27, 1849. An advertisement in the *Wochenblatt* on September 2, 1848, shows that from about that time until October a paper called the *Tagesanzeiger* was edited there by Ernő Hazai (Heim), whom we shall meet again in spring 1849 at the head of a radical paper in Pest. A short-lived thrice-weekly fashion paper edited and published by Dávid Wachtel began publication in October: *Der Südungar*, subtitled "Zeitschrift für Belletristik und Soziales Leben in Ungarns Südosten," which boasted a supplement called *Südungarns Beiwagen*. These were printed on the press of Viktor Hazai (Heim), which was set up in 1848 but closed soon afterwards.

Within the German-language press, the fourteen papers that catered for the Transylvanian Saxons (most of which antedated the revolution) were ventures of a different kind. The papers' "national" character was tied up with the earlier, privileged position of the Saxon "nation" and with its adherence to the House of Habsburg. *Der Siebenbürger Bote* had been appearing in Nagyszeben since 1792. It was published by the Hochmeister press along with two supplements, the *Intelligenzblatt* und *Transsilvania*. The mother paper was edited by Joseph Benigni, while editorship of *Transsilvania* was taken over from Theodor Steinhausen on March 27 by Frederick Hann, a teacher at the Nagyszeben Academy of Law who was one of the quite small group of Saxon advocates of a liberal, pro-Hungarian cultural policy. The paper sounded a new note in the press of the Saxon community, which clung tenaciously to its privileges. On April 10 the paper published an article by Wächter, another teacher at the Academy who hailed the Hungarian reforms and, if he did not support the idea of union between Transylvania and Hungary, did not reject it either. But these bourgeois liberal journalists were soon thrust aside. After a short interregnum, direction of the paper was resumed on May 5 by the former editor. Another Nagyszeben paper was *Der Siebenbürgerische* (later *Siebenbürger*) *Volksfreund*, which was published by the press of Sámuel Filtsch. Originally a weekly, it came out twice a week from March 23, 1848, and was edited by the publisher or from time to time by Johan Michaelis. The third paper in the town, *Unterhaltungen aus der Gegenwart*, was founded on May 8, 1848, with Heinrich Schmidt as editor. A total of twenty small, book-sized pamphlets appeared irregularly until October 11. The other, lesser centre of the Saxon press was Brassó (Kronstadt, Braşov), where the *Kronstädter Zeitung* was published twice a week by the press of Johann Gött, accompanied by two supplements: the *Siebenbürger Wochenblatt* and *Stundenblumen der Gegenwart*.

The Slovak Papers

The first recognition on the part of the Slovaks of the significance of what had been achieved by the revolution of March 1848 came from the *Slovenskje Národňje Noviny* (Slovak

National Journal), edited and published since 1845 by Ludevit Štúr and printed twice a week in folio format at the Wigand press in Pressburg. "For the time being," Štúr wrote on March 21, "we may rest content with this and receive freedom with whole-hearted enthusiasm. Had we received from the national point of view that which we certainly have need of we might be wholly free and content. And we should have received it if we had been prepared." In an appeal to the Slovak people on April 11, Záboj Hostinsky (Péter Kellner), signing himself "Z.", declared that if the Hungarian government really strove for liberty and equality "the happiness and future of Hungary will develop and be renewed on this firm foundation." He argued that while Hungarian should be "the language of diplomacy in the National Assembly and the national offices," following the initiative of Liptó County the Slovak language should be "legally introduced." In the April 8 issue of the paper's supplement, *Orol Tatranski* (Tatra Eagle), the legal, official primacy of Hungarian was recognized by Karol Kuzmány (1806-66), a Lutheran minister, teacher, and Slovak national poet. But he added, "Hungary must remain the mother of the Hungarians, of the Slovaks, and of the Germans." On May 3 the paper extolled the abolition of serfdom in a poem. However, in that month Štúr moved to Vienna. The editorship was taken over for a while by the young Bohuslav Nosák and then by J. Štúr and L. Dohnány. Shortly after that the paper closed. The last extant issue is dated June 9, 1848, and the supplement appears to have ended its career on July 6.

At about the same time another paper was founded in Pressburg. The *Slovácke Noviní* (Slovak Journal), which first appeared on July 3, 1848, was opposed to Štúr's political line, although it likewise adopted the Slovak literary language and showed a friendly attitude towards the Hungarians. It was printed in folio format on the press belonging to the successors of Belnay. The editor and publisher, András Kostelni (or Kostolný), was a Pressburg lawyer who had been a tutor in the Borsiczky family and enjoyed good connections among the landed nobility. A plan for the paper had been put before the government on May 8 by József Justh, the *comes* of Bars County, who requested that this "Slovak paper in support of the ministry" be approved without having to lodge caution money. The Ministry of the Interior denied the exemption but promised favours and indirect support. Szemere put in a request to the Finance Ministry on the paper's behalf for 800 forints as a fee for publishing official announcements, saying that "interests of state" prescribed that the people not be abandoned to the influence of the "Pan-Slavist" paper, which was still appearing at the time. Some evidence points to the caution money's being put up by Justh, along with Count Károly Zay and Baron János Jeszenák. Szemere, on the other hand, wrote on September 18, "I arranged the caution money for the Pressburg Slovak paper." In October 1848 the paper requested financial support from the National Defence Commission as well. An article in *Kossuth Hírlapja* on August 9 signed by a certain Berényi singled out this "Slovak newspaper in a Hungarian spirit" for praise. It continued to appear twice a week until December 7, 1848.

Plans for a similarly pro-Hungarian Slovak paper, or rather a paper addressed to the Slovaks in the traditional biblical Czech language, were supported in a letter on April 25, 1848, by Lajos Beniczky, government commissioner of the Upper Hungarian towns with mining privileges. He too used the argument that the government needed a paper which would counter the Pan-Slavist propaganda. The proposal originated with the local Lutheran bishop, Ján Seberiny, who headed the "Old Slav" movement. The editor of the *Uhersko-Slovenské Noviny* (Hungarian Slovak Journal) was to have been István Launer (1821-1901), a teacher at the Selmec (Banska Štiavnica) secondary school for girls. Launer opposed the efforts of the Štúr faction on behalf of the everyday Slovak language, which he despised, and insisted upon the traditional Czech language of the Bible out of a belief in the linguistic and national unity of the Czechs, Moravians, and Slovaks. At the same time he adhered to Hungary as a political mother country and had produced a pamphlet supporting the Hungarian government and the cause of the war of independence. On May 27 the *comes* of Hont County asked the government to put up the caution money, and Szemere made a similar proposal to Batthyány on September 18. But the competition between the two Slovak papers was eventually won by the undertaking that had already been started in Pressburg. The Hungarians, betraying total ignorance of the disputes between the various lines of thinking among the Slovaks, recommended that Launer ally himself with Kostolný. Launer did not give up. On October 6 he applied once again for a permit to start the paper, and the Ministry of the Interior informed him in a letter dated October 13 that he would be granted assistance of 600 forints. However, the protracted affair was shelved for a while at the end of the year and revived only in the following spring. Other efforts of a similar kind appear to have been made. At the beginning of November 1848 the National Defence Commission is known to have turned down an application from György Pejkó, who had requested a permit to launch a Slovak political paper without depositing caution money.

The Slovak version of the *Nép Barátja* was called *Priat'el Ludu* and edited by the Pest lawyer Lukács Mácsai (or Máčai, 1816-81) and László (or Andor) Szeberinyi (or Szeberényi). Although some authors date it from October 1848, in fact it started on June 8 in Pest, where it ceased publication in December. A new start was made for a time in Debrecen in the spring of 1849. The accounts of its influence are likewise contradictory. Some historians have considered that the sharper tone taken against the dynasty after the turn of events in September was a tactical error, as it elicited an unfavourable response among Slovak readers. In contrast, the Austrians seem to have rated the paper's effectiveness highly, since they went to the trouble of preparing forged copies and distributing them in the Slovak counties.

There soon appeared Roman Catholic "popular papers" in Slovak as well. One of them was *Wůdce z Trnawi* (Trnava Leader), written in biblical Czech orthography, which was started in Nagyszombat (Tirnau, Trnava) on July 12 by Ferdinand Pelikan, a teacher of theology, the caution money being supplied by the town's Catholic clergy. It also had a weekly supplement entitled *Bohumil*. The advent of these papers was welcomed on July 4 by *Religio és Nevelés*, which saw them as serving the purpose of "resuscitating religion, the firmest foundation for the bestowal of happiness on the public, and leading our Slav compatriots to a sober perception and enjoyment of our political position." Soon after, however, the head of the Pressburg post office sent in a report complaining that "it seems to be edited with the aim of arousing the Papist population against the Lutherans." In the September 15 number of *Kossuth Hírlapja*, L. Sz-i (Lajos Szeberényi) made a strong attack on Pelikan and his paper under the title "A Jesuit," accusing both of pro-Habsburg sympathies and hostility to the Protestants. The argument was resumed in *Kossuth Hírlapja* on October 1, when Pelikan described Szeberényi's accusations as unjust and personally offensive. Apart from that, the Pest publishers of the *Katholikus Néplap*, the Good and Cheap Book Society, also began in the autumn of 1848 to advertise a forthcoming Catholic popular paper in Slovak under the title *Katolické Noviní* (Catholic Journal) with Simon Klempa, an assistant priest in the Józsefváros district of Pest, as editor. In the event it appeared only somewhat later. In addition there are mentions of a paper in Nagyszombat called the *Trnavski Posel* (Trnava Deputy) and of a small paper in Pressburg called *Svetozor* (World View).

In the spring of 1849 Launer made another attempt to start a paper and this time managed to obtain authority to do so. On May 6 in that year he issued an appeal for subscriptions giving his objectives as defence of the country and furtherance of understanding among nations. But the paper never actually got under way. Meanwhile Štúr and his associates prepared to launch a Slovak newspaper in the spring of 1849 on the Austrian side of the fence, but they were beaten to it by the imperial authorities, who started a Viennese Slovak paper called *Slovenské Noviny* (Slovak Journal) on July 10, 1849. The editorship went to Ondrej Redlinský (referred to as András Radlinsky by Szinnyei), a Catholic parish priest and religious writer. To provide a denominational balance, the associate editor was the Lutheran minister Daniel G. Lichard, a teacher from Selmec. From April 5 to September 27, 1848, Lichard had published a weekly paper in Szakolca (Skalica) called *Novini pre hospodárstvo, remeslo a domáci život* (News for Agriculture, Industry, and Domestic Life). From April 1849 he was responsible for a paper called *Slovenský Pozornik* (Slovak Observer), again in Szakolca, and for a time this also had a supplement called *Žitva*, after the locality.

The Romanian Papers

Of the papers in Romanian the twice-weekly *Gazeta de Transilvania*, printed on Johann Gött's press in Brassó, had been a vehicle for the national aspirations of the Romanians since 1838. Its founder and editor was Gheorghe Barițiu, who came from a family of impoverished nobles, his father having been a priest in the Romanian Orthodox Church. He had attended secondary school in Kolozsvár and then theological college in Balázsfalva (Blaj) and in his mid-thirties risen to be the leading Romanian journalist of his day. The *Gazeta* also had a supplement called *Foaie pentru minte inima și literatura* (Pages for Reason, Sentiment, and Literature) a literary paper that in 1848 was largely concerning itself with political matters. In the April 5, 1848, number of it, Barițiu began a series of articles entitled "What the Transylvanian Romanians Want." He welcomed the March revolution and the great transformation in Hungary, not least the declaration of the freedom of the press. With the exception of union between Transylvania and Hungary, the Pest Twelve Points too received his general endorsement, since by them "all barbarous, tyrannical, and oppressive privileges are annihilated." Like Štúr on the Slovak side, Barițiu considered that "the events of the recent past have found us unprepared," but he began nevertheless to outline the national demands of the Romanians. He recalled the *Supplex Libellus* (1791) and attached certain conditions to the union, in particular the rights of the Romanian language, pointing to multilingual Switzerland as a pattern. On April 10 the *Foaie* contained a report from A. Papiu Ilarianu (1828-76), who was later to be a government minister of Romania but at the time was a young clerk in the royal court of appeal in Marosvásárhely. He said that some thirty Romanian trainee lawyers had joined the young Hungarians in celebrating March 1848, and unlike the Saxons they approved of the union as well, but some, including Avram Janeu and the young writer himself, considered prerequisite the abolition of serfdom without compensation. During the spring Barițiu became steadily more opposed to the policy of the Hungarian government, particularly after the Balázsfalva meeting, which voiced national demands that could no longer be reconciled with the position taken by the Hungarians. In the spring of 1849 Barițiu thought it best to abandon his paper and flee to Wallachia but there found himself imprisoned for a time by the Russian authorities.

In contrast, the weekly "ecclesiastical, political, and literary" *Organulu Luminarei* (Journal of Enlightenment) took a line friendly to the Hungarians and supported the union. It was edited by Timotei Cipariu, a Romanian Uniate canon in Balázsfalva, where it was printed on the press of the local seminary. From May 12, 1848, it took the name *Organulu Natiunale* (National Journal) and continued to appear until June 3. Its supplement, the *Inventiatoriulu Poporului* (People's Magazine), appeared between May 12 and October 6. Initially a peaceable line was also taken by Aron Pumnul (1818-66), a Balázsfalva teacher who was one of Cipariu's associate editors, but he soon joined the Romanian movements that turned against the Hungarian government and so thought it wiser to withdraw to Bucharest.

The Romanian version of the Pest *Nép Barátja* was the weekly *Amicu Poporului*, which appeared between June 15 and October 18, 1848, supporting, of course, the policy of the Hungarian government and joint Hungarian-Romanian efforts. Like its Hungarian equivalent it used everyday language to explain events to the people, and its Transylvanian Romanian vernacular contrasted strongly with the heavily Latinate style of the priests of Balázsfalva. The editor was Sigismondu Pop (1817-89), known in Hungarian as Zsigmond Nagysomkúti Papp, who came from a family of Romanian nobles in Szatmár County. After completing his studies at the law academy in Nagyvárad and at the seminary there, he became a secondary schoolteacher in Belényes (Beiuş). In 1848 he resigned, however, and offered his services to the Hungarian government, which appointed him captain-general of the Kővár (Chioar) district. As a member for Zaránd County in the 1848 National Assembly he spoke in favour of separation of the Romanians from the supremacy of the Serbian Orthodox Church. Understandably enough, the paper was not a simple translation of its Hungarian equivalent but an independent edition of it publishing its own articles and correspondents' reports. For instance, on June 24 it told of the election in Lugos (Lugoj) to the National Assembly of Euthim Murgu (1805-70), who on April 8 had been released from prison by the revolutionary forces in Pest. Thereafter Murgu supported the policy of the Hungarian government and reconciliation between the Hungarians and the Romanians, earning himself a four-year prison sentence from the Austrians after the defeat. *Amicu* ceased publication in the autumn. A successor entitled *Democraţiea* was started in Pest on June 24, 1849, but it seems probable that only one issue ever appeared. Pop, who was editor of the new venture as well, said in a statement of intent in the new paper, "We wish to work on the basis of and in accordance with the principle of democracy. We do not wish there to be any exceptional class whose power allows it to rule over others"; in the new country "the people will govern, and do so, moreover, according to their own will." One reason for the paper's rapid disappearance may have been the distaste with which it was received by the government. An indignant Szemere sent Kossuth a copy on June 26: "I ask you to read it through; can this be a popular paper, a government paper"? In his leading article assessing the government's programme and membership, Pop had taken the liberty of delivering various warnings and critical observations. Szemere was said to have "more of a French than a Hungarian character," while Görgey was praised as "a gentleman of great talent; he possesses the heroism of Napoleon, he produces much out of nothing." Foreign Minister Kázmér Batthyány was called "a man of modest standing," and László Csányi was accused of having "surrounded himself with a vile, washed-out aristocracy" in Transylvania.

A new Romanian paper called the *Espatriatul* (Expatriate) was started in Brassó on March 25, 1849, once Bem's army had expelled the Austrian forces from the town. The editor and publisher was Cesar Boliac (or Bolliac), who had taken refuge in Transylvania after the failure of the Romanian revolution in Wallachia in the previous year. The paper welcomed Bem as one "who struck down the demons of tyranny and cleared the sky" and supported the Hungarian war of independence and Hungarian-Romanian reconciliation, particularly against Russia as the common enemy. "All Europe," Boliac wrote by way of introduction, "is influenced by one struggle: the battle of freedom and of tyranny waged between the peoples and the dynasties. The ruling houses are becoming reconciled to one another, so that they may defend their ramshackle thrones shoulder to shoulder, and they place their one hope on the inequality and strife that exists between the peoples. If the peoples will but recognize their true interests one day, the battle will be at an end." Boliac censured the Romanians, hoodwinked by the camarilla, for turning not against the common enemy but against the Hungarians, who had liberated the Romanian serfs as well as the Hungarian. His paper continued until June 10, 1849.

The Serbian and Croatian Papers

For a considerable time after the mid-1820s the centre of the Serbian press and of the *Matica Serbska*, the first Serbian literary society, was Pest-Buda. From the 1830s the secretary of the society and the editor of its paper was the writer and journalist Teodor Pavlović (in Hungarian Tivadar Pavlovics), who was born in Torontál County and was one of the literary pioneers of the Serbian national awakening. The paper, called the *Srpske Narodne Novine* (Serbian National Journal) at this time, was printed on József Beimel's press and appeared twice a week. In the April 9, 1848, number there was poetic appeal by associate editor Jákov (or Jakab) Ignjatović (1824-89), the son of a rich merchant of Szentendre who had qualified in law in Pest, travelled abroad, and served for a time in the imperial cavalry. He urged the people of the principality of Serbia and the South Slavs as a whole to rise and shake off the Turkish yoke. This failed to evoke a favourable reaction from either the Serbian or the Hungarian government, for the latter wished to maintain good relations with the Turkish empire. On April 16 the official *Srpske Novine* in Belgrade objected to the idea because of the international treaties that were in force. Ignjatović incidentally was invited to work for a while as lay secretary to Patriarch Rajačić, but when he realized that the patriarch's Serbian followers were coming out against Hungary he left his service. Szinnyei relates that after a time Pavlović's championship of Serbian national aspirations put him in a difficult position in Pest. Eventually he left the city, and the paper came to an end in October 1848.

Hungarian press bibliographies have so far expressed even less certainty about the career of the other Serbian paper, the *Vjestnik* (Herald). The editor was Konstantin Bogdanovic (or Bogdanovich, 1811-54), who had been born in the Szerémség district, had his schooling in Karlóca (Sremski Karlovci) and Szeged, studied theology in Pest, and then lived in Serbia for a period during the 1840s. On April 18, 1848, he is known to have declared his intention of continuing to publish the paper under the terms of the new press law. After that there is only uncertain evidence of its subsequent appearance in Zimony (Zemun) and then Újvidék (Novi Sad) or nearby Karlóca.

In the Hungarian press in the broadest sense of papers published in the lands belonging to the Hungarian crown must be included the press of Croatia, which at the time was an autonomous unit politically attached to Hungary. In the case of these papers no distinction can be found between papers for and against the Hungarian government such as can be observed in the press of other nations and national minorities in the country, if one discounts the publication in Pest from June 8 to December 7, 1848, of a Croatian edition of the *Nép Barátja* entitled *Pučki Priatelj*, which received Hungarian government support and was edited by Iván Bujanovics. All the Zagreb papers essentially subscribed to "Illyrian" national endeavours that looked to the Habsburgs for support. One such was Ljudevit Gaj's *Novine* (Journal), which was already influential earlier in the 1840s, along with its supplement the *Danica* (Dawn). Another was the *Slavenski Jug* (South Slav), begun in October 1848 by Bogoslav Šulek (or Schulek), a man of Slovak origin from Nyitra County. This was probably the Croatian paper with the highest standard and the first to attempt to address fairly broad sections of the population. Ever since 1839 Šulek had subscribed to Gaj's school of thought and to the Croatian movement, from which he expected the liberation of the Slavs to emerge, although in the mean time several relatives of his in Hungary were fighting on the Hungarian side in the war. But not unexpectedly there were some traces in the Croatian press of the growing disappointment of the national liberals when the court turned a deaf ear to their aspirations at the end of 1848. The December 12, 1848, issue of the *Novine* contained an article which expressed an opinion common among the leaders of the liberal line of thinking. Ivan Kukuljević and the poet Ivan Mazurević had a hand in formulating it. In the event, it declared, it had not been right of the Croatians to take up arms against the Hungarian revolution, since their reward "on the part of Vienna is to be a shameful ingratitude." Nevertheless, the underlying tendency in the Croatian press at the time was against Hungary. To complete the picture one should mention the existence of the *Agramer Politische Zeitung,* which was printed by Gaj's press in German, along with supplements called *Luna* and the *Intelligenzblatt*. From January 1849 the paper continued as the *Südslawische Zeitung*.

Hungarian Papers Abroad

Finally one comes to a few Hungarian attempts abroad to counteract the unfavourable attitude of the local press and introduce and popularize the case for the Hungarian revolution in a foreign language. Such attempts were made in two cities, Vienna and Paris.

The March revolution and the freedom of the press brought a multiplication of the number of papers published in Vienna in the spring of 1848. At the end of 1847 there had been twenty-eight, but by the middle of the following year the capital of the Habsburg Monarchy boasted seventy-eight papers of various kinds. Of these only the radical papers showed any inclination to sympathize with Hungary. The more moderate and generally more cautious papers opposed Hungary to varying degrees. This applied not only to papers close to the court and anti-revolutionary circles but to the papers that represented the Austro-German grande bourgeoisie, which had felt its interests and monopoly position threatened by the policies of Kossuth ever since the days of the Industrial Protection Association and now had the added concern that the Hungarian government was refusing to take over a share of Austria's state debt. But among the opponents of the Hungarians there were also papers of as low a standard as the *Zuschauer* or the *Geissel*, which on more than one occasion adopted an abusive tone. The official *Wiener Zeitung* may have refrained from stooping to the same tone but was increasingly decided in its disapproval of the measure of independence Hungary had attained in March. Various shades of opinion within this consensus were represented by the government-subsidized *Donau-Zeitung*, the semi-official *Presse*, the conservative bourgeois *Journal des Österreichischen Lloyds*, and the *Fremdenblatt*, which last called for the incorporation of Hungary into Austria and gave fulsome praise to Jelačić. One particularly stubborn and dangerous foe to the new independent Hungary was the *Allgemeine Österreichische Zeitung*. The editor was Ernst von Schwarzer, who held the post of minister of public works for a time in the summer of 1848. His ostentatiously constitutional, liberal expressions of friendship for the people and his attacks on the now vanished camarilla won him widespread popularity, but at the same time he was an Austrian centralist who had a strong sense of being German, hated the Slavs, and roundly condemned the policies of the Hungarian government, Kossuth's in particular. To all this the Hungarian press, particularly *Kossuth Hírlapja,* reacted strongly in its turn.

The main person who tried to remedy a far from easy situation was the intelligent and agile Ferenc Pulszky (1814-97), a young state secretary at the so-called Hungarian Foreign Ministry in Vienna who was closely aligned to Kossuth. He took to visiting the Daum Coffee-house in the Kohlmarkt, which was frequented by journalists. There he sought supporters among them by talking them round or even by offering them money. In his efforts he was assisted by his friend Imre Henszlmann (1813-88), later a noted art historian but at the time an assistant clerk at the Hungarian Foreign Ministry and a kind of press officer for it as well. Through personal connections and bribes Henszlmann sometimes managed to place articles of rectification, propitiation, or information in the *Wiener Zeitung*.

Of more direct concern to our subject is that Pulszky managed to launch a German-language paper to represent Hungary's interests, using a subsidy he received from Batthyány. Called *Der Völkerbund*, it appeared as a "sociales Blatt mit besonderem Hinblick auf Ungarn" three times a week from May 30, 1848, onwards. The editor was the Pressburg lawyer József Orosz (1790-1851). He had started the *Országgyűlési Tudósítások* with Kossuth but had soon changed direction and been given charge of the government paper, the *Hírnök*. While in exile in France after the defeat, Orosz committed suicide. According to *Kossuth Hírlapja* on July 26, this paper "edited with skill and good tact has set itself the task on the one hand of presenting the affairs of Hungary to the German reading public in a truthful light far clearer than that in which they have appeared in any other German paper hitherto." The paper was certainly written and edited in a practised style, but it was an old-fashioned, colourless one that the Viennese public, accustomed to sensation and a radical approach, was little inclined to read. Eventually Pulszky was reduced to distributing copies free in the coffee-house.

Still less influence was exerted by another short-lived German daily that began publication in Vienna on July 5 under the title *Ungarn und Deutschland*. Subscriptions were sold by the booksellers Hügel and Mainz and in Pest by Gusztáv Emich. The editor, Miklós Töltényi, was a lively journalist and pamphleteer with an incisive style who nevertheless ran this paper along remarkably boring lines. In any case he showed less interest in the affairs of Vienna and Austria than in those of the greater German nation as a whole. A notice of it headed "New Political Newspaper in Vienna" appeared in the August 2 number of *Kossuth Hírlapja*.

On July 22 Henszlmann recommended to Batthyány that an attempt be made to win over to the Hungarian side the mildly liberal *Presse* and the radical *Constitution*, which was showing appreciable goodwill towards Hungary. Certainly Töltényi and the senior staff member Ludwig Haug later wrote articles in support of the Hungarian revolution in the latter paper, to which Pulszky gave financial support. After the suppression of the Viennese revolution Haug fled to Hungary and saw active service under Bem. After the defeat he was shot in the head by order of Haynau.

In August 1848, a radical, republican German journalist named Anton Schütte informed Pulszky and Kossuth that he was prepared to put up an effective defence of Hungarian interests in a Vienna paper he was about to found. But after the reoccupation of Vienna he too was obliged to flee.

As the crisis heightened, the Viennese press attacked Hungary with increasing force, and in mid-September Pulszky asked Batthyány for special funds to counteract this. Batthyány viewed the friendship expressed towards Hungary by the radical German papers in both Vienna and Pest with rather mixed feelings, but he was prepared to put up a couple of thousand forints. This later featured among the charges against him, as if he had intended the money for fomenting revolution in Vienna.

There is no opportunity here to review the varied and broad spectrum of the French press in Paris after the February revolution, even from the point of view of its reactions to events in Hungary. It is enough to note that although the left-wing press, unlike the official papers, by and large supported the movements for national liberation, they often gave accounts of the Romanian and South Slavic efforts against their Hungarian "oppressors" and on more than one occasion viewed the event of the Hungarian revolution and war of independence in reverse and with scant approval. The situation was less than favourable, although it contained positive features as well. The first to carry news of the revolutionary turn of events in Hungary was *La Réforme*, a left-wing, democratic, republican paper which had been instrumental in preparing for the February revolution. It did so in a number of articles that appeared from April 2, 1848, onwards. The author of these, who wrote under the name of József Boldényi, was Pál Szabó, Jr. He had been a merchant in Fiume (Rijeka) and then a dishonest director of the Hungarian Commercial Society. Having also abused the trust of Kossuth, he had managed to flee to Paris with a large sum of embezzled money. Curiously, this prepossessing crook, who did more than a little harm to the opposition reform movement, seems for unfathomable motives to have tried hard to draw the attention of the French public to Hungary's cause. After writing these articles, which were radical and republican in tone, he then tried to establish a paper. His weekly *La Hongrie* was launched on July 29, 1848, but only two issues seem to have appeared. A part in the venture was taken by the husband of Countess Emma Teleki, August de Gérando (1820-49), who had published some important work in French on Hungary in support of the reform opposition. Alongside a piece by de Gérando on the question of national minorities in Hungary, writings by E. Marguerin, J. Fleutelot, and M. Havez-Montlaville appeared in the paper, which also had a correspondent in Hungary named Elek Bartay. According to an introductory article the paper's purpose was to "present the importance of Hungary as a nation from the European political point of view" and "provide an accurate picture of Hungary's efforts on behalf of its freedom and independence." News of the venture was given under the title "Gazette of Hungarian Interests in Paris" on August 23, 1848, by *Kossuth Hírlapja*, which hastened to wish it success. It chose specially to mention the articles by the editor and by de Gérando and also a piece of writing which "discusses the attitude of the French press towards Hungary and singles out the papers which have fallen into the snare of Pan-Slavism and operate even from the banks of the Seine as disseminators of the Pan-Slavist lines of argument." It was not long before Mór Mérei in the August 31 number of the radical *Nép-elem* was likewise drawing his readers' attention to the new weekly in Paris. Nor did he even object to its flattering character sketches of the members of the first responsible Hungarian ministry; as he put it, "What concern are our private troubles to those abroad"? One remarkable fact is that *Kossuth Hírlapja* and the *Nép-elem* both identified the editor not as Boldényi but as one Lajos Bogdán, who "wishes to place the Hungarian homeland and its interest before the free French people." From that circumstance some Hungarian literary historians have tried to posit the existence of one Lajos Bogdán as an otherwise unknown radical Hungarian journalist, but in the absence of any other information about him and in the certain knowledge that the editor of *La Hongrie* was Boldényi one is more inclined to surmise that the press at home was reluctant to praise the swindler Szabó, alias Boldényi, for the new venture and so found him a new *nom de plume*. In October 1848 Boldényi made another attempt to found a paper. With his *La Hongrie en 1848, recueil politique, historique et littéraire* he sought to compensate for the fairly unfavourable views on the national minorities question put forward in articles on Hungary in the Paris press. Again it was short-lived, for only four issues appeared. A contributing factor was the arrival in Paris as Hungarian envoy of Count László Teleki in September. Neither he nor his colleagues, including Frigyes Szarvady, were prepared to collaborate with an embezzler like Boldényi, and their objections were later vindicated when Boldényi succeeded in defrauding the family of the émigré Bertalan Szemere out of what remained of its fortune. Instead Teleki and his group attempted in company with de Gérando to place as many sympathetic unsigned articles as possible in the moderate, bourgeois liberal paper *Le National*, which was coming increasingly to the fore as the left wing was pushed back, giving the most favourable reports on events in Hungary on the national minority issue and opposing the stance taken by the official *Journal des Débats*, which showed Habsburg sympathies. In the spring of 1849, by the way, the news of the Russian intervention produced the most feverish period in Teleki's activity as a journalist in France. He also made plans for a series of pamphlets that would resemble a periodical and keep French public opinion informed on the events that followed the Russian invasion. A publication entitled *De l'intervention russe*, which Hungarian scholars long considered to be a simple pamphlet, was in fact the first in the series, and there are reports that a second appeared as well. However, lack of subsequent news and the approach of defeat combined to prevent him from publishing any more.

Bibliography

János Lupas, "Barițiu György, az erdélyi román hírlapirodalom megalapítója" (György Barițiu, the Founder of Transylvanian Romanian Journalism), *TSz*, 1915, pp. 382-405 and as an offprint; Viktor Cherestesiu, *A magyarországi román sajtó politikai vezéreszméi és munkája a szabadságharc előtti évtizedben; Adalékok az erdélyi román intelligencia, kivált Barițiu György politikai gondolkozásának jellemzésére* (The Guiding Political Ideas and Activity of the Romanian Press in Hungary in the Decade before the War of Independence: Contributions to an Analysis of the Political Thinking of the Romanian Intelligentsia, Particularly György Barițiu) (Budapest, 1917); Lajos Steier, ed., *Beniczky Lajos . . . visszaemlékezései és jelentései az 1848/49-iki szabadságharcról és a tót mozgalomról* (The Reminiscences and Reports of Lajos Beniczky on the 1848-49 War of Independence and the Slovak Movement) (Budapest, 1924); Béla Pukánszky, *A magyarországi német irodalom története a legrégibb időktől 1848-ig* (The History of German Literature in Hungary from Earliest Times to 1848) (Budapest, 1926); Lajos Sipos, *A magyar szabadságvisszhangja a francia irodalomban, 1848-1851* (The Reaction to the Hungarian War of Independence in French Writing, 1848-1851) (Budapest, 1929); Emil Sigerus, *Die deutsche periodische Literatur Siebenbürgens, 1778-1930* (Sibiu, 1930); Rózsa Ösztern, *Zsidó újságírók és szépírók a magyarországi németnyelvű sajtóban a Pester Lloyd megalapításáig, 1854-ig* (Jewish Journalists and Men of Letters in the German-Language Press in Hungary until the Establishment of the *Pester Lloyd* in 1854) (Budapest, 1930); Piroska Szemző, *Német írók és pesti kiadóik a XIX. században, 1802-1878* (German Writers and Their Pest Publishers in the Nineteenth Century, 1802-1878) (Budapest, 1931); Emilia Kardos, *A pécsi német sajtó és színészet története* (The History of the German Press and Stage in Pécs) (Budapest, 1932); Heinrich Réz, "Deutsche und österreichische Mitarbeiter der deutschungarischen Zeitschriften und Zeitungen, 1819-1852," in *Festschrift für Gedeon Petz* (Budapest, 1933), pp. 225-29; idem, *Deutsche Zeitungen und Zeitschriften in Ungarn von Beg . . . bis 1918* (Munich, 1935); Elemér Ungár, *A magyarság a hazai német folyóiratok tükrében, 1819-1848: Tanulmány a nemzeti érzés fejlődésének történetéhez* (Hungarians as Reflected in the Country's German Periodicals, 1819-1848: Study towards a History of the Development of National Sentiment) (Pécs, 1937); Rapant Daniel, *Dejiny slovenského povstania r. 1848-49* (History of the Slovak National Uprising in 1848-49), vols. 1 and 2 (Sv. Martin, 1937-50); E. Weisenfeld, *Die Geschichte der Publizistik bei den Siebenbürger Sachsen* (Frankfurt a.M., 1939); Jean Kósa, "L'Opinion française et la Hongrie au siècle dernier", *Nouvelle Revue de Hongrie*, March 1940; Piroska Szemző, *A 'Pester Zeitung": Egy XIX-ik századbeli kormánylap története* (The *Pester Zeitung*: The History of a Nineteenth-Century Government Paper) (Budapest, 1941); Károly Vigh, *A tizenkilencedik század szlovák hírlaptörténete* (The History of Slovak Newspapers in the Nineteenth-Century) (Budapest, 1945); Dezsényi, *Az időszaki sajtó*; László Szikhay, *Launer István, egy 1848. évi szlovák röpirat szerzője* (István Launer, a Slovak Pamphleteer of 1848) (Budapest, 1848); Jenő Zsoldos, *1848-49 a magyar zsidóság életében* (1848-49 in the Life of Hungarian Jewry) (Budapest, 1948); *1848-1849. évi iratok a nemzetiségi megbékélésről* (Writings of the Years 1848-1849 on Reconciliation of the National Minorities) (Budapest, 1948); Paul Bouteiller, *La Révolution française de 1848 vue par les Hongrois* (Paris, 1949); Vladimir Klimeš, *Počátky Českého a Slovenského novinářstvo* (The Beginning of the Czech and Slovak Press) (Prague, 1955); Zoltán I. Tóth, "The Nationality Problem in Hungary in 1848-1849", *Acta Historica* 4; 235-77. Marko Miloš, "Kotázkam publicistickej činnosti L'udovita Štura" (On Questions concerning the Journalistic Activity of Ludovit Štúr), in *L. Štúr, Život a dielo, 1815-1856* (L. Štúr, Life and Works, 1815-1856) (Bratislava, 1956), pp. 297-302; Vladimir Zapkay and Julius Horváth, *Slovenskje Národnje Novini, 1845-1848* (Slovak National Journal, 1845-1848), vol. 4 (Bratislava, 1956); Gábor G. Kemény, "Pest nemzetiségi lapjai 1848-49-ben" (The National Minority Papers of Pest in 1848-49), *Budapest*, May 1968, pp. 42-23; József Kiss, "Petőfi in der deutsch-sprachigen Presse Ungarns vor der Märzrevolution," in *Studien zur Geschichte der deutschungarischen literarischen Beziehungen* (Berlin, 1969), pp. 275-97; idem, "A Nemzeti Dal egykorú fordítói és fordításai" in Lukácsy and Varga, *Petőfi*; Josip Horvat, "Društveni spektar stoljeća novinstva Hrvatske, 1835-1935" (A Century of Croatian Journalism in Its Social Context, 1835-1935), *Jugoslavenski Istorijski Časopis* (Yugoslav Historical Review), 1968, no. 3-4, pp. 39-56; Maria Vyvijalová, *Slovenskje Narodňje Novini: Boje o ich povolenie, Študia a dokumenty* (The *Slovak National Journal*: Struggles for Its Authorization, Studies and Documents) (Martin, 1972); Ambrus Miskolczy, "George Barit a román-magyar szövetségért 1848-ban" (György Barițiu on Behalf of the Romanian-Hungarian Alliance in 1848), *Tiszatáj* (Tisza Region), 1974, no. 6, pp. 42-46; Zoltán Sárközi, *Az erdélyi szászok 1848-1849-ben* (The Transylvanian Saxons in 1848-1849) (Budapest, 1974); Emil Niederhauser, *A nemzeti megújulási mozgalmak Kelet-Európában* (The Movements of National Renewal in Eastern Europe) (Budapest, 1977); Márta Lengyel, "Egy fejezet 1848-i sajtónk történetéből: Julián Chownitz 'Die Opposition-ja'" (A Chapter in the History of the Hungarian Press: Julián Chownitz's *Die Opposi-

tion), in *Az Országos Széchényi Könyvtár Évkönyve 1978* (The Yearbook of the National Széchényi Library, 1978) (Budapest, 1980), pp. 471-91

16. The Early Months of 1849

The Hungarian press had been developing rapidly, but at the beginning of 1849 came a great setback, almost amounting to an interruption, which is all the more conspicuous after the growth caused by the revolution in the previous year. As the capital fell and the government retreated beyond the River Tisza the number of papers declined sharply and the spectrum of the press narrowed. Several major political papers ceased publication entirely, and attempts to resuscitate others after varying lengths of time were not always successful. Nothing more was seen of the literary fashion papers. In an effort to express the change numerically, József Fitz calculated that the number of titles in the period from the beginning of 1849 to the defeat in the war of independence was hardly more than half what it had been: 74 instead of 149, counting all publications in all languages. Within this total the number of papers in Hungarian fell from 65 to 36 and in German from 65 to 23. The figures, moreover, include new titles that were founded from scratch after the initial period. A graph would show the greatest setback occurring at the beginning of the year, followed by a steady, gradual recovery. After the successful campaign and the recapture of the capital in the spring there were signs that the press would enter a new period of growth and regain lost ground so long as external power relations permitted. But in the event the time was too short, and the new ventures died one after the other while still in their cradles. We shall observe the spectrum of the press during two consecutive periods, one lasting roughly from January to May and the other continuing until August.

The first thing to note is that there was a schism in the press at the beginning of 1849, for certain papers continued to appear in the capital during the Austrian occupation. One such was the *Pesti Hírlap*, which carried on as an unworthy shadow of its former self. The editor was the young Sándor Szilágyi (1827-99), who would undertake many things. The paper was eventually banned by Windischgrätz on January 23, 1849. By then the conservative *Figyelmező* had been revived as a daily. It began publishing again on January 21 and was still edited, with the benefit of Windischgrätz's patronage, by Károly Vida, who was prepared not only to oppose Kossuth but to support the old historical, constitutional rights left over from feudal times. One need hardly add that the *Figyelmező* now relentlessly attacked the leaders of the Hungarian revolution and war of independence, describing Kossuth and company as currency forgers and rebels. With the approach of the Hungarian army the paper understandably ceased publication on April 21. Vida fled to Pressburg and on July 2 attempted to resume publication there. The year before, the *Pesther Zeitung* had felt that it could not emphasize too strongly the Hungarian colours it wore in its capacity as a kind of semi-official paper, but under a new editor, I. Seiz, who took over on January 16, just after the Austrian occupation, it hastened to applaud the liberation of the city from revolutionary coercion and express joy at being able to serve the "real" interests of the whole empire, including Hungary, by guiding its readers back to the "only correct political notions." After a short intermission the *Pesther Courier,* edited by Simeon Philipovics, also began to appear every day and continued to do so until April 21. On January 20 came the revival of Zsigmond Saphir's *Spiegel*, expanded into a daily. It ceased publication on April 22, a day later than the previous two papers and for similar reasons. *Religio és Nevelés* also continued until April 22. Its editor, János Danielik, took over as publisher as well on January 23 when Károly Somogyi resigned. In a later note Somogyi said he had done so because Danielik wanted to turn *Religio* into "a political organ," what is more into one "in the service of the oppressive German authorities." We also learn from him that for the same reason Danielik later republished all of the forty issues that had appeared between January 2 and April 22 in a revised form. Somogyi himself brought out the *Katholikus Iskolai Lap* (Catholic School Journal), a "periodical of teaching and educational affairs," during the Austrian occupation, but he tried to steer clear of sensitive political issues and so was able to continue publishing it right through until June 30, after the capital had come under Hungarian control again.

Not so the thrice-weekly *Magyar Őr* (Hungarian Guardian), a "Catholic political journal" edited and published by Pál Nagy from January 25. Many historians have asserted that it ceased publication after only four issues following a ban by Windischgrätz, but in fact it continued until April 12, when it was closed because of the approach of the Hungarian army. The weekly *Gazdasági Lapok* (Agricultural Pages), which had been advertised in *Kossuth Hírlapja* towards the end of the previous year as the successor to the *Magyar Gazda*, actually got under way on January 1, and as a specialized paper unconcerned with politics it managed to survive the arrival of the Austrians and their departure without experiencing any special difficulties, continuing until July 1, when the Hungarian government was preparing to withdraw for the second time. Its editor was László Korizmics (1816-86), an agronomist and former engineer on an estate who was a well-known authority on irrigation. He had received a post as secretary in the agricultural department of Gábor Klauzál's ministry but as far as possible had remained aloof from political activity.

After this interlude let us now accompany the revolutionary press to the new, temporary seat of government in Debrecen. For almost five months the government, the depleted staffs of the ministries, the National Assembly, and all who followed them were packed into the town. According to the memoirs of Mrs Sándor Vachott, the writers and journalists tended to lodge in Csapó utca. It was hardly possible for the municipal press, which printed the two local papers, to cope with the mass of decrees, official publications, and newspapers that poured out of Debrecen, and printing capacity remained fairly modest even after extra machinery had been brought in. Nor was that the only difficulty facing the press. There was also a shortage of paper, problems with the post and other communications, and a very much reduced reading public.

The Alföldi Hírlap and the Közlöny in Debrecen

The arrival of the government in Debrecen temporarily enhanced the importance of the local *Alföldi Hírlap*. At the beginning of January 1849 it was for a while the only Hungarian political paper on the government side. In its first issue of the year on January 3, it published Kossuth's appeal on the removal of the seat of government and the continued pursuit of the war, and on January 7 it carried Kossuth's message to the people of Debrecen. One of the editors, József Szanka, had returned from the battlefront in the Arad district only on January 5, while the other, László Telegdi, was away at the Transylvanian front until the end of February. Szanka wrote the National Assembly reports for the paper. In No. 3 on January 10 there was an enthusiastic appeal from Petőfi, an article by Mór Szegfi in which he urged the government to launch a paper in German, and a piece of writing by Mihály Táncsics. This last, entitled "The Guilty Must Be Punished," cited the example of Robespierre, whom people had been wont to depict as a merciless tyrant but whom "his later descendants recognize as a man who punished a few of the wicked that he might spare the hundreds of thousands of good citizens. Let the guilty pay, whatever their rank, so that the innocent blood of millions may be spared." The paper later published an appeal from Táncsics for subscriptions to his own paper, and it followed with interest the activity of the Egalitarian Society, which was revived on January 28, 1849. But in other respects the paper followed a moderate line of support for Kossuth. On February 14 it criticized the articles in favour of peace contributed to the *Közlöny* by Jókai. Apart from those already mentioned, contributors in this period included János Pálffy, József Tóth, József Reviczky, Zsigmond Csernátoni M(olnár), Gábor Nagy, and Mihály Könyves Tóth. Also included was poetry by József Lévay, Károly Szász, and Hiador (Pál Jámbor). The paper's provincial correspondents were not members of the county nobility like those of the *Közlöny*; most had been students in Debrecen. *Marczius Tizenötödike* sometimes made slightly condescending, ironical mention of the paper, but a sign that it was strengthening was its appearance three times a week from March 11, with a print run of a thousand that shortly afterwards rose to thirteen hundred. On March 29 the *Alföldi Hírlap* repeated its advice to the government to supply the Transylvanian Saxons and Romanians "as soon as possible with a paper in their own language, so that they may be brought as soon as possible to recognize the righteousness of our cause and the efforts by the Austrian tyrants to demoralize them and bring them under subjection may be countered." When the government moved again, the paper reverted to its original, more modest role, but apart from an enforced break of three weeks it appeared right up until August 2. On the following day Debrecen was occupied by Russian troops.

The first national paper to revive in Debrecen was, as one might expect, the *Közlöny*, whose first issue there appeared on January 14, 1849. It was printed on the "state press" that came into being when, as will be remembered, a mechanical press and two hand presses, along with the necessary type and staff, were dispatched to Debrecen from the university press in the capital. That same press later followed the government on its subsequent journeys—back to the capital in May, on to Szeged in July, and finally to Lugos. But the relaunching of the *Közlöny* went far from smoothly. In the flight from Budapest the list of subscribers had gone astray, and the Debrecen post office failed even to supply a list of the new ones. There was a dispute over powers between the National Defence Commission and the national police bureau, ending in a compromise whereby supervision of the *Közlöny* would be the task of Nyáry of the Commission, while Madarász of the police would look after the distribution. Here again Kossuth took a personal hand; considering it "in the interest of our cause that the *Közlöny* arrive in the provinces of the country in as great a number and extent as possible," he decreed that the paper be sent automatically wherever it had been sent in the previous year. Later the Commission also prescribed that irrespective of all subscriptions "the *Közlöny* must be distributed to as many communities as possible." Initially so little comfort could be drawn from the result of these measures that at the end of January a scandalized Kossuth reprimanded Madarász, pointing out that subscribers even in the neighbouring county of Szatmár, not to mention places farther afield, had yet to receive a single copy. Not long after he imperatively urged Madarász again to see that the paper was distributed better and faster: "I really cannot see how this happens, since my almost daily warnings on this subject receive the answer that the requisite measures will be taken." Madarász really tried to do his best, and if he was less than fully successful the reason would seem to have been that he was unable to exact accurate, effective work from his administrative apparatus. However, the main problems had an objective basis. Whereas Madarász ordered a print run of seven thousand copies at the end of January (for copies were needed by the army as well), it emerged that the press brought from Buda was unable to produce more than thirty-five hundred. In the second half of February, therefore, the government had some machines brought from Kolozsvár on which extra copies of earlier issues were prepared.

"With the change in circumstances," the paper wrote on January 14, "there needs to be a change in the content of our paper, and we should not be fulfilling our calling if we continued to confine ourselves to official statements and the dry presentation of events. In future, therefore, we shall also include reflections upon this country's affairs." In other words, the *Közlöny* was attempting under the new circumstances to develop into a real political paper. Initially this was reflected in the publication of appeals and other statements from the Commission and in the stance it took on January 18 as a result of the National Assembly debate on January 13: "Never before has such a scandalous trick been played on a free, independent, constitutional nation. . . . As the wages of peace the tyrant foe demands our nation's death." The prime mover behind this development of the *Közlöny* was Kossuth himself. The decrees he wrote or inspired essentially served as the paper's leading articles. Kossuth was in frequent touch with Gyurmán, sometimes going so far as to correct even the war reports himself. But as soon as it emerged that the *Közlöny* was able to influence political opinion, the paper itself became a target of influence. One after another, the political tendencies that confronted each other in the National Assembly and even on the Commission sought to bring the paper under their sway: first the radicals and then the moderates, who around this time began to be known as the peace party. A sign of the first attempt came at the end of January, when Csernátoni, formerly a senior member of the *Marczius* staff, began to write for the *Közlöny*, obviously with Gyurmán's consent. From January 27 to January 30 Csernátoni wrote an article in three instalments in his chatty style, very different from the paper's official tone hitherto. He condemned the "black-and-yellow" pro-Austrians who had remained in Pest, calling the series "Letter from Debrecen to a Budapest Lady." On January 30 a writer signing himself "Sz." pointed out that in this war "there can be no place for compromise or a middle road of any kind," since the question was this: Did Hungary wish to be a self-governing, independent country or not? On January 31 Csernátoni made a sharp attack on the Habsburgs—the robber kings—and their highwayman friends. On February 1 a writer signing himself with the Greek letter lambda, perhaps Csernátoni again, directly criticized the government in its own official paper, protesting that the public administration was disorganized, the ministerial portfolios not "in the hands of individual, independent and responsible gentlemen" or else not assigned, and many civil servants unsuited to their jobs, as a result of "blind faith and bluster."

The National Defence Commission speedily reacted in a statement on the very next day, February 2. It observed that "there appear in the official *Közlöny* articles by individual writers which in content and tone neither accord with the serious nature of an official paper nor reflect faithfully the views of the government." It had therefore arranged, it announced, that the *Közlöny* would in future "provide, alongside the official columns, articles which will disseminate information and guidance for the reading public in gaining a true understanding of the patriotic standpoints and measures which the National Defence Commission considers effective in ensuring the success of our sacred cause of our country in good times and in hard."

Although the main target of this statement was Csernátoni, we find in the same number an article by him denouncing traitors and adding, with the strengthening peace party in mind, that traitors included those who did not wish to fight or behaved faint-heartedly. "Tomorrow," he wrote, "I shall say who the cowards are, how they talk, and how they must be treated." Tomorrow, however, never came. Presumably the members of the peace party intervened to prevent the official paper of the government from serving as a radical mouthpiece. On February 3 the issue came before the National Assembly, where László Madarász, as the official responsible and the one who voiced Kossuth's views, denied that "the National Defence Commission has exerted any influence on the editing of the *Közlöny*" and advised the National Assembly to delegate two of its representatives to act as "monitors" of the paper. In such a measure, he added, there was "no censorship and no restraint upon the press to be seen." On behalf of the peace party Pál Hunfalvy stated that "a degree of confusion has reigned in the ideas of the newspaper world, and this has caused a good deal of trouble, because the policy of the National Assembly has differed from the one that might be read in the columns of the official paper." Clearly aiming at Csernátoni, he added that "the last few days" had seen "men who work in offices of the governmental bureaux expressing ideas which the National Assembly cannot espouse." In the end the House preferred to Madarász's proposal one from Bezerédy, who thrust the responsibility back onto the government: "Let the government choose an editorial staff that accords with the views and desire of the National Assembly and of the government."

The National Defence Commission thereupon assigned one of its own members, the well-known novelist Baron Miklós Jósika (1794-1865), to "undertake the supervision of the *Közlöny*" and inspect the articles in it before they were published. At the same time it considered that "a permanent column" should be opened for "political articles," which it commissioned Jókai to write. "He alone" was to be "responsible for this," in other words, he was not even to be subordinated to Gyurmán. The appointment was made on the recommendation of Nyáry, who had been exerting a growing influence on the young Jókai since the previous year as the latter gradually abandoned his initial radicalism. What Nyáry aimed to do was to turn the *Közlöny* into a vehicle for the views of the peace party, and Jókai fulfilled his expectations. Nyáry explained that a more peaceable note had to be struck on the subject of the Habsburgs because of the foreign powers and the army. Jókai complied in the February 9 number, perhaps making use of articles he had written previously for the *Pesti Hírlap*: the Hungarians, he said, were not perfidious, since they were only defending their rights; once those were secured they were prepared for reconciliation. "We have never called the king perfidious" because "we did not wish to close the door to conciliation. . . . We do not want to depose the king; we want him to fulfil his obligations." This was a view similar to the one Nyáry had put forward in the House of Representatives on January 13. On the following day, February 10, Jókai again took a position of unambiguous opposition to the radicals, who were demanding that an independent republic be declared. Responsibility for the war, he argued, rested not with the ruling house but with the imperial aristocracy; "to consider forms of government and prepare a new constitution, peaceful times are needed."

Of course these articles aroused great indignation on the other side. In its thirteenth issue, the *Alföldi Hírlap* said that confusion was caused because people "a week ago read in the official paper that anyone who still sought a compromise was a traitor and as such deserved the gallows, while now it is precisely conciliation that is being recommended." The radicals would have liked to use the incident to bring about Nyáry's downfall. In a formal question József Madarász enquired whether the Commission had put the House's decision on the *Közlöny* into practice and whether it subscribed to the views in the articles that were being objected to. The House was dissatisfied with Nyáry's evasive reply that the articles had passed through Jósika's hands, for this hinted that they had been considered satisfactory. During the debate Dániel Irányi said that the things written in the *Közlöny* failed to correspond with the principles of the House, the majority of which aimed at a "declaration of this country's independence." The debate was cut short by Kossuth, who wished to help sustain a front of national unity by remaining neutral. He began by regretting that in difficult times such as these the House should be debating about newspaper articles, his implication being that this was not a matter of essential political concern. He described how the enemy was intent on casting aspersions: "In Pest one can read in the *Figyelmező* that one cannot speak freely or write freely here," whereas precisely the opposite was the case. Originally the *Közlöny* had been "nothing more than an official notification of facts and decrees." When the fall of the capital meant, "so to speak, that apart from the *Alföldi Hírlap* Hungarian journalism was reduced to the *Közlöny*," the government had tried to make use of it "to clarify matters through the free chafing of opinions" in material that would appear "in the unofficial section of the *Közlöny* as opinion or argumentation." Of course, he said, care had to be taken that the articles did not conflict with the views of the government, but from that it did not follow that the government had to own to all that appeared. Jósika, who had been requested to exercise supervision, had been content to give general instruction; "thus the National Defence Commission had no prior cognizance of the articles in question." As to whether the government owned to what was written in the *Közlöny* one could not, he said, reply in general terms. "Consequently I am not prepared . . . to own entirely to newspaper articles, just as one cannot direct someone to say in what way he does not own entirely to an article, because it contains things to which he owns and things to which he does not own." What finally concerned the policy of the government, he said, was that if "someone were to ask the National Defence Commission what kind of policy it would be pursuing in three months from today I should be unable to respond, because politics is the science of measuring the requirements. . . . For us who stand in the country's line of defence our task can be only two things, viz., to guard against wanting to tie the future, which is unknown to us, to the cord of present circumstances and to defend this country in such a way that no path to the honourable settlement of Hungary's affairs may be cut off." On the following day, in the February 13 number, Jósika issued a loyal statement in which he announced that as "the greatest friend of the free press and the most decided enemy of all that even smacks of censorship" he had indeed refrained from inspecting the *Közlöny*'s articles individually. "Thus my entire conduct consisted . . . of putting forward the views of the government in a friendly conversation with the editorial staff, announcing beforehand that I was not going to look over the articles." He had defined the policy of the government as to bring about the defeat of the enemy and "to enforce, perpetuate, and honour the national rights safeguarded by the 1848 laws."

After the *Közlöny* had spent its fleeting hour amid the crossfire of political debate, a balance was achieved for the time between the radicals and the members of the peace party. Certainly it was the radicals from whom Jósika preferred to distance himself, but Jókai, once Kossuth had summoned him and spoken to him personally, immediately changed his tone. On February 13 he declared that "whoever attacks us and our constitution by force of arms is an enemy and perfidious, not a king." By way of excuse he added, "We have wished to draw the nation's attention to the fact that those who say they struggle in the king's name are lying and pursuing their own self-interest. . . . Should we have strayed, our purpose has still been a good and true one." On February 15 he wrote of the enemy more strongly than ever, as having "murdered and plundered" the country "for four hundred years." But once Jókai had fulfilled Kossuth's wishes he showed himself in a more moderate light again. At the end of the month he parted company with the *Közlöny*, having gained the more important position of editor of the peace party's *Esti Lapok* (Evening Pages).

The less colourful political articles that subsequently appeared in the *Közlöny* were largely written by Károly Szathmáry, who toned down and selected various opinions. On February 27, for the anniversary of the 1848 revolution in France, "Muratáji" presented the Hungarian revolution as a component in the struggle for the freedom of the world, even though "Hungary remains the only territory in which the struggle for freedom has still not been abandoned." On the anniversary of the Pest revolution, the paper published one of Petőfi's poems. Yet on March 23 it spoke as if the change in the spring of 1848 had not been brought about by a revolution at all, for "it was by a constitutional path through our legal organs /of state/ and with the agreement of the king that we won freedom for the people and returned to the country the independence of which it had been robbed." In mid-March the National Defence Commission announced that war reports would in future be received from the president's office by all the papers, not just the *Közlöny*, and that proceedings would be taken against damaging articles. This was mainly the period to which Lázár Mészáros was referring when he wrote, "Since the events of the war consisted of several unfortunate and very few good facts, it was the task at the *Közlöny* to gloss the first over and in the case of the second to make a little go a long way." The paper's domestic reports had dried up, apart from news of military promotions, with which a great deal of space was filled by Mór Ballagi, a clerk at the Ministry of War. At a session of the upper

House on March 30 Ödön Beöthy reproached the *Közlöny* for not providing enough up-to-date foreign news either. The National Defence Commission instructed the paper to publish "notable items of foreign news" immediately, accompanied by comments. Here the main problem was that the foreign papers were reaching Debrecen infrequently and with some difficulty. Not even the government was always accurately informed about the latest international developments, and efforts were being made by Madarász to obtain French, English, and German papers from the east, through Transylvania.

Yet in spite of all its deficiencies and difficulties, the *Közlöny* undoubtedly fulfilled its function very well, at least as the informational and organizational paper of the leadership during the war of independence.

On March 24 the paper's coverage of the Olmütz manifesto of March 4 showed that by then even the official press was beginning to prepare for a declaration of independence. "The fateful moments are approaching," it wrote. "In a couple of days the curtain which is draped across the future of Hungary, Austria, and perhaps all of Europe will be rent in twain. . . . Monarchy . . . is but a human institution than which the mind of man has already created a better and more serviceable." On the following day Kossuth delivered to the House of Representatives the speech in which he first referred openly to dethronement. It was published in the *Közlöny* on March 30: "Nothing now remains but the battle, and at the end of the battle the message for the nation: self-reliance, independence. . . . Unless we want to brand the nation with the stamp of historical ignominy . . . the National Assembly should express its will concerning the Olmütz manifesto and arrange its government accordingly." The peace party's *Esti Lapok* responded with yet another reference to conciliation, and Kossuth wrote in a letter from the camp at Tiszafüred on March 29 calling for a rejoinder to it: "It would be well if Gyurmán were to give the lie to this cowardly dalliance in a forceful leading article. . . . It is time Gyurmán made forceful use of the ungodliness of the Austrian house and particularly of the provocation provided by the Russian intervention." The articles he requested soon appeared. The leading article on March 31 stated, "We must prepare . . .

for a festive, splendid decision"; if this were delayed, "later generations would curse us" for having "voluntarily placed our head under the tyrant's axe." The second article appeared in two parts on April 1 and 3. The title was "Austria and the Russian Intervention", still referring of course to the earlier, lesser intervention on the border of Transylvania, the conclusion being that Europe could no longer ignore Hungary's struggle. On April 17 the *Közlöny* reported the historic April 14 session of the House of Representatives, Kossuth's speech, and the declaration of the dethronement of the Habsburgs, and several articles in subsequent issues were devoted to praise in keeping with Kossuth's arguments for the declaration of independence, stressing that it meant the Hungarians had joined the ranks of independent European nations and that "the path of conciliation was cut off forever." Daily from the beginning of May the paper carried statements of allegiance by local authorities and institutions. On May 2 Kossuth issued a written order to Gyurmán to go to Pest and have the issues of the *Közlöny* reprinted in two thousand copies, and this was done on Kozma's press. On May 3 the paper published the list of members of the new government. Thereafter the affairs of the official *Közlöny* were supervised by Szemere.

The government's other publication, the *Nép Barátja*, resumed publication in Debrecen on January 16, 1849, two days after the *Közlöny*. It was printed on the city press. A month or so later the city council of Debrecen sought to ban the paper on the grounds that the editor, Gereben Vas, had failed to lodge the deposit for it. This local move against it must be considered rather curious, since the paper could be said to have been an official one. The subject of caution money had in fact been cleared up the previous year, and on December 10 the National Defence Commission had promised 10,000 forints to the editor if he would ensure a regular print run of five thousand in 1849. Ferenc Csürös, an earlier researcher into the history of the Debrecen printing press, postulated that the move had been suggested to the city fathers by no less a person than László Madarász because of certain adverse comments the paper had made about him. Later chroniclers have ignored the problem. However, on February 24 Kossuth himself is known to have taken the matter in hand after Vas had addressed an application on February 21 to the bureau of police, in other words, to Madarász. Kossuth told the city council that the National Defence Commission had already granted permission for the *Nép Barátja* to continue on the basis of the caution money lodged earlier in Pest. From March 16 Vas alone appeared as editor on the title page of the paper, which was published in Debrecen until April 28, when it moved back to the capital. For a while (from the beginning of April to May 26) the *Nép Barátja*'s Slovak edition, *Prjat'el Ludu*, was also published in Debrecen, where it was printed "on the press brought here from Kolozsvár".

New Initiatives by Táncsics

The third attempt to resume publication in Debrecen was made by Mihály Táncsics, who had far less success than his official competitors. Táncsics left Pest in a peasant's cart on the bitter cold night of January 5. He was ill-clad and arrived chilled to the bone in Debrecen, where his memoirs relate that the city's "houseowning citizens, male and female, thoroughly understood how to exploit our national misfortune." His first concern was to take the "steps necessary" for publishing the *Munkások Újsága*. His paper had been banned in the capital, "but I believed no one would obstruct the continuation of it here," especially because "the many papers which had been published in the capital had all ceased to appear" and "under our critical circumstances" there was a great need "on the part of the uneducated multitude for a paper that would provide instruction on various matters." Táncsics encountered his first obstacle at the printing press, which was hardly able to cope with the assignments it already had, and he decided he would try and publish a "piecemeal" paper "untied to any time" until conditions improved. Initially, it would seem, this took the form of the *Debreczeni Vásárfia* (Debrecen Fairing), whose subtitle declared it was provided "as a courtesy" by Mihály Táncsics. According to his *Életpályám*, the "first box," in other words, the first number, began with his New Year's good wishes to "his worker friends," the same words with which he had greeted them "in the first number for 1849 of the *Munkások Újsága*," which had remained undistributed. The greetings were followed by a succession of short, ironical political comments which defined as fairings such "objects" as the "Rope" for a traitor's neck, the "Liquor" to be knocked back by the one "who hauls the traitor up onto the gibbet, lest pity assault his heart," the "Powder and Shot" for cowardly deserters, and the "Commemorative Coin" as a bonus to the people of Debrecen who demanded so much house rent.

A significant study on the *Munkások Újsága* written twenty or so years ago differed from earlier ones in stating that the paper never appeared at all in 1849 because "there was no way it could, in January because of the conditions at the printing press and later because of punitive measures." But what were the measures taken against if there was nothing to punish? Táncsics later recalled that "after some printers arrived in Debreczen from Kolozsvár, I too started up the *Munkások Újsága*, but only a few issues could appear as it was banned here as well." Apart from that evidence, there is a photograph of the title page of the *Munkások Újsága*'s new first issue, dated January 21, 1849, for everyone to see in one of the appendices to the monograph on the Debrecen printing press. The paper's new motto was "Let the guilty be punished, for if the evil-doer receive not his deserts the best of laws will be worth nothing." The comment was a return to the basic line of argument in Táncsics's piece on January 10 for the *Alföldi Hírlap*; it emerges from the text that he was speaking of those who committed crimes against their country. It also emerges that subscriptions to the paper, which Táncsics planned to publish three times a week, could be taken out at post offices or at the bookseller Lajos Telegdi's at a price of 2 forints 24 krajcárs for the first six months of 1849. Táncsics began the paper by explaining again how "the first number of this year appeared earlier in Budapest, but it proved impossible to send it out by post." Apart from the greetings from the editor, which "can be seen in the *Debreczeni Vásárfia*," this number had contained articles by Lajos Hajdú and Lajos Kenézi. Táncsics, under the title "Our Task," went on to reply to the paper's opponents: "Many are angry with the *Munkások Újsága*, perhaps because we are certainly wont to tell the truth in it." Moreover, "Usually, in truth's case, the more it is attacked the more it triumphs. Beware, you who decry my paper right and left, for by doing so you do yourselves mischief, since you fall into being enemies of truth, which from your point of view may be dangerous." And he added, "I shall be presenting my policy bit by bit."

But we also have knowledge of a paper bearing the inscription "*Munkjások Újsága*, January 21, No. 1" on which the subtitle "*Debreczeni Vásárfia*, 2d box" can be read. It contained comments similar to those of the earlier "fairing," among others the "Scaffold" on which the traitors had to be executed. From this one would assume that the *Vásárfia*, which had begun as an irregular publication, then appeared as a supplement or supplementary paper to the regular one.

However, it is probable that only one and at the most three issues of the Debrecen *Munkások Újsága* ever saw the light of day. Action against it was taken by the city council with remarkable speed, probably at the behest of the National Defence Commission or, more particularly, Madarász. Táncsics was straightaway summoned and required to lodge the caution money without delay. The deputy town clerk István Boros told Madarász that as the editor of the *Munkások Újsága* had so far failed to pay the deposit prescribed by law and had himself frankly admitted this at the council meeting to which he was summoned on this matter, he had instructed the city court to institute proceedings under Paragraph 31 of Act 18 of 1848 and suspended publication of the paper until the proceedings were heard. The city court acted with similar haste. On February 3 Madarász was told that Táncsics had been fined 500 forints for not lodging the caution money and that the fine had been collected from him; "concurrently," it was reported, "he has been prohibited from publishing the paper he edits until the statutory conditions have been fulfilled, which decision it is intended shall be communicated to the manager of the local press in the form of an extract from the records." The ban by the city council was subsequently published in the *Közlöny* on the instructions of the National Defence Commission's police department. On February 15 Madarász also issued an order published on the following day by the *Közlöny* instructing post offices to refund subscriptions received for the *Munkások Újsága*, which was "according to the verdict of the court unfurnished with the legal requisites and therefore banned."

Of course the caution money was patently just a pretext

of which use could formally be made, as Táncsics realized. Such swift proceedings against one who not a year earlier had been freed by the revolution from prison (to which he had likewise been sent on that occasion for a press offence) and who at this time was a member of the House of Representatives and the Egalitarian Society showed plainly how nervous the government was made by the attempt to resurrect the *Munkások Újsága*. Initially Táncsics may have hoped to win Kossuth over against Madarász. At least, something of that kind seems to have been mentioned in an undated letter signed by the leading persons of Mezőkeresztes and addressed to him as the "former editor" of the *Munkások Újsága*. Táncsics tried unsuccessfully to get the letter published in *Marczius*, but in the end it appeared only in his book *Életpályám*. The letter-writers related that the paper, which "faithfully interpreted" their demands, was read in Mezőkeresztes almost as a prayer book; it had encouraged them to provide soldiers, money, and clothing, but now they would remain without counsel. However, they were convinced, they said, that Kossuth would not allow the true cause to be suppressed merely for lack of money, for "if your paper had been banned for taking a dangerous line or exerting a harmful influence, basic evidence for this would have been presented." This tactic, if that is what it was, proved unsuccessful. On February 27 the *Közlöny*, in an assessment of "how many Hungarian papers appear in this country," remarked pointedly that "the *Munkások Újsága* is dead," an assertion to which Táncsics wanted the right of immediate reply. Since Gyurmán would not publish his objections, they eventually appeared in No. 14 of *Marczius*. Pálffy by no means subscribed to Táncsics's views but remained true to his own in not imitating the government by turning against him. In *Marczius* on February 28 appeared a short, sharply worded statement by Táncsics entitled "Popular Papers":

> We say of Robert Blum, of our own earlier Martinovics, and of many others not that they are dead but that they were executed, beheaded. . . . The *Munkások Újsága* was in flourishing health, and it did not die a natural death, for it was murdered. . . . There is no power that can cause the *Munkások Újsága* to die. It will live a long time yet, as long as the spirit of any paper can live. . . . Have no fear, my village brethren, for while I myself live I shall not desert you, and I shall support your

cause until I breathe my last. . . . . While I cannot continue my work of mobilization for your benefit under the title *Munkások Újsága* or any other, make use of the issues which have already appeared and of my other studies. One day I shall tell the tale of who murdered my paper and why.

Not long afterwards Táncsics published "a little book" entitled *Új alkotmány-javaslat* (New Constitutional Proposal) to mark the anniversary of the March revolution. This he distributed free, "sending numerous copies of it to Szeged and Kolozsvár as well." Among its contents were demands for the nationalization of church property and the abolition of the remaining feudal services and a proposal that all landless cottars who took part in the war of independence receive 20 holds (28.4 acres) of land each out of estates confiscated from traitors to their country. Táncsics then sought another solution, "being unable to publish a newspaper," and started a series of pamphlets entitled *Forradalom* (Revolution) in octavo book format, each being a sixteen-page printer's sheet in length. These were printed on the city press and could be subscribed to in advance from the booksellers Csáthy and Telegdi for 6 "silver" krajcárs each. Táncsics used them to put forward his revolutonary programme, which went beyond the secularization of church estates and confiscation of traitors' property to suggest a maximum landholding of 2,000 holds (2,840 acres). The first two of these were printed in Debrecen on the city press in April 1849, after which Táncsics, along with others, returned to the capital, where in May and June he had five more printed at the press of Lukács and Partner. In his memoirs he wrote that the remaining pamphlets were in the press when "the printing staff fled in dismay at the news of the Russians' approach." The manuscript of them was lost. Shortly afterwards Táncsics himself followed the government to Szeged.

The Resumption of Marczius Tizenötödike

Marczius Tizenötödike belied its reputation for agility by managing to be only the fourth paper to resume publication. The new first issue came out on February 14. The city press had been unable to take on the printing of *Marczius*, and so Pálffy had had to wait for the press the government had ordered from Kolozsvár. The diary entries of its manager, Lukács Bartók, record that it began operation on January 31 with a staff of eleven and two iron presses from the Catholic girls' school and one from the Reformed Church College. Bartók wrote, "I printed the *Marczius Tizenötödike* every day on half-sheets, sometimes in eight hundred and sometimes in six hundred copies." Later the "press transferred temporarily from Kolozsvár to Debrecen" issued the declaration of independence and for a time, while the "state press" was on its way back to the capital, the *Közlöny* as well. It remained in Debrecen until June 4.

Some historians have expressed surprise that the government was prepared to help a traditionally opposition paper in this way. In fact Pálffy and his group, as radical supporters of the war of independence, had now become of some assistance to the National Defence Commission against the strengthening opposition from the peace party; moreover, Pálffy had become a counsellor at the Ministry of the Interior and Csernátoni one of Kossuth's presidential secretaries. Indeed, *Marczius* hastened in its very first number to take issue with the articles in favour of the peace party which Jókai had contributed to the *Közlöny*. Csernátoni, having just closed the unfortunate episode that arose out of his radical articles for the *Közlöny*, was delighted to find himself for a while Pálffy's associate editor, on the "unconstrained ground" of *Marczius*, "where I can speak and write as the mood takes me and my convictions dictate." But for the young radicals Debrecen was no substitute for Budapest, the basis of the revolution. It was easier to elicit a response to reaction than to radicalism among Debrecen's guildsmen, burghers, and well-to-do peasants. The situation later prompted Petőfi to write in the summer of 1849, angrily and in many points unfairly, "Debrecen is even more dangerous than on Friday, so much so that if Hungary's independence miscarries, we shall be able to attribute it to nothing other than the fact that it was declared in Debrecen." *Marczius* too was affected by the shrinkage in the public, the response, and the corps of contributors. Apart from Pálffy, who sometimes wrote anonymously and sometimes, for his ironical pieces of polemic; used the pseudonym "Gedeon Nagy," it was Csernátoni who featured most frequently. Ferenc Tomor continued to contribute writings with a republican slant. There were a host of pen names and initials—"Karika" (Wheel), "Montagnard," "Nagyőr" (Great Sentinel), "Papramorgó" (Liquor), "Radicalis," "Reggeli" (Breakfast), "Péter Téli" (Peter Winter), "Terrorista," "V.," etc.—and it is difficult to fit names to them. The paper carried a sample of Hiador's "Songs of Freedom," which could be bought, the advertisement said, in pamphlet form at the newspaper's offices. For the anniversary of the revolution József Erdélyi wrote a commemoration. It is known to have taken Pálffy a lot of persuasion and a high fee to gain Károly Szász for the paper, since he otherwise tended to be influenced by the peace party views of his father, a state secretary. Notably, however, it published Petőfi's poem "Nyakravaló" (Collar) against Lázár Mészáros on February 20.

But it soon emerged that Csernátoni could no longer write exactly as the mood took him. In the February 17 and 19 issues he could still comment with impunity in connection with the earlier debates in the House of Representatives that the National Defence Commission should "free the hands of the head of government from the tendrils binding them" by dismissing one member or another, for that accorded with the old desire of the radicals to bring Kossuth fully over to their side. Csernátoni was again defending Kossuth when on February 20 he criticized János Pálffy's arguments in the February 11 number of the *Alföldi Hírlap* for modernizing the running of the National Defence Commission and reorganizing the government, which amounted to an indirect suggestion that Kossuth's powers be curtailed. But on February 23 Csernátoni, writing about the surrender of Eszék (Osijek), combined a sharp attack upon Mészáros with unaltered appreciation for Görgey, whom both Kossuth and Madarász had come to see as more and more dangerous since the Vác declaration and during the campaign in Upper Hungary. The lightning struck at once, in the shape of Kossuth's letter of February 24 from which I have already quoted, in which he called him to account and recalled his past criminal record. As a result of that letter Csernátoni felt it necessary to withdraw from the work he had been doing for the paper and from his position as a presidential secretary. In *Marczius* on the same day was a strong reaction by Csernátoni to an article by Jókai in the previous day's *Közlöny* against the emergency courts and their "terrorist" appearance. The radicals, Csernátoni said, were indeed among the "men of ill will" who wished "to terrorize the betrayers of the country by means of the emergency courts." There was no future, he said, for one who "caressed the enemies of freedom and humanity, the betrayers of the country," and he added, "I have addressed myself to Mr J/ókai/; Ny/áry/ too should learn from it." But in the same number *Marczius* had news of the launch of a new paper, the *Esti Lapok*, with none other as its editor than Jókai, last year's "extreme left-winger" who now leaned towards the other side. "It has just come to our knowledge," wrote Csernátoni bitingly in his "Scapegraces" column on February 24, "that the *Figyelmező* has been hounded out of Budapest, although that has not disturbed Mr Vida, who has simply arrived in Debrecen and already started up a paper called the *Esti Lapok* under the pseudonym Mór Jókai." He did not have to wait long for the counter-attack. In the fifth issue of the *Esti Lapok* Jókai used information from Lajos Kovács to expose his adversary's past: "A certain Lajos Cseh, who emerged from prison in Vienna two years ago, where he certainly was not incarcerated for a political crime, is now publishing 'Scapegraces' under the name of Csernátoni." The latter's response was the article quoted in an earlier chapter in which he chose as the lesser of two evils to relate the story of his youthful misdeeds. But even though Csernátoni was temporarily silenced, *Marczius* pursued a running debate with its new adversary, Jókai's paper.

The Esti Lapok

The *Esti Lapok* started as a daily in quarto format on February 22, 1849. It was printed on the municipal press and remained in Debrecen until May 31, after which it continued in Pest. From the very first issue it was apparent that the paper supported not a break with the dynasty and a fight to the last but lawful self-defence and if possible a policy of compromise, by and large in accordance with Nyáry's resolution, which had been defeated in the House of Representatives on January 13, 1849. The introductory article said that although the paper considered the war of independence justified, if the destiny of the country were to be placed at risk in pursuing it, it would prefer peace. In another passage it said that "every moment of our present" must be so arranged "that we do not thereby block the path to any opportunity in the future." Jókai, in a recognizable pass at Kossuth's policy, especially condemned the "pettifogging" spirit of looking always at what can be considered justified and not at the true interests at stake. It is not surprising that the *Esti Lapok* should have aroused contradiction and protest from the start.

Jókai, who doubled as responsible editor and as publisher, by and large followed the line taken by the *Pesti Hírlap*, which had closed down by then, although he altered the tone to suit the altered circumstances. For the didactics and consistency of principle that marked the erstwhile paper of the centralists Jókai substituted his humour and his changeable, sometimes even inconsistent attitude, which none the less covered a plain enough political objective—that of the "moderate" noblemen who as members of the House of Representatives in Debrecen were "peace partisans." When Jókai spoke in later years of those who had worked for the paper it was principally a number of these whom he named. Among them were Gábor Kazinczy and Lajos Kovács, two organizers of the friendly get-togethers, and János Pálffy, Antal Zichy, and Rudolf Szunyogh, who stood security for the caution money (although the police authorities later tried to stir up trouble on that score: on March 1 Madarász is known to have temporarily banned postal distribution of the *Esti Lapok* on the grounds that Jókai had still not lodged the deposit). But there were more modest, less politically prominent contributors too, such as József Kolmár, who had previously worked for *Kossuth Hírlapja* and even for radical papers. It was largely Kazinczy, Kovács, Nyáry, and to some extent Pál Hunfalvy who influenced the political line taken, along with Zsigmond Kemény, who did not appear much in public or even write for the paper but was among the leaders of the group. Jókai mainly took care of the paper's popular tone and the way it was expressed, as well as running the "humorous column" headed "Charivari".

"The *Esti Lapok*", Samu Szeremlei wrote hardly twenty years later, "was filled with personal tattle, and the soberest views were clothed in a robe of humour." This peculiar humour, certainly directed at times at individual persons and employed by Jókai with a serenely artistic sureness, was fundamentally among the traditional weapons of the county-based politics of the nobles. The aim was to attack the personal weaknesses of political opponents, to make use of their vulnerable points, to depict their features in caricature, and to ridicule and compromise them with scathing anecdotes. As we have seen, the first target was Csernátoni, but right from the start action was commenced against Madarász and his colleagues as well. They were presented in issue No. 2 as loafers, and in No. 3 it was remarked of their chief that though "a man may be a republican from tip to toe he can be a thoroughly bad minister of police" into the bargain. Kemény wrote in 1850 that they had begun in February to plan Madarász's downfall, which was to have been followed by moves against Kossuth.

When it came to their own role and the dangers, the "terrorization" by Madarász, that faced them, Kemény and his companions exaggerated wildly in their extremely biased memoirs. They presented matters as if the "Kazinczy-Kovács coterie" had amounted to an organized party which had pursued its objectives resolutely and deliberately from the outset. The very conduct of the *Esti Lapok* demonstrates that there cannot have been any revolutionary "terror" in Debrecen. If there had, no toleration would have been shown for a paper whose purpose, according to the later reminiscences, was to put an end to Kossuth's *ad hoc* administration and instead of "self-important illusion . . . provide scope for manifestations of concern and opposition," a paper which not only emphasized that it stood for what was legal and not what was revolutionary but actually attacked the radical chief of police. Moreover, it would be an exaggeration to speak of this phenomenon as an organized party or as having the appearance from the opposite side of a political and even military plot large and effective enough to constitute a serious threat to the cause of the war of independence. Initially, the "peace party," if one can call it that, represented the common anxieties, fears, disgruntled demands, and cautious conversations of some ten to fifteen representatives in the National Assembly. Its political importance did not lie in its level of effectiveness or organization. What began to make it dangerous was the general retreat by the nobility from the revolution, a broad, national process that caused a certain shift in the centre of gravity on the now restricted political stage of Debrecen. Nor is it very surprising that the horizons of the *Esti Lapok* and of its radical opponents should have narrowed to the Debrecen stage and its actors, as if their tactical measures chiefly and basically determined the great sociopolitical processes taking place in the country. The illusion was fostered by the shortage of news and information of a broader kind, particularly in an international context; often they had to be content with rumours. "The foreign papers had ceased to arrive," Szeremlei wrote, "and the newspaper editors themselves knew nothing for certain about the position in Pest, Vienna, or foreign countries." Szeremlei even inclined to the view that "the government seemed to approve of this dreadful hiatus of knowledge, because it actually confiscated the foreign papers for quite a while, thus purposely keeping the domestic press and the representatives of the nation in ignorance of developments in the world of politics abroad." In fact, as we have seen in relation to the *Közlöny*, the government itself, and more specifically Madarász's office, managed to obtain the foreign papers only laboriously, irregularly, and late.

At first it was *Marczius* that defended Madarász from the charges in the *Esti Lapok* that he distributed the *Közlöny* irregularly and ran a "happy-go-lucky administration." In the February 26 number of *Marczius* an article signed "No Representative" described it all as a pretext; Madarász was being execrated because he was energetic and a republican and therefore viewed as "a Danton or a Marat." In the same number "Radicalis" continued an enthusiastic eye-witness account begun on February 23 of Görgey's northern campaign. The writer considered that in Görgey "a vast organizing intellect has been gained by the army," which had to a large extent been no more than a "disorderly mass of people." He added that "as Kossuth made the most fortunate choice in Görgei, so Görgei did in his brigade commanders."

The Debreczeni Lapok

On February 27, just five days after the peace party's venture,

Madarász's *Debreczeni Lapok* (Debrecen Pages) was hurriedly launched as a counterweight. The publisher was Madarász's younger brother József, who did most of the editing as well. It was printed three times a week in quarto format on the press "transferred temporarily from Kolozsvár to Debreczen." One should add right away that it did not survive long. A break came hardly more than two weeks later, on March 14. Having made a new start on March 30, it ended on April 4. In all there were only nine issues, in which the Madarász brothers fought their rear-guard action until the enemy managed to secure their political downfall. No small part in the paper's ill-fortune may have been played by the Madarász brothers' convoluted style, which has been encountered earlier. Jókai wrote venomously of how the subscribers were supposed to have sent in a request that the head of the paper "translate what he writes into Hungarian, because they cannot understand Persian." But style was not the basic issue in the battle. After all, the paper's other decisive political figure besides Madarász was Dániel Irányi, and he expressed himself very clearly. The essence was apparent from the first number: on constitutional matters, at least, the new paper took an even more decided stance than *Marczius*. It pressed for a final break with the dynasty and the declaration of a republic and spoke out against the "legalistic campaign" of the *Esti Lapok*, the paper's impugning of the war's revolutionary nature, and the men who were "considering a compromise" and thus "in the same camp as the enemy." "A war of independence is indeed one of life and death" was the watchword provided by László Madarász. Meanwhile Irányi declared in an article in several parts entitled "For Guidance in Debrecen" that the peace party consisted partly of honest but timid men and partly of selfish lords fearful for their possessions, who "honour their parchment /i.e., noble/ privileges and their ancestral estates, though mortgaged to double their value, more than they do the liberty of their country." On March 1 Irányi wrote in commemoration of the anniversary of the French revolution of February 1848.

There were now two radical newspapers embroiled in debates with the *Esti Lapok*. On March 2 came an attack on the peace party paper in *Marczius* by "Terrorista." Meanwhile Pálffy reported that the paper had received many letters objecting indignantly to the "ignoble treatment" accorded to Csernátoni and published one of them, from Rákóczy, who was a colleague of Csernátoni's at the National Defence Commission. Rákóczy considered that on the part of Jókai, who had "worn such a big red feather in Budapest," it was a piece of baseness and "meanness of soul" to upbraid Csernátoni with an offence for which he had already atoned. "Csernátoni's fault, if any, was to express his convictions to all without any regard."

As we have seen, *Marczius* too was ready to defend Madarász against the *Esti Lapok*. Yet the two radical papers did not stand for the same things, and the discrepancy between the papers of the March Youth and of the petty noble radicals became increasingly apparent. It can be observed most of all on three topics: Görgey and the high command, the national minority issue, and social progress, the peasant question.

The Madarász brothers were against Görgey, a fact that emerges as clearly from the early issues of the *Debreczeni Lapok* as from the subsequent memoirs of József Madarász. In the paper reservations were expressed about the appreciative words which had appeared in *Marczius* on February 23, and it was stated that it was still far from clear whether Görgey's northern campaign had been useful or harmful. *Marczius*, on the other hand, in a leading article on March 6, was delighted to report that Kossuth had returned from the camp at Tiszafüred (where he had been looking into the conflict between the Polish General Dembinski and certain high-ranking Hungarian officers) and that henceforth "the supreme command of our camp is entrusted to Görgey, on whose outstanding talent as a leader we have reported in more detail in a great many issues of our paper." In the past, if the truth be told, *Marczius* had also castigated those who had turned against Dembinski, but it now appeared that the Polish general had not been set aside "for political reasons"; and "when Görgei crossed the Tisza again yesterday uttering the guiding principle that the Hungarians would fight on and if a chance of peace opened up would attach conditions proportionate to their victory, that which was the sole wish of every good patriot and thinking politician had come to

pass." In the same issue "Radicalis" had further praise for
Görgey's abilities as a commander and his vigilance during
the northern campaign. Two days later, on March 8, "Terrorista" devoted a whole leading article to the way the opinion
held about Görgey by some—to wit, the peace party—had
changed. At first they had been against him, particularly when
they saw that in turning northward he did not concern himself
with their safety. Then, after the Vác proclamation, they
had thought he was a monarchist and their man. Now there
were wry faces again when they learned that he was preparing for combat and not compromise. In fact, the writer continued, Görgey was a soldier and "a Hungarian yearning for
freedom" who wanted to win. The staff of *Marczius*, he went
on, was delighted that Kossuth and Görgey had met in person without their retinues, knowing "that it would suffice for
them to be together for an hour, indeed for a few minutes,
in which the two pure patriot characters could recognize one
another and diminish the misunderstandings that may have
existed to their due values, in a word, for them to become
perfectly content with one another." However, "Radicalis,"
in the same March 8 issue, reacted to the news that Görgey
might not after all be the commander-in-chief of the whole
army by saying that if he were not, he should become so as
soon as possible, for a "dual command" could only have ill
consequences. But on the same day, March 8, the *Debreczeni
Lapok* was making its target plain enough in calling for death
to descend upon the head of every recalcitrant, "be he the most
outstanding general or the simplest private soldier." It saw
Kossuth's weakness in the fact that he was "very humane, very
compliant" and even referred to the dangerous desires of the
"parleying party" and to the possibility of having a military
dictatorship. On the following day, March 9, an unsigned
leading article by Pálffy in *Marczius* brought up the matter
of the supreme command, which had been thrown open again,
and plainly showed its support for Görgey. "The worst thing
in the world," Pálffy wrote, "is irresolution and indecision,"
and that was what it amounted to "if one appoints a commander-in-chief for twenty-four hours and then repents of
it forthwith." The appointment of General Antal Vetter, he
said, had taken everyone by surprise; "it seems that an
influence on the guidance of the greatest affairs of our country

is exerted through certain intrigues behind the scenes." Indirectly, the tactful phrases of the charge were directed at the president of the National Defence Commission as well. "Kossuth's name is great and glorious in the land," Pálffy wrote. "Therefore let us not see in anything a measure that would point to Kossuth's having yielded to influences from any source whatsoever." It was certainly to this that the *Közlöny* reacted on March 11 with a warning to editors not to divulge news about military operations in their papers. The following day's *Marczius* included Pálffy's reply in the form of a satirical letter from "Gedeon Nagy" dated from the imaginary village of Kutyabagos (from *kutya*, "dog"). That, he said, was not what the argument was about, and so there was not much sense in the move that had been made. The *Debreczeni Lapok* failed to appear in the latter half of the month, but Madarász is known to have gone to see Kossuth on March 24 to demand the dissolution of the House of Representatives and the trial of Görgey by military court.

Political Controversies

The two radical papers also differed strongly over the national minorities. In the previous year even the March Youth had been content with stressing the common liberty of the individual. But at this juncture *Marczius* made a big advance and showed no small courage in recommending that Hungary's whole policy towards the national minorities should be reviewed. In two unsigned articles on March 6 and 10 it was argued that the Hungarian revolution could win over the country's national minorities, which had turned against it, only by recognizing them as such and offering them more than the Habsburgs were prepared to offer. The Hungarians had to realize, the paper said, that "we can no longer ignore the national minorities existing in this country," who had to be won over with a promise "of greater liberty and nationhood resting on clearer foundations." The best course would be to declare that "Hungary, Transylvania, Croatia, and even, if they desire it, the Slavic population of the Upper Hungarian counties" should be "federative republics." And if some considered federalization "one of the tasks for the future," none the less "we must arrange to state in good time the foundations upon which the federative republics united under the Pest government can one day be built" and introduce a "communal system" from which "the consequence will be that localities . . . may conduct their own affairs in the language of their own choosing." Here the historical importance lies not in the specific solutions put forward, which in any case were not elaborated upon further, but in the initiative in principle. This marked the first attempt to escape from the traditional Hungarian assessment of the national minority question, one that was to continue dominant for a good while to come. It marked a search for a new perspective on the issue within the old boundaries of the country. One hardly need add that in their attempt Pálffy and his fellows went far beyond the traditional notions of the "moderate" nobility and those of the radical petty nobility as well. The *Esti Lapok* wasted no time in accusing them of wanting to carve Hungary up. In the *Debreczeni Lapok* one of the most authoritative of the radical noble politicians, László Újházy, had the blessing of the Madarász brothers when on March 10, right after the first article had appeared, he addressed an open letter to *Marczius* on several issues, of which the national minority issue was given most emphasis. Újházy asserted emphatically that because the unity of the state was supremely important, "we cannot share with our brethren . . . of different tongues in anything other than public liberty, equality, and affection," which would certainly have sufficed for them had it not been for the "counter-revolutionary intrigues of the perfidious dynasty." The second article in *Marczius*, which appeared that very evening, reacted to this oversimplification of the problem:

> We agree with Újházy that it would be a glorious thing if we managed to establish out of the peoples who live within our old historical borders a country that rested upon a strong, free, and purely Hungarian national entity. But in our view this is no longer among the possible outcomes from which a long and secure future can be hoped. /Among the Slavs and the Romanians/ has arisen a sense of nationhood, and although we might suppress this by force of arms there would be little to be thankful for in such a victory.

Marczius saw the principle of *Gleichberechtigung*, equality of rights, which Austria had proclaimed as a promise designed to mislead, as exerting an influence on the various national minorities: "We must show that standing by Austria is tantamount to being disappointed, while standing by Hungary is tantamount to lighting upon that which the national minorities seek," for it "will provide more advantage." In effect, *Marczius* was already prepared to jettison for the sake of the future the traditional principle of the Hungarians' historical rights: "In what a politician does he must always look to the future and not to how long we can sustain certain unnatural, historical rights that are a hangover from the Middle Ages. . . . Now, in advance, it would be better to settle the whole national minority issue radically, or at least place it on a good track along which it might securely roll forward."

On the third subject one finds little said in the press at this time, a fact that in itself is significant. We know that some of the March Youth really began to take note of the problems of the peasantry in the spring of 1849. One of them, István Kléh, submitted a report to the National Defence Commission at about this time. The war of independence, he said, could not be waged successfully without harkening to the peasant demands. After a time this new position of Kléh's, as we shall see later, found its way into the political programme of *Marczius* as well. But there is little sign of a similar development in the thinking of the radicals among the nobility. In the House of Representatives on January 18 Madarász proposed a proclamation that the nobility "has always striven to alleviate the lot of the people and make the people free together with them" but that the court and its adherents had prevented them. It was not hard for Nyáry to reply and score a point for his own policy: "I consider it mistaken and unworthy on our part to want to blame the events of the past directly upon the king, the dynasty, and the ruling house. Had the Hungarian aristocracy returned the people their rights a hundred years ago the dynasty and the camarilla would not have gained the power to injure Hungary so shamefully." On February 12, 1849, the Egalitarian Society, headed by József Madarász, issued a new programme in which it recommended the creation of branch societies wherever twelve members were "to be found," but it continued to confine itself in seeking new members to proclaiming equality of rights, without taking up the social problems. Even on March 25 its fear that the peace party was growing stronger led it to accept the counsels of Táncsics only so far as to demand that the estates of traitors be parcelled out among returning Hungarian soldiers. Nor was there any word about developing the methods of eradicating feudalism or the laws of 1848 to accompany the demand for an independent Hungarian republic in the programme of the Radical party formed on April 5, 1849, under the chairmanship of László Újházy. In the social sphere the radicalism of the nobility lagged behind the views of Kossuth, who at least issued a decree on April 20 preventing the coercion into the performance of feudal services and the expulsion from land classified as manorial of persons whom the landowners considered manorial cottars but who considered themselves former urbarial peasants.

Meanwhile two events occurred in which the press played a large part. One was the downfall of Madarász, engineered by the growing peace party. The other was Kossuth's proclamation of independence in an attempt to halt the peace party's growth.

The attack on Madarász began on March 17, when Gábor Kazinczy asked in the House about the suspected misappropriation of some diamond studs which were among the valuables confiscated from the estate of Count Ödön Zichy, who had been executed for treason in the autumn of 1848. The details of the case and the studies of it cannot be gone into here. Suffice it say that it was likely that the National Defence Commission itself had made use of the more valuable of the missing pieces in its diplomatic activities in connection with the Turks and the Romanians. But all those involved remained silent on the subject, and the entire blame fell on Madarász, whose office, irrespective of that, had proceeded with a demonstrable lack of care and control. On March 19 the campaign was taken up by the *Esti Lapok* and pursued with increasing stridency. For a while the affair became the paper's major concern, and it did not omit to couple pursuit of it with propagation of its own political ideas: "Let us not compromise what can be achieved for the sake of what cannot," it wrote on March 21 in a clear reference to the goals of agreement and of independence, just as if the Habsburgs would be willing to agree with the peace party and there were no

need for the utmost efforts even to achieve agreement. On
March 23 the *Esti Lapok* declared that Madarász had "clearly lied before the sacred House." Between March 24 and 30
it published in instalments a decisive biography of the "present chief" of police under the title "Pro memoria." The break
in the publication of the *Debreczeni Lapok* left the battle
against the peace party's paper to be carried on by *Marczius*,
which preferred to steer clear of the Madarász affair when
it could. On March 21 Csernátoni wrote a few lines to Pálffy,
beginning with his usual salutation "Berti, my friend," saying that as circumstances had changed he would like to be
a regular member of the paper's staff again. He then contributed an address to the electors of Komárom County, who
wished to put him up for a vacant seat in the House of Representatives. In the electoral address he declared his objective
to be a "democratic republic" and expressed his conviction
that the counter-revolution could not be defeated "without
severity and terror." He concluded by sarcastically rejecting
the statement of "Z" in the *Esti Lapok* that "we do not represent a revolutionary standpoint." Seeing the progress being
made by the peace party's campaign, the Madarász brothers,
accompanied by one or two of their adherents, visited Kossuth on March 24 looking for protection and putting forward
a plan for counter-attack under which Kossuth would dissolve the House, take the executive power into his own hands,
and appoint László Madarász as prime minister or minister
of the interior. Kossuth would not agree to this and under
the circumstances could not have done so. But he did want
to stop the peace party in its tracks, and before setting out
to visit the army on the following day, March 25, he sought
a guarantee from the House of Representatives that no political change of any kind would be made in his absence. Without mentioning any names he expressed strong and unambiguous condemnation of the *Esti Lapok*'s campaign against
Madarász. "Be good enough to look back over the activity
of the press in the last few days," he said. "It is horrifying
and repulsive. Anyone who holds the word 'country' in greater esteem than satisfaction of his own personal feelings must
be horrified by what the press is currently doing." Turning
to Lajos Kovács, he went on,

> I have a duty to say this much: this exasperated press debate has revolved in paricular around a man who is a member of the government, and clearly he has been faced with accusations which if true preclude him from belonging to the government and if untrue demand the punishment of the accusers. In this respect I inform the House of Representatives that the government deems it necessary to order that every document referring to this question being debated with such exasperation in the press be printed, and that we have at the same time arranged according to the law to summon a jury which will be instructed to proceed in accordance with the law.

Naturally the political debate in the press went on during Kossuth's absence. On March 26 the *Esti Lapok* again distanced itself from republicanism: "Let us fight and win under the present form of state." On the same day the peace party paper was attacked in *Marczius* by "Gedeon Nagy" and by Csernátoni, who used the "Scapegraces" column to ridicule Lajos Kovács, Rudolf Szunyogh, and their fellows under the title "Renegade Creed." He did the same thing again on March 27, while in the same issue a writer signing himself "V" followed up the attack on the *Esti Lapok*. On March 29 "Gedeon Nagy" and Csernátoni condemned their adversaries' manoeuvres in the press and in the House of Representatives, where the majority were not prepared to recognize the validity of the election of Csernátoni and other new radical representatives on formal grounds. But apart from this open skirmishing, an underhand trick was tried by certain elements that remain undiscovered to this day: an attempt was made to turn the army officers against the *Esti Lapok* by spreading false reports of it. This can clearly be seen in a letter that Kossuth sent from Tiszafüred to the National Defence Commission on March 29. It related how Klapka had asked if it were true that the *Esti Lapok* had published an article expressing readiness to make peace with Austria even at the price of providing forty thousand soldiers to fight against the Italians. According to Kossuth, "Righteous anger flashed through the army like the wrath of a thunderbolt—those crazy people will provoke the army into some kind of political outbreak in the end." Interestingly, Kossuth to some extent treated the report as true and immediately gave orders to Gyurmán about what the *Közlöny* should do to counter it. But, as the reply from the National Defence Commission soon made clear, no such article had ever appeared in the *Esti Lapok*.

The end of March also saw a growing reflection in the press of efforts to ensure that Hungary would react to the Olmütz manifesto by declaring independence. It could be seen, among other things, in the revival of the debates around the form of state. On March 30 József Madarász declared in the *Debreczeni Lapok*, which had resumed publication, "We decisively desire a republic in Hungary." The paper even advocated a temporary suspension of freedom of the press so as to silence the adversary and defend radicalism. "First we want a free country," it wrote, "and then freedom of the press, in the sense that if freedom of the press should obstruct the achievement of freedom for our country, we consider that the country's representatives and government would have both the right and the obligation to suspend the former while it continued to constitute a danger." The *Esti Lapok*, in contrast, took the view that the form of state was but a tool and as such a matter of secondary importance. On March 30, however, it warned that it would be inadvisable to introduce a republic in Hungary at that time because of the disorganized state of public morality. On the same day *Marczius* turned the argument on its head: the form of government was a tool indeed. Monarchy was a tool in the hands of tyranny for oppressing the people. A republic was likewise a tool "in the hands of the people and freedom," one with which it might "become strong and powerful, brighten the nights of darkness, efface and relieve misery, uproot crimes, and elevate humanity." The sharpening of the debate makes it all the more surprising at first sight that Jókai should have changed his political colours again at this juncture. Hungarian historians have usually explained it by saying that not even the *Esti Lapok* could shake off the influence of the growing public enthusiasm for independence. In any case, Jókai declared on April 2, under the title "Political Horoscope," that Hungary no longer recognized the Habsburg king, that the dynasty had signed "the death sentence on its own rule" with the Olmütz manifesto, and that the independence of Hungary would basically accord with the economic interests of Britain and of the new, emergent Germany. Unexpectedly, Jókai also gave his support to a republican form of state, again partly for foreign policy reasons. He argued that since the enemy (Austria) could never defeat Hungary, the struggle would eventually be resolved by the intervention on Hungary's side of the European democracies. To choose another foreign dynasty at that point would certainly turn one or more powers against Hungary. Since there could be no question of a "national" king, the best thing was to declare a republic. One's impression, however, is that Jókai was less influenced by public opinion than by the constraint of a possible new tactic on the part of the peace party. Friends had warned that it would be impossible under any circumstances to prevent Kossuth from declaring independence. In that case it would be preferable for Kossuth to be the designate head of state of a republic than of a national kingdom. The impression is reinforced as one examines subsequent issues of the *Esti Lapok*, in which its position is put in arguments in favour of a republic but not infrequently in a contradictory fashion that is even mixed with nostalgia for the monarchy.

On April 2, while Kossuth was away, there was even a mention in the House of Representatives of the rumour current in the army that the *Esti Lapok* had printed an article advocating bargaining. István Gorove asked the government if there were "reliable knowledge of incitement taking place in the army and aspersions being cast on members of the National Assembly." The reply came from Nyáry, who said that "after a member of the government had read every number of the *Esti Lapok* again," the Commission had established that the news was "a downright lie" and had written to tell Kossuth so. But that was only a prelude to a counter-attack by the peace party on the two radical papers. On March 30 the *Debreczeni Lapok* had gone beyond a recommendation that independence be declared to call for the dissolution of the House and the summoning of a new constituent National Assembly elected on a broader basis. On the same day the thirty-ninth issue of *Marczius* had written that after the expected victory "we shall send" the present National Assembly "into retirement." The liberal representatives of the peace party felt that ideas of this kind were directed at them and hastened to object in the name of the National Assembly as the true repository of power. János Pálffy began by asserting in general terms that he considered "activity and behaviour of this kind" on the part of the radical papers, which "defamed" the National Assembly, so "scandalous" as to call for trial before the emergency courts, but "not being a man of extremes" he would consider it sufficient if the House were "severely to censure" the press "in the minutes." When Irányi, from the radical side, demanded specific instances, Gorove recalled the two papers' incriminating assertions quoted above, putting forward as an object-lesson the French Revolution, in which similar moves had presaged "all the monstrosity and bloodshed" of the Convention. "But I trust that the people," he went on, "will prefer to honour their representatives, whom they freely elected, than to tolerate their being dispersed by a few scurvy individuals." The idea of instituting a press trial was then opposed by Imre Szacsvay, who was not one of the peace party: "Press freedom has countless concomitants, but if we desire freedom we must tolerate the bad." A bad press would kill itself in any case, he said. The people did not think highly of *Marczius*, and the *Debreczeni Lapok* had "managed to achieve nothing" because it had "not even managed to make itself comprehensible to the people." Kazinczy described as a piece of underhand corruption and "an unforgivable crime" the charges by the radical press that Debrecen contained "a secret party" whose members "want to sell Hungary out." Eventually the debate ended without any specific resolution's being passed. In the *Debreczeni Lapok* on April 4 an indignant József Madarász explained in his tortured style how the session had "hounded" the radical papers and almost taken him to court. But that was the final issue of his paper.

Shortly afterwards *Marczius* was able to report on the first big successes in the spring campaign. The April 10 number began with the report Kossuth had sent to the National Defence Commission. Then came a letter from Görgey sent from Gödöllő on April 7, from whose direct, familiar tone and use of the second person singular it emerges that he was on close personal terms with those running *Marczius*. "God bless you," Görgey wrote after the victorious advance. "I am incapable of writing down two lines of a respectable sequence of ideas. After all, we are very close to Pest, to which, as you know, all kinds of interests attract me. Today's order of the day to the army was this: Forward at all costs! Long live this country!" After that came a dispatch from Csernátoni, who was also with the army. However, the *Esti Lapok* chose this of all times to assert that the war of self-defence should only "be continued until it can be ended without endangering our future." The writer signing himself "N", whose article entitled "We and You" has just been quoted, was far more vigorous in waging war on the radicals and the Madarász brothers: "Your purpose is revolution; according to your complaints you are like fish out of water in Debrecen. You have not found material for it among the sobriety of the Great Plain people. To you the prosperous, peace-loving working people of Debrecen are an abomination; your legions of freedom are the vagabonds of Pest. . . . You would take revolution as far as you could; you preach guillotine, dictatorship, republic, Convention, etc."

But by this time the declaration of independence was imminent. It was considered not least to put paid to the hopes of the peace party. "The time has come," *Marczius* wrote on April 13, the "moment anxiously awaited for three centuries" when Hungary could become independent. On April 16, after the ceremonial act, Csernátoni recalled the resolution declaring the dethronement of the perfidious dynasty under the title "April the Fourteenth." In the same issue he analysed Lázár Mészáros; although he was "a student of the old era . . . unable to break out of his settled ideas" and not even a good war minister, he was none the less an upright, honest patriot. Independence, by the way, was enthusiastically celebrated by the whole press, including the peace party's *Esti Lapok*, which as an afternoon paper managed to scoop all its rivals by praising the great watershed on the same day, April 14, in a leading article by Jókai. Even so, it gave greater coverage, stretching over three columns, to the statement of the investigating committee on the Zichy valuables and the Madarász affair. But even under a new situation in which independence had been accepted by the peace party for want of something better, the balance of forces had shifted still more in favour of the liberal nobility. The alliance made between Kossuth and the radicals in the autumn of 1848 had come apart. The real defeat was suffered by radicalism, particularly Madarász and his adherents. On April 20 Imre Szacsvay, as spokesman for the investigators in the House of Representatives, gave a statement saying that "integrity in handling" the Zichy valuables had not been observed.

However, there were only uncertain suspicions as to how the "errors of negligence and abuse" may have been compounded by "the scandalous outrage that certain of the aforesaid valuables were misappropriated," and the task of pursuing further enquiries was entrusted to the government. Although Madarász had had more than a month in which to prepare himself, he exacerbated a tricky situation by replying with so tangled and obscure a statement that it appeared to be a deliberate evasion of the issue. Perhaps it was an example of the characteristic remarked upon earlier: the harder he tried, the less he was able to express himself clearly. The majority of the House was against him. On the following day, April 21, the *Esti Lapok* exclaimed in a burst of *Schadenfreude* that Madarász's "political life is at an end." On May 4 it added a note of triumph: "Many harkened to our words. . . . And Madarász disappeared. And Táncsics was silent. . . . And the flamingoes (out-and-out radicals) are noticeably thinning in the market-place of public affairs." Madarász resigned his seat in the House as well and returned to Fejér County. Although he was re-elected to the constituency of Csákvár, he played no further part in public affairs. His younger brother József wrote in his memoirs in that strange style of his that the responsibility largely belonged to the press: "When the official paper of prime minister Szemere showed the way in the fabrication and dissemination of rumours and aspersions, it was hardly a miracle that the *Esti Lapok*, the *Népbarát*, and these papers that gnawed upon fabrications, by trumpeting farther and wider, perplexed and misled the public." And he went on to charge the now "unfortunate" Kossuth, as he put it, with having surrounded himself with servile sycophants and possibly nursing a desire to be a king.

After the declaration of independence, plans were afoot in Debrecen for "ministerial combinations," as *Marczius* wrote on April 17. Csernátoni opposed the idea the *Esti Lapok* supported of Kossuth's being given a ministerial or prime ministerial post, judging that it might put his popularity at risk. Among the ministerial candidates mentioned in *Marczius* was Szemere, who had long ago become disillusioned in his old partisanship for Batthyány, but the first to suggest him as prime minister was the *Esti Lapok*. The idea almost certainly derived from Zsigmond Kemény, who reckoned that

Szemere might prove useful against Kossuth. And Szemere for his part sought the cooperation of the former adherents of the peace party, for rather similar reasons.

For a while it was as if the old antagonisms had been smoothed over, even the *Esti Lapok* having accepted independence and a republic. This may partly explain how a former member of the March Youth, Pál Vasvári, who is known to have taken part in the battles in Transylvania against the Romanians, came to contribute an article entitled "The Wallachians in Revolt" to the *Esti Lapok* on April 23 and in it to present a view of the national minority question that departed to no small degree from the norm. Vasvári too underlined that the enemies of the revolution had to be defeated and restrained, but he added that "the restraint of the Transylvanian rebels is a merciless honour," for essentially the Romanians had been turned into enemies because Transylvania's Hungarian nobility had "despised them, scorned them . . . and used them as beasts of burden." Even after the revolution the local nobility had wanted "to remain tyrants over the peasantry of Wallachian race," and "at a time when the abolition of urbarial dues had been proclaimed in the Hungarian lands the Transylvanian landowners were still exacting unpaid labour unmercifully."

All that remains is to mention briefly the modest provincial press to be found outside Debrecen in the early months of 1849. In Szeged on January 3, 1849, a paper called the *Tisza Vidéki Újság* (Tisza District Journal) began to appear twice a week in quarto format, printed on János Grünn's press. On the front page was an engraving that symbolized the new brotherhood of man: landowner, artisan, and peasant linking hands. The publisher and editor responsible was the town clerk, Pál Molnár, a lawyer who had previously worked for the *Jelenkor* and the *Nemzeti Újság*. However, the paper was banned by the government at the end of March because Molnár failed to lodge the requisite caution money. As a continuation, Molnár on April 21 issued the first of a series of "political pamphlets." Three in all appeared at irregular intervals under the title *Tiszavidéki Emlék* (Tisza District Memento). Meanwhile, at Szabadka a paper called *Közlöny kivonata* (Digest of the Gazette) began appearing on March 1, 1849, "as a weekly paper containing a digest of the battlefield (reports) and National Assembly speeches in the official gazette, to make up for the lack of newspapers." It was edited by Ferenc Szép and printed in poster format on both sides. To our knowledge five issues appeared. The proprietor of the press that printed it, Károly Bittermann, was imprisoned after the defeat.

Bibliography

Sándor Szilágyi, "Az Esti Lapok Debreczenben" (The *Evening Pages* in Debrecen) in *A magyar forradalom*, pp. 74-75; Samu Szeremlei, *Magyarország krónikája az 1848. és 1849. évi forradalom idejéről* (The Chronicle of Hungary in the Time of the Revolution of the Years 1848 and 1849), vols. 1 and 2 (Pest, 1867); Lukács Bartók, "A kolozsvári kath. lyceum nyomdája Debreczenben 1849-ben" (The Press of the Catholic High School of Kolozsvár in Debrecen in 1849), *Vasárnapi Újság*, no. 33 (1871); Pál Gyulai, "Jókai mint hírlapíró" (Jókai as Journalist), *Budapesti Szemle*, 1875, no. 9, pp. 202-16, and in *Bírálatok* (Critiques) (Budapest, 1911), pp. 132-52; Gusztáv Beksics, *Kemény Zsigmond, a forradalom és a kiegyezés* (Zsigmond Kemény, the Revolution and the Compromise) (Budapest, 1883); Madarász, *Emlékirataim*; Pál Hunfalvy, "Rövid visszapillantás a forradalomra" (A Brief Review of the Revolution), *Budapesti Szemle*, 1883, no. 34, pp. 268-76; Lajos Kovács, "Az 1849-iki pártok és az 'Esti Lapok'" (The 1849 Parties and the *Evening Pages*), *Hazánk*, 1884, no. 1, pp. 196-200; Lajos Hentaller, "Sajtómegrendszabályozás 1849-ben" (Control Exercised over the Press in 1849), in *Vérrózsák* (Blood Roses) (Budapest, 1906), pp. 204-10; Kálmán Mikszáth, *Jókai élete és kora* (Jókai's Life and Times), vol. 1, Összes Művei (Collected Works), vol. 18 (Budapest, 1910) Ferenc Csűrös, *A debreceni városi nyomda története, 1561-1911* (History of the Debrecen Municipal Press, 1561-1911) (Debrecen, 1911); Mór Jókai, *Forradalom alatt írt művek* (Works Written during the Revolution) (Budapest, 1912); idem, *Az én kortársaim: 1848-as emlékek* (My Contemporaries: 1848 Reminiscences) (Budapest, 1913); István Szabó, "A debreceni sajtó 1848-49-ben" (The Debrecen Press in 1848-1849), *Hajdúföld* (Hajdú Country), November 20, 25, and 29, and December 2, 4, 6, 8, 16, 21, and 23, 1923; idem, "A szabadságharc debreceni hírlapjai" (The Debrecen Papers in the War of Independence), *Debreceni Képes Kalendárium* (Debrecen Illustrated Almanac), 1924, pp. 55-58; Endre Csobán, "A közvélemény problémái" (The Problems of Public Opinion), in *A szabadságharc fővárosa, Debrecen* (Debrecen, the Capital in the War of Independence), ed. István Szabó (Debrecen, 1949), pp. 205-60; Géza Juhász, "Az írók szerepe" (The Role of the Writers), ibid., pp. 261-328; András Borossy, "Az országgyűlés" (The National Assembly), ibid., pp. 329-84; István Barta, ed., *Kossuth Lajos az Országos Honvédelmi Bizottmány*, vol. 2, *1849 jan. 1-ápr. 14.* (Lajos Kossuth at the Head of the National Defence Commission, vol. 2, January 1 - April 14, 1849) (Budapest, 1953); Windisch, *Közlöny*; Sándor Lukácsy, "Táncsics Mihály elfeledett cikkei" (The Forgotten Articles of Mihály Táncsics), *Alföld* (Great Plain), 1964, pp. 159-63; Kálmán Benda and Károly Irinyi, *A négyszáz éves debreceni nyomda* (The Four-Hundred-Year-Old Debrecen Press) (Budapest, 1961); János Varga, "A 'gyémántos' miniszter" (The "Diamond" Minister), *Élet és Tudomány* (Life and Science), 1964, pp. 24-25; Margit Busa, "A Religio és Nevelés 1849. évi második kiadásáról" (The Second Publication in 1849 of *Religion and Education*), *MKsz*, 1966, pp. 157-58.

17. The Final Phase

The starting point for surveying the second phase in the history of the press in 1849 is the end of April, after the recapture of Pest. Amid the joy of the liberation new papers arose and old ones were revived to replace those that had disappeared under the Austrian régime. However, a few papers went on publishing in Debrecen for a while. For example, the first issue of the *Közlöny* to come out again in Pest was dated June 5. But for these papers too the declaration of independence and the formation of the Szemere government at the beginning of May meant a realignment of political tendencies.

With the arrival of the Hungarian army in the capital, the *Figyelmező* fled with the Austrians towards Pressburg and ceased publication for a good while. Some other Pest papers closed down as well, but the *Pesther Zeitung* changed editors again instead: Ede Schwarz filled the post from April 25, followed by B. Mauksch from June 15. Having previously served Windischgrätz, the paper now turned into an enthusiastic advocate of Kossuth and expressed its delight that Hungary had broken with the Habsburgs. For want of any other there was a need for this semi-official German paper, to cater among others for the German-speaking citizens of the capital itself.

The Temporary Revival of the Press in Budapest

Three Hungarian papers were launched in the capital on the same day, April 24, 1849. One was a paper called *Szabadság, Egyenlőség, Testvériség* (Liberty, Equality, Fraternity), which was printed in folio format on Vazul Kozma's press. The publisher and responsible editor was Imre Kocsiss, the Pest lawyer who has earlier been mentioned as a member of the staff of Táncsics's paper the previous year. Thus it counted as a left-wing venture, and this may be why it thought that the new circumstances required it to emphasize in the third issue that "by equality we do not mean anarchy, we do not mean communism. This great concept . . . we interpret as follows: there shall be no regulations in the social order that hinder movements for the elevation of individuals." But in No. 4 it declared as its aim that in the Hungarian republic "the rule of oligarchs as members of particular castes should be rendered impossible, starting out from the great principles of liberty, equality, and fraternity on the widest possible basis, and the people should be its own sole and exclusive master." But on April 28, after only four issues, it came to an abrupt end for which no formal or underlying reasons can be given to this day.

April 24 also saw the resurrection of the *Pesti Hírlap*, which managed to survive for rather longer. It appeared in its traditional folio format, published and printed by Landerer. The first number was edited "until the return of Mór Jókai" by Sándor Szilágyi, but he gave place on the very next day to the playwright Károly Obernyik (1815-55), a friend of Kölcsey's in his youth and later of Petőfi's. The previous year he had used Lamartine's work to compile "Történeti képek" (Historical Pictures) from the "first French Revolution" for the *Budapesti Divatlap*. The swift change followed uproar over the appearance of Szilágyi's name, since he had also brought the paper out under Windischgrätz. At first some even wanted him taken before the emergency court, but the affair was smoothed over. Hardly a month later Szilágyi risked making a statement in the May 21 number of the new non-radical Pest version of *Marczius Tizenötödike*, claiming that under his control the *Pesti Hírlap* had been "edited in the freest possible way" and that the Austrians had repeatedly threatened and finally banned it. To this text, which contained no small measure of moral indignation, he added, "Moreover, I was forced to publish the proclamations." Yet who had forced him to be editor and thus land himself in such a predicament under Austrian rule? In any case, the episode is usually omitted from biographical sketches of Szilágyi. On May 1 the editorship was taken over by Jókai. The *Pesti Hírlap* wrote enthusiastically of the military successes in the spring campaign, compared the declaration of independence with the American one of 1776, and pointed out the far greater justification for the indictments made in the Hungarian document. The last number appeared on July 8, 1849.

The Final Phase

One should add here that Jókai was soon running more than one daily in Pest. The *Esti Lapok* continued to appear in Debrecen until the beginning of June, but on April 30 a parallel paper with the same title was launched in the capital, with Jókai as its publisher and Landerer as its printer. This fourth new paper to be launched in Pest was edited until May 8 (No. 8) by Mór Ludasi (Gans, 1829-85), a journalist and counsellor at the Ministry of the Interior who had been born in Komárom. After the defeat he spent the next fifteen years or so in Vienna as a successful conservative journalist, a spokesman for the old conservative Hungarian aristocracy, and a millionaire landowner. On June 4 the post of responsible editor for the paper, which now continued solely in Pest, was taken over by Jókai, who retained it until the last number appeared on July 7.

To return to April 24, the third new paper in Pest was published by László Lukács and bore the familiar title of *Marczius Tizenötödike*. It purported to be a direct continuation of the radical *Marczius* which had ceased publication at the beginning of 1849, even to the extent that the first issue was labelled No. 4 and the statement made that "we pick up today the thread of *Marczius Tizenötödike* that was tyrannically and forcibly broken on January 5." This was actually an advertising stunt and a somewhat misleading piece of manoeuvring. As I have said, the real *Marczius* continued in Debrecen under its original editor, Albert Pálffy. Yet, this real *Marczius* was referred to by the Pest paper as "our Debrecen namesake." The assumption, or rather misappropriation, of the title was all the more misleading because the new paper was by no means a parallel Pest edition imbued with the same spirit as the Debrecen one. Behind a handful of pseudo-revolutionary catchwords it represented the cause of consolidation of the liberal nobility. "Moderate" forces were being mobilized behind a radical façade. Gone from the front page was the old slogan rejecting *"táblabíró* politics." In its place was the traditional motto of the Hungarian Academy of Sciences, "Sunshine after cloud." The paper's first concern, in a sentence in remarkably bad taste, was to attack and dismiss Pálffy as "compromised" and "one of the most partial adherents of the long-armed Madarász." Who was responsible for this as editor is not known, as no name was mentioned apart from an announcement on the back page that "we have been fortunate in gaining József Gaal as editor of our paper from tomorrow." József Gaal (1811-66) was a well-known playwright, a poet, an amusing raconteur, a corresponding member of the Academy, an ironical critic of the backward nobility in the age of reform, an advocate of liberal progress, and since youth among the friends of László Szalay, but he was clearly miles away from revolutionary radicalism. He served for a while in 1849 as secretary to Sebő Vukovics, the minister of the interior. The end of the war found him alongside Damjanich in Arad, where the Austrians interned him for a couple of years. Little is known of the paper's staff, as they generally wrote under pseudonyms such as "Mentő" (Saviour), "Tövis" (Thistle), "Nekérdi," "Galamb" (Dove), and "Etel." On May 21, Gábor Jászkürty wrote on the patriotic women of Pest and György Tóbiás on the capture of Buda, and László Kisbéri tried to start a series entitled "Traitor's Gallery in Budapest." Erdélyi, Hiador, and Zalár supplied poems, and from the provinces came contributions from, for instance, Antal Erdődy, Mikola Budán, and Andor Kokas. A good deal of material, such as war reports and speeches by Kossuth, was lifted from the *Közlöny*, but in other respects the paper preferred a conversational, jovial, anecdotal tone that differed substantially from the pungency of the real *Marczius*, except perhaps once, when on May 31 "Kisértet" (Ghost) attacked László Madarász in an abusive article entitled "Laczi Again!" for what he had attempted in Fejér County. When the paper turned on April 28 to assessing the members of the Szemere government, it questioned the wisdom of appointing Görgey as defence minister. He was, it said, "a commander, of whom we have few, but he may turn out to be a bad minister." What, it asked, was the purpose of this? "Do they intend to retire the creator of plans for battle and turn the lion of combat into a churchmouse"? On May 28 a leader signer "A. V." expressed strong optimism over "the ever more sanguine prospects of a European war," in other words, of the Hungarians' not being left to fight alone. "We strongly believe," the writer went on, "that . . . we could even overcome the Russians if they came." The same article referred to an oral statement by József Irinyi, just back from Paris, that Louis-Napoléon had "not been overthrown yet" but "clearly has little time left in which to play the inveigler" and that foreign sympathy for Hungary was "constantly growing." Imre Váhot chose this paper in which to break the news that he would be forced to delay his plans for reviving the *Divatlap* and the *Nemzetőr* because a senior clerk at the post office had followed the Austrian troops with the subscription fees in his pocket, and in which to announce later that they would reappear on July 1 (which they did not). Meanwhile there was an announcement on June 5 (No. 40) that the paper would at last be edited by Albert Pálffy again from June 7 onwards.

Republican Slogans and Genuine Radicalism

This little episode was a sign, to some degree, of the changes taking place in the political press as a whole. Ostensibly there was no longer any peace party paper; all became noisily republican and called for a war to the bitter end. Some, as has been shown, sheltered behind a radical name. Even the peace party's own creation, the *Esti Lapok*, was full of republican phrases and denied any supposition that it inclined towards a compromise with the Austrians. The *Közlöny* was now the official paper of a new government with a republican policy. But in fact these and other papers within the war camp increasingly served the cause of the consolidation of the liberal nobility in Hungarian society and politics. Kossuth's declaration of independence had been designed to cut the ground from under the peace party and prevent it from seceding, but this political tactic was insufficient to stop the growth in the influence of a "moderating," regressive noble tendency within the frames of the war of independence and the new state, which was independent in principle. Much could be contained within this new political form of state; one could remain a moderate liberal while wearing republican colours.

It has been mentioned in the previous chapter that Szemere and some former members of the peace party had come to terms, not least in opposition to Kossuth. Szemere had called his government republican, and by this time not even Zsigmond Kemény (with a group of other ministers) had any aversion to the term. As Kemény later wrote, he expected this form of state to provide a better curb on Kossuth's lust for power. This immediately provides an explanation for what the *Esti Lapok* wrote on May 7: "We know that revolutionary power in the hands of Szemere and his colleagues is quite different from what it would be in those of Madarász and his accomplices, for example. . . . Words frighten us least of all." The intermediary between Szemere and Kemény had been Csengery, who thought better than the others did of Szemere, later describing him in positive terms in his book *Magyar szónokok és státusférfiak* (Hungarian Orators and Statesmen /1851/). Certainly it was a sign of agreement that on May 9 Szemere appointed Kemény and Csengery as counsellors in his own Ministry of the Interior. On the other hand, the *Esti Lapok* gave voice to a succession of desires of the liberal nobility that were aimed at winding up the revolution, and these the Szemere government tried to varying degrees to fulfil. One such desire was abolition of government commissioners as an institution. On May 12, Szemere recalled the government commissioners from more than a dozen counties. Another was the dissolution of the emergency courts, explained by the *Esti Lapok* as follows: "Europe fastens its eyes upon us", and nothing "can do greater harm to true liberty than if we allow the opinion to gain ground that order and a monarchy, on the one hand, and communism and a republic, on the other, are equivalent notions." On May 22 Jókai described the consolidation by the liberal nobility as a "victory for the Hungarian Girondins over the Jacobins, the enemies of order and liberty," and underlined that "we can expect support from the West only if we can guarantee that the war of independence will not turn into communism and anarchy." The paths of the former March Youth had diverged: this was shown by Jókai's standpoint, on the one hand, and Pálffy's, on the other.

The only radical paper to keep faith with itself within the new political spectrum was Pálffy's *Marczius*. In May, while it was still appearing in Debrecen, it made increasingly sharp attacks on the revival of the power of the *táblabírók* now that the war of independence seemed to be heading for victory and on the "moderate" Szemere government, which paid lip service to a republican platform while actually representing the restoration of the nobility. Csernátoni, whom Kossuth had sent to Paris with the declaration of independence, no longer wrote for the paper, but others were there: "Barnabás Borona," "Proletarius," and "C. A.," and then "S. B.," who sent news of Bem, Márton Zeney with a report from Transylvania, Péter Kis, and Benedek, who continued to defend Csernátoni against the *Esti Lapok*. On May 5 Ferenc Mentovich, later a teacher in Nagykőrös and a materialist natural scientist, contributed a "Self-Justification", having been attacked for working for Szilágyi's *Pesti Hírlap* under Windischgrätz. In reply to Mentovich the editors of *Marczius* agreed that as an individual he had not turned against his country and that the *Pesti Hírlap* had retained "some lingering scent of the nation's cause," since it had been banned. But the editorial described it as a mark of gross political ignorance to have supposed that the "base Austrian government of terror would allow the smallest scope for free statements in the press." On May 9 an article signed "Democrata" again criticized others who sought to justify themselves retrospectively for having written under the Windischgrätz régime. In the same number Józsa Nyiri reported on the investigation going on into the affair of the Zichy diamonds. He would not "cast a stone" at his former superior (Madarász), he said, but he was in no wise compromised himself. Andor Várady sent dispatches from Vértes, György Jura Jr from the Máramaros area of north-eastern Hungary, and Antal Várady from Pest, describing the horrors of the bombardment. The paper made several attacks on the "new republicans," those who had hastened to climb on the bandwagon after the recent victories. This brings us to one of the main purposes of the paper, which was to combat the return to power of unprincipled, power-hungry noblemen. One can read in the May 11 number how "the soul is saddened by contemplating this tribe, which seems to believe all that occurs, the blood shed by thousands, is designed solely to assist this class to continue monopolizing all that is good and great. Moreover, they do not care in the least what they are called; so long as they can grasp this monopoly they will readily become royalists or republicans, for no smart Hungarian pays any attention to a name." One can go on to read what a "Village Clerk" from Szatmár wrote in a letter on May 14 about the landowning class: "Those lords have no other design than to turn by any means the so-called urbarial losses into urbarial profits. . . . The quondam-liberal *táblabírók* have secretly wrung all meaning out of the urbarial laws, so that in many places unpaid labour continues as ardently as it did in the days of (the early sixteenth-century) King Ulászló." These words are worth noting because they show unambiguously that Pálffy and those of the March Youth who followed the same path had remained faithful to their earlier ideas and even developed and broadened them just when the nobility was drawing back. That very withdrawal may have been what helped Pálffy to recognize the true significance of the peasant question, to which he had initially paid scant attention. Thus *Marczius* came to see in the "complete abolition of feudal relations" the essential condition for democracy. As one of the last and increasingly isolated spokesmen for the dissolving, crumbling left wing, Pálffy spoke out with increasing instead of decreasing vehemence and with an almost feverish resolution against the return to power of the time-serving *táblabírók*: "Hungary is free," he wrote on May 18:

> Come, esteemed *táblabírók* and *szolgabírók* (district administrators), who for the last thirty years have spent alternate three-year periods as liberals and time-servers, behold the bumper harvest, here is the groaning board, come, and let us declare that nothing here has altered save that the regal throne has been replaced by the presidential seat. Let us help one another, let us divide the offices among us, let us pass good, fat compensation laws. . . . Do not take fright at silly words like revolution, republic, or democracy.

The allusion to the presidential seat was obviously addressed to Kossuth, perhaps as a bitter warning but certainly as a sign that the radicals no longer believed they could rely on his support as they had in the summer and autumn of 1848. This left them in an even weaker position against the line of thinking represented by Szemere's republican platform, which *Marczius* on May 23 called nothing but a "self-styled democratic republic of the county nobility."

The debate at this time was still set in Debrecen, where the government's official paper appeared as well. However, the *Közlöny*, where Kelmenfy was standing in during Gyurmán's absence, found no reason to engage in any substantial debate with its opponent. It preferred to keep its readers supplied with reassuring news. On May 8, for example, it declared, "The dawn of freedom has begun to break in Russia too," for a plot had been discovered and the tsar would lack time or inclination to march against other nations. On May 17, however, the paper merely hoped that the rest of Europe would not stand idle while Russia intervened. Szemere's main concern seems to have been to see the *Közlöny* circulated more widely and more effectively. Understandably, it was practically impossible to ensure the regained counties of Transdanubia adequate supplies of an official paper from Debrecen, but very few copies were reaching other distant regions such as the Székely country either. On May 16, Szemere ordered that "all larger villages or, so far as the shortage of printing equipment here allows, all villages receive gratis a copy of the *Közlöny* which it shall be the duty of the *vicecomes* to circulate." Presumably because he realized how ineffectual the *Nép Barátja* was, he also ordered the *Közlöny* to "open a short section of articles for popular enlightenment, which should contain comments tailored to the comprehension of the people," since there was no paper "which can influence the disposition of the people using their own language." He went on to prescribe that these articles be read out to the villagers on feast days. On May 27 an article by Mór Szegfi describe Hungary's victory as certain and praised the government, "before which the traitor is struck dumb and intrigue put to shame."

At the end of June the papers of the government and the radical opposition finally returned to Pest. The *Közlöny* came out in the capital again on June 5 and *Marczius* on June 7. The battle between them continued, although it was rather one-sided, since Pálffy did most of the attacking. He was far more isolated than he had been a year earlier. There was no real political force to back him, even though several radical or seemingly radical papers were being published in German again. *Die Opposition* was edited by A. Pfeilbogen from April 29 and then from June 19 until July 8 by Mór Vasfi (perhaps Mór Eisler). *Der Ungar*, again edited by Zerffi, resumed publication on May 1 and likewise closed down at the beginning of July. Zerffi then left the capital and at the end of July and the beginning of August tried, perhaps as a continuation, to publish another paper in German in Pancsova (Pančevo) called the *Südungarische Grenzbote*. By this time he was to all intents and purposes supporting the Szemere government, and he seems not to have taken it kindly when on July 1 a new German paper to the left of his own appeared. He did not hesitate to express his scorn of *Der Vierzehnte April* (named after the date independence was declared), describing it as a "gutter paper." It was published by László Lukács and edited by Ernő Hazai (Hazay or Heim, 1819-89) and survived until July 7. Hazai came from a bourgeois family in Temesvár and had studied agriculture in Hohenheim, after which he had set up a press in Temesvár on which he printed revolutionary posters. He and two younger brothers of his served the cause of the Hungarian revolution and war of independence with enthusiasm. After the defeat he fled to Turkey, and although sentenced to death *in absentia* he managed to obtain a pardon. In the 1850s he was on the staff of the *Pester Lloyd* and later became a supporter of Deák and the Compromise. In the collection of character sketches Sándor Szilágyi published in 1850 during the new period of absolutism, he described Hazai as a *"rouge republicain*, a communist, a Raspail on the banks of the Danube."* (The politician and chemist François Raspail (1794-1878) took part in the French Revolution of 1830, became the leader of the Society for Human Rights and in 1834 editor-in-chief of the radical *Réformateur*, founded a paper called *L'Ami du peuple* in 1848, and on May 15, 1848, was prosecuted for intruding into the National Assembly.) The words or phrases "red republican" and "communist" had come into use in the spring of 1848 among the "moderates" and conservatives as derogatory terms for the radical left-wingers. Undoubtedly Hazai belonged among the latter, an assumption confirmed by the fairly close connection his paper had with János Horárik. On the other hand, the article in which the paper set out its programme, which was signed "The Editors," declared that "the programme of our endeavours all the task of our campaign will be a democratic republic with all that follows from it" but described as an impossibility the talk in Hungary about communism, reasoning that it was a rich country in which "almost all" were landowners and the rest did not live in the kind of poverty that would have made the principles of communism even "conceivable" among them. The article went on to say that there was one man against whom no word of criticism or distrust should be uttered, and that was Kossuth: "And if this man were once to place the cursed crown on his head" the people would be moved to fall upon their knees and pray in the churches "since the land of bliss had come." Such expressions on the part of a radical paper are not a little surprising, even when one considers that the republican programme of Szemere and his followers was aimed in part at reducing Kossuth's power, so that a stand on behalf of Kossuth might be aimed at them. This is an added reason for agreeing with the most recent research findings, which contradict Ervin Szabó's assumption that this article was written by Horárik. At the same time, Horárik was being less open than before about propagating Utopian socialist and communistic ideas to avoid provoking further attacks on the radicals as communists, and he could by no means let himself be carried away by radical republican ideas. But in No. 5 he took issue in a piece entitled "To the Editor and K. I." with the programme article. Although he had himself written about Kossuth with the greatest respect, he disagreed with the press adulation of him: "You have turned Kossuth into an idol of yours and uttered confused words about certain perpetuity and certain fidelity; you are swearing things for certain as if you were twelve-year-olds. . . . In assessing a political personality let us go no farther than his deeds, than today, in other words, and tomorrow let him be described and vindicated by his deeds again." When the paper was attacked by Zerffi in the columns of *Der Ungar*, Horárik rejected the "assault" in an open letter to the editors of *Der Vierzehnte April* in the June 9 number, repeating his opinion about the opposition critique and the question of Kossuth. Zerffi's sneer that Hazai's was a "gutter paper" was in Horárik's view "obviously meant to denote something like a proletarian paper," which he was ready to admit, along with what he had said earlier against idolizing Kossuth. "No living man could rise high enough to be my Washington or my Timoleon, although I can and do appreciate all the good that our fellow citizen Kossuth has performed. I shall never adore him as an idol; I shall never grovel before him." In other respects Horárik certainly did recognize the significance of Kossuth, and in 1849 he translated and published Meyer's pamphlet *Szózat Némethonból, Habsburgház és Kossuth Lajos felől* (An Appeal from Germany, concerning the House of Habsburg and Lajos Kossuth), which proposed as a possible development an anti-Habsburg alliance of the nations of the Monarchy with Kossuth at its head. The debate between the two papers did not prevent Horárik from publishing his letter "To Our Fellow Citizen the Minister of Transport" in the June 13 number of *Der Ungar*, pointing out that capital was the "plague of the working people" and that the railways as a source of income "would turn the thousands of people working for them into proletarians and result in their being cheated out of their human rights." He proposed that the people "should themselves take over and appropriate" capital, in other words, capital should be "transformed into people's capital," with half the profits to be "handed over to the treasury and the other half distributed among the workers." We know that Horárik also intended to expound his in many respects Utopian ideas about state-owned factories and mines, but he was prevented from doing so by the defeat in the war of independence.

The Közlöny, Respublica, and the Futár

After the *Közlöny* returned to Pest it suffered from a lack of direction, and although the technical side was managed capably by József Kolmár, Andor Szeberényi, and József Máday, it entered a rather critical period. It published almost nothing but decrees and appointments, failed to provide factual information on the war situation, and on more than one occasion chose to ignore unfavourable news. Moreover, Lázár Mészáros said in his memoirs that little credence was given to it when it tried to deny the disquieting rumours that were being fabricated and spread in Budapest. *Marczius* hastened to fill the vacuum. On June 7, in the first number to appear again in Pest, *Marczius* devoted most of its space to prior events in Debrecen and announced that the "democratic-republican society" had chosen the paper to represent it. In this connection it repeated that certain personages who had scattered during the days of calamity had now returned to the fore, pinned red cockades to their breasts, and done their utmost to "become republicans." But these "April republicans" had adopted the "new label" only so that "they might the more easily rob it of its practical meaning," for "this former county nobility with sizeable estates" had decided "that all the honours of victory should be the exclusive property of a particular class." An article entitled "Amnesty" in the same issue sharply criticized the Debrecen emergency courts for their bias, which came to light because those higher up on the social scale were acquitted while the "miserable Slovak student" was sentenced to be shot through the head. On June 12 *Marczius* again attacked the government's paper: "The most pitiful predicament in the world is that of someone who would like to learn something of the country's position from the *Közlöny*." Two days later it returned to the fray: "The good-natured villager reads reverentially through the *Közlöny*, which seems, in imitation of the *Wiener Zeitung*, to report ever since the battle at Szőny as if nothing had happened in the mean time," and only a tiny item of news on some victory informed him by the by that some county or other had "gone to the devil goodness knows how long ago." On June 17 it addressed the *Közlöny* directly: "You do not know what a republic is, you leave monarchy in peace; you know neither revolution nor democracy. To read you would disturb neither a well-to-do Debrecen citizen nor a Pressburg *Spiessburger*; each could read what he would. . . . Thy name, O *Közlöny*, is Scandal! You are a true squaring of the circle." On June 22 there was a conspicuous addition to the title of a war report signed "Red": "Not after the *Közlöny!*" The June 28 number contained the acid remark, "Those who have chosen the *Közlöny* as their source of information could rest their heads on their pillows in peace of mind even last night, thinking that the people called Muscovites might not exist at all, or at least that they were not the devourers of men they were taken for, or at the very least that they certainly lived much too far away to feel inclined to come here."

Szemere himself had been planning to turn the *Közlöny* into a political paper of a high standard, but he realized how hard it would be to create a paper of that kind on behalf of the government as a whole. Therefore he chose instead to found a political daily of his own called *Respublica*, whose first number came out on June 17, 1849. It was printed on László Lukács's press, and the subscription for six months was 8 forints in Pest and 9 forints 12 krajcárs by post to the provinces. The preparations had begun a few weeks earlier. Szemere gained János Erdélyi as editor and as staff members Zsigmond Kemény and Antal Csengery, former editors of the moderate liberal *Pesti Hírlap*, with whom he had established relations in Debrecen. As early as June 9 the *Esti Lapok* wrote openly, "There is to be a fine addition to the press with the title *Respublica*. Of the staff one can mention first of all Csengery and Kemény, who were on the staff of the *Pesti Hírlap*. Apart from its title, this certainly is the strongest recommendation for the paper." On June 15 the *Esti Lapok* reported again that *Respublica* would rely on the renewed strength of the old *Pesti Hírlap* staff. The first issue of the new paper also mentioned the connection when it published by way of a programme Szemere's answer dated December 2, 1848, to a letter from Csengery and Kemény, declaring himself to be a republican. Later Kemény was strenuously to deny he had ever written a line for *Respublica*, but he had certainly made an initial promise to take part. Towards the end of June he thought it better to keep out of the venture, partly because of the Russian intervention and the looming defeat and partly because of the growing discord within the government, to which he considered that Szemere contributed in aspiring to bypass Kossuth and Görgey and obtain for himself the position of dictator. Later Szinnyei too came to feel from his perusal of the press at the time that Szemere had added to the confusion with "a couple of articles" that "by exposing the relations between Kossuth and Görgey seemed, albeit in a disguised way, to rebuke Kossuth." János Erdélyi (1814-68) was an excellent scholar, a progressive writer, and in 1848 director of the National Theatre, but he took little interest in politics. It took some determined persuasion from Szemere to make him accept the editorship "despite his own sympathies and his customs hitherto." The job was taken over from him on July 5 by István Szokolay, who has featured earlier as the writer of progressive sociopolitical articles in *Kossuth Hírlapja* on the abolition of the remnants of feudalism. Two days later, on July 7, Szemere announced that he had broken off "all his intellectual connections" with the paper, "since my principles only allow me to be connected with a paper that will refrain from abandoning the sphere of higher debate for that of personal abuse." Two days after these lines had appeared in No. 16, *Respublica* concluded its three-week career with its eighteenth issue. During that time it had published poems by Arany, Petőfi, and Károly Szász and in unsigned articles had eschewed the vital political and social concerns in favour of aspects of education, communications, legislation, and finance, upon which it had neither time for nor hope of reaching any conclusions.

On June 20 *Respublica* had written about the expected launch of a new popular paper to be called *Népszabadság* (People's Freedom). The new paper, it wrote, would not idly prattle away or "curry popularity" by addressing its readers with the rustic, familiar "you"-form *kend* as Táncsics's had done. Instead of foisting old saws on them it would instruct the people in a serious, intelligent way. The latter thrust was aimed at Gereben Vas, who quickly responded by saying how enthusiastically he had agitated for a republic in Debrecen while Erdélyi had been "comfortably laughing in one of the stalls of the National Theatre." He assured his opponents that the *Nép Barátja* would continue under his editorship and with official support. In asserting this Vas relied on Kossuth, who had in June ordered the payment of his salary for six months. He managed to place his response in *Marczius* on the same day, for against Szemere Pálffy and his staff were even ready to defend such a one as he. Szemere, by the way, saw a need for the new venture not least as a counterweight to Táncsics's pamphlet series *Forradalom*. Bypassing Vas, whom he considered incompetent, he managed to obtain János Arany as an editor. Arany had been an assistant clerk in Szemere's Ministry of the Interior in Debrecen for a while, and Szemere was already familiar with his excellent editorial principles. *Népszabadság* was first advertised in the *Közlöny* on June 30. It was to be published twice a week, on Sundays and Thursdays, as a supplement to the official gazette. The other editor alongside Arany was to be Dániel Gondol, the son of a minister in the Reformed Church. At the time an assistant clerk in Szemere's Ministry of the Interior, he had successively been a student of the Reformed Church College in Pápa, a tutor, a man of letters, and a translator in the 1840s of Dickens, Shakespeare, and James Fenimore Cooper, meanwhile becoming a corresponding member of the Academy of Sciences. (Later he was a clerk in the Hungarian Chancery in Vienna.) But time ran out before the paper could appear. The government departed for Szeged, and Arany returned to his family in Nagyszalonta. Meanwhile the first issue of *Democratiea*, the revived Romanian version of the *Nép Barátja*, came out on June 24, edited by Zsigmond Papp. However, no subsequent issues of this successor to the *Amiculu Poporului*, of which publication had been suspended, are known today.

In the mean time Szemere also tried to reform the *Közlöny* itself. A plan by Károly Zeyk, a head of department at the Ministry of the Interior, would have given the official paper two editors, so that one at least would always be on hand. The first was to be "responsible directly to the Ministry of the Interior" and the other, along with the rest of the staff, subordinate to him. On the last day of June, Gyurmán quit the editorial board. Little is known of the background to this. One can only suppose that he intended to involve himself with Kossuth and a new paper he was planning rather than with Szemere. His successor was Dániel Emődy (1819-91), a lawyer who had contributed to the *Pesti Hírlap* in Csengery's time, been one of the March Youth, and become an assistant clerk in Klauzál's Ministry of Agriculture and Commerce. Later still he had helped organize the military and prepared to accompany Ödön Beöthy to Bucharest for negotiations with the Romanians. After the defeat he was let off lightly with a temporary ban of his practising as a lawyer, and he subsequently taught law at Sárospatak College. Just before these changes took place, Szemere wrote in the June 30 number of the *Közlöny*, "The new circumstances have assigned a new task to the official paper." Henceforth, he said, it would not confine itself merely to publishing decrees but "enter a new phase, start a new life, put itself in an active position, and be champion, defender, representative, and interpreter of the government's principles." This was followed in the same number by an editorial by Emődy setting out the paper's programme. The standard of the official section of the paper would be raised, he said, and the unofficial section would "henceforth pursue a programme and a defined line of policy" which would be "democratic and republican." In 1848 the situation had been complicated by "the task of balancing the requirements of the selfish monarchy with the demands of the people's will," but since April 14, 1849, "a new era has opened up before us." Szemere, the prime minister, "identified in his inaugural address the promised land towards which the government intends to lead us. . . . He expressed ideas that await accomplishment, and we believe they will be accomplished." Having outlined this programme, which tended to confine itself to generalities, Emődy said that the *Közlöny* in future would cover international relations more thoroughly, since "an active part" in Europe was also "awaiting us." However, it would not indulge in polemic: "We shall try to retain a tone of dignity even towards our enemies."

But again, this new *Közlöny*, the active political paper of the Szemere government, was unable to get started in the capital. At the beginning of July the government removed itself to Szeged, and on July 3 the official paper's printers and printing presses set out after it. Despite orders from Kossuth that in the interim "the *Közlöny* should appear continuously in Pest, even if only as half a printed sheet, and that once its own presses had been moved it should be printed on another press," the *Közlöny* did not appear at all between July 4 and July 12, and as a substitute the government started a temporary official column in *Respublica*. On July 4 *Marczius* objected to the government's "depriving itself of one of its mightiest weapons, the press," and on July 6 it accused Szemere of suspending the *Közlöny* with the intention of raising the circulation of *Respublica*, which "at present has the fewest subscribers of any Hungarian paper." It has been mentioned already that Szemere had broken off his connection with the *Respublica* by that time.

The *Közlöny* in any case could not have become the *common* official paper of the government, for Kossuth did not wish to identify himself with Szemere's new *Közlöny*. On June 21 the *Esti Lapok* contained an announcement entitled "On Kossuth Hírlapja" by the paper's former editor, József Bajza. As editor and proprietor he would relaunch his paper on July 1, exactly one year after the first version had started. The successor paper, called the *Futár* (Messenger), did actually appear when planned, printed on Vazul Kozma's press as a folio broadsheet. Setting out its programme, Bajza remarked that it might be "superfluous to say that the *Futár* will disseminate republican ideas. I wish to have a republic based upon the widest sovereignty for individual freedom and the fullest equality in civil rights." But the paper's first number was its last. Bajza followed Kossuth and the government as far as Arad. After the defeat he tried to go into hiding for a while, but he soon suffered a breakdown and ended his life mentally deranged a few years later.

By appearing once the *Futár* had accomplished more than several other papers being planned at that time. During the final weeks of the war of independence a succession of papers old and new advertised in Pest for subscriptions for the second half of the year. Imre Vahot planned to revive the *Divatlap* and the *Nemzetőr* at the beginning of July. Even János Illucz Oláh was getting ready to resume publishing the *Nemzeti*. But in the event the flight of the government meant the end for the papers already in existence. The last known issue of *Der Ungar* is dated June 27. The *Közlöny*, as has been mentioned, left the capital on July 3. We shall return later to *Marczius Tizenötödike*, which ended its career on July 6. The *Esti Lapok* and *Der Vierzehnte April* came to an end on July 7, the *Pesti Hírlap* and *Die Opposition* on July 8, and *Respublica* on July 9. But on July 10, after all the other papers had closed down, there appeared as the last effort a new paper called *Forradalom* (Revolution). Although it bore the subtitle "Political Pamphlet," it was designed, according to its front page, to appear daily. The editor and publisher was Arthur Erdélyi, whose real name was Imre Zalay. He was the son of a Pest public prosecutor and in 1849 had been fighting in Transylvania with Bem's army. After being wounded, he published in Kolozsvár a "democratic pamphlet" entitled *Múlt, Jelen, Jövő* (Past, Present, Future) in which he revealed himself to be an enthusiastic follower of Kossuth's, armed at the same time with an updated defence of the interests of the landed nobility. Erdélyi sought "social reforms" to forestall troubles similar to the uprising of the French proletariat, which would lead to a "bloodbath of the whole nation." His proposals had something of a Utopian slant to them, but more as a sign that he was well-informed, since he was opposed to the radicals, whether Pálffy's circle or Táncsics's. His sole truly Utopian gesture was to have his paper printed at that time in that place, on László Lukács's press. The second and last number appeared on July 11 within hours of the appearance of Haynau's troops on the streets of Pest.

The Suppression of Marczius

One story that remains to be told concerns how *Marczius Tizenötödike*, the first-born of the revolutionary press, ended its life before the final defeat. As time went on Pálffy attacked Szemere's government and policy with an increasing sharpness one might call a personal passion, since he saw it as promoting the restoration of rule by the nobility. His radicalism did not fade; indeed, we have seen that on social problems it became more profound. Nor can one omit to say that on several occasions he hit the mark, even though he used a form of murderous caricature to do so. Two changes since the previous year had modified the function and the scope of *Marczius*. One was the end of the wave of revolution both elsewhere in Europe and increasingly in Hungary, particularly among the nobility, in the provinces and the capital alike. The little vanguard of the March Youth had dispersed, and there was less and less of the specific set of circumstances which had allowed *Marczius* a year earlier to speak and exert influence on behalf of the revolutionary forces. Pálffy's growing personal passion was certainly a mark of defiance in isolation as well. The other fundamental change was, of course, the military reverses suffered by the cause of Hungarian independence, which as the rear-guard action of the European revolutions was abandoned to a pincer movement by the two great powers. On the one hand, this led to an agonizing and feverish quest for a way out, just in case the process might still be reversed by taking appropriately energetic measures, but as the catastrophe approached the fundamental issue of survival or non-survival increasingly overshadowed the objective significance and realism of the debates over the alternatives that were, or were thought to be, open. If historians in Hungary were more concerned with historical psychology, it would be possible to identify more clearly certain features of this kind of situation, for example, the tendency to believe that subjective efforts can compensate for a lack of objective conditions, to attribute exaggerated significance to personal motives, tensions, contradictions, or hopes, which inevitably narrows one's outlook. In any case, this applies neither solely nor chiefly to Pálffy, for it appears among the entire government and leadership in the war of independence as an inescapable historical phenomenon.

On June 20, Pálffy outlined in a *Marczius* editorial "our minimum demands of a revolutionary, republican, and democratic government". Among other things he called it scandalous that National Assembly representatives should have been appointed on a mass scale "to the highest offices", because the "tyranny of a parliamentary majority consisting of officials" would certainly be no more pleasant than the rule of Metternich, Windischgrätz, or the Habsburgs. The only cure for this was "open revolution," in other words, a new revolution within the new system born of revolution. In the final phase of the war and after the changes mentioned, this could indeed be conceived of only as a subjective desire. On June 27 there appeared an unsigned article with a personal edge to it: "Two Piquant Clues as to What Sort of Genuine Democrat Bertalan Szemere Is." One clue, it said, was the 1848 press law; in its final form it had turned out to be a tool of the rich against the poor, and in Szemere's original draft it had been worse still. "We have burned (that draft) here in Pest, in the market-place by the city hall, as a piece of Jesuit handiwork that made a mockery of the freedom of the nation." The other clue was the latest regulation on the wages of county officials, which would place the "landed lords and their bastards" in a position of advantage.

It was also on June 27 that the government took its first counter-measure. Kossuth issued a decree on the way to proceed against papers that divulged military secrets. It had been worded by Szemere and also signed by him as minister of the interior and then published on June 28 in the *Közlöny*. The frequency with which *Marczius* wrote about the meagreness of accurate reports on the war in the *Közlöny* has been mentioned. The new decree now weighed upon those who published too much. It claimed that "the most authentic and the speediest reports are being given to our country's enemies by our newspapers" and argued that this might have grave consequences through either carelessness or ill will. The decree went on to say that because repeated warnings and admonitions had proved ineffective, papers committing such offences in future would be immediately banned and the editor taken before a summary court.

"Distribution of newspapers and any other printed matter will be possible in Budapest only after perusal and permission from the central department of police and publications printed elsewhere only with the permission of the chairman of the local authority."

Limitation of information in a dangerous situation of war can certainly be justified. In December 1848, when Windischgrätz was approaching the capital, the National Defence Commission had rightly warned the press to take care not to publish any news that might be of use to the enemy. But it did not introduce such drastic measures as these, which amounted to reintroducing the prior censorship abolished on March 15, 1848, although in December there had been far more papers inclined on occasion to publish unnecessary detail about operational matters. Going through the papers of June 1849, when the situation was far graver, one can find hardly anything in them that could qualify as a betrayal of war secrets or information of a military nature, apart, of course, from indirect information in *Marczius* about a sharpening of the debates within the Hungarian leadership and the condemnation of the government by the opposition press for concealing the true state of the war. To put it clearly, the decree against divulging was secrets, plausible though it was in itself, was a convenient legal catch-all, a pretext, if you like, for ending the specific radical opposition attacks in *Marczius*.

Pálffy obviously realized this, but it never occurred to him for a minute to retreat. *Marczius* reacted sharply to the government decree in an article signed "Richardo" on June 29: "As is known, yesterday the government abolished freedom of the press and reintroduced censorship. . . . This will make a fine piece of news abroad. . . . In our view this act of infamy against the freedom of the press is the most impertinent piece of ingratitude ever perpetrated by any government on this earth." Moreover, it was in the writer's view quite without justification, "since there was never a more modest and honest press in the world than the Hungarian one." Debates took place in the papers, he said, but not one attacked or injured the sacred common cause.

On June 30 *Marczius* reproached the government in an unchanged tone, saying that it had taken fright at the news of the defeat in the battle of Győr and seemed to have "lost its head" at a time when no faint-heartedness was permissible. It went on to say that no one should doubt that there would be victory despite the Russian intervention. Moreover, it floated in question form the ideas of whether "the Muscovite intervention will lead to intervention by the Western European nations on our side" and whether "in general our war of independence will become a European war." *Marczius*, as a desperate hope, was ready at that point to give credence to news of goodness knows what origin that President Louis-Napoléon of France had been removed and Ledru-Rollin made president of a provisional government. Of more significance was an article signed "D." which said that the National Assembly's main task at its meeting on July 2 would be "to abolish the remnants of feudalism." If that did not happen "there would be an irreparable diminution of the people's confidence (in the National Assembly), a confidence for which there is so immense a need in the interest of saving the country. . . . We regret enormously that a year later we should have to urge the National Assembly to do what the impulse of the revolution should have made it do." But if the National Assembly should prevaricate, it continued, "the government should do it" and "not only be revolutionary in words but make use of revolution's means."

The sharp attacks from *Marczius* were silenced when the government suppressed the paper. The order, dated July 7, was worded by Sebő Vukovics, the minister of justice, and corrected by Szemere. Besides their signatures it bore Kossuth's. The text, which was not published in the *Közlöny* until July 14 in Szeged, merits attention for its unusually harsh tone and for the arguments it used:

> Under the present difficult conditions nothing is more injurious to the deliverance of our country than mockery of the government's decrees and incitement against them, confidence-destroying defamation of those in government, and base imputations against them, which serve to stifle the efforts at defence. . . . /The government/ has no more sacred obligation than to avenge such odious attempts with the full force of the law. . . . /*Marczius Tizenötödike*/ has continued with daily more boldness its incitement against the government and the measures for conducting the war, an incitement that endangers public peace and hampers and impedes the defence of the country, and in Nos. 63, 64, 65, 66, and 67 the incitement against members of the government went so far as to advocate assault and battery upon them.

The Final Phase

The editor, it went on, had repeatedly failed to present his paper for acceptance and had "committed the very crime" (betrayal of war secrets) that the obligation to present the paper prior to publication was designed to prevent. Consequently, the paper was being suppressed and its responsible editor was to be "tried by jury for his harmful incitement against the defence of the country," the necessary measures having been taken "to prevent him from becoming a fugitive from the law."

Marczius, however, had been attacking the Szemere government for some time, one might say ever since it came into office, and this makes one wonder what directly caused this severe measure to be taken at this particular time.

István Barta, who meticulously compiled the fifteenth volume of Kossuth's collected works, republished this decree with the comment that articles in the issues cited had "charged the government primarily with neglecting to take defence measures." But part of this statement is not quite accurate and part so general that one immediately suspects it of disguising something that seemed in 1955 too "delicate" to be gone into in detail.

When one considers it thoroughly, one is also not entirely convinced by another, far more specific version of the story. According to József Ferenczy, Kossuth banned the paper when Pálffy extended his criticism to Kossuth's family circle, the "female camarilla." Szinnyei too ascribed the ban to *Marczius*'s having gone so far as to attack "the president himself." The same version features in the memoirs of Vukovics, who was one of the main figures in the case: "So long as the paper merely abused the ministers, Kossuth showed no resentment at all. But when the debate on Görgey led the paper to castigate Kossuth, and in particular what was known as the female camarilla, he also thought the time had come to cut the scandal short." Vukovics went on to describe Szemere's insistence that the decree also bear both their signatures, so that Kossuth might "share in the odium of the measure." The opinion Vukovics formed of the March radicals, by the way, shows clearly the unparalleled extent of the rift and the hatred between them and the new political leaders of 1849. Vukovics, citing Csányi's authority as well, stated in all seriousness that "the gravest suspicion was entertained" of Pálffy: according to the extraordinary theory, he was "a traitor to his country and inciting people against the Hungarian government in the service of the enemy." Moreover, the staff of *Marczius,* of whom Vukovics mentioned Józsa Nyiri and (erroneously, of course) Gereben Vas by name, had made use, "out of anger over the fact that the government, and Szemere in particular, disregarded the immodest demands they put forward for the gift of offices," in other words, for personal revenge, of "base defamation" in attacking the leadership of the country.

Vukovics's version is still far from satisfactory, particularly because Pálffy at this stage was still talking of Kossuth personally with unchanged respect and expressing himself very guardedly even about Kossuth's immediate circle, although in general he was extremely outspoken. One should recall that something very similar had occurred previously, at the beginning of March. From the issues cited in the ban it is immediately apparent that the strain was caused by the same thing in both cases: the subject of Görgey's role as commander. In March it had led only to a veiled warning from the National Defence Commission that the press not betray military secrets. At that time a personal meeting had restored Kossuth's confidence in Görgey, which was reinforced by the successes of the spring campaign. But at this juncture Kossuth actually broke with Görgey and according to Vukovics kept in personal touch with Perczel instead. It became inevitable in so delicate and difficult a situation that *Marczius*'s repeated and decided championship of Görgey would lead to the paper's being banned. In all probability that was the main reason for Kossuth's harshness, while the references to those around him would have been an additional reason at most. *Marczius* had betrayed no operational secrets, unless one seriously considers the furore around Görgey to be one. This version also explains the "delicacy" of the question Hungarian historians appear to have evaded in the 1950s. It was understandably hard, on the one hand, to laud the radicalism of *Marczius* while condemning the regressive efforts of the peace party and, on the other, to say that this same radical *Marczius* had continued at the cost of imperilling its own existence to be the most militant advocate of the very Görgey who was conventionally considered a peace party conspirator and traitor. Or could Pálffy, one of the main initiators of the revolutionary press in Hungary, a man who had identified so clearly the dangers in the inclination to surrender and in the return of the nobility to power, have been utterly misinformed, blind, and obtuse on this particular point? Silence was not going to banish that problem, or the other one of what made Kossuth turn so decisively against the last and most progressive organ of Hungarian radicalism. Could it really have been wounded personal vanity? If so, how could that unworthy aspersion be reconciled with the image created of the celebrated leader of the revolution?

Marczius loosed its final blast of protest in No. 65 on July 4, when the news spread that Görgey had been replaced as commander-in-chief by Lázár Mészáros. Only a few words need be said here about the events leading up to this. On June 26, 1849, the council of ministers accepted Görgey's proposal that the lesser of the two enemies, Austria, which was already in the country, had if possible to be defeated before the arrival of the greater, the tsar's army, because once united the two would form an invincibly superior force. The plan was for all the Hungarian forces to concentrate at Komárom as soon as possible to deal a series of blows against Austria. But the concentration never took place. On hearing news of the loss of Győr on June 29, the council of ministers modified the plan in the absence of Görgey, who was minister of war. The government decided instead on a retreat to Szeged, where Görgey was to follow. The modification was certainly motivated not only by the dire situation and the danger of becoming surrounded by the enemy but by disagreements among the leadership. When Görgey demurred, Kossuth on July 1 removed him from command of the armed forces and placed Mészáros in his stead with Dembinszki as his second-in-command. But by the time the two joined the army the Battle of Ács had taken place. Albeit with difficulty, the Hungarian forces had managed to drive Haynau's army back without any reinforcements, and Görgey had received a wound in the head. In view of the mood among the troops, Kossuth thought it better to retain Görgey as commander-in-chief for the time being but to subordinate him to Mészáros. On July 11 the Upper Danube army began its long, devious retreat southwards.

On July 4 Pálffy was prompted by the news of Görgey's removal to write, "The whole capital seems to be discussing the latest changes in the leadership of the army, and the sense of outrage is indescribable. . . . No one can conceive what fault certain people can find in Görgey again this time." He continued on a sharper note: "Whoever the initiator may be, this cannot be tolerated. Considering the latest appointments, one does not know what to think. Who is in command in Hungary? Do we have a responsible government, or is there a secret national defence camarilla ruling alongside it"? After that remark, which was chiefly aimed at Perczel, Pálffy pointed out that if Görgey had really showed plain disobedience he would have merited shooting in the head, not just removal. But what if he had merely proposed something else, some better plan? "Away with a ministry so wretched that it does not dread to encourage scuffles among the leaders in dangerous times like these! Away with it still more because its miserable directions do harm to our greatest bulwark"! (meaning Kossuth). In this way, Pálffy continued, all were made to believe that "the symptoms, the influence of the surroundings which hitherto only peered from behind the crown will reappear in altered forms." And "are the ministers incapable of shielding the name of the governor" from such "misunderstandings? Horrifying!"

In fact this article contained the essential point. It was merely complemented by another in the same number that asked whether "ours is a government" at all and answered, "It is not," and by subsequent support for Görgey on July 5 and 6. These included unambiguous statements that Görgey's chief concern was to defend the great cause of the country and not to ensure the personal safety of certain people or cover their flight. There were condemnations of those who wanted to remove Görgey from his post as commander-in-chief even though he had always helped to save the country and only refused to do what he had considered dangerous from the country's point of view; "the God of the Hungarians fashioned Görgey in his good humour and presented him as a gift to the cause of our liberty."

To put matters precisely, what led to the suppression of *Marczius* was not its attacks on the government either in general or more directly for "neglecting to take defence measures." Nor was the whole reason that it had begun to criticize those close to Kossuth politically and so indirectly Kossuth himself. The direct reason was that it argued in favour of Görgey as commander-in-chief and against the measures aiming at removing him, even after Kossuth had made the none-too-easy decision under the circumstances to have done with him. That was the moment at which Kossuth suppressed the paper. Pálffy escaped being taken to court only because the government, on the eve of its flight, had no time to assemble a jury. He was not arrested, as he had bound himself in a written statement at the desire of the minister of justice to follow the government and attend at his own trial. Pálffy in any case did not wish to "flee" from justice and followed the government with a manly calm and resignation as far as Arad and the defeat that brought an end to far greater things than the proceedings against him.

Szeged and Kolozsvár

Meanwhile, on July 13, the first number of the *Közlöny* to be published in Szeged sought to calm its readers while publishing the usual decrees and appointments. "The struggle that will attain freedom for the people of Europe will be the one which is directed from here, in Szeged." On July 15 it wrote as another encouragement that the European powers were considering Hungary's cause as their own. Britain was seeking a "resolute, strong ally" in the east, where Austria could no longer be relied upon. None the less, the paper was obliged to write on July 18 that the Western nations were providing no help, although it stressed that, trusting their own strength, Hungarians were "prepared to stand against the attack of the greatest tyrant in the world." The next day it returned to the same theme: The French and British had failed to help, but "while our fate depends on our own will and our own strength why should we despair? Our battle is a hard one and may last a long time," but victory was certain. On July 21 the *Közlöny* went on to examine why the Russian intervention had not led to support from the other powers: "Europe thinks of our struggle as the struggle of absolutism with communism; and it seems more inclined to prefer the first to avoid being swept away by the second." An article signed "D" therefore explained that in Hungary there was no "communist" agitation, there was not even a proletariat. Moreover, "the abolition of feudalism will turn the people in general into such well-to-do landowners that no desire for land will disturb the peace of our state." The official paper had clearly taken note of the waning of the European revolutions and the retreat from social progress by the Western bourgeoisie, but it thought that the cause of the Hungarian war of independence might be made more presentable if it were deprived of its revolutionary character and an attempt were made to paint a reassuring, idyllic picture of Hungarian society. At the end of July, however, the government was forced to flee farther, and Szeberényi was ordered to arrange for the transporting of the press, which arrived in Arad after an adventurous journey on the evening of July 30. There three issues of the *Közlöny* were published (on August 5, 10, and 11). They were edited by Kelmenfy instead of Emődy, who was ill. The last number is thought to have reached galley-proof stage at Lugos on August 13, but it was never printed or distributed.

As Samu Szeremlei put it, the government's move to Szeged "suddenly raised" the *Szegedi Hírlap* (Szeged Journal) "from its previous obscurity and unpretentiousness," for "apart from the *Közlöny* it was the only paper in the seat of government." It was published from May 2, 1849, as a continuation of earlier local attempts which had fallen by the wayside. It came out twice a week initially and in its final days from July 16 every day, the editors being Mihály Havi and Mihály Szabó. The latter had been a trainee teacher with the Piarists and then a militiaman before turning to journalism. It was printed on the local press of János Grünn, who had previously concentrated on calendars and pulp literature. The publisher, proprietor, and real manager of the paper was Mihály Tóth, a Szeged lawyer and chief justice whose election after the revolution had been heartily welcomed in Táncsics's *Munkások Újsága*, since he was a former "inciter of the people." Certainly this connection and political sympathy were behind a proposal the *Szegedi Hírlap* put forward on July 28 that Táncsics be appointed "as a main factor, a main tool" in the defence administration; he was so loved by the people that "no man other than our Kossuth is more dear to them." None of those directing the struggle "is a better patriot than he . . . none loves his country more dearly . . . however red the feather he wears."

Understandably, the nation's problems and even the tensions within the leadership were reflected more directly in the local paper during the two weeks in which the city served as a temporary seat of government. Among those to write more general articles of this kind was Dániel Dózsa, a member of the *Közlöny* staff. It is worth noting how the *Szegedi Hírlap*, now that *Marczius* had been suppressed, made some rather more cautious attempts to defend Görgey and to promote a reconciliation between him and Kossuth. On July 17 it reproved those who were "throwing mud" at Görgey. Then came a longer article in several instalments discussing the anxiety that someone might arise who "like Napoléon will expel the convention and use a military dictatorship to drive out the Muscovites." Kossuth, the article went on, was accused of fearing for his power, but if that were so he would never have raised Görgey up in the first place. Görgey, on the other hand, was charged with monarchism, but if a monarchist he would have laid down his arms when the government proclaimed itself republican. The article concluded that the need was for agreement between Kossuth and Görgey and that it was a crime to disturb that agreement by sowing suspicion. On July 21 the paper again spoke out against the manoeuvrings against Görgey: "You do not know this man's character, you do not know what secret strands have suddenly been woven around his overthrow, but if you did you would pity those who misconstrue his most sacred intentions and the most ardent endeavours that flare from his love of his country." Articles on a similar note were published on July 25, when several speakers at a closed session of the National Assembly expressed views of the same kind, on July 26, when the paper hinted quite plainly at the antagonism to Görgey felt by those around the president, and again on July 28, when it was remarked that "Kossuth and Görgey together might be the saviours of the Hungarian land" and so those who tried to turn them against each other were a curse. On July 30 the *Szegedi Hírlap* ceased publication. So too, presumably, did the *Freiheitsbote,* the local German paper edited by Bernát Mauksch, of which the only evidence of existence we have is an advertisement in the July 28 number of the *Szegedi Hírlap*.

On July 16, in the final phase of the war, plans for a new "political newspaper" called *Szabadság* (Freedom) were published in Kolozsvár by Miklós Krizbai (Dezső), a former *Kossuth Hírlapja* contributor who was to be responsible editor, and János Tilts, a bookseller, described as the "publishing proprietor." The prospectus stressed that despite the hard times facing the country there was no breaking it so long as it drew strength from freedom. They therefore intended to launch the paper "at the beginning of next month." Their purpose would be "careful nurture of the people's freedom and defence of it with alert attention against the ravages of anarchy, the machinations of absolute power, and the treacheries of the aristocratic faction that flirted with it and only mocked at the supremacy of the people." Subscription to the "first series," from August to October, cost 3 forints 30 krajcárs. It mainly aimed to deal with events in Transylvania. *Szabadság* represented liberal progress and hoped till the very last moment for a peaceful compromise. Its career ended on August 14, the day after the capitulation at Világos (Şiria).

Military Papers

The group of papers to survive longest was the section of the press in the war of independence commonly known as the military papers. In spite of the name these were not professional military papers. Alongside the events of the war in the narrow sense, they tried to provide general information for soldiers and civilians at the centres of military operations, where the national papers were hardly available or not available at all. This shows up in the fact that they were published not at the changing seat of the National Assembly and the government but farther afield, some of them in Transylvania, in Kolozsvár, Brassó, and the Székely country, and others in Komárom. The wartime press came into being at the end of 1848 and the beginning of 1849, during the critical period when the government was forced back onto Debrecen and the slowly reviving press at the new centre was unable to serve the public in remoter parts of the country.

The military press began life in Transylvania at the very end of 1848 as a result of Bem's victories and chiefly at his instigation. Since mid-November, when the *Kolozsvári Híradó* had closed down, Transylvania had been without a paper in Hungarian. Bem attached importance to keeping the public informed, and he initiated and promoted publication of local papers at several places, in particular by using his military authority to license them so that the caution money prescribed under the press law did not have to be found. The first place was Kolozsvár, where Bem's good offices ensured that on December 28, four days after the city's liberation, a daily called the *Honvéd* began to appear, at first in quarto format and from June 25, 1849, as a folio broadsheet in Hungarian and German. The editor was Ferenc Ocsvay, who had gained experience as a journalist while running the *Kolozsvári Híradó*. This paper became the central organ of the military command in Transylvania and attained the highest standard of any of the military papers. In the article setting out its standpoint, the editor said the paper would propagate "Hungary's freedom and independence in the highest sense of those words," along with "equality before the law irrespective of any private interest." Ocsvay is commonly said to have represented the county nobility, in spite of his occasionally radical tone, but he remained faithful to the cause of the war of independence, a loyalty for which he paid, after a long period in hiding, with several years' imprisonment. One colleague of his worth mentioning by name was Lajos Medgyes (1817-94), a Reformed Church minister in Dés (Dej) and an acquaintance of Petőfi's. Short stories and poems by Medgyes had been appearing in a variety of papers since the end of the 1830s. In his political articles for the *Honvéd* he criticized the aristocracy, and on April 25 he gave an enthusiastic welcome to the declaration of independence. No. 104 of the *Honvéd*, on April 28, published Bem's famous war report of April 23 criticizing General Vécsey. This had been translated from French into Hungarian by Petőfi and led to a clash between Petőfi and Klapka. As is known, Bem later complied with Kossuth's wishes by issuing a statement saying that his criticism had been based on a misunderstanding and as such was to be considered null and void, and this was published in the *Közlöny* on June 13 and 14. As early as April 14 the *Honvéd* was writing that "the watchword all over this country is republic" and that "what we talk of today may become reality tomorrow." None the less, on July 27 Ádám Székely warned readers against the perils of a possible popular uprising: "Our crusade should not be . . . like that of György Dózsa" (the leader of the 1514 Peasants' Revolt). The last number of the *Honvéd* appeared on August 14.

Bem was obviously aware that circumstances in Transylvania did not permit his own central paper to reach all places either. To avoid leaving parts of the army and the country without any information and encouragement, he instigated the publication of smaller-scale, local military papers with print runs of two to three hundred. One such was the *Brassói Lap* (Brassó Journal), which was started in mid-April in Brassó after his victorious campaign and with his encouragement. It was printed twice a week in quarto format on János Gött's press. But it was short-lived: when it ceased publication on May 24 only twelve numbers had appeared. The editor, Károly Veszely, was a Catholic chaplain and teacher, who saw one aim of the paper as promoting cooperation with the neighbouring peoples. He later spent two years in irons, Haynau's initial death sentence having been commuted. Later another local publication of the same kind appeared in Csikszereda (Mercurea Ciuc). Called the *Hadi Lap* (Military Journal), it started on May 27, 1849, with Sándor Bíró, a captain in the Hungarian army, as its editor. Beneath the title was inscribed, "It appears once a week on Mondays on half a printer's sheet, and if by their subscriptions the enthusiastic warriors of liberty show enough sympathy for our paper to cover its expenses, it will appear twice a week, on Mondays and Thursdays." But except for a short period around mid-June, it did not manage to appear twice a week. The paper came to an end with No. 9 on July 2. From June 4 to June 14, 1849, the *Hadi Lap* had a weekly supplement, the *Csíki Gyutacs* (Csík Percussion Cap), edited by Sándor Bíró and Mózsa Simó and issued in Csíksomlyó (Simleu), where it was printed in octavo format at the Franciscan friary using a two-hundred-year-old press and type. Its purpose was to sustain enthusiasm in its readers with encouraging reports of the war. Perhaps three numbers appeared in all, and copies are now extremely rare. Another military paper was started on June 7 in Kézdivásárhely (Târgul Sâcuiesc). It was called the *Székely Hírmondó* (Székely Courier) and was edited by János Fogarasi. For this Bem presented to the town his own camp press, which he had brought from Debrecen. As the editor wrote in his introductory article, "Kézdivásárhely, which has sacrificed so much for the defence of the country, no other town having done more in proportion to its population, has received this press as a reward for its faithful struggles from the town's liberator, Lieutenant-General Bem." But the paper, which was supposed to appear twice a week, ceased publication or June 17, and only four numbers of it are known.

At this point one should mention a plan for a military paper which Aurél Kecskeméthy (1827-77) was to have started on Görgey's behalf in Pest under the title *Való* (Reality). Kecskeméthy was only twenty-two at the time. He was the son of a penniless former petty clerk to the Lieutenancy Council and had originally studied to be a lawyer, but he seems to have shown promise of being a talented journalist and at the end of 1848 was already aspiring to start a paper. That aspiration of his coincided with Görgey's intention of giving expression to a line based upon the "real" situation, both in the National Assembly, which was to due to convene again in the summer, and if possible in the press. In Görgey's view Kossuth had acted incorrectly and rashly when he declared independence in Debrecen, giving as one of his reasons the alleged desires of the army, for by doing so he had caused dissension among the officers precisely at a time when a successful advance was being made. He thought that the ill effects of this could be remedied by returning to the basis of 1848, although when he met adherents of the peace party in passing he weighed them in the balance and found them wanting. The incident demonstrates how Görgey, whose true genius as a commander showed him what to do in military terms, made very uncertain and belated moves when very reluctantly he tried to resolve a quite alien situation caused by the political contradictions among the leadership. The launch of *Való* was planned for the beginning of July 1849, but it never saw the light of day. All that Kecskeméthy produced was a prospectus for the paper dated "June" and obviously based upon Görgey's instructions. Despite the victories in military organization, it said, there remained a great deal of "stumbling along untrodden paths, improvisation born of shortage, disorganization, and corruption" at a time when thoroughgoing organization was "very important amid European conditions of a dubious turn." For those reasons it was necessary for "a strictly military paper to exist." Those who "can conceive that the future or the death of the country depends on our army," in whose ranks "the greater part of the noblest and most enthusiastic and educated sons of the country are fighting . . . will understand the close bearing of the war portfolio on the other branches of government and its political weight among them far better than to imagine or desire that the paper should be exclusively military." On the paper's political line the editor wrote, "We are not unconditional apostles of any particular forms of government," but on behalf of the noble principles which "were written on the victorious banners of the new democracies: liberty, equality, fraternity" and consistent realization of them "we wish to live and are willing to die."

Another important centre of the military press was Komárom, whose noteworthy fortifications ensured that it never passed into Austrian hands even after the Hungarian army made its general withdrawal at the end of 1848, from which time it remained a Hungarian enclave until the beginning of October. Clearly this little blockaded area, which could keep in touch with the outside world only through special messengers and individual acts of daring, was in need of a press of its own. The first military paper of this kind was the *Komáromi Értesítő* (Komárom Bulletin), which was started on January 9, 1849. The editor was József Mack, an artillery major soon to be promoted to lieutenant-colonel. He had been sent by the National Defence Commission across enemy lines to the fortress at the very end of 1848 to provide the necessary organization for the artillery. He has been mentioned earlier as a radical contributor of articles and a curious figure. He himself related that he and the likewise radical Zsigmond Rosty had planned in October 1848 to start "a military paper that would satisfy public demand and not only contain dry military facts, lessons, and descriptions of manoeuvres but serve as the organ of the Hungarian army." If not exactly in this form, he now had a chance to fulfil his plan to found a paper, which some historians consider that he had probably mentioned to the Commission. Early in January he gave legal notification of his plan to the mayor of the town, adding that he would ask the National Defence Commission to excuse him from lodging the caution money, which he could not do. The city council granted him an extension, and Miklós Puky, who was government commissioner for Komárom County from the end of January, did in fact pass on his request to the Commission on the grounds that "no other paper is regularly available here and for this one it is not possible to raise the caution money required although it is doing a great deal to encourage the people." In a reply dated February 22 Kossuth decreed that "in view of the present circumstances, the *Értesítő* published in Komárom is temporarily permitted to appear without lodging caution money." But he warned Puky to be on the watch "lest its attitude take a turn detrimental or even dangerous from the point of view of the nation's cause" and instructed him to "put the paper before the mixed commission in the event of any offences." In the meantime the running of the paper was taken over, at first in practice and from March 12 formally, by Mátyás Rózsafi (Ruzicska, 1828-83), a young colleague of Mack's who was his main contributor. He was locally born, had previously trained for the priesthood, and was an enthusiastic revolutionary. At twenty years old he was the youngest editor in the press at this time. When he subsequently wrote his memoirs on this period he had long lived in the New World, as an émigré and then as a colonel on the side of the North in the American Civil War. He also died in America. Discussing the aims of the paper in the January 14 number, he emphasized the importance of "energetic, sharp, open, and sincere appeals to shake up those who have fallen asleep, scourge the evil in spirit, preach courage, lend confidence to those tormented by fear, and add new light to the star of hope in our future, which has become dimmed in the eyes of some people." Later he wrote that the editorship had been "thrust into my lap without my seeking it, during the hours of danger, a few weeks after I returned from Vienna, where I had been a seminarist in the Pázmány Institute and occasional correspondent of two Hungarian papers and where as a university student I had first smelled gunpowder on the street barricades." The *Komáromi Értesítő* appeared daily, surviving until July 6, although it failed to publish between March 19 and March 26 and from then until May 8 came out only infrequently and irregularly. It was printed on the local press of the Siegler brothers under fairly difficult circumstances. The premises had burnt down in the autumn of 1848, and the press had to be moved several times during the siege and bombardment of the town. Initially the paper was printed in three hundred copies, but at the end of January six hundred were being sold at 3 krajcárs each. The March 15 number was a special, festive one printed in gold. Rózsafi recalled that apart from the printing expenses, "the *Értesítő* cost nothing either to edit or distribute, since the first I did with volunteers and the second was done by my thirteen-year-old sister during the few hours' break in the daily bombardments."

In the "Editorial Announcement" on February 16 Rózsafi wrote that he had received a succession of letters "unconditionally recommending a republic," but he feared that if he published them the majority of readers would turn against the paper, as they had not been "gradually made accustomed to the idea of a republic. . . . I feel that although it is natural to applaud a republic, it is not appropriate at present. . . . But I do not mind if ideas that prepare the ground for a republic are smuggled" into the articles "in a decent way." On February 20 he made space for some reflections on this by First Lieutenant Henrik Szudy: that because "there is only one sound basis for the transformation of Hungary: a republic," the idea of it had to be made popular. Rózsafi's political sympathies certainly played a prominent part when he defended his old editor, Lieutenant-Colonel Mack, after his arrest at the beginning of April for gross neglect of duty. Mack was not released until August 23, when he said that he would defend himself as a free man, although in the event he never had the chance to do so. This study does not set out to expose the chaos of intrigue, mutual mud-slinging, and personality clashes so sadly characteristic of the claustrophobic little world of Komárom in the first half of 1849. Suffice it to say that it seems likely that an important factor in the affair, alongside his eccentricity, was his radicalism, republicanism, and opposition to the forces of the nobility. On April 18 Kossuth turned down a proposal that Mack be promoted: "Because of some gross piece of negligence, which has also been put down to mental disturbance, he is in custody in Komárom." But on July 12 Kossuth urged that the matter be decided quickly. Rózsafi too had his problems with the local leaders (in May, for instance, General Richard Guyon wanted to try him in a military court over an article of his in which he had accused a high-ranking officer of miasppropriating food supplies), and he constantly pressed in his paper for a swift conclusion to the investigation against Mack. On June 7 he published a separate defence of Mack in Jókai's *Esti Lapok*, where he emphasized Mack's professional competence and patriotism. Moreover, he later took part in the somewhat adventurous undertaking in which Mack, with the authority of the émigré Kossuth, attempted to organize a plot in the Székely country which came to a disastrous end in 1851. On August 23, 1849, however, a new military paper, the *Komáromi Lapok* (Komárom Pages), published the news that "the founder of the Hungarian army's artillery, a lieutenant-colonel whose mysterious fate is the concern of all honest patriots . . . has been released from custody."

Rózsafi was quietly replaced as editor of the *Értesítő* by István Friebeisz (1822-90), who arrived in Komárom with Klapka at the end of June. The paper ceased publication with some farewell words from Rózsafi in No. 73 on July 6, the *Komáromi Lapok* replacing it on July 11. This too was edited by Friebeisz, who had been an official in Pest County and later a parliamentary reporter and a diary editor, in the meantime contributing a variety of pieces to the *Regélő* and the *Honderű*. In the autumn of 1848 he had become a second lieutenant in the Hungarian army before serving as one of the reporters for the military history the National Defence Commission intended to send to the various units of the army in March 1849. While an editor he remained an army officer, and at the time of the capitulation he had risen to the rank of major. In the upper left-hand corner of the paper's front page was written, "This paper is published every evening except Sunday. Due to the present confused circumstances, no subscriptions can be taken yet. The price of one copy is 3 krajcárs." As a motto under the title appeared "Let us not trust in God alone, as we have done. Let our country arise from our human integrity. Petőfi."

The paper, which was the sole source of information in the isolated world of Komárom, was purchased and read by a great many people when it was distributed after five in the evening to its points of sale. At first the print run was six hundred copies, but when some interesting news reached the town, sales doubled. The general interest was not lessened by the fact that the leading articles offering encouragement were interspersed with quite a few literary pieces lifted from earlier papers, particularly the *Életképek*, and that the news was sometimes embroidered or fabricated. The first leader by Friebeisz described the paper's line as "republican in the full sense of the word," but this is known to have been a composite notion embracing a variety of views at this time. On July 12 the paper contained an enthusiastic poem by Kálmán Lisznyai Jr, once one of the "reporters" sent to Görgey's camp by the National Defence Commission and a friend of Petőfi's. The poem lauded Görgey as a "revolutionary meteor." On August 8 there was Béni Egressy's poem "The German Flees," but on August 20 an article signed "Kunfi" read, "If we can save our country only through the monarchy, we shall become monarchists." From September 1 to September 6 the paper failed to appear, the reason, according to József Szinnyei's diary, being that "Friebeisz was arrested for an exaggerating article of his, and his paper was banned; quite a few people did not seem to mind, since the whole thing, as they put it, was a pack of lies." More precisely, the trouble was that Friebeisz, who as a second lieutenant was subject to military discipline, had referred, in an article written on receipt of the first news of negotiations for a capitulation, to a point of military law under which a fortress commander who showed an inclination to become a traitor could be removed from his command. Naturally the military authorities impounded the issue, and Klapka ordered that the author be arrested. But after twenty-four hours' house arrest Friebeisz was able to move freely again, and his paper was soon back in circulation. Indeed, the sensation made it sell out more quickly than usual. On September 24 Károly Bulcsu published a disillusioned poem entitled "The Honours of the French Nation" about the assistance the French had

The Final Phase

failed to provide. The last issue, No. 68, of the last military paper came out two weeks after arms had been laid down at Világos—on October 1, 1849. In his farewell article Friebeisz quoted a saying of Montesquieu's: "Write no more than three lines, and if they wish, they can hang your for it!" With that ended the history of the press during the Hungarian revolution and war of independence.

Bibliography

Péter Szillányi, *Komorn im Jahre 1849* (Leipzig, 1851); *Mészáros Lázár emlékiratai*; Dániel Hamary, *Komáromi napok 1849-ben* (Komárom Days in 1849) (Pest, 1869); Mór Szegfi, "Bujdosásaim idejéből" (During My Time in Hiding), in *A Honvédmenház könyve* (The Book of the Soldiers' Almshouse), ed. Kálmán Tóth (Pest, 1970); Stefan Giegl, "Die Felddruckereien im Jahre 1848," *Tipographia* 16 (1884); Miklós Puky, "Emlékeim" (My Reminiscences), *Hazánk*, March 1885, pp. 163 ff.; Mátyás Rózsafi, "Komárom 1848/49-iki történetéhez" (Towards a History of Komárom in 1848-49), ibid., August 1887, pp. 63 ff.; Miklós Puky, "Komáromi dolgok" (Komárom Affairs), ibid., pp. 154-57; József Szinnyei, *Komárom 1848-49-ben: Naplójegyzetek* (Komárom in 1848-49: Diary Notes) (Budapest, 1887); Lajos Naményi, "A szabadságharc Közlönyének aradi számai" (The Arad Issues of the *Közlöny* in the War of Independence), *Arad és Vidéke* (Arad and District), no. 160 (1889); Zoltán Ferenczi, "Bem hadijelentése a 'Honvéd'-ben" (Bem's Military Bulletin in the *Soldier*), *Petőfi Múzeum*, 1892, pp. 131-42; *Vukovics Sebő emlékiratai* (Memoirs of Sebő Vukovics), ed. Ferenc Bessenyei (Budapest, 1894); Zoltán Ferenczi, *A kolozsvári nyomdászat története* (History of Printing in Kolozsvár) (Kolozsvár, 1896); József Krivácsy, "Mack Komárom várában" (Mack in the Castle of Komárom), *Történeti Lapok* (Historical Pages), May 1896, pp. 95-96; "A sajtótermékek köteles példányaira vonatkozó intézkedések történetéhez" (Towards a History of the Regulations on the Compulsory Provision of Copies of Press Publications), *MKsz*, 1902, pp. 204-5; Ferenc Szinnyei, "Nagy Ignác" (Ignác Nagy), *ItK*, 1902, pp. 47-61, 174-96, 319-35, and 467-92 and as an offprint; József Szinnyei, "Egy öreg újságíró naplójából" (From the Diary of an Old Journalist), in *A budapesti újságírók almanachja* (The Budapest Journalists' Yearbook) (Budapest, 1909), pp. 83-90; József Pogány, "Raspail a Duna partjain" (Raspail on the Banks of the Danube), in *Harcok emberei: Irodalom és politika* (Men of Battle: Literature and Politics) (Budapest, 1911), pp. 71-79; Ernő Czóbel, "Arany János tervezett néplapja, a 'Népszabadság'" (János Arany's Planned Popular Paper, *People's Freedom*), *It*, 1917, pp. 479-89, and in *Válogatott írásai* (Selected Writings) (Budapest, 1963), pp. 386-97; György Kristóf, *Az erdélyi magyar vidéki hírlapirodalom története 1867-ig* (History of the Transylvanian Hungarian Provincial Press to 1867) (Kolozsvár, 1939); József Lukács, *Katonai hírlapok a magyar honvédség felállításáig* (Military Newspapers until the Establishment of the Hungarian Army) (Budapest, 1942—offprint from *MKsz*, 1941); idem, *A magyar katonai hírlapok és folyóiratok bibliográfiája*, vol. 2, *Rákóczi Ferenctől napjainkig, 1705-1941* (Bibliography of Hungarian Military Newspapers and Periodicals, vol. 2, from Ferenc Rákóczi to the Present, 1705-1941) (Budapest, n.d. /1941/); idem, "Előkerült a 'Csíki Gyutacs' két száma" (Two Issues of the *Csík Percussion Cap*

Come to Light), *MKsz*, 1942, pp. 50-52; György Kristóf, "Az 1849-iki *Hadi Lap* történetéhez" (Towards the History of the 1849 *Military Journal*), ibid., pp. 301-4; József Lukács, "Kecseméthy Aurél 1849-es katonai lapjáról" (The 1849 Military Paper of Aurél Kecseméthy), ibid., pp. 429-30; Béla Dezsényi, "Tábori nyomdák és nyomdászok 1848-ban és 1849-ben" (Camp Presses and Printers in 1848 and 1849), *MKsz*, 1944, pp. 57-61; József Lukács, "Csíki Gyutacs," *Élet és Tudomány*, March 14, 1949; József Bajza, *Válogatott cikkek és tanulmányok* (Selected Articles and Studies) (Budapest, 1954); István Barta, ed., *Kossuth Lajos kormányzó elnöki iratai, 1849 ápr. 15 - aug. 15* (The Presidential Documents of Governor Lajos Kossuth, April 15-August 15, 1849) (Budapest, 1955); István Barta, "A kormány parasztpolitikája 1849-ben" (The Peasant Policy of the Government in 1849), *Századok*, 1955, pp. 849-81, and 1956, pp. 4-68; Dénes Kovács, "Hadi Lap," *A Csíki Múzeum Évk.* (The Csík Museum Yearbook), 1957, pp. 83-86; G. Gábor Kemény, *Társadalom és nemzetiség a szabadságharc hadi lapjaiban* (Society and Nationality in the Military Papers of the War of Independence) (Budapest, 1957); Windisch, *Közlöny*; Endre Pálvölgyi, "Bem József és a magyar nyomdászat" (József Bem and Hungarian Printing), *Magyar Grafika* (Hungarian Graphics), 1961, no. 1, pp. 73-77; Imre Lengyel, "Az Alföldi Hírlap 1849-ben: Adatok egy vidéki hírlap társadalmi szerepének vizsgálatához" (The *Great Plain Journal* in 1849: Notes towards an Examination of a Provincial Paper's Role in Society), *A Déri Múzeum Évkönyve 1966/67* (Yearbook of the Déri Museum 1966-67) (Debrecen, 1968), pp. 319-42; Imre Szántó, "Szeged az 1848-1849-es szabadságharc alkonyán" (Szeged during the Decline of the 1848-1849 War of Independence), *Acta Universitatis Szegediensis, Acta Historica*, 124 (1984): 3-25.

Epilogue

The defeat and the severe repression that followed it disrupted the press for quite a time. Many journalists fled abroad, and others were imprisoned or went into hiding. A number of papers vanished, and the standard of the press fell considerably, particularly during the first period of Austrian neo-absolutist rule (1849-59). Even the conservative *Figyelmező* was suppressed in 1850 for having supported the "historic rights" of the country. Once again a relatively major role came to be played by papers of an educational, entertaining, literary, or scientific character. The comic papers, a special genre that helped people to vent their feelings indirectly, gradually came into fashion. Open political opposition could manifest itself only abroad, in the foreign press, which it did particularly during the international crisis of 1859-60, when the Hungarian émigré community under Kossuth's leadership set up press centres in Brussels and Paris and Széchenyi, who was recovering from a nervous breakdown near Vienna, began to organize the "illegal" international press campaign against absolutism that he continued until his death in 1860.

The second period of neo-absolutism (1860-66) was somewhat different in character. After the Hungarian Diet was convened in 1861, the political spectrum of the press became wider and more differentiated. There were signs of the measure of recovery one would expect in a society which had been changed by the bourgeois revolution. The development included a gradual modernization of the internal structure of the papers, a growing variety of literary publications, and a widening of the scope for professional reviews (economic, technical, medical, linguistic, historical, etc.). The number of papers published grew from 15 in 1850 to 44 in 1860 and 119 in 1867.

The Compromise of 1867 with Austria was more or less inevitable. Hungary alone was not strong enough to overthrow the Habsburg Monarchy, which enjoyed the support of the major powers in Europe. Moreover, the ruling classes of Hungary (and everywhere in Europe at the time) refused to start a new revolution. The preferred solution of the most influential groups was to reorganize the Habsburg Monarchy, which they had begun to view as a political umbrella protecting them from new dangers of an international political character. The principles for the compromise between Hungary and Austria had been defined as early as 1865 by Ferenc Deák in the *Pesti Napló* (Pest Diary), a paper representing liberal noblemen with Zsigmond Kemény and Antal Csengery at its head. But Austria needed one more defeat, in the Prussian war of 1866, before it could be brought to accept the idea. Incidentally, the Compromise of 1867 gave the Hungarians a degree of national autonomy and a favourable position they had not enjoyed for any length of time since the early sixteenth century. The era of dualism featured rapid economic and cultural development and a major expansion of a modern, liberal press. Yet that relatively favourable position could not have been attained without the immense revolutionary efforts of 1848-49, which had aspired to something greater—independence—but finally allowed a solution that was more realistic for its time.